Equal Recognition

Equal Recognition

The Moral Foundations of Minority Rights

Alan Patten

PRINCETON UNIVERSITY PRESS

Princeton & Oxford

CONTENTS

PREFACE

To many of my American friends and acquaintances, the subject matter of this book needs some explaining. The United States has always been a culturally diverse society, and new waves of immigration add to this diversity every day. To mention just one measure, a startling one out of five Americans reports using a language other than English at home. To most Americans, however, the country's cultural diversity is not deeply consequential for its political morality. Cultural diversity is one more source of the differences that are pursued and expressed in the private realms of family, neighborhood, market, and civil society. The enjoyment of these differences is appropriately safeguarded by the liberties entrenched in the American constitutional tradition. But many believe that these generic protections of private life are all that is called for in the way of respect or accommodation of cultural diversity. Most Americans would have little sympathy for the idea that public institutions ought officially to protect or accommodate the cultural differences that exist in their country.

Attesting to this general skepticism about public claims based on culture is the relative absence of any major social movement devoted to preserving or promoting distinct cultures within the United States. In recent decades American society has been reshaped in dramatic ways by social movements defined around issues of race, class, gender, disability, and sexuality. There are also some signs today of a nascent movement to assert the rights of irregular migrants. But for the most part, these are all movements geared toward a goal of integration. They aim for the full inclusion of marginalized or subordinated groups into a unified American citizenship. What one does not observe is any large-scale campaign in favor of the rights of minority cultures to remain different. There are no large-scale organized efforts to extend equal status to Spanish alongside English in public institutions. Nor are there claims to self-determination or demands for self-government by national minorities. In general, one finds little feeling among Americans that the United States is imperfectly just by virtue of the ways in which it does or does not respect and accommodate its linguistic, cultural, and national minorities. Of course, southern secessionism played an enormous role in American political development, and echoes of these secessionist sentiments can still be heard now. But for most Americans—even in the South—these sentiments are the proverbial exception that proves the rule.

To many readers, then, my topic will seem, if not exotic, then at least awfully Canadian. It is true, I should disclose from the start, that my interest in the questions addressed in this book was nurtured by an upbringing in Canada.

Many of my formative political memories as a child and a young adult were a product in one way or another of Canada's struggles with cultural diversity. Indeed, one of the very first memories of my childhood is walking hand in hand with my father up Redpath Place in Montreal to see the soldiers guarding the home of a prominent resident during the October Crisis of 1970. My father, a New Englander with liberal inclinations on most issues, maintained a lifelong admiration for Pierre Trudeau's decision to declare martial law in response to the kidnappings by the Front de Libération du Québec. "Just watch me," he was fond of saying, quoting a line from one of Trudeau's press interviews at the time. An even more vivid childhood memory is watching the returns from the 1976 Quebec provincial election in a glum room full of my mother's family. My mother's parents had fled Nazi Germany in the 1930s and raised their six children in the 1950s and 1960s as members of Quebec's Anglophone community. They could not help but see the election of the strongly nationalist Parti Québécois as a disturbing return to the bitter European conflicts they had left behind.

Subsequent events would keep nationalism, language, and culture at the center of Canadian political life. These included the adoption of Bill 101 by the Quebec National Assembly in 1977 to promote and protect the French language; the referendum in Quebec in 1980 on "sovereignty association"; the "patriation" of the Canadian Constitution in 1982; the failures of the Meech Lake Accord of 1989 and the Charlottetown Accord of 1992, each of which sought to secure Quebec's assent to the 1982 Constitution; and the bare defeat, by a 50.6 to 49.4 percent margin, of a second referendum on the secession of Quebec in 1995. Meanwhile, Canadians bitterly debated free trade with the United States, with opponents arguing inter alia that the Free Trade Agreement of 1987 and the North American Free Trade Agreement (NAFTA) of 1994 would hasten the demise of a distinct Canadian culture.

My earliest interest in the topics addressed in this book was certainly stimulated by an upbringing amid these Canadian events and debates. They raised fascinating questions about justice and the nature of liberal democracy. Trudeau's vision of liberalism approved of federalism, official bilingualism, and Canadian nationalism but disapproved of secessionism, demands for "special status," and Quebec's public privileging of French over English. Was Trudeau's the correct interpretation of liberal principles, or could they, perhaps should they, be understood in some different way?

But while my interest in questions of nationalism and culture has its origins north of the border, the questions have much broader relevance. In important ways, the rest of the world looks much more like Canada than it does the United States. Many of the world's leading democracies are home to established linguistic and national minorities, which organize themselves to assert their own rights and status. To be sure, each of these countries has its own history, its own political traditions, and its own peculiar sociodemographic profile. There is no Canadian model readily available for export around the world because Canada's approach, even were it generally regarded as a success, is adapted to its own specific circumstances. Nevertheless, there is a set of problems and puzzles concerning the nature and value of culture that is familiar from the Canadian experience and that arises in some shape or form in every region of the world.

Moreover, if one thinks long enough about these problems and puzzles, one starts to see their relevance even for the United States. In part, this is for the obvious, "Wilsonian" reason that the United States is an international actor with global power. It is expected to take a position on demands for cultural recognition and self-determination that are regularly made on the world stage. How should the United States have responded to the cultural claims of national groups as Yugoslavia and the Soviet Union were breaking up? Insofar as the United States used its influence to secure language rights or self-government rights for national minorities, was there a consideration of principle at stake? Is the threatened destruction of Tibetan culture itself a reason for the United States to oppose China's occupation of Tibet? How should the United States respond to secessionist movements in Scotland and Catalonia (not to mention Quebec)?

The questions explored in this book are also relevant to an American reader because the right approach to cultural minorities within the United States is not fully settled. Some ongoing debates occur on the fringes of American political life. They concern the claims of Native Americans, for instance, and the status of Puerto Rico. Other debates are likely to become more central, as growing numbers of Spanish-speaking immigrants populate regions of the country. As this population grows in size, confidence, and level of self-organization, it may prove hard to keep questions about minority cultural rights off of the agenda.

A further perspective on the issues to be studied in this book is gained by considering the rights and claims of cultural minorities from the standpoint of national majorities. Questions about what minorities may legitimately demand have as their obverse a set of questions about nationalism and the permissible use of state power by the controlling majority. To what extent can a national or cultural majority use the instruments of state power to impose its values, traditions, and narratives onto the society as a whole? May the national majority think of the state and its territory as its own "homeland" and inscribe its identity in more or less modest ways into public institutions and public spaces? These questions about what if any forms of nationalism are acceptable arise in every state. They are connected, in the United States and elsewhere, with questions about religious establishment, since the national majority will often think of its identity in partly religious terms. But they also arise with respect to a range of nonreligious issues, such as the designation of an official language, decisions about education curriculums, the choice between unitary and federal systems of government (and the allocation of powers in the context of the latter), and the selection of flags, symbols, anthems, place names, and other conspicuous markers of public identity. The importance of these and other questions about majority nationalism is hard to deny.

As we shall see in chapter 1, theories of liberal democracy do not speak with one voice about minority rights or majority nationalism. In the post–World War II decades, the major statements of liberalism were articulated by American theorists writing first and foremost for an American readership. For the reasons mentioned at the outset, questions about nationalism and minority rights did not figure very prominently in these accounts. It was not so much that this or that position on these questions was rejected, but that claims about justice were not made to depend one way or another on how the state deals with minority-majority dynamics.

Beginning in the 1980s, however, a new generation of theorists started to challenge this incurious agnosticism about problems of culture. One group of philosophers began to argue that the principles of liberal democracy mandate the recognition and accommodation of minority cultures. Many of these same thinkers also embraced liberal forms of nationalism. Both minority rights and liberal nationalism were regarded as remedies to overly thin and antiseptic versions of liberalism that ignored the cultural dimensions of liberal political community. In general, the suggestion was that national minorities ought to enjoy the same opportunities to engage in liberal forms of nation building as were already the legitimate prerogative of national majorities.

Soon after these theories of liberal multiculturalism and nationalism were formulated, a group of liberal critics began arguing that the earlier, orthodox statements of liberal theory did not neglect the claims of culture simply out of oversight. According to these critics, there are deep reasons of liberal principle for rejecting many of the claims associated with multiculturalism and nationalism. For these thinkers, a key point is that human diversity goes all the way down to the individual. Insofar as liberals take liberty and individuality seriously, they should resist schemes of cultural and national recognition that impose a false homogeneity onto a fluid and diverse human experience.

In general this book sides with the multiculturalist interpretation of liberalism. I argue that, under a fairly broad spectrum of empirical circumstances, liberal principles do mandate specific minority cultural rights, including language rights, self-government rights, and rights to other forms of equal recognition by public institutions. At the same time, the account to be developed here differs from existing theories of liberal multiculturalism in two major respects. First, for reasons that will be explained, I find many of the criticisms of liberal multiculturalism to be quite convincing. Theorists of multiculturalism have not done a good job of responding to the charge that they "essentialize" culture, nor have they adequately formulated the connection between foundational liberal principles and minority rights. The first and most important aim of this book is to rebuild the foundations of liberal multiculturalism on a more solid basis.

A restatement of the moral foundations of minority rights leads to a second major difference with the existing multiculturalist literature. In my view, theorists of multiculturalism have been too quick to embrace liberal nationalism. It is true that many minorities have nationalist aspirations. They seek to control the territory that they regard as their homeland with their own institutions. But not all minorities fit this pattern. Even setting aside immigrant minorities, there are small and scattered minorities who could never aspire to significant forms of self-government, and "internal" minorities (minorities within minorities) whose aspirations to self-government conflict with the self-government of the national minority that constitutes the local majority. An account of minority cultural rights ought to be able to illuminate these cases as well, and not be too closely tethered to a vision of cultural minorities as nations. More important, from the fact that spokespersons for cultural minorities often articulate nationalist demands, it does not follow that, as a matter of liberal justice, these demands ought to be met. Which of the claims made by cultural minorities ought to be met, and to what extent, depends on the reasons that justify cultural rights in the first place. In the view developed in this book, minority cultural rights are ultimately based on an idea of liberal neutrality. The liberal state ought to be neutral in its treatment of majority and minority alike, a principle that will sometimes mean extending equivalent culturally specific resources and facilities to each. There is nothing in this rationale that supports the liberal nationalist notion that national minorities should enjoy all the traditional prerogatives of the nation-state within some restricted territory. National majority and minorities alike are entitled to equal recognition, on the account I propose, and this will typically have implications for how internal boundaries are drawn. But however those boundaries are configured, the claims of equal treatment that can be made by all citizens do not disappear. On the proposal to be developed in this book, then, liberal multiculturalism stands in some considerable tension with *both* orthodox, noncultural forms of liberalism *and* liberal nationalism.

I wish I could say that the philosophical claims I defend in the book lead back to a specific set of conclusions about the particular controversies that originally stirred my interest in this topic. But long-running scholarly projects are rarely this tidy. One of the things I have learned in years of thinking about the topic is how complex and difficult it is. The competing claims of majorities and minorities have a legal and constitutional character specific to the national context in which they are made. These claims are also made against a backdrop of fiercely contested historical narratives. Specialized literatures in law, history, literature, and other disciplines try to make sense of majority nationalism and minority rights using their own approaches and methods. In addition, many of the questions that arise in contemplating these issues are appropriately referred to the social sciences. What causes majority nationalism and minority mobilization, and when are such movements likely to be successful? What social effects will alternative regimes of accommodation and recognition each have under various possible conditions?

I do not offer a general theory of multiculturalism or nationalism here, nor a complete recipe for solving particular conflicts. I try to think rigorously about the philosophical issues with the confidence that they are one dimension of the overall problem. The conclusions I argue for illuminate normative policy choices by suggesting what questions to ask and what criteria to apply, but they do not fully determine those choices since there are crucial factual issues that need to be studied rigorously in another forum. The philosophical inquiry of the present book can indicate what *kinds* of facts are relevant to policy choices, but it will not reveal what those facts are.

It is not that, as a rule, political philosophers shy away from making all-things-considered judgments or offering specific remedies to particular real-world problems that interest them. In fact, some of the very best recent work on multiculturalism is highly contextual and not at all reluctant to advocate solutions to particular problem cases. Some parts of the book, especially in the final three chapters, do get fairly close to important policy questions, but much of the book has a more theoretical ambition. As valuable as the more case-driven and policy-oriented contributions have been, I worry that they are too impatient with, and inattentive to, some of the underlying philosophical issues of a more foundational character. The contextual theories produce polished conclusions that will have great intuitive appeal to people who are already sympathetic with the projects of liberal multiculturalism and nationalism. But they are less well equipped for responding to the deeper, more principled challenges that critics of these projects sometimes articulate.

It is in restating the philosophical foundations of minority cultural rights that I hope to make my chief contribution. In a sense, then, I haven't lost my fascination with the particular controversies that fueled my original interest in the book's topic. I have come to realize, however, that there is more than one way to make progress in thinking about these issues. I try to do so, not by confronting the policy questions head on, but by seeking to illuminate them more indirectly through an exploration of the key underlying philosophical questions.

Work on this project dates back to the mid-1990s when I first started working on some papers about liberalism and cultural rights. The book's completion took much longer than I wanted, and probably much longer than many of my friends or family ever imagined any professional project could take. I look forward to Thanksgiving dinners when I don't have to explain why the book is still not completed.

Over the years I have accumulated some sizable debts to colleagues and students who have discussed the book's ideas with me. In many cases they generously sent me written feedback. I am especially grateful to Arash Abizadeh, Ayalet Banai, Chuck Beitz, Eamonn Callan, Joseph Carens, Javier Hidalgo, Jacob Levy, Don Moon, Will Kymlicka, Steve Macedo, David Miller, Jan-Werner Müller, Philip Pettit, Jonathan Quong, Helder de Schutter, Jeff Spinner-Halev, Annie Stilz, Daniel Weinstock, and Leif Wenar—each of whom offered support, encouragement, and penetrating critical feedback on more than one occasion. I also owe debts of gratitude to Richard Arneson, Rainer Bauböck, Eric Beerbohm, Colin Bird, Michael Blake, Charles Blattberg, Corey Brettschneider, Phil Buckley, Simon Caney, Dario Castiglione, Andrew Cohen, Ryan Davis, Kyla Ebels-Duggan, William Edmundson, Chris Eisgruber, George Kateb, Niko Kolodny, David Laitin, Dominique Leydet, Christian List, Andrew Lister, Catherine Lu, Ian MacMullen, Margaret Moore, Véronique Munoz-Dardé, Michael Murphy, Kai Nielsen, Ryan Pevnick, Denise Réaume, Rob Reich, Gideon Rosen, Nancy Rosenblum, Shahrzad Sabet, Michel Seymour, George Sher, Sarah Song, Nenad Stojanovic, Sarah Stroud, Lucas Swaine, Robert Taylor, Philippe Van Parijs, Jay Wallace, Andrew Williams, and Lea Ypi. Two anonymous readers for Princeton University Press gave me valuable feedback on the penultimate version of the manuscript. And Rob Tempio was a wise and patient editor whose advice and judgment I relied on at important moments. Chris Ro, Javier Hidalgo, and Shahrzad Sabet all provided research assistance at various points in the writing.

I'm grateful to university audiences at Virginia, Stanford, Queens, Yale, Oxford, Georgia State, Syracuse, Washington University, UC Davis, UC Berkeley, Toronto, McGill, and Princeton—as well as to audiences at various professional conferences in the United States, Canada, Europe, and Japan. Early portions of the research enjoyed funding from agencies of the Canadian and Quebec governments (SSHRC and FCAR, respectively). More recently I benefited from the munificence of the Department of Politics and the Center for Human Values, both of Princeton University.

Some parts of the book are based on previously published work. A slightly shorter version of chapter 2 appeared in the *American Political Science Review* in November 2011 under the same title (copyright © 2011 by Cambridge University Press; reprinted with permission). A considerably shorter version of chapter 4 was published by the *Journal of Political Philosophy* (Wiley-Blackwell) in September 2012 under the same title. Chapter 7 is a heavily revised descendant of a paper first published in *Ethics* in April 2002 under the same title (copyright © 2002 by the University of Chicago Press). And chapter 6 borrows some material from several different published papers on language policies, including Alan Patten, "Political Theory and Language Policy," *Political Theory* (Sage Publications, 2001); Alan Patten, "Liberal Neutrality and Language Policy," *Philosophy & Public Affairs* (Wiley, 2003); Alan Patten and Will Kymlicka, "Introduction: Language Rights and Political Theory: Contexts, Issues, and Approaches," in *Language Rights and Political Theory*, edited by Will Kymlicka and Alan Patten (Oxford University Press, 2003); Alan Patten, "What Kind of Bilingualism?" in *Language Rights and Political Theory*; and Alan Patten, "Survey Article: The Justification of Minority Language Rights," *Journal of Political Philosophy* (Wiley, 2009).

This book is dedicated to my wife, Matilda, and to our three wonderful children, Felix, Agatha, and Raphael.

Equal Recognition

CHAPTER 1

Introduction: Liberalism and the Accommodation of Cultural Diversity

1.1 Competing Interpretations of Liberalism

Conflicting claims about culture are a familiar refrain of political life in the contemporary world. On the one side, majorities seek to fashion the state in their own image. They want to see their own values, traditions, norms, and identity expressed in meaningful ways in public institutions. From the majority's perspective, the expression of their culture in collective decisions is simply a matter of majority rule or democracy. It is normal for states to be shaped by the majority's culture, and there is nothing objectionable about such shaping so long as certain liberal limits are observed on how it is done.

On the other side, cultural minorities often press for greater recognition and accommodation by the state. They want public institutions to be designed in such a way as to leave them spaces in which to express and preserve their own distinct cultures. For minorities, these demands for recognition and accommodation of their distinctiveness are consonant with liberalism's concern about tyranny of the majority, its commitment to tolerating difference, and its ideals of equal citizenship.

We can observe these different claims in a variety of contexts. One important area is language policy. Majorities frequently prefer to establish their own language as the principal medium of public communication—the language in which services are offered to the public and in which public business is conducted. Minorities, by contrast, ask the government to provide services in their languages and to make it possible for them to use their own languages when they participate in public institutions. Another area in which claims of culture are voiced is in the design of democratic institutions. Statewide majorities tend to be comfortable with a unitary state, which reflects their sense of political community and which allows their preferences to predominate. Minorities, by contrast, typically want institutional and jurisdictional spaces to be carved out in which they can enjoy a measure of autonomy and self-government. Other flashpoints include the school curriculum, the use of public space, and the designation of symbols, flags, anthems, and other conspicuous markers of identity.

We might think of the differing claims about these issues as claims of *majority nationalism*, on the one hand, and *minority rights*, on the other. These claims are in considerable tension with one another. Suppose we understand the majority nationalism claim as saying that no injustice is produced when state institutions and policies are made to reflect the values, traditions, narratives, and identity of the majority, so long as standard liberal constraints are satisfied. And let us take the minority rights claim to be insisting that, as a matter of justice, the state ought to recognize and accommodate the cultures of minorities by leaving spaces in which at least some institutions and policies can reflect minority values, traditions, narratives, and identity. Without significant further qualification, these assertions cannot both be true. If it is consistent with justice for the majority to shape the state's institutions and policies according to its own culture, then it cannot be a requirement of justice that some of the state's institutions and policies be shaped by minority cultures. For instance, if there is no injustice in the statewide majority declaring its own language to be the sole official language of public communication, then it cannot be true that providing minority-speakers with rights to the public use of their language is a matter of justice. If it is not wrong for the statewide majority to establish a unitary system of government that corresponds to its sense of political community, then an autonomy scheme designed to empower some cultural minority cannot be considered a requirement of justice. And so on.

There is no single view among liberals about the merits of these competing claims. In practice, many liberal democracies around the world do offer some recognition and accommodation of cultural minorities. A list of states extending significant language rights to minority language speakers would include dozens of entries. Canada, Belgium, Switzerland, Spain, the United Kingdom, India, Israel, and South Africa are just a few of the most prominent examples. Many states have also incorporated arrangements into their constitutions, such as regional and other forms of autonomy, that are aimed at giving cultural minorities a measure of self-government. Federalism in Canada, Belgium, India, and Iraq can be understood, in part, through this lens, as can Scottish and Welsh devolution in the United Kingdom, the Swiss system of cantons, Spain's autonomous regions, and various experiments around the world with indigenous self-government. Examples of states providing accommodations and exemptions for cultural and religious groups are also quite prevalent. Some well-known cases include special hunting and fishing rights for members of indigenous groups; exemptions from workplace helmet requirements for Sikhs; requirements that publicly funded cafeterias (e.g., in public schools) be sensitive to the religiously and culturally based diets of those they serve; and exemptions from sport, school, and workplace dress codes.

While the practice of extending recognition and accommodation to cultural minorities is widespread, it is certainly not universal. The political traditions and reigning ideologies of many states remain deeply suspicious of minority rights. In France, and in countries influenced by the French republican model, there is a tradition of identifying equal citizenship with the notion of a common public culture and with the relegation of particular cultural and religious identities to the private sphere. Inevitably the common public culture is aligned in certain respects with the majority culture: it is the majority's language that serves as the common language of the republic; it is the majority's sense of political community that determines the boundaries and internal constitution of the republic; and it is the majority culture that influences the choice of public symbols and norms. While harder to encapsulate in a single model than the French tradition, the American case has also been an important example of a successful state built around a single, common language and a strong and generally shared sense of national identity. Although the United States is notable for its tradition of accommodating religious differences, Americans remain reluctant to extend significant language or self-government rights to cultural minorities. Indeed, if anything, the political impetus has been pushing in the opposite direction, with English-only and English-first laws and ordinances finding support in many states and municipalities, and with politicians rarely missing an opportunity to remind immigrants of their obligation to learn English.[1]

So practices of both minority rights and majority nationalism are well established in liberal democracies around the world. Something of this same mix of attitudes is discernible among the political theorists who have thought and written about claims of culture from within the broadly liberal tradition. Over the past quarter-century or so, one of the remarkable developments in political theory has been the groundswell of interest in questions relating to culture, identity, and difference. A group of theorists, including Will Kymlicka, Joseph Raz, Charles Taylor, Yael Tamir, David Miller, and Joseph Carens, have sought to mobilize the resources of liberal political thought to make a principled case in favor of minority cultural rights.[2] Although the language and argumentation vary from person to person, the distinctive claim made by these theorists is that particular minority cultural rights are, *as such*, a requirement of justice conceived of in a broadly liberal fashion (I explain the "as such" qualifier below).

---

[1] On language policy in the United States, see Schmidt 2000; Schildkraut 2005; Rodríguez 2006. Puerto Rico is an important exception to the privileging of English.

[2] Kymlicka 1989b; 1995; 2001a; Raz 1994; Taylor 1994; Margalit and Raz 1990; Tamir 1993; Miller 1995; Carens 2000. Other notable contributions to this literature include Spinner 1994; Margalit and Halbertal 1994; Tully 1995; Parekh 2002; Gans 2003.

Kymlicka has called this thesis "liberal culturalism."[3] Liberal culturalism, he says, is "the view that liberal-democratic states should not only uphold the familiar set of common civil and political rights of citizenship which are protected in all liberal democracies; they must also adopt various group-specific rights or policies which are intended to recognize and accommodate the distinctive identities and needs of ethnocultural groups."[4] As Kymlicka lays out the view, both "liberal nationalism" and "liberal multiculturalism" fall under the umbrella of liberal culturalism. Liberal nationalism calls for recognition and accommodation of the national cultures and languages—both majority and minority—that fall within the boundaries of a state. And liberal multiculturalism claims that nonnational cultural groups, such as immigrant groups and religious minorities, "have a valid claim, not only to tolerance and nondiscrimination, but also to explicit accommodation, recognition, and representation within the institutions of the broader society."[5] Each of these views claims the mantle of liberalism in virtue of two main considerations. They are said to be derived from liberal ideas of freedom, equality, and justice. And they recognize a variety of limits that are motivated by liberal principles on what can and should be done to accommodate and recognize particular groups: liberal forms of accommodation and recognition do not violate standard rights and liberties; they operate with inclusive conceptions of membership; they do not impose membership in particular groups on individuals; they do not facilitate aggression by one group against another; and so on.[6]

In reaction to the wave of liberal-culturalist scholarship, another group of liberal theorists has argued that the older understanding of liberal political theory, typified by the principles of justice defended by John Rawls, is perfectly adequate for thinking about the claims of cultural minorities, even if it was not originally developed with those claims in mind.[7] The theorists I have in mind include prominent political philosophers such as Jeremy Waldron, Brian Barry, Anthony Appiah, and Samuel Scheffler.[8] These philosophers have challenged liberal culturalism on a number of points: they have drawn attention to various perverse effects that might be associated with the culturalist program; they have taken issue with the claims about freedom and equality made by liberal culturalists; and they have challenged the conceptualization of culture relied on by proponents of minority cultural rights. For the most part, these thinkers do not go out of their way to praise majority nationalism as an alternative to minority rights. But their understanding of liberalism does not

---

[3] Kymlicka 2001a, chap. 2.
[4] Ibid., 42. See also the formulation in Raz 1994, 172–73.
[5] Kymlicka 2001a, 41.
[6] Ibid., 39–42.
[7] Rawls 1999a; 2005.
[8] Waldron 1992; 2010; Barry 2001; Appiah 2005; Scheffler 2007. Other notable critiques of liberal arguments in favor of cultural rights include Danley 1991; Kukathas 1992; 2003; Blake 2002.

contain grounds for condemning majority nationalism, so long as core liberal principles are respected.

Although the debate was barely ten years old at the time, by 1998 Will Kymlicka was suggesting that a consensus had started to form in favor of liberal culturalism. Theorists continued to disagree about why, exactly, culture matters to people in ways that should elicit liberal attention. And they disagreed about how the principles of cultural justice should be applied and institutionalized in particular contexts. But, in Kymlicka's view, there was no clear competitor with liberal culturalism out on the field, and thus "liberal culturalism has won by default, as it were."[9]

As major parts of this book will reveal, I am generally very sympathetic with Kymlicka's theory of cultural rights. Indeed, part of my ambition in the book is to develop Kymlicka's theory further and to try to place some of its major claims on more secure foundations. It is a premise of this project, however, that Kymlicka's declaration of victory was somewhat premature. Of course, insofar as I seek to defend a version of liberal culturalism, I provide one more data point confirming Kymlicka's hypothesis that, in Nathan Glazer's phrase, "we are all multiculturalists now."[10] But I think that Kymlicka's declaration both overestimates the strength of the existing arguments in favor of liberal culturalism and underestimates the coherence and plausibility of a rival, nonculturalist interpretation of liberalism. What is needed, and what I aim to provide in this book, is a restatement of the ethical foundations of liberal culturalism. Such a restatement needs to confront, and to take seriously, the powerful alternative conception of liberalism that retains a grip among many liberals.

Rethinking the foundations of liberal culturalism will have important implications for how that view is formulated. Kymlicka and other liberal culturalists are actually quite sympathetic with majority nationalism. They object to the idea that the *statewide* majority should be able to impose its preferences throughout the state. This would leave insufficient space for the legitimate cultural aspirations of minorities. But they do not reject the narrower claim that majorities should be able to impose their preferences *if* appropriate substate autonomy arrangements are established so that there are several majorities. Their central contention is that minorities ought to have the same opportunity to form (local) majorities and to use their majority power to express their culture as is enjoyed by the statewide majority at the national level. For these theorists, then, minority cultural rights are not opposed to nationalism but instead represent a demand to pluralize it: to give more than one group within the state the chance to have its own political community and to express itself culturally through the public institutions of that community.

---

[9] Kymlicka 2001a, 43; also 33.
[10] Glazer 1998.

In my view, this widely endorsed version of liberal culturalism is much too cozy toward liberal nationalism. Cultural groups do not always have a nationalist agenda and are not always in position to pursue one. Even where they do pursue such an agenda, it should be looked on with some suspicion whenever it affects a culturally diverse population. In reexamining the foundations of liberal culturalism, we shall discover that the best reasons for affirming such a view are also reasons for a more general rejection of nationalism. The idea of accommodating national minorities through substate autonomy arrangements is an important and worthy one. And there may be secondary, pragmatic considerations that counsel in favor of deferring to nationalist claims. But we should resist the suggestion that justice ultimately consists in majority and minority each enjoying the opportunity to culturally dominate some part of the state.

1.2 Why the Case for Liberal Culturalism Needs to Be Restated

One reason why a restatement is needed is that a number of the existing arguments in favor of liberal culturalism seem vulnerable to serious objections. One prominent strand of argument in liberal culturalist writings has appealed to the liberal value of autonomy or freedom. The claim is that culture is a necessary part of the background context in which individuals make a succession of choices about how to live their lives.[11] As Kymlicka formulates the claim, "freedom involves making choices amongst various options, and our societal culture not only provides these options, but also makes them meaningful to us."[12] Since liberals plainly attach great value to protecting and fostering individual freedom and autonomy, they would seem to have a compelling rationale for supporting forms of recognition and accommodation that help to secure vulnerable cultures.

Commentators since the early 1990s, however, have consistently pointed out the problem with this argument.[13] It may well be true that, in some sense, people rely on culture for a context of choice. But it does not follow that the culture they rely on has to be *their* culture if that means the culture in which they were brought up and with which they identify. Since people can (and regularly do) assimilate into new cultures, the autonomy argument does not, on its own, provide a special reason why any particular culture ought to be recognized and accommodated.

[11] A number of the main liberal-culturalist authors have forwarded an argument of this form. See Kymlicka 1989b, chaps. 8–9; 1995, chap. 5; Tamir 1993; Raz 1994; Miller 1995, e.g., 86, 146. For a critical overview, see Patten 1999b.

[12] Kymlicka 1995, 83. See also Tamir 1993, 36, 84; Raz 1994, 175–78; Miller 1995, 86, 146.

[13] Waldron 1992; Margalit and Halbertal 1994; Tomasi 1995; Forst 1997. I discuss the problem in Patten 1999a; 1999b; and in chapter 3.

A second strand of argument in the liberal-culturalist enterprise is designed in part to address this shortcoming in the first. As many writers on cultural rights have observed, culture can be an important basis for individual identity. People often care about their culture and feel attached to it. Their cultural membership makes a difference in their practical reasoning in a variety of situations. Their culture is important to their sense of who they are, and the loss of the culture may even have psychologically devastating consequences. These considerations, it is suggested, help to explain why individuals have a legitimate interest in enjoying a context of choice in their own culture.[14] More generally they mean that individuals have a valid claim on state recognition and accommodation of their culture.

Here I think that the argument suffers from something like the opposite defect of the previous argument. One can make out how strong "culturalist" conclusions might follow from the premises of the identity argument. But it is less clear what those premises have to do with liberal principles in the first place. Whereas the idea that liberals should protect and promote the conditions of individual autonomy is immediately intuitive, the notion that a liberal state has any obligation to ensure that people are able to realize the commitments that happen to be associated with their identity is not. Theorists who make the identity argument have not, in short, explained why, and in what ways, identity is something that liberals should care about.

A third strand of argument was absent from the earliest statements of liberal culturalism but has become increasingly prominent since the publication of Kymlicka's *Multicultural Citizenship*.[15] This argument appeals to the idea of neutrality or, to be precise, the inevitable nonneutrality of the state when it comes to culture and identity. The idea is to drive a wedge between the possible liberal responses to religious and cultural pluralism. Whereas the liberal state can handle religious diversity through a policy of disestablishment—a refusal to privilege or promote any particular religious faith—the same solution is not available for dealing with cultural diversity. The state cannot avoid decisions about language, internal boundaries, school curriculums, public symbols, and so on—all of which work to advantage some particular cultures and identities and not others. Because the state is necessarily not neutral in these areas, there is no fundamental objection to it pursuing various liberal forms of nation building based around the majority national culture. But then it follows that, as a matter of fairness, "all else being equal, national minorities

[14]Margalit and Halbertal 1994; Kymlicka 1995, 89–90; Forst 1997. Taylor (1994) also makes an "identity" argument of sorts.

[15]Kymlicka 1995, 107–15; 2001, introduction and chaps. 1–2; Moore 2001, 130–31; Norman 2006, 49–57. The limits of the liberal idea of neutrality in matters cultural are also emphasized by Young 1990; Spinner 1994; and Carens 2000.

should have the same tools of nation-building available to them as the majority nation, subject to the same liberal limitations."[16]

In its present form, this neutrality argument also strikes me as inconclusive. It operates with an impact- or effects-based conception of neutrality (the state is neutral only when its policies do not generate a net advantage or disadvantage for any culture or conception of the good) that liberals who call for neutrality have rarely if ever endorsed.[17] Liberals who instead adopt a justificatory conception of neutrality have no trouble condemning certain forms of nation building (which *aim* to promote a particular national culture) even while allowing that the state will inevitably need to make decisions about language, boundaries, curriculums, and the like that will predictably have an impact on particular cultures and identities. So long as these necessary decisions are made on the basis of general liberal values, and not on the grounds that some particular culture or conception of the good is superior, there is no departure from neutrality.

There are at least prima facie reasons, then, to think that liberal culturalism rests on shakier normative foundations than its defenders like to believe. At the same time, there are also grounds for thinking that the rival, nonculturalist interpretation of liberalism, which was the standard view before the 1990s, is more coherent and plausible than its liberal-culturalist critics allow. One major reason for this has just been given. Kymlicka maintains that the nonculturalist position "faces the problem that its traditional pretensions to ethnocultural neutrality can no longer be sustained."[18] But, as we have just seen, if neutrality is conceptualized in terms of justifications rather than effects, this particular problem disappears.

A further consideration is that the nonculturalist position can go much further than one might expect in accounting for the legitimacy of certain protections for minority cultures. Nonculturalist liberals reject the thesis that certain minority cultural rights are, *as such*, a requirement of liberal justice. They do not think that recognition and accommodation are directly demanded by justice. The rejection of this thesis still leaves them with plenty of resources, however, for justifying many of the policies advocated by liberal culturalists.

Consider some of the ways in which nonculturalist liberals can still justify rights and policies that provide significant opportunity and protection to cultural minorities:

- The standard set of civil rights endorsed by all liberals provides considerable space for cultural minorities to express and organize themselves. For example, one does not need to be a liberal culturalist to think that

---

[16] Kymlicka 2001a, 29.

[17] For this criticism, see Barry 2001, 27n20; Arneson 2003, 194n7. The point is nicely elaborated in Stilz 2009. For a related discussion, see Kukathas 1997, 422–23.

[18] Kymlicka 2001a, 43.

it would be wrong for the state to prohibit minorities from publishing books or newspapers in their own language or from organizing into clubs and associations aimed at furthering their culture and identity.

- Widely supported claims of distributive justice may also provide a reason to support certain kinds of policies specifically targeted at cultural minorities. Minority-culture status often interacts with and reinforces socioeconomic inequality. If certain group-specific policies help to alleviate inequality and disadvantage, then culturalist and nonculturalist liberals alike have a reason to adopt those policies that has nothing to do with promoting or recognizing culture as such.

- Liberals of every stripe also acknowledge certain democratic political rights. On issues where justice neither obliges nor prohibits a particular policy from within a range of possibilities, the test of legitimacy is endorsement by the democratic political process. By virtue of their democratic rights, cultural minorities are entitled to struggle politically for permissible laws and policies that accord them a measure of recognition and accommodation. The rationale for these laws and policies is not a principle of *cultural* justice but a requirement of *political* justice that all citizens be given the right to participate as equals in the shaping of public policy.

- Finally, an important principle for all liberals is the rule of law. States should respect the laws they have adopted, the treaties they have entered into, and the constitutional provisions that bring them into existence in the first place. This means that they now have a strong, principled reason to respect laws, treaties, and constitutional provisions that extend recognition and accommodation to cultural minorities, even if justice did not require that they adopt those measures in the first place and would not require them to adopt or respect those measures now if it were not for the importance of the rule of law.

To be clear, the suggestion is not that societies claiming to be liberal have generally observed these principles. Clearly, often they have not. Rather, the point is that we need not encumber liberalism with principles of cultural justice to have the theoretical resources necessary to articulate what is going wrong when liberal societies reject all rights that offer protection to cultural minorities. Applied with a certain amount of cultural sensitivity, noncultural liberalism already gives us some purchase on such cases.

It should be clear from this that the difference between culturalist and nonculturalist interpretations of liberalism is not necessarily about advocacy. For some of the reasons I have just been citing, liberals of both allegiances may end up agreeing on what the right policy is. In these cases, their disagreement concerns *why* the policy in question is the right one, with nonculturalists emphasizing the ways in which the policy furthers standard, nonculturalist liberal concerns, and culturalists arguing that the policy also realizes principles of cultural justice. In addition, the policy differences between culturalists and nonculturalists are likely to be further muddied by the fact that both will have to trim their sails in certain situations to take into account pragmatic and other contextual considerations. As we shall see below, good policy is typically more complicated than simply applying the relevant abstract principle.

The disagreement between culturalist and nonculturalist liberalism is first and foremost, then, a philosophical one. It is a disagreement about the *grounds* for thinking that the state should adopt certain measures and policies and refrain from adopting others. Once this question of justification is worked out, however, there will almost certainly be some implications for advocacy. The culturalist view will approve of certain measures and policies where the nonculturalist view would disapprove or be indifferent. The policies favored by the nonculturalist view are likely to have certain predictable characteristics. They will tend to protect cultural difference in private contexts rather than in public institutions. Where they do impinge on public institutions, it will often be on a temporary and transitional basis. And where they do apply to public institutions in a more permanent fashion, it will likely be in a somewhat haphazard fashion, depending on the accidents of constitutional history and majoritarian politics. By contrast, the culturalist view, as I shall develop it throughout this book, is mainly concerned with the *ongoing* treatment and standing of cultural minorities in *major* decisions about *public* policy and the design of *public* institutions.

The principal aim of the present book is to explore and evaluate the differences between culturalist and nonculturalist forms of liberalism. Are the theoretical resources supplied by the standard, nonculturalist interpretation of liberalism adequate on their own for understanding how states ought to treat their cultural minorities? Or do those resources need to be supplemented by the liberal-culturalist idea that certain minority cultural rights are, *as such*, a requirement of liberal justice? As I have hinted already, the main claim of the book is that we should prefer the second of these alternatives. My thesis is that there are basic reasons of principle for thinking that cultural minorities as such are owed specific forms of recognition and accommodation. I shall sometimes refer to this as the *strong cultural rights thesis*. Strong cultural rights are moral rights, which are grounded in basic reasons of principle, to certain forms of recognition and accommodation.

In developing this thesis, I shall take as the main opposing hypothesis the view that there is no basic liberal reason for thinking that cultural minorities as such are owed particular forms of accommodation and recognition as a matter of principle. My imagined opponent can acknowledge what I shall call "pragmatic" and "derivative" reasons for supporting certain policies of accommodation and recognition. She can even grant that it would be permissible for cultural groups, working through the democratic political process, to win for themselves certain accommodations or forms of recognition. What she does not accept—and what distinguishes her view from the one that I shall defend—is that there are strong cultural rights.

As noted earlier, a defense of the strong cultural rights thesis will inevitably have implications for how such rights are understood. The argument I develop points away from a nationalist conception of strong cultural rights and toward a more fully inclusive conception. I shall return to this theme in section 1.4. First, however, let me be more precise about the overarching disagreement between culturalist and nonculturalist liberalism.

1.3 Four Distinctions, Plus One More

To further isolate the disagreement and motivate the discussion, it is useful to introduce four distinctions. One is between principled and pragmatic reasons why a liberal might adopt policies of cultural accommodation and recognition. The second is between basic and derivative senses in which liberal principles might be said to mandate policies that offer accommodation and recognition to cultural minorities. The third is between the view that accommodations are owed to cultural minorities themselves as a matter of basic principle and the view that there are impersonal and/or third-party-regarding reasons of basic principle for adopting policies of accommodation and recognition. And the fourth is between the view that accommodations are *owed* to cultural minorities and the view that it would be permissible for a liberal political community to make such accommodations. My claim, as I have said, is that there are *basic* reasons of *principle* for thinking that certain policies of recognition and accommodation are *owed* to *cultural minorities* as such. By discussing the four distinctions, I attempt to explain and motivate the italicized terms.

The four distinctions not only isolate the claim I am interested in defending but also help to show that the claim is a very strong one—one that is very far from being obviously true. Indeed, by the time I finish describing the fourth distinction, some readers may have decided that the claim is highly *un*likely to be true. The fifth and final distinction I introduce mitigates the strength of the claim somewhat, without rendering it trivial. This is the distinction between saying that a particular right or normative requirement retains its full force in all contexts (it is context-invariant) and the claim that it has full force in some but not all contexts (context-dependent).

PRINCIPLED NOT PRAGMATIC

To think about the principled reasons for adopting some policy is to think about the intrinsic merits of the policy and the consequences that would result from people following the rules and procedures, and enjoying the benefits, established by the policy. A principled reason for adopting some policy of cultural accommodation, then, would refer to desirable properties of the policy of accommodation itself or to desirable results that would be achieved by the actions of people enjoying the accommodation. By contrast, someone interested in the pragmatic reasons that count for or against some policy emphasizes that people do not always comply with the rules and procedures established by particular policies or take advantage of the benefits that they offer. People may instead break the rules established by a policy that they do not like, or they may circumnavigate the policy by choosing some alternative option that is also available to them. Pragmatic reasons for or against some policy point to the consequences that would ensue as a result of people acting outside the framework established by the policy.

The distinction between principled and pragmatic reasons is seen, for instance, in debates about extending special forms of political autonomy to regionally concentrated national minorities. According to some people, the most salient consideration in these debates is not whether the forms of autonomy in question are required by justice but whether extending them would help to avert a secessionist crisis. People who reason in this way are emphasizing pragmatic rather than principled reasons. They are, in effect, saying that, even if justice does not require regional autonomy for national minorities, one has to take into consideration the likely behavior of national minorities who are denied the autonomy arrangements. National minorities would not necessarily resign themselves to living within an autonomy-denying, unitary political system but might increasingly turn to a secessionist alternative, thereby raising the likelihood of an unacceptable outcome. Under different conditions, the pragmatist might reach the opposite conclusion. Even if justice does require the provision of autonomy for some national minority, the pragmatic considerations might tilt in the other direction. It might be argued that regional autonomy would embolden local elites to drive for full independent statehood. The debate about Scottish devolution in the 1990s was largely conducted in these pragmatic terms, with proponents of devolution arguing that the new arrangement would ward off a nascent secessionist movement in Scotland and opponents claiming that devolution would hasten the dissolution of the union by giving secessionists a platform from which to broadcast their grievances.

Or, to take a second example, consider the debates over the public school curriculum in the United States. Many commentators express principled reservations about accommodations for evangelical families who object to the ways in which religious faith is discussed and presented in the classroom and in textbooks. Some of these same commentators concede, however, that accommodations might be a good idea for pragmatic reasons. Offering accommodations within the public schools would discourage families from opting for even less desirable options that are permitted to them, such as private religious schools or homeschooling.[19] The point is not that accommodations are intrinsically desirable or that desirable outcomes would come about when families take advantage of them. Rather, it is that families will not necessarily resign themselves to using the public system if a system of accommodations is not established but may instead choose some other option that comes with even more worrying consequences.

For the most part, my focus in the present book will be on principled rather than pragmatic arguments in favor of accommodating and recognizing cultural minorities. My central question is not whether there are *any* kinds of reasons for supporting specific forms of cultural accommodation and recognition as such, but rather whether there are principled reasons of this kind. Since pragmatic considerations clearly do have some weight in certain circumstances, it follows that the conclusions I shall argue for do not necessarily dispose of the practical question facing citizens and officials. I shall seek to clarify the principled considerations that are at stake, but this does not quite answer the "What should be done?" question since sometimes what should be done depends on pragmatic considerations.

Despite the relevance of pragmatic reasons, the principled reasons for or against accommodation and recognition policies are worth thinking about for their own sake. In part this is because it is sometimes appropriate to prioritize principled over pragmatic considerations. We are uncomfortable, for instance, about Lincoln's statement that "if there be those who would not save the Union unless they could at the same time *destroy* slavery, I do not agree with them. My paramount object in this struggle *is* to save the Union, and is *not* either to save or to destroy slavery."[20] Avoiding a secessionist crisis might have been a good pragmatic reason for compromising with the southern states on the issue of slavery, but many people today would prioritize justice over national unity in such a case.[21]

A second motivation for focusing on reasons of principle is that the pragmatic consequences may not be very pronounced one way or another, or they

[19] Macedo 1995, 487–88.

[20] Lincoln 1862. Lincoln went on to say that "I have here stated my purpose according to my view of *official* duty; and I intend no modification of my oft-expressed *personal* wish that all men everywhere could be free"—reaffirming that, as a matter of principle, he continued to hold that slavery was wrong.

[21] To call a consideration "pragmatic" is to not to deny that it is ultimately motivated by moral considerations. Lincoln's belief in the value of national unity was based in part on a moral judgment about the significance of the American experiment with liberty and democracy for the progress of world history. For discussion, see Callan 2010, esp. 257. In fact, the considerations favored by pragmatists (e.g., unity and the avoidance of civil conflict) almost always have some recognizable moral basis. The point is that the reasons privileged by pragmatists come into play only because it is expected that some people will break the rules or circumnavigate the institutions that are based on immediate principle. Rather than accept that slavery is an illegitimate and immoral institution, for instance, they attempt to secede. For the reasons mentioned in the text, I am interested in thinking about the considerations of immediate principle. I am grateful to Jeff Tullis for encouraging me to clarify this point.

may be very difficult to discern. When this is true, and there is no strong pragmatic reason to act one way or another, citizens and officials are left with considerable latitude to follow principle. Clearly it is both interesting and important to think about the principled considerations for their own sake.

BASIC NOT DERIVATIVE

The second distinction is between two different kinds of principled considerations that might be advanced on behalf of specific policies of accommodation and recognition. Accommodation policies are sometimes defended in terms that suggest they are directly required by general liberal values and principles. As we saw in the previous section, liberal-culturalist authors have suggested that the case for minority cultural rights can be based directly on liberal values of freedom, equality, neutrality, and so on. Policies that could be defended in this way would be morally required even if it could not be shown that they make some further beneficial contribution to the realization of other principles of liberal justice. When a policy can be defended in this way, I shall say that there is a *basic* reason of principle that can be advanced on behalf of the policy.

In other cases, the argument for adopting the policy simply is that the policy would make a beneficial contribution to the realization of some other specific principle of liberal justice. In these cases, the argument for accommodation or recognition offers a *derivative* reason of principle. There is some other specific liberal principle that does not itself directly call for accommodation or recognition, and the argument is that the policy of accommodation or recognition would contribute to the realization of that other principle, either instrumentally or as an application of the principle.

In the previous section we noted a range of different derivative reasons that a nonculturalist liberal might emphasize as a means of reconciling nonculturalism with certain cultural protections. For a specific example of a derivative reason, consider the long-standing attempt by Turkish authorities to suppress the use of the Kurdish language. Although the situation seems to have improved somewhat in recent years,[22] an earlier policy made it illegal to publish newspapers or to make radio or television broadcasts in Kurdish. This policy was, of course, targeted at a particular cultural group, but one does not need to believe that there are basic reasons of principle supporting the accommodation or recognition of the Kurdish language to think that there was a violation of liberal justice. It is enough to recall that freedom of expression is an important liberal principle and to note that the freedom to decide which language to express oneself in is part of the freedom of expression.

---

[22] See chapter 6, n. 6.

Whether advanced by culturalist or nonculturalist liberals, derivative reasons are, in fact, routinely offered in debates relating to multiculturalism and cultural rights. Many multicultural policies aim to reduce discrimination against, and ignorance about, minority cultures. For instance, government agencies offer education and "sensitivity training" to teachers, police officers, judges, health-care workers, and other professionals who deal with a culturally diverse clientele on a daily basis. The rationale for these policies does not rely on any idea of cultural recognition or accommodation as goods in themselves. Rather, the point is to promote the responsiveness of the professionals in question to a normative consideration—the effective and unbiased delivery of their service—that, in itself, has nothing to do with recognition or accommodation. Transitional bilingualism approaches in the classroom have a similar rationale. At root their point is not to recognize or accommodate the ongoing use of minority languages but to prevent minority-speakers from falling too far behind in other areas (e.g., literacy, numeracy) while they learn the normal language of instruction in the school.

It is sometimes suggested that fairly far-reaching policies of accommodation and recognition can be defended on the basis of derivative reasons. When the Quebec government introduced dramatic new language legislation in 1977 aimed at making French the normal language of public and economic life in the province, one of the main rationales given for the policy referred to the history of discrimination that French-speaking Quebecers had been subjected to by the small but powerful English-speaking minority.[23] The claim was that French-speakers would likely never be equally treated in an economy operating in English and that the only way to ensure that Francophones did not continue to suffer from discrimination was to make the economy operate in French. A similar claim is occasionally advanced concerning Spanish-speakers in the United States.[24] Since discrimination against Spanish-speakers is endemic, even after they have learned English, the only way to protect their basic claims of justice, it is suggested, is to develop a Spanish-speaking society and economy in the United States. These arguments do not assume that the minority language accommodations they call for are directly required by justice but instead claim that they are essential to preventing other forms of injustice that themselves make no reference to cultural accommodation or recognition.

Jacob Levy has sought to develop the idea that there are derivative reasons in favor of certain policies of accommodation and recognition into a full-scale theory of multicultural rights. In Levy's view, the tendency for majorities to oppress and discriminate against cultural minorities is deep and pervasive.

---

[23] Laurin 1977, 47–49.

[24] Some political theorists have suggested a trade-off between learning English and Spanish-language instruction in the public schools (see sec. 6.6). In response to this form of argument against rights to bilingual education, Stephen May (2003, 136) claims that "English is almost as inoperative with respect to Hispanic social mobility in the USA as it is with respect to black social mobility."

One does not need fancy normative theories of cultural justice to see why constitutions should often extend minority rights to cultural groups. Instead, all one needs is a morally minimal concern to prevent oppression and fear, combined with the observation that the point of constitutions is, in part, to counterbalance prospective threats to liberty, security, and other basic interests. Once one takes seriously this insight about liberal constitutionalism, it may be possible to justify regional autonomy for national minorities, separate (or multilingual) institutions for linguistic minorities, and so on, without resorting to any difficult argument that justice inherently requires these arrangements.[25]

Although derivative reasons of principle play a crucial role in justifying some policies of accommodation and recognition, my focus in this book is on exploring whether there are any basic reasons of principle for supporting such policies. In part, the motive for zeroing in on the question of basic reasons is philosophical in character. However important derivative reasons might be in practice, they seem theoretically straightforward. By contrast, the claim that there are basic reasons to support policies of accommodation and recognition is widely disputed and is clearly in need of further elaboration and investigation.

If the motive for focusing on fundamental reasons of principle were merely philosophical, it might be hard to justify an entire book on the subject. But there is more to it than that. As I suggested in the previous section, there is reason to expect that the derivative and basic strategies of argument will support different policy conclusions. In general there is reason to suppose that, on their own, derivative reasons will justify a more minimal set of policies than would an approach that recognizes both derivative and basic reasons. It would be surprising if fundamental reasons justified no new policies at all that were not already supported by derivative reasons. We should expect that the policies supported by the derivative reasons are likely to be more focused on private contexts, more limited to transitional arrangements, and/or more dependent on the vagaries of constitutional history and electoral politics than policies supported by basic reasons. Derivative reasons would apply to, and last as long as, the cultural trait that makes a person vulnerable to mistreatment remains salient. If that person could be fully integrated into the mainstream culture—for example, by fluently mastering the majority language—it would be harder to find a derivative reason for thinking that the original culture requires some special accommodation if the person is to be protected from oppression.

As mentioned earlier, there are accounts that attempt to justify fairly far-reaching accommodation policies on the basis of derivative reasons. But these accounts underestimate the complexity of the relationship between policies of cultural accommodation and recognition, on one side, and core elements of liberal justice (e.g., minimizing fear and oppression) on the other. Judg-

[25] Levy 2000; 2003; 2004.

ments about this relationship will often be highly conjectural and vulnerable to reversal with changes in empirical assumptions. As the earlier example of Spanish-speakers in the United States suggests, it may simply not be clear what a concern for minimizing fear, oppression, or discrimination counsels one to do. There is certainly some plausibility to the suggestion that a robust set of Spanish-language rights would be bulwark against certain forms of discrimination and oppression to which Hispanic Americans might otherwise be subject. But there are also reasons to be hesitant about this conclusion. On the one hand, the United States (like other states) has had some success at integrating cultural minorities into mainstream society without recourse to cultural rights or accommodations. Ethnic groups, such as Irish Americans and Italian Americans, and religious groups, such as Catholics and Jews, now enjoy rough equality with other Americans along a variety of dimensions of concern to liberals, even though they were not granted significant cultural rights or accommodations. For someone whose sole concern was to minimize noncultural injustices toward Spanish-speaking Americans, it would be tempting to try to follow this strategy of integration. On the other hand, minority cultural rights are themselves no panacea when it comes to minimizing injustice. Policies of accommodation and recognition empower new majorities and new elites who may be disposed to adopt discriminatory or oppressive policies toward dissident members of the accommodated group or toward nonmembers. Before accepting the proposition that a robust set of Spanish-language rights would serve to minimize noncultural forms of injustice, we would want to know, for instance, how Hispanic Americans who prefer to use English would be treated under the proposed linguistic regime and also how Anglo Americans living in areas with heavy concentrations of Spanish-speakers would fare. I am not suggesting that these questions are unanswerable, nor am I arguing against Spanish-language rights in the United States. I am simply underlining how difficult it can be to form a reliable judgment about whether some proposed cultural accommodation would be good or bad from the standpoint of realizing noncultural elements of liberal justice.

A derivative-reasons-based approach does, I think, offer a firm basis for defending certain kinds of accommodations, including, as I have mentioned, those of a transitional character. But beyond a minimal set of transitional accommodations, it is far from clear what policies and constitutional arrangements relating to cultural minorities would do the best at minimizing noncultural injustices. In this respect, the derivative-reasons-based approach is similar to utilitarian and sociobiological arguments made in other arenas. If one feeds in the right empirical assumptions, these arguments can get you the desired conclusion. The problem is that if those empirical assumptions get tweaked slightly the conclusion changes. In this sense, the derivative principles approach does not, on its own, provide a secure and robust basis for defending policies of cultural accommodation and recognition. Given this conclusion, it is important to explore whether there are basic reasons of principle, in addition to derivative ones, for supporting policies of the kind we are interested in.

MINORITY-REGARDING NOT THIRD-PARTY-REGARDING OR IMPERSONAL

A third distinction that helps to isolate the claim I want to make is between several different categories of reasons of basic principle that might be advanced in favor of cultural accommodations. Some such reasons refer especially to burdens that individual members of cultural minorities would face should the laws and institutions of the society not extend a particular accommodation to them. I call these *minority-regarding* reasons of basic principle.

Minority-regarding reasons can be contrasted with both *third-party-regarding* and *impersonal* reasons of basic principle. Third-party-regarding reasons do not, in arguing for a particular accommodation, privilege the standpoint of individuals belonging to the cultural minority that would enjoy the accommodation. Instead they refer to the interests of some other or broader group, typically all members of the society in question or even all people in the world. At the limit, the claim made in appealing to such a reason is that *everyone* would benefit if some particular accommodation were to be made. Impersonal reasons depart even more radically from minority-regarding ones. Unlike both minority-regarding and third-party-regarding reasons, they invoke a kind or dimension of value that is not ultimately reducible to the interests or well-being of individuals.[26] The claim made in offering such a reason is that the failure to extend an accommodation would result in a loss of value in the world that does not reduce to the diminished prospects of individual persons.

It is common to hear all three kinds of reasons in debates about cultural accommodations. When Britons debate whether to provide more Welsh-language services, the claim is sometimes made that Welsh-speakers themselves have such a significant interest in this being done that others have an obligation to accommodate them even if that means bearing some net cost. This of course is a minority-regarding form of reasoning. But different kinds of argument are also made. Sometimes the claim is that everyone benefits from living in a linguistically diverse society. With more languages, people have more options, and this enhances their capacity to direct their own lives.[27] Linguistic diversity is good, in this sense, in part because some people might want to choose to lead a life of Welsh-speaking. But it is also good because

[26] In Michael Blake's phrase (following Joel Feinberg), cultural loss, in this view, is a "free-floating evil," which is independent of any reference to human interests. For discussion and critique, see Blake 2002, 644–48. Another insightful critique of the attempt to derive cultural rights from a notion of cultures as intrinsically valuable is Johnson 2000. Johnson argues that such a view has trouble making sense of the basic fact that some cultural practices are "reprehensible"; this fact makes more sense in a view that connects cultures with human interests. For a third good critique, see Weinstock 2003, 252–56.

[27] Goodin 2006.

the existence of other language communities is likely to generate new options and experiments in living that would never occur to people speaking some particular language with its own conceptual scheme and patterns of discourse. At other times the argument is that preserving Welsh is analogous to conserving a species, or a piece of great art, or protecting an unspoiled place of natural beauty. Even if no individual's interests would be adversely affected by the loss of Welsh, the world would lose something valuable if it were to die out.

The focus in this book is on exploring the minority-regarding reasons that can be advanced on behalf of cultural accommodations. I am interested in whether there are considerations of justice *to* minorities that support the provision of such accommodations, and not in the broader question of whether there are *any* (basic, principled) reasons for their provision. By their very nature, the third-party-regarding and impersonal reasons would not leave minorities themselves with any special stake concerning the treatment of their culture. When third-party-regarding reasons are invoked, it is everyone's interests, minority and majority alike, that are said to be burdened. When the appeal is to impersonal reasons, the setback is to the universe, so to speak, and not to any particular person's interests or well-being. Since so much of the debate about cultural rights revolves around whether cultural rights are owed to minorities, it is worthwhile exploring this question in its own right.

To be sure, an exploration of impersonal and/or third-party-regarding reasons would also be an interesting exercise. For what it is worth, I am skeptical about whether a satisfactory account of cultural accommodations could be constructed on the basis of these categories. In each case, the losses and benefits that are invoked seem rather weak. Consider first the third-party-regarding reasons. The general benefits they point to—such as a greater diversity of options for all to choose from—are genuine goods, but it is far from clear that liberal principles require that they be provided. Individual autonomy does depend on the availability of what Mill calls a "variety of situations" and Raz terms an "adequate range of options." But an adequate range of options is not the same as a maximal one. At a certain point, additional options do not enhance autonomy, and even if they do, they do not enhance it beyond the point that the liberal state is committed to ensuring.

Moreover, even if adding options is something the liberal state is required to do in a given situation, it does not follow that extending cultural accommodation is necessarily the best way of going about it. Once one adopts a third-party-regarding perspective, one should be tough-minded about which policies will best produce the general benefits being sought. Accommodation policies involve money, time, political energy, and institutional capacity, and they have to translate somehow into accessible options if they are to produce the advertised benefits. Perhaps these resources would produce even greater general benefits if they were used differently? Investments in the arts and education, and support for civil society and for research and development efforts by the private sector, seem like alternative ways of encouraging a greater diversity of options. It is not enough for proponents of the third-party-reasons approach to show that cultural accommodations would produce some general benefits. They have to show that those accommodations would produce *greater* (or at least equivalent) benefits than any alternative, permissible use of the resources that would be expended.

The weightiness of impersonal reasons also seems contestable. It is true that we have powerful reasons not to tear down centuries-old cathedrals or to despoil the Grand Canyon. Although, at first glance, the strength of these reasons seems to suggest that impersonal reasons can be weighty, this initial impression is misleading. It fails to factor out the personal reasons we have for conserving such wonders, such as the value for present and future people of experiencing them.[28] Once these personal reasons are filtered out, it is not clear that any particularly urgent reason is leftover. Imagine that at some considerable expense to contemporary society a number of special rockets could be launched into space that would collide with one another (or with something else) on the far side of the galaxy to produce an extraordinary (and long-lasting) visual effect of the most unique kind. Unfortunately the effect will occur so far away, and so far into the future, that no human being (or sentient being, for all we know) will be able to experience it. From the point of view of value in general, there might be a pretty strong reason to develop and launch the rockets. But from our perspective, this reason does not seem especially weighty. It looks like the sort of reason that people might voluntarily act on using their own resources, in something like the way that private associations undertake costly projects for religious reasons (building cathedrals, etc.). What we do not have here is the sort of reason that it would be right to invoke (even by a democratic majority) to justify imposing significant costs on people against their will.

The weakness of both the third-party-regarding and impersonal reasons can be seen in another way. Both reasons point to ways in which it would be good if a culture is preserved. Preserving a culture, as we shall see in chapter 2, means that current members need to make decisions to participate in certain institutions and practices that transmit the culture to new generations. If they do not make those decisions (for whatever reason), the culture is doomed to disappear. It seems, then, that members of the culture have a special role to play in preserving the culture, and thus in producing the benefits that others enjoy or that are valuable in an impersonal sense. If these benefits are truly substantial, then one might expect the members of the culture to have a duty

---

[28] Scanlon (1998, 220) notes that the personal reasons may derive their force, in part, from the impersonal value that is at stake. The fact that the Grand Canyon has great impersonal value may help to explain the strength of the personal reasons people can claim to have the opportunity to visit and admire it. I don't make much use of this point in the chapters to follow, but I think it is broadly supportive of the thesis I defend. Insofar as cultures and languages have impersonal value, this strengthens the claims of people who want to enjoy and participate in them. It is all the more important that these claims get their due.

to carry on their culture. But many people would resist this conclusion. They think that cultural minorities ought to have the option to preserve their culture if they want, but that they have no duty to do so. This last idea is hard to reconcile with the suggestion that third-party-regarding and/or impersonal reasons are especially weighty.[29]

For all these reasons, I will concentrate on exploring the case that can be made for minority-regarding reasons of basic principle. Of course, it may turn out that there are no such reasons, in which case, if there are *any* reasons of basic principle, they would be third-party-regarding or impersonal ones. But the latter categories of reasons seem shaky enough that it is worth devoting some sustained attention to the question of minority-regarding reasons.

Required Not Permissible

One more distinction that is helpful for locating my claim is the distinction between requirement and permission. In general, a policy is required if a failure on the part of some decision-making body to adopt it would give rise to a legitimate complaint of justice. Given the previous distinctions, I am obviously especially interested in cases where the complaint is principled, basic, and minority-regarding. In these cases, when the policy is required, cultural minorities have a *right* to the policy—what I have been terming a "strong cultural right." A policy is permissible, by contrast, so long as, in adopting it, a decision-making body would not give rise to a legitimate complaint of injustice (of any sort).

Virtually all policies contain at least some provisions that are not required from the point of view of normative principle. The implementation of normative principles involves all sorts of conjectures and judgment calls, which reveal themselves in variations from decision maker to decision maker and from jurisdiction to jurisdiction. Given that disagreement about these judgments and conjectures is often reasonable, people do not necessarily have a legitimate complaint of justice if a particular principle is not implemented in the way that they would have preferred. Within a range, several different courses of action are permissible. There may also be reasonable disagreements about certain principles themselves. Rawls argues, for instance, that "there are many liberalisms and related views, and therefore many forms of public reason specified by a family of reasonable political conceptions."[30] The core commitments of liberal thought can be interpreted in different ways and can give rise to different substantive principles.[31] Where there is reasonable disagreement about

---

[29] See Kymlicka 1995, 122–23; Weinstock (2003, 255–56) also makes this point in a slightly different context.

[30] Rawls 2005, 450.

[31] Ibid., 451.

principles, a zone is established in which decision makers have permission but not an obligation.[32]

If the permissible exercise of discretion is a normal part of policy making, however, then so is conformity with certain obligatory principles of justice. If liberal arguments about civil and political rights are sound, for instance, then disagreement about whether these rights should be protected is not reasonable. Of course, there may be a variety of institutional means of protecting such rights, and it is possible that there could be legitimate disagreement about which of those means is the most effective. But *that* disagreement is heavily constrained by the requirement to protect the right that is being implemented in the first place.

Virtually every policy involves some permissible exercise of discretion, as well as some boundaries, more or less tightly drawn, that are required by justice. In this book, my focus is mainly on the question of requirements. My claim is that, under a range of standard conditions, particular forms of accommodation and recognition are a requirement of liberal justice in something like the way that civil and political rights are such a requirement.

Against this focus on requirements, it is sometimes objected that there is a deep tension between democratic politics and the idea that justice might require some policies. Suggesting that the leading theories of language rights are "allergic to politics," David Laitin and Rob Reich maintain that "there is a large and desirable area of indeterminacy where liberal principles offer no clear prescription in regard to language policy."[33] What makes this area "desirable" is, in part, the fact that it offers a space for the exercise of democratic politics. The implication is that political theorists who lay too much emphasis on articulating normative requirements are preempting a discussion that should really be conducted and decided democratically. A related suspicion is that there is something objectionably "juridical" about the enterprise of laying down requirements of justice (cultural or otherwise) for everybody.[34] This enterprise looks doubly problematic when it is observed that, rather like the judiciary, professional political philosophers tend to come from fairly privileged, majority-culture strata of society, and the principles they come up with may, in subtle ways, be colored by that background. Why then should we treat those principles as having any special authority? Would it not be preferable to generate the relevant principles "politically," through an inclusive, democratic process?

---

[32] Carens 2000, 6–8, 28.

[33] Laitin and Reich 2003, 93; Laitin 2007, 114–15, 118.

[34] Williams 1995. The idea that leading theories of justice are problematically "juridical" is a theme of Honig 1993.

These "democratic" objections to the enterprise of exploring normative requirements are confused about the proper relationship between normative political theory and democratic politics. We should distinguish between two questions that might be asked about cultural rights. The first concerns *authority*: who should have the authority to make decisions about the recognition and accommodation of cultural minorities? The second, by contrast, concerns the *substance of deliberation*: what substantive principles and normative criteria should guide the decisions of whoever it is that is legitimately tasked with making decisions about cultural rights?

Those who press the objections from democracy presume that the important question is the authority question. They argue that the democratic process should be the ultimate maker of decisions about cultural rights. Without filling in a conception of the democratic process, it is not clear what this answer to the authority question is meant to exclude. As a first approximation, we might take it as excluding government by bureaucrats, judges, and panels of professors.

Our question is not the authority question, however, but the substantive question. We are interested in whether there are any basic reasons of principle for thinking that minorities are owed accommodation and recognition. Indeed, for much of this book, the authority question is rather tangential to my concerns. I certainly do not mean to argue *against* the idea that the democratic process should have the ultimate authority to make decisions about cultural rights. The important point is that answering the authority question in a democratic way does not put to rest the substantive question. *Even citizens of a democracy need to address the substantive question.* Democracy is not just a mechanism for expressing raw, uninformed preferences. At its best, it is a process in which citizens try to decide what to think about the issues they face and then act (by voting, campaigning, protesting, etc) according to their best judgments. Given this understanding of democratic citizenship, it is wrong to think of democracy and political theory as somehow rival enterprises. There is a role for political theorists to contribute to the public discussion by seeking to clarify concepts and principles and to work out their implications. It is something like this aim that I have in mind when I set out to explore whether a justification can be given for strong cultural rights.

Against this attempt to reconcile political theory with democracy it might be objected that a properly "political" and "democratic" approach to thinking about cultural pluralism is bound to be more relational and contextual than an approach whose ambition is to elaborate a general theory. It is for this reason that the correct substantive test of legitimacy refers, not to some abstract general theory, but to actual public deliberations having an appropriate character. Actual public deliberations tend to be suffused with claims about relationships, context, facts, and so on, to such an extent that general theorizing is a poor substitute or proxy.[35]

It seems to me, however, that this objection underestimates the extent to which people engaging in actual public deliberation appeal to general ideas of equality, liberty, neutrality, culture, and so forth, to make their case. There is a role for political theory, not as a substitute for deliberation, but as a reflective effort to clarify and evaluate the status of certain general kinds of reasons that are advanced with great regularity in actual debates. In this way, political theory serves, not as a proxy for democratic deliberation, but as a resource that those engaged in deliberation can draw upon to illuminate, and make more rigorous, their concepts and claims.

By now it should be clear that the main thesis I intend to defend is a rather demanding one. It would be easy to justify various cultural protections if one could help oneself to pragmatic as well as principled reasons, or derivative as well as basic reasons, or if one could limit the task to showing that such protections are permissible rather than required. Rather than take the easy route, for each of these alternatives I want to take the tougher of the options and argue that the case for policies of recognition and accommodation can still be made. Taking the tougher route should, I hope, make the argument more theoretically interesting. More important, if the argument is a success, it will make the case for minority cultural rights deeper and more robust than it would be if pragmatic and derivative considerations were admitted freely into the mix or if permission was all that was established.

Some readers might wonder if I have not chosen such a difficult trail that I cannot possibly make it to the top. It is one thing to announce a thesis that is counterintuitive—this can make the ensuing discussion more interesting— but quite another to embark on a quixotic attempt to demonstrate something that is obviously mistaken. A leading reason for skepticism of this sort has to do with the notion of "requirement" that I have been assuming, and with the related notion of "rights" (e.g., when I refer to "strong cultural rights"). To see the problem, and also to situate my claim against it, we need a fifth and final distinction—this time between context-dependent and context-invariant requirements.

Context-Dependent Not Context-Invariant

In general, the state is required to adopt a policy when it has a reason for so doing that is strong and urgent enough that it should pursue the policy even in the face of other valid, countervailing reasons. The distinction that I now

---

[35] For an attempt to articulate a "political" approach to thinking about cultural difference that is distinct from a "theoretical" approach, see Laden 2007; Owen and Tully 2007.

wish to introduce turns on the fact that a claim that some policy is required in this sense can be more or less robust in the face of variation in the background context. On the one hand, the claim might be valid in *any* context. In this case there are no possible background circumstances or mitigating conditions that would make the requirement invalid. It is often said that the requirement that states refrain from torture (and the corresponding right not to be tortured) has or approaches this level of absoluteness in that the validity of such a requirement is robust to great variation in background context. I call requirements of this sort "context-invariant."

On the other hand, there are clearly some requirements that are valid under one set of conditions and not under another. I shall call these requirements "context-dependent." Some of the rights enshrined in the *Universal Declaration of Human Rights* are best thought of as context-dependent in this sense. The declaration enumerates various socioeconomic rights that could plausibly be satisfied directly in some economic and social contexts but not in others.[36] For instance, simplifying somewhat, one might expect the right to "periodic holidays with pay" to be immediately binding in countries that have achieved a certain level of income and wealth but not in countries that have not. For countries in the first class, the requirement to guarantee holidays is robust: its validity does not vary, for instance, with year-to-year fluctuations in the economy, with the intensity of competition from foreign economies, with attitudes about work held by the majority cultural or religious group, or so on. But the requirement weakens as one crosses over the relevant threshold of income and wealth, and in this sense its validity does depend, to some extent, on context. In one sense, indeed, the requirement does not just weaken but disappears altogether: on balance, a state is not required to guarantee paid holidays when it falls below the relevant threshold. In a different sense, however, the validity of the requirement does not disappear. The underlying human interests that are served by paid holidays remain, and they continue to generate reasons for the state (and, in the case of human rights, for the international community). Under unfavorable circumstances, where the right cannot be directly fulfilled, these reasons continue to imply a set of goals and guidelines that are relevant to the eventual fulfillment of the right. For example, they count in favor of states selecting forms and models of economic development that would eventually be compatible with guaranteeing adequate paid vacation for all.[37]

---

[36] The *International Covenant on Civil and Political Rights* explicitly acknowledges the context-dependency of the rights that it specifies, allowing that "In time of public emergency which threatens the life of the nation and the existence of which is officially proclaimed, the States Parties to the present Covenant may take measures derogating from their obligations under the present Covenant to the extent strictly required by the exigencies of the situation." See Beitz 2009, 30, for discussion of the fact that "not all of the human rights of contemporary doctrine can plausibly be regarded as preemptory."

[37] I am influenced here by the discussion of "manifesto rights" in ibid., 120–21.

To avoid misunderstanding, the distinction between context-invariant and context-dependent requirements is not entirely a matter of the strength of the requirement. The obligation to secure various socioeconomic conditions might be very strong and yet also context-dependent (in some contexts, scarcity or social conflict make it impossible to secure the conditions in question). To call something a requirement is already to say that there is a strong and urgent reason to perform it. Instead, the distinction I am pressing here concerns the robustness of the requirement: the extent to which a requirement remains in force with variation in background conditions.

If one thinks of strong cultural rights as highly robust or context invariant, then the strong cultural rights thesis is almost certainly mistaken. As we shall see at various points in the book, there clearly are circumstances in which states are not directly required to extend certain forms of recognition and accommodation to cultural minorities. Major examples of such circumstances include those in which recognition/accommodation would

- pose a serious threat to international and/or intra-state peace and security;
- create a space in which human rights violations are much more likely than they would be in the absence of such policies;
- have a significant weakening effect on the basic sense of social solidarity needed to support the provision of public goods and the protection of basic liberal values;
- consume the time and resources of the state to a degree that is disproportionate to the importance of such policies in a liberal-democratic framework; and
- make a significant contribution to the social marginalization and exclusion of members of the minorities in question, by fostering conditions under which members of those minorities will predictably lack the skills, capacities, and access to valuable social networks they need to be able to enjoy an adequate range of options across the different areas of human life.

These circumstances are not far away in some distant possible world but are likely to obtain in some places in the world as we know it today. If the strong cultural rights thesis really did embrace context-invariance, it would have to insist that the requirements of recognition and accommodation continue to have full force even in circumstances such as these, and this I take it would be highly problematic.

If the strong cultural rights thesis is understood to be context-dependent, however, this problem is averted. One can grant that there is no basic, principled requirement for states to recognize or accommodate minorities in circumstances such as the ones mentioned above, while still insisting that in other contexts there is such a requirement. To be sure, if one limited the validity of strong cultural rights only to extremely propitious conditions, then the thesis would start to look weak and uninteresting. But I shall be arguing for a middle-ground position in between these extremes. In the view that I shall defend, strong cultural rights are roughly comparable to the socioeconomic rights recognized as human rights. The cultural rights are certainly not context-invariant, but so long as certain thresholds are met (which I specify in various places throughout the book), they are robust to a variety of circumstances and conditions. The analogy with socioeconomic human rights holds in another respect too, in that, even if the context is such that a state should not adopt policies accommodating or recognizing some particular cultural minority, the reasons that count in favor of adopting such policies do not disappear. They are instead deflected into the goal of establishing conditions that are more propitious for the eventual adoption of the policies in question.

1.4 The Main Argument of the Book

The core case I develop in favor of strong cultural rights revolves around two main claims. The first holds that the liberal state has a responsibility to be neutral toward the various conceptions of the good that its citizens affirm. The second claims that, in certain domains, the only way for the state to discharge its responsibility of neutrality is by extending and protecting specific minority cultural rights. Although various qualifications and provisos are introduced along the way, and the rights that are justified must defeat countervailing considerations, the argument demonstrates why, in some contexts, specific strong cultural rights are indeed a requirement of liberal justice.

The suggestion that minority rights might be grounded in liberal neutrality will immediately seem unpromising to many readers. As we have seen already, some political theorists claim that cultural neutrality is impossible and cite this impossibility as part of a justification for cultural rights. I want to claim the opposite. A liberal state can, in principle at least, be neutral between majority and minority cultures. And the possibility of this neutrality is not a reason for rejecting or ignoring minority rights but, in fact, carries with it the implication that certain minority rights ought to be recognized. In a range of situations, a state that is neutral toward culture is not one that takes no notice of culture, or disentangles itself from culture, but is one that extends equal recognition to each culture.

To make this argument, I elaborate a new conception of neutrality, which I call "neutrality of treatment." The state treats two or more conceptions of the good neutrally, I propose, when it is equally accommodating of those different conceptions. It is equally accommodating of two or more conceptions of the good, in turn, when, relative to an appropriate baseline, it extends the same forms of assistance to each and imposes the same forms of hindrance on each. I argue that this understanding of neutrality is distinct from two more familiar views, which are known in the literature as "neutrality of intentions" and "neutrality of effects."

The new conception helps to make clear why it is a mistake to equate neutrality with indifference (taking no notice) or disentanglement, and why equal recognition of majority and minority cultures is a form that neutrality can take. Indeed, I argue that equal recognition is often the *only* form that neutrality of treatment can take for a range of decisions that a state must take about what I call the "format" of its institutions—the language, symbols, boundaries, and so on, that are associated with those institutions.

By developing a distinctive conception of neutrality defined in terms of "treatment," I shall also be in a position to address a different challenge, which is that many theorists now question whether neutrality belongs in the pantheon of liberal principles at all. By showing that neutrality of treatment is not a species of neutrality of effects, I avoid reliance on a view that liberal political philosophers have quite rightly disavowed. My defense of neutrality of treatment also avoids a claim that has got neutrality of intentions into trouble in some situations, namely, the claim that the liberal state has an *obligation* to be neutral. In the view that I defend, the liberal state has a strong presumptive (or *pro tanto*) reason to be neutral, but that reason is potentially outweighed (although never totally erased) by countervailing considerations. Departures from neutrality do not necessarily indicate an injustice. But there *is* an injustice if a state departs from neutrality without a sufficiently good reason. This pro tanto character of my basic claim about neutrality carries forward into the analysis of minority rights. I do not claim that a failure to extend such rights is always a form of injustice. Sometimes there are urgent and weighty liberal reasons for insisting on greater cultural uniformity in public institutions, although the aim of creating conditions that allow for the recognition and accommodation of difference never slips entirely from view. What I do claim is that there is an injustice when minority cultural rights are refused without a sufficiently good reason.

At a more fundamental level, I shall seek to explain why neutrality of treatment deserves to be considered an important liberal value. I rely here on two key ideas. The first, which is taken for granted in the book, is the idea of a state that represents all its citizens. Liberal values exclude the notion of a *Favoritvolk*, a privileged religious or cultural group that is given special concern or respect by the state. At some sufficiently abstract level, the state ought to be equally responsive to the interests of all its citizens.

The second idea says something more specific about one of the interests to which the state ought to be responsive. Of the several interests that citizens have, one of them is an interest in self-determination. This is the interest that a citizen has in being able to pursue and enjoy the conception of the good that he or she happens to hold, so long as that conception is permissible and at least minimally worthwhile. This interest, I argue, is a weighty one, especially as it pertains to conceptions of the good, or components of such conceptions, that have certain features. When a preference occupies a pivotal role in a person's conception of the good, or when it has a nonnegotiable character, or when it is salient to the individual's enjoyment of the recognition and respect of others, then there is reason to think that the individual has a particularly strong interest in being able to fulfill that aspect of her conception of the good. Cultural aspects of a person's conception of the good often possess one or more of these features, and thus persons normally have a weighty interest in being able to fulfill their cultural values.

Putting these two ideas together: the state's abstract obligation to be responsive to the interests of all its citizens implies a more concrete obligation to extend a fair opportunity for self-determination to all its citizens. This more concrete obligation is the basis of the state's pro tanto reason to extend neutral treatment to the various conceptions of the good valued by its citizens.

An important feature of my position is that the rights I defend are not rights to cultural preservation nor indeed to any particular cultural outcome. They are rights to equal accommodation and, hence, equal recognition. What cultural outcomes emerge out of such a framework will depend on the preferences, choices, interactions, etc., of the various citizens acting within the framework. It might be that some cultures flourish and others struggle or even disappear altogether. If a framework of equal recognition, together with other conditions of liberal justice, is in place, then the outcome is just whatever it is. In addition, the specification of the framework of equal recognition is not itself predicated on a goal of producing any particular outcome but instead is grounded in an independent idea of fairness. So, in the view I defend, outcomes play neither a direct role (justice does not require any particular outcome to be realized) nor an indirect one (the conditions that make up a justice-conferring framework are not based on the goal of realizing any particular outcome).[38] I call this outcome-independence of the position its "proceduralism." John Rawls argued that, by establishing fair background conditions, the basic institutions of society set up a system of "pure procedural justice" in which any outcome that arises could be considered just by virtue of

---

[38] Most leading theories of liberal multiculturalism avoid a direct appeal to outcomes. They defend rights to cultural options, not duties to preserve cultures. But, unlike the approach developed here, many do rely indirectly on outcomes. For instance, both Kymlicka (2001, 213) and Van Parijs (2011a, chap. 5) endorse Laponce's "territorial imperative" argument, which has as its premise the desirability of language preservation (see sec. 6.9). And Kymlicka's "context of choice" argument (which other theorists echo) is naturally construed as a point about outcomes, not unfairness of procedures (see chap. 3 below). It points out a potential threat to autonomy that liberals would normally be concerned to avert, even if they wouldn't forcibly avert it by locking people into a culture against their will. The theory developed in this book does not derive its content from assumptions about which cultural outcomes it would be good to produce or avert.

the background conditions under which it came about. Rawls believed that the various institutions implied by his two principles of justice were sufficient for procedural justice in this sense.[39] One way to think about my project is to see it as proposing equal recognition as an additional element that ought to go into a satisfactory specification of fair background conditions, when thinking about procedural justice under conditions of cultural diversity.

In working out this account of strong cultural rights, I do not suppose that I am adding some entirely novel form of justification to the existing arguments made by liberal culturalists. There are clearly important continuities between the "identity" and "neutrality" arguments that I described near the beginning of the chapter and the case that I have just been sketching.[40] (A version of the "freedom" argument also makes several appearances in the book as well, especially in chapters 3 and 6.) What my argument does contribute, I hope, is a restatement of the ethical foundations of liberal culturalism that is deeper and more secure than the existing approaches and that responds to, or allows a response to, some of the standard objections against such a view. If my argument is successful, it should be clearer than it was before how the considerations

---

[39] Considering whether his theory of justice as fairness is "fair to conceptions of the good" that struggle for survival and success, Rawls (2005, 198) writes: "The objection must . . . hold that the well-ordered society of political liberalism fails to establish, in ways that existing circumstances allow—circumstances that include the fact of reasonable pluralism—a just basic structure within which permissible forms of life have a fair opportunity to maintain themselves and to gain adherents over generations. But if a comprehensive conception of the good is unable to endure in a society securing the familiar equal basic liberties and mutual toleration, there is no way to preserve it consistent with democratic values as expressed by the idea of society as a fair system of cooperation among citizens viewed as free and equal." My account preserves the procedural character of this response to the objection—what matters is "fair opportunity," not the actual success of conceptions of the good—but proposes that "equal liberties" and "mutual toleration" can (and should) be supplemented explicitly with a requirement to extend equal recognition consistent with a concern for democratic values.

[40] The best early statement of a neutrality-style argument is the account of evenhandedness in Carens 2000, 8–14, 77–87; also 1997. Carens equates neutrality with a "hands-off" approach to culture and identity and contrasts this with an evenhanded approach that involves "a sensitive balancing of competing claims for recognition and support" (12). My account is much indebted to Carens, but there are several differences worth noting. Most obviously, there is a semantic difference: whereas Carens opposes evenhandedness to neutrality, in my account evenhandedness is one of three possible forms that neutrality can take. More substantively, there is a difference of structure between the two accounts. Carens regards evenhandedness as an overall approach to fairness and thus admits a variety of different considerations into the "sensitive balancing" that goes into determining what evenhandedness involves in a given case. In my account, by contrast, neutrality has a more specific structure based on the idea of equal accommodation. It is a pro tanto obligation of the liberal state, and other factors and considerations enter in as potentially competing (or strengthening) reasons. Most important, my account tries to go quite a bit further than Carens in exploring the foundations of neutrality and evenhandedness in liberal principles and commitments. I try to take seriously skepticism about neutrality and devote considerable space (especially in chap. 4) to explaining why neutrality is an appealing idea and how it is rooted in liberal commitments. All three of these differences are in the spirit of Carens's own remark that he has "not yet worked out a general theoretical account" of how neutrality and evenhandedness are related to one another (14). My own earliest sketches of the equal recognition approach are in Patten 1999c; 2000.

adduced by the identity and neutrality arguments are grounded in liberal principles and thus why it would be problematic for somebody committed to such principles to reject them.

As a related payoff, my approach contributes a distinctive perspective on some important policy questions relating to cultural justice. In policy discussions, the default assumption of many defenders of minority cultural rights is that the point of such rights is the preservation of vulnerable minority cultures. The policy recommendations are oriented to that goal, and so is the assessment of whether a particular policy is successful. If a given policy is failing to secure a culture's preservation, then, in a standard view, one ought to conclude that it is not doing enough.

The theory that I develop, by contrast, has a rather different set of implications for policy. The point of cultural rights is not to guarantee the preservation of any particular culture but to secure fair background conditions under which people who care about the survival or success of a particular culture can strive to bring about that outcome. The policy recommendations are geared, then, toward establishing fair background conditions (through equal recognition), not to securing a particular outcome. From the fact that a particular culture's preservation is not secured by equal recognition, it cannot be inferred that that policy is a failure. The relevant question in assessing a policy regime of equal recognition is whether recognition is truly equal. Are public policies structured in a way that is evenhanded between majority and minority cultures, or is there some kind of bias in favor of the former?[41]

As noted earlier, another tendency in existing debates is to elide the protection of minority cultural rights with the accommodation of substate minority nationalism. This tendency is quite explicit in some of Kymlicka's writings. In certain of his formulations, a leading rationale for minority rights is to offset the nation-building efforts of a state's national majority. Since the national majority uses the national government to engage in forms of nation building, substate national minorities should have, as a matter of fairness, the right to use the governments of subnational units for minority nation building. In other places, this tendency to "nationalize" minority rights is a consequence of the previous tendency, the tendency to think of cultural preservation as the point of cultural rights. It is argued that preservationist projects face a kind of "territorial imperative." To have any hope of preserving a culture, a group

---

[41] The distinction between preservation and equal recognition is relevant to an evaluation of Canada's official languages policy. Critics have sometimes assumed that preservation is the metric of success and have pointed to high levels of assimilation among Francophones outside of Quebec as evidence that the policy is not working. For reference to this view, see McRoberts 1997, 204–5; Kymlicka 1998a, 133. Equal recognition offers a different lens through which to evaluate the policy. Facts about assimilation are not by themselves indications that the policy is failing. What matters is whether the two languages truly are recognized equally in various contexts.

must, in effect, be a national group, endowed with its own territory, and with ample control over, and domination of, that territory.

In contrast with these existing accounts, the approach developed in this book attempts to denationalize the nature and content of minority cultural rights. Such rights are not, in general, rights to engage in nation building but in fact place constraints on the legitimate forms of nation building that any level of government can pursue.[42] Cultural minorities are not neatly concentrated into homogeneous territories but typically live, to some extent at least, side by side with members of the majority. There are territories in which national minorities form local majorities, but those territories are also typically home to members of the national majority who find themselves in the local minority, as well as to other minorities. In general, the obligations of fairness that ground the idea of equal recognition apply to all levels of government, and thus there is no reason to think either that the state as a whole belongs to the national majority or that substate jurisdictions containing concentrations of the minority somehow belong to that minority. The exclusion of a *Favoritvolk* goes all the way up, and all the way down. Since the point of cultural rights, in my account, is not cultural preservation, there is also no reason to nationalize such rights based on a territorial imperative.

So minority rights are not to be equated, in my account, with rights to engage in minority nation building. In this respect, the account developed here challenges the prevailing tendency to see a close connection between minority cultural rights and liberal nationalism. In two further respects, however, the account I propose is compatible with insights highlighted by liberal nationalism. First, the account can allow that there are sometimes legitimate reasons for governments to engage in nation building geared around the majority's culture. I mentioned earlier that the claims of minorities might sometimes have to be balanced against considerations based on values such as social solidarity, social mobility, and administrative efficiency. It may be that an energetic program of majority nationalism can be justified on the grounds that it is the best means of securing these values, even though such a program entails the nonneutral treatment of minority cultures. As I argue in chapter 5, how-

---

[42] I do not want to exaggerate the disagreement here since Kymlicka and others do acknowledge constraints on legitimate nation building. For Kymlicka (2001a, 29; see also 2001b, 27; Norman 2006, 56, 166), "all else being equal, national minorities should have the same tools of nation-building available to them as the majority nation, subject to the same liberal limitations." Still, I think there is a difference that will emerge in this book between two variants of the liberal approach to minority rights. For Kymlicka, and for those who follow him in this respect, a major rationale for minority rights is to give national minorities an equal opportunity for nation building. The limitations Kymlicka seems to have in mind are fairly minimal. He says that liberal principles preclude "ethnic cleansing, or stripping people of their citizenship, or the violation of human rights" (2001a, 29; for a fuller catalog, see Kymlicka 2001b, 54–58). As noted in the text, the view I develop is mainly concerned with limiting nation building by circumscribing the range of contexts in which it is acceptable for government (at any level) to favor the majority's culture.

ever, I do not think that such a trade-off is invariably justified: there are difficult empirical and normative questions that would need to be asked about the degree to which the values in question are in fact jeopardized, the magnitude of the contribution to securing those values that would in fact be made by majority nationalist policies, and the precise respects in which minority cultures are to be treated nonneutrally. Even where this calculus does come out in favor of majority nationalism, a residue of the pro tanto considerations favoring neutrality remains. The residual value of neutrality directs the state to encourage conditions that make it possible eventually to honor the claims of cultural minorities (such as rethinking the content of the national identity and encouraging second-language acquisition).

The second respect in which my account can be reconciled with liberal nationalism is more speculative but less ambivalent. It seems possible that nationalism can take a sufficiently inclusive form that the concerns about disadvantaging and alienating minorities I have been highlighting do not arise in a significant way.

An inclusive brand of nationalism is, in part, one that hews closely to principles of liberal democracy. It leaves citizens space to hold their own beliefs and to pursue their own diverse projects. It does not connect full membership in the political community with ethnicity or religious affiliation. It affirms liberal rights and makes decisions through democratic procedures. And so on. But such a nationalism also acknowledges that there are multiple modes of belonging to the political community. It recognizes that for some the statewide political community is a primary affiliation, while for others it is a more attenuated, perhaps more instrumental, connection. Such a nationalism need not eschew all reliance on particularity or emotion. As with any form of nationalism, it can adopt its own symbols, advance its own narratives, and foster feelings of pride and loyalty among citizens. But it is not sectarian, and it is not aligned to particular cultural traditions and symbols. It need not limit itself to purely generic symbols, such as the scales of justice, but there is no doubt that the public self-presentation of the inclusively nationalist state manifests a tendency toward the ecumenical and the evenhanded. A nice example of an inclusive symbol that illustrates both tendencies is the post-2001 badge of the Police Service of Northern Ireland. The badge evenhandedly incorporates images of the crown, the harp, and the shamrock and also features the more ecumenical symbols of the torch, the olive branch, and the scales of justice.

I do not argue that inclusive nationalism is easy to bring about, or even that there are many (or even any) examples of it in the world as we know it. The point is the more theoretical one that the ideals of neutrality and equal recognition that I develop in the pages of this book are not necessarily "postnationalist" ones, if that implies a sharp break with nationalism in all its forms. A recognizable nationalism of sorts can still be realized in a state that commits itself to those ideals.

1.5 Overview

The core argument about neutrality and equal recognition that I have been describing is mainly developed in chapters 4 and 5. Chapter 4 examines the idea of liberal neutrality in isolation from the book's more narrow concerns with cultural justice. It introduces and defends "neutrality of treatment." Chapter 5 then explores the implications of neutrality of treatment for the justification of minority cultural rights. It is in this context that I distinguish between procedural and nonprocedural accounts of cultural justice and, within the former category, between "basic" and "full" liberal proceduralism. The major argument is that neutrality of treatment mandates the latter form of proceduralism, which incorporates a concern for what I term "equal recognition." The second half of the chapter considers and responds to several objections to this defense of cultural rights.

Although chapters 4 and 5 present the core argument of the book, other chapters set up and fill out that argument and add important additional ones as well. Chapter 2 considers a major threshold question that any contemporary account of cultural rights must tackle. According to a popular recent line of argument, any attempt to develop a case for strong cultural rights is scuppered from the outset. The problem has to do with the concept of culture itself. Drawing on the well-known critique of essentialism, the contention of a number of commentators is that there is no defensible way of identifying distinct cultures, or of determining how they are faring, that is consistent with the normative agenda of multiculturalism.

The ambition of chapter 2 is to respond to this threshold objection to the project by developing a conception of culture that can withstand the essentialist critique, while at the same time providing a basis for the normative claims made later in the book. Culture, in the view proposed in the chapter, is what people share when they have shared subjection to a common formative context. A division of the world, or of particular societies, into distinct cultures is a recognition that there are distinct processes of socialization that operate on different groups of people. Since culture in this view is the precipitate of a common social lineage, I refer to this as the "social lineage account" of culture. Although there may be some weak sense in which the social lineage account remains "essentialist," I argue that it is not essentialist in an objectionable manner. It is compatible with, and indeed helps to account for, the patterns of heterogeneity, contestation, hybridity, and so forth, that commentators have rightly emphasized in pressing the essentialist critique.

The account of culture in chapter 2 also prepares the ground for an account of why culture matters to people. Why is it a bad thing for one's culture to disappear, or for one to be denied the opportunity to participate in some cultural practice? I take up this question in chapter 3, where the aim is to develop an account of why culture matters that is salient to the strong cultural rights thesis. The main answer I consider is, in effect, a generalized version of the "freedom argument" mentioned earlier. The thought is that it is bad for people to lose their culture, or to be denied certain cultural opportunities, because the options that are open to them are thereby diminished in an unacceptable way. I argue that any account of this form is vulnerable to a dilemma, and that an important implication of the dilemma is that strong cultural rights should not be thought of as rights to cultural preservation. The dilemma does, however, leave scope for the neutrality-based, proceduralist argument developed in chapters 4 and 5.

Chapters 6 and 7 work out further the general model developed in chapters 4 and 5 by considering two particular areas in which minority rights have been contested. Chapter 6 explores the justification of minority-language rights. The main existing approaches to language rights—which I term the "nation-building" and "language preservation" models—each understand language policy making to be primarily a question of what might be called "language planning." The policy maker, or institutional designer, identifies some desirable outcome—language convergence or language maintenance—and then determines how public institutions can best help to realize these outcomes. Building on the idea of liberal neutrality developed in chapter 4, chapter 6 introduces a third approach to language policy—the "equal recognition" model. The distinctive feature of this approach is its rejection of language planning. The task of language policy is not to realize some specific linguistic outcome—be it convergence on a common public language or the survival of minority languages—but to establish fair background conditions under which speakers of different languages can strive for the survival and success of their respective language communities. Following the argument of chapter 5, I claim that, in general, fair background conditions are realized only when the state extends certain minority rights to speakers of minority languages. Overall the chapter defends a hybrid approach to the justification of language rights, which draws on each of the three principal models. A concluding section of the chapter discusses some of the distinctive policy implications of adopting this perspective on language rights.

Chapter 7 then turns to the problem of self-government rights. To what extent do national minorities have a legitimate claim on some form of self-governing autonomy within a multinational state? When, if ever, does this claim—or its frustration—support a further claim to independent statehood? By drawing on the idea of equal recognition, the chapter develops a distinctive way of thinking about the justification of multinational federalism and other forms of autonomy for substate national groups.

The chapter explores this issue in the context of a further question that has been debated by normative political theorists in recent years—the moral status of secessionist claims. The two main views on this question have been the plebiscitary theory and the remedial rights only theory. The former re-

gards a secessionist claim as morally legitimate if and only if it is democratically mandated and is consistent with a set of further conditions (e.g., respect
for liberal rights), none of which involve protecting or respecting schemes of
self-government for national minorities. The remedial view maintains that a
group's secessionist claims are morally legitimate only if the group has been the
victim of injustice at the hands of the state.[43] In Allen Buchanan's influential
version of this theory, a right to secede is given only to those groups that can
(1) reasonably complain of a pattern of serious human rights violations at the
hands of the state, or (2) establish that they were unjustly incorporated into
the state.[44] Drawing on the idea of equal recognition, chapter 7 attempts to
chart a middle course between the plebiscitary and remedial (as formulated by
Buchanan) approaches. My proposal does not require that the seceding group
be able to demonstrate that it has been the victim of one of the forms of injustice highlighted by Buchanan. A right to secession *can* be claimed against
"minimally just" states (i.e., states that satisfy Buchanan's conditions). Against
the plebiscitary approach, however, I argue that, under certain fairly common
conditions, a democratic mandate does not generate a right to secede from a
flawless state. For such a right to be generated, there must be *either* a violation
of the conditions of minimal justice à la Buchanan *or* a distinct failure by the
state, a failure of equal recognition. Where a state avoids both of these kinds
of flaws, it need not worry about legitimate secession: a democratic mandate
does not, on its own, generate a right to secede.

Finally, chapter 8 examines a more general problem that arises with respect
to minority cultural rights, including both language and self-government
rights. The problem arises from the fact that most states are home to dozens,
even hundreds, of cultural groups. Their members speak different languages,
have different practices and traditions that they want to maintain, and, in
some cases, would like for their group to enjoy some autonomy over its own
affairs. Some cultural rights claims do not come with a great deal of cost and
could conceivably be granted to all such groups. This is especially likely to be
the case for rights that are "derivative" in character (to use my earlier vocabulary) but may even apply to some that are "basic." Many strong cultural rights
could not, however, be universalized to all claimants without risking grave
damage to other legitimate public purposes and priorities. To extend a full set
of language rights or self-government rights to every group that claims them
may cripple the liberal state's ability to pursue its legitimate objectives. In these
cases, some principle is required for deciding which cultures ought to enjoy a
full set of strong cultural rights and which should not.

[43] Buchanan 1997; 1998a; 2004.
[44] Buchanan 1997, 37. As I discuss in the chapter, Buchanan (2004) subsequently added a third condition that is triggered when states violate intrastate autonomy agreements. This condition moves in the
direction of the account I defend but still falls short of it in a way that I shall explain.

Chapter 8 considers two different approaches to this problem. The first attaches categorical significance to the distinction between "national" and "immigrant" groups. It argues that, in areas where universalizing rights is impossible, some priority ought to be extended to the claims of the former over those of the latter. This priority is grounded in the idea that immigrants waive certain kinds of claims on cultural rights as a condition of admission into the receiving state. The second answer proposes that one or more general principles be made the basis for determining the allocation of cultural rights. By "general principles," I mean principles that attach no weight to the fact that a group is immigrant or national but instead decide on the basis of criteria that could, in principle, be associated with either sort of group (e.g., group size).

Will Kymlicka is famous for defending a version of the first answer, and, in the critical reception of his work, few of his arguments have been subjected to more repeated or intense criticism.[45] Chapter 8 discusses some of the weaknesses in Kymlicka's position but argues that the sort of answer that Kymlicka offers (in favor of a limited immigrant/national group dichotomy) can be defended. The argument as I develop it rests in part on a reconsideration of what it what it would take for immigrants voluntarily to waive their rights. A key claim is that the standard of voluntariness ought to take into account the degree to which it is reasonable to impose the particular conditions that are attached to the provision of the benefits in question. A further part of the argument consists in suggesting that, for a limited class of cultural and linguistic rights, a liberal society is acting permissibly and reasonably in prioritizing the claims of national minorities over those of immigrants. I thus offer a reappraisal of Kymlicka's controversial theory that immigrants voluntarily relinquish their cultural rights, one that is meant, not as an interpretation of Kymlicka's original intentions, but as a proposal that stands on its own feet and, indeed, gains some of its plausibility through disentanglement from other elements of Kymlicka's theory.

---

[45] Kymlicka 1995, 95–100. For the critical reception, see references in chapter 8 below.

CHAPTER 2

Rethinking Culture: The Social Lineage Account

2.1 The Dilemma of Essentialism

Normative theories of multiculturalism have come under attack in recent years for a number of reasons. Many critics challenge the positive arguments offered on behalf of multicultural policies, questioning whether the values of liberal democracy entail that the state ought to recognize and accommodate the distinctive concerns of minority cultures.[1] Others highlight the potential costs of multicultural policies. Even if such policies do promote liberal democratic values in some respects, they compromise those same values in other respects. Familiar formulations of this second form of critique suggest that multiculturalism is "bad for women," that it ghettoizes vulnerable minorities, and that it fosters intolerance and extremism.[2]

In this chapter I consider a distinct kind of challenge to multiculturalism, a challenge that has been around for a while but has received some of its most forceful statements within the past decade.[3] According to a growing number of critics, a fundamental problem with normative theories of multiculturalism is their reliance on a concept of culture that is empirically and morally naïve. The theory of multiculturalism is founded on an essentialist picture of cultures as determinate, bounded, and homogeneous, a picture that is empirically false and morally dangerous. When cultures are conceptualized as fluid, interactive, and overlapping, and as internally contested and heterogeneous, they become more acceptable empirically and normatively. But then culture is no longer serviceable within a multicultural framework. Defenders of multiculturalism are left without a culture concept that allows them to make judgments about the treatment, survival, and revival of distinct minority cultures.

---

[1] Waldron 1992; Barry 2001.

[2] Okin 1999; Barry 2001, 103–9; Sniderman and Hagendoorn 2007.

[3] Barry 2001, 7, also chap. 7; Benhabib 2002; Appiah 2005, chap. 4; Scheffler 2007. See also Waldron 1992; 2010.

I shall call this challenge the *dilemma of essentialism*. According to the dilemma,

> *either* culture is understood in an "essentialist" way, in which case multiculturalism is empirically and morally flawed; *or* culture is understood in a nonessentialist way, but then the concept no longer supplies multiculturalism with the means of making the empirical judgments and normative claims that matter to it.

Whichever horn of the dilemma one opts for, the upshot is that normative defenses of multiculturalism should be dismissed.

My aim in this chapter is to defend multiculturalism against this challenge by arguing that the dilemma of essentialism is false. I do this by grabbing the second horn of the dilemma and showing that it is possible to elaborate a plausible nonessentialist concept of culture that is serviceable to the normative agenda of multiculturalism. By "plausible" I mean a concept that is responsive to both empirical and normative desiderata. To be plausible, a concept should pick out as sharing a culture at least some of the groups that multiculturalists have in mind when they make their normative claims. And the concept should help us to see—in at least some cases—why culture is valuable to people. It should help us to make sense of the idea that, in a central range of cases, it is good for people when their cultures are respected and preserved.

Although nothing guarantees that there is a nonessentialist culture concept that satisfies both of these desiderata, I argue that there is such a concept. Culture, I propose, is what people share when they have shared subjection to a common formative context. A division of the world, or of particular societies, into distinct cultures is a recognition that distinct processes of socialization operate on different groups of people. Because culture in this view is the "precipitate" (to borrow Kluckhohn's term[4]) of a common social lineage, I shall sometimes refer to this as the social lineage account of culture. Although there may be some weak sense in which the social lineage account remains essentialist—it does say that members of a culture uniquely share a particular property, namely, the property of having been shaped by a common set of formative conditions—it is not essentialist in an objectionable manner.[5] It is compatible with, and indeed helps to explain, patterns of heterogeneity, contestation, and hybridity that commentators have rightly emphasized in pressing the critique of essentialism.

The next section takes a closer look at the problem of essentialism, explaining why it is such a serious issue for multiculturalism and how existing

---

[4] Kluckhohn 1950, 34.

[5] Some accounts of essentialism (e.g., Mallon 2007) maintain that a definition of a kind, to count as essentialist, must refer to "nonrelational" properties. In this understanding of essentialism, the social lineage account is not essentialist at all.

responses to the problem have fallen short. The chapter's main conceptual proposal is developed over the course of the three sections that follow. The chapter then considers, in section 2.6, why culture matters normatively. Although I leave this issue for the end and postpone detailed exploration of the issues for subsequent chapters, it is a crucial part of the response to the dilemma of essentialism. The dilemma does *not* say that there could be no nonessentialist culture concept. Rather, it says that there is no such concept that is supportive of multiculturalism. To respond effectively, it is necessary to show how the social lineage account might be called on in support of multiculturalism.

2.2 The Critique of Essentialism

Any attempt to articulate a culture concept for multiculturalism has to address the important critique of cultural essentialism that anthropologists and political theorists have developed in recent decades. In general, essentialism consists in the identification of kinds in the natural or social world through the singling out of some relevant property (or set of such properties) that are possessed by all and only the individuals who belong to that kind. The critique of essentialism consists in pointing out that the individuals belonging to the various kinds that are commonly supposed to exist do not, in fact, uniquely share a relevant property or set of properties. There is both variation within the members of the putative kind and commonality between members and nonmembers.

Applied to culture, the critique of essentialism amounts to the argument that all the usual features that are taken to define culture run foul of the problems of internal variation and external overlap: the relevant features are not shared by all and only the members of the groups that are generally said to share cultures. The critique is often thought to follow from, or be associated with, certain commonplace observations about human beliefs and practices. In groups of any size, beliefs and practices are heterogeneous and contested. They change and fluctuate over time. And they are formed interactively and dialogically with members of other groups, often taking on a recognizably hybrid character as a result.

To see the critique of essentialism in action, consider the familiar conception of culture as a shared framework of beliefs and values. There are actually two versions of the familiar conception, the first of which requires that all and only the members of a distinct culture hold some particular set of beliefs and values.[6] If this is the proposal, however, then it is obviously a nonstarter.

---

[6] Geertz (1973, 250) attributes such a view to Talcott Parsons, whose account dominated postwar anthropology for a generation. On Parsons's view and its importance for an era of American cultural anthropology, see also Kuper 1999, 227.

In virtually any of the groups that are usually thought to share a culture, one can find significant variation of beliefs and values. There is unlikely to be any significant belief or value, or set of beliefs and values, that is shared by all and only the members of the group. A closely related problem is variation over time. The familiar view seems to imply that a distinct culture would cease to exist whenever its members revised or abandoned the beliefs or values that constituted it. This implication leaves insufficient space for the distinction between cultural disappearance and cultural change.[7]

A different version of the familiar conception takes a cue from Clifford Geertz's dictum that "culture is public because meaning is."[8] Geertz draws on well-known accounts in the philosophy of language to argue that the meaning of words is settled publicly, by social conventions, and not by agreement of private beliefs. In the same way, he suggests, practices and established forms of social behaviors are associated with particular meanings that are settled publicly. Winking (to use Geertz's example, borrowed from Ryle) has a specific meaning in a given context, whether the winker has certain beliefs in his or her head or not. The suggestion, then, is that cultures might be defined as the "socially established structures of meaning" in terms of which people engage in social behaviors of various sorts. In this picture the relevant framework of shared beliefs and values for identifying distinct cultures is not identified by inspecting the private beliefs and values of different individuals but by recovering through interpretation the beliefs, values, and meanings that are embodied in particular practices and institutions. The implication is that a society can be said to contain several distinct cultures when it is home to several distinct public structures of meaning of this kind.

But once the claim is put in this way, it immediately looks vulnerable to the same challenges that undermined the first version of the familiar conception. The main problem is that meanings in a society are typically contested. For many practices and bits of social behavior, there will be several publicly established meanings that people enact in their behavior.[9] There is *a* socially established structure of meaning only if "structure" is meant to encompass the possibility of difference and disagreement. But making this move produces a

---

[7] Perhaps sharing culture is a matter, not of sharing some specific beliefs or values, but of having some threshold number of beliefs and values from a longer, culture-defining menu of beliefs and values? People share a culture when they all surpass the threshold from the same menu. But this too looks unpromising. If the threshold is set at a very high level (so that one has to have most of the beliefs and values on the menu), then intragroup variation remains a problem: some in the group will pass the threshold and others will not. If the threshold is set too low, on the other hand, then one is likely to find intergroup commonality. One will not have succeeded at identifying something distinctive about the group that justifies considering it a distinct culture. Perhaps in some cases a magic combination of menu and threshold can be identified that puts just the right people inside and the others outside, but this seems unlikely to work very generally.

[8] Geertz 1973, 12.

[9] Wedeen 2002, 716.

dilemma. Are lines of cultural difference demarcated by these differences of signification, or can a single culture be home to divergent understandings of the relevant meanings?

If the former, then the contours of shared cultures are going to look nothing like the contours of the groups that are typically thought of as cultures: Those groups contain a great deal of disagreement about meanings, often because at least some of their members interact in various ways with other groups and are attracted, in at least some measure, to the meanings and forms of signification that predominate in them. If, on the other hand, it is allowed that cultures can be home to divergent understandings of the relevant meanings, then the conception does not yet offer any basis for distinguishing different cultures.[10] Why not just say that the whole society (or the whole world) contains one single culture, albeit a culture that is subject to considerable fragmentation of meanings and values? A similar problem arises with respect to the question of disappearance versus change. Does the culture disappear every time one or more of the meanings embodied in its practices is revised? Presumably not. But then how do we determine when a culture has disappeared and when it has been preserved?

These arguments retrace the familiar critique of essentialism. To be clear, the objection is *not* to the idea that there are shared beliefs and values, nor to the idea that there are socially enacted, publicly established meanings. Rather, the point is that commonality and variation in these beliefs, values, and meanings do not track the cultural differences that are commonly supposed to exist. There is variation within, and overlap between, these putative cultures.

If familiar conceptions of culture fail to satisfy the empirical criterion stipulated earlier, they also do poorly by the normative criterion. Attempts to protect distinct cultures risk being oppressive to the many people within groups who do not, in fact, hold the beliefs and values that are supposedly constitutive of the group's culture.[11] Moreover, if the supposedly constituting values are illiberal, then the familiar concept would end up pitting cultural preservation against liberalism. A culture would have to maintain its illiberal values and practices or disappear altogether.[12]

One possible reaction to the critique of essentialism is that it must go wrong at some point, because people clearly do engage in actions that are "cultural." They communicate with one another, attempting to exchange, negotiate, validate, subvert, and otherwise manipulate meanings and symbols. For these actions to be possible, it is occasionally argued, there must be some of kind of shared framework in the background that provides a common vocabulary and

---

[10] Consistent with her suggestion that "cultures are constituted through contested practices," Benhabib (2002, viii–ix) says that she does not believe in "the possibility of identifying them as meaningfully discrete wholes."

[11] Ibid., 4; Mason 2007, 227.

[12] Kymlicka 1989b, 168–70.

set of meanings. For instance, Kymlicka responds to a version of the critique of essentialism (pressed by Waldron[13]) by arguing that "cultural materials" are only "available" or "meaningful" to people "if they become part of the shared vocabulary of social life—i.e., embodied in the social practices, based on a shared language, that we are exposed to."[14]

But this response to the critique of essentialism remains unconvincing. From the fact that people exchange meanings with one another, it does not follow that there must be some framework of shared meanings hovering in the background. In reality, only a minimal amount of commonality is needed to get a fruitful discussion, or an exchange of meanings and signs, off the ground. Persons who, if the world were to be divided into discrete cultures, would clearly not be considered to share a culture can still improvise a meaningful dialogue with one another, so long as there are sufficient resources or situational clues in the immediate context for interpreters to form plausible theories about what speakers are trying to convey.[15] This is sometimes called "cross-cultural" or "intercultural" dialogue.

Not surprisingly, many theorists of multiculturalism acknowledge the force of the critique of essentialism and opt for the second horn of the dilemma of essentialism. Joining the chorus of critics of cultural essentialism, they announce that their defense of multiculturalism will be grounded in a nonessentialist culture concept. I am obviously sympathetic to this general strategy for responding to the dilemma, but the attempts so far to execute it seem unsatisfactory. Many of the theorists adopting this approach do a good job of presenting the critique of essentialism but then become painfully circumspect about what precisely the alternative conception is supposed to be. The effect is to reinforce the suspicion voiced by critics of multiculturalism that essentialism is continuing to play an unacknowledged role in the view's foundations.

In his early work, for instance, Kymlicka introduces a distinction between cultural "character" and the cultural "structure" or "community," which is designed in part to guard against the critique of essentialism. The cultural structure is something that persists even while the character of the culture changes. Quebec's culture, to use Kymlicka's example, survived the dramatic transformations of the Quiet Revolution of the 1950s and 1960s. Although the example seems promising, Kymlicka never tells us very much about how to identify cultural structures. How do we know if a society contains one or several, if it is not by looking for frameworks of meaning that have distinctive characters? Kymlicka concedes that defining cultural communities is a "vexed problem" but insists that "we know that such communities exist."[16] Given that

[13] Waldron 1992; 2004.
[14] Kymlicka 1995, 103; see also 1989b, 165; Raz 1994, 176–77.
[15] Popper 1976; Davidson [1986] 2006; Waldron 2004.
[16] Kymlicka 1989b, 168n2.

challenges based on the dilemma of essentialism continue to be repeated, a fuller account is clearly needed.

The failure to elaborate an alternative to an essentialist view of culture is also apparent in James Tully's book *Strange Multiplicity* (1995). The opening chapter contains a memorable statement of the critique of essentialism, directed against what Tully dubs the "billiard-ball" concept of culture. Elsewhere in the book, however, Tully routinely talks about cultures and their continuity as if his opening critique did not present weighty reasons for abandoning multiculturalist claims about culture altogether.[17] He claims in various places to be working with a "dialogical," or "intercultural," conception of culture, but it is never clear what exactly the concept of culture is that the adjectives "dialogical" and "intercultural" are meant to modify.

A third example of the simultaneous problematization of, and reliance on, the culture concept can be found in Phillips's book *Multiculturalism without Culture* (2007). Much of her argument proceeds squarely within a framework that is critical of multiculturalism. She rehearses the standard critique of culture as essentialist and reifying and argues that narratives of culture are often harmful to women and others. But Phillips cannot quite bring herself to drop multiculturalism in favor of a cosmopolitan focus on individuals. In part she has various unrelated objections to existing formulations of cosmopolitanism. But she also finds a "kernel of truth" in the multicultural claim that "majority and minority cultural groups" should be treated equally and regards this as a good reason not to abandon the discourse of multiculturalism.[18] The puzzle about Phillips's position here is what entitles her to talk of cultural groups in this way given her explicit antiessentialism.[19] What concept of culture is at work in the distinction between majority and minority groups and in the judgments about how such groups are treated?

In sum, then, the critique of cultural essentialism is a deceptively powerful one, and existing theories of multiculturalism do not tend to do a very good job of responding to it. Although many proponents of multiculturalism now

---

[17] Tully identifies "cultural continuity" as one of the three conventions that ought to guide "post-imperial" reflection on intercultural constitutionalism (1995, 117; see also 3, 21, 172, 186). Barry alleges that there is a tension between Tully's official denunciation of essentialism at the start of his book and an unacknowledged but indispensable essentialism that creeps into the argument at later points (2001, 256–61; 2002, 207–11).

[18] Phillips 2007, 71–72.

[19] See ibid., 167. Alluding to the title of her book, Phillips writes, "When I say I want a multiculturalism without culture, I mean I want a multiculturalism without particular *notions* of culture I have found unhelpful. But while I think that cultures have been reified and cultural conflict exaggerated, it is not part of my argument to deny that people are cultural beings" (52). Phillips has quite a lot to say about why certain views of culture are unhelpful (chaps. 1–2), but surprisingly little to say about what an adequate view of culture would be. Song's (2007, chap. 2) discussion of culture is characterized by a similar pattern, with a lengthy discussion of problems with essentialist conceptions of culture and very little development of the positive alternative that she relies on later in the book.

recognize the problem, they end up tiptoeing verbally around it rather than fully articulating an alternative conception of culture that avoids the pitfalls of essentialism. The remainder of the chapter elaborates just such a conception.

2.3 Cultural Continuity

Normative multiculturalism assumes that it is possible both to identify distinct cultures and to distinguish between cases of cultural change (which presuppose an underlying continuity) and cultural disappearance. Without a means of identifying distinct cultures, judgments about how cultures are faring become impossible. And if there were no way to distinguish change from disappearance, there would be no way of judging the results of multicultural policies, and perhaps no reason to embark on them in the first place.

It is tempting to collapse these two problems of individuation and continuity into one, and to say that C2 is continuous with C1 just in case C2 and C1 are one and the same culture. But collapsing the two problems leads to a difficulty.[20] It is plausible to think that both the French culture and the French Canadian culture circa 1800 were continuations of the French culture circa 1600. But by 1800 the French and the French Canadian cultures were clearly not one and the same. And, if they are not identical, then they cannot both have been the same as French culture in 1600. This suggests that there must be some different interpretation of "being a continuation of" that is weaker than "being identical to." I begin by trying to identify this weaker notion of continuity and then turn to individuation in the next section.

A passage in Kymlicka provides a helpful place to start. In his previously mentioned remarks on the distinction between a culture's "structure" and its "character," Kymlicka notes that it is "right and proper that the character of a culture change as a result of the choices of its members," but things are different when the "very survival of the culture" is jeopardized "as a result of choices made by people outside the culture."[21] Although not presented as a conceptual claim about the difference between continuity and disappearance, Kymlicka's suggestion points to a way of understanding that difference. Perhaps continuity involves relations of choice and disappearance their absence? When the abandonment of some relevant form of belief or practice, and its replacement with some other, is the result of the choices of members of the culture, then we can say that the culture has been continued (in changed form). When it is the result of conditions imposed from the outside, then it is better to say that the culture has ceased to exist.

---

[20] The argument in this paragraph follows Parfit's (1984, 262) distinction between identity and continuity, and his discussion of "branching."

[21] Kymlicka 1995, 104; see also 1989b, 167.

The appeal of this suggestion is obvious. It aligns cultural preservation with individual choice and thus with something of clear normative significance. But, as is, the proposal suffers from the fundamental difficulty that cultures sometimes disappear as a result of the choices of their members. Choice does not always imply continuity. An example illustrates the problem with the choice-based proposal and also points the way to a better one. The case is borrowed from John Terborgh, who presents it in the course of a discussion of cultural loss:

> *Misael's Loss.* Misael is a member of the Machiguenga culture, which inhabits a remote area in the Peruvian Amazon. Despite his legendary skill with the bow and arrow—a skill that is useful and highly valued in traditional Machiguengan settings—Misael has recently moved his family away from his home village to the multiethnic riverport town of Boca Manu. Here Misael's skills are in little demand and he is forced to take the menial work that he can, "while suffering," as Terborgh puts it, "the indignities of second-class status." Despite the personal cost that he faces as a result of the move, Misael's motivation for it is clear. In the remote village where Misael had lived, the school is run by missionaries and is of inferior quality. The school in Boca Manu is better, and the knowledge and skills that it can impart to Misael's children "offer the vision of a better life."[22]

Terborgh concludes that "here culture is being lost." In part he means that Misael's children are losing their ancestral culture. Raised and educated in a setting where the Machiguenga people are not in the majority, they are quickly integrated into the multiethnic, Spanish-speaking, motorized-boating population that makes up Boca Manu. At the same time, Terborgh sees Misael's choice as fairly representative. In a generation or two, as many individuals make choices like Misael's, Machiguenga culture itself will disappear.

Misael's story illustrates why the distinction between cultural continuity and loss is not merely a matter of choices being made or not made by members of the culture. Misael does seem to be making a choice of sorts. In Terborgh's recounting, there is little suggestion that he is driven by poverty or oppression to flee his ancestral village; indeed, his skill at a locally valued activity is "legendary." Misael is moved by the prospect of a better education and better economic opportunities for his children. If we agree that Misael's culture is about to be lost, then we are forced to recognize that individual choice is insufficient to establish cultural continuity.[23]

---

[22] Terborgh 2002.

[23] Even if Misael is not making a choice in the relevant sense (e.g., because of poverty), the general point is still valid. Substitute for Misael a member of a reasonably prosperous minority culture and it remains conceivable that such a person would move his family to a majority-culture setting in search of even

So how then should we understand the opposing ideas of continuity and loss? Terborgh's reflections on this conceptual question are problematic. In support of his contention that Machiguenga culture is lost to Misael's children, he points to various practices that they will not engage in, skills that they will not possess, and forms of thought and feeling that they will no longer experience. Misael's children will not share their father's facility with the bow and arrow, they will speak Spanish rather than Machiguenga, they will not "think like a Machiguenga," and so on. But as Yu and Shepard note, Terborgh seems to be relying on a "notion of culture as a static, species-like entity."[24] They point out that, although Machiguenga culture is now undergoing a major transformation, this has been true throughout its history. The Machiguenga culture has always been in a state of transformation or flux. It has continuously been formed and reformed through interaction with the Incas, the Spanish, the Peruvian state, Protestant missionaries, the rubber and oil companies, the pan-indigenous movement, and so on. In other words, Terborgh's conception of cultural loss does not deal well with the critique of essentialism. Terborgh replies by suggesting that these earlier transformations had been "incremental" rather than "fundamental," whereas what is happening today, as Misael's children and others like them "forsake traditional life to partake in Peru's public education system," is a fundamental break with historical continuity.[25] But, by itself, this reply risks underestimating the possibility that a culture might survive even a fundamental change in its forms of thought and practice.

Still, I think that Terborgh's intuition about the Machiguenga is basically correct, and that his own account of their situation contains the resources needed to develop a defensible account of cultural continuity and loss. The lesson to draw from Terborgh's story is not that cultural loss occurs whenever people abandon fundamental aspects of their thought and practice, but that it occurs when there is a significant disruption of the processes by which the culture is transmitted from existing members to new generations and other newcomers. The facts in Terborgh's story—especially the emphases on migration, schooling, and language—fit this "disruption-of-transmission" account of cultural loss as well as, or better than, they fit the "loss of fundamentals" account presupposed by Terborgh himself.

What does it mean for the transmission of a particular culture to be "disrupted"? The suggestion adapted from Kymlicka is that choice is the key factor, but we have seen that this suggestion fails to explain an important case. A factor that does a better job of explaining the range of relevant cases is *control*. If existing members of a culture control the socialization of some set of new-

---

better opportunities. So long as choices of this kind are sometimes made, and it is agreed that their cumulative effect can occasionally be cultural disappearance, choice is no guarantee of a culture's continuation.

[24] Yu and Shepard 2003. For reasons I mention in the next section, I think that the comparison with species is inapt.

[25] Terborgh 2003.

comers (e.g., the next generation), then to that extent there is no disruption, and the culture of the socialized group can be considered continuous with that of the group that socialized it. If, on the other hand, the existing members of the culture lose control over the socialization of a next generation, either because they choose to surrender it or because it is taken away from them, then the transmission of their culture has been disrupted. There is no group whose culture can be considered a continuation of the culture of the existing group.

By "socialization" I have in mind a broad range of different formative processes that work, in one way or another, to shape the beliefs and values of the persons who are subject to them. Socialization often occurs through participation in particular institutions and through exposure to particular practices and forms of social behavior. The family is obviously an important institution of socialization, as are the schools, the workplace, institutions of government and public administration, the media, popular culture, and even language and forms of discourse.

An institution or practice involved in socializing a new generation is "controlled" by the members of a particular cultural group if members of that group occupy most of the key positions of power and responsibility in that institution or practice, and/or if most of the other participants are incipient members of the cultural group in question, in the sense that they have already received some socialization into that group in other contexts (e.g., the family). Thus the schools are controlled by members of culture C if the majority of teachers and key decision makers in the schools are members of C, and/or if a significant number of students in the schools hail from family backgrounds in which one or both of their parents belong to C.

A number of the key facts in Misael's story are facts about socialization processes. Misael's decision to move to the town makes his children subject to a number of new socializing influences. If my proposal is correct, then it is exposure to these new forms of socialization, and the disruption of the previous processes in which the beliefs and practices of members of the Machiguenga culture had been transmitted to new generations, that accounts for our sense that the culture is on the brink of disappearance.

In their original community, Misael and his fellow Machiguengas used the Machiguenga language and were continuously exposed to the concepts and forms of discourse that happened to predominate in the language at the time. Their children might have gone to school in a setting where at least some of the teachers and officials, and perhaps all the children, come from Machiguenga backgrounds. Many of them would go on to live, work, and worship alongside other Machiguengas. By contrast, once Misael and his family arrive in Boca Manu, they begin participating in formative practices and institutions that transcend the Machiguenga community. Of course, they bring with them whatever Machiguenga socialization they received prior to their departure. They also retain their family environment, and they may maintain some contacts with their home community and with a local diaspora. But notwithstanding these continuities, Misael's children will soon find themselves subject to a powerful set of socializing institutions and practices that are largely administered and populated by members of the non-Machiguenga majority. These include the economy, political institutions, and education system of the town (and perhaps the larger Peruvian society that the town is part of); the language (Spanish), narratives, and forms of discourse that predominate in the town; the main forms of popular culture and entertainment of the town; the commercial and neighborhood life of the town; and so on. Misael's children will go to school with non-Machiguengas and the teachers will be non-Machiguengas; when they grow older they will work alongside non-Machiguengas and answer to bosses who are non-Machiguengas. They may marry non-Machiguengas and raise their own children in a manner that is even further removed from a Machiguenga upbringing.

Misael's story is one possible illustration of how cultural disappearance occurs, but there are other routes to the same outcome. In general, migration, economic change, rising literacy, access to new media and forms of popular culture, improvements in transportation and communication, and other broad social changes of this kind all have a tendency to expose people to new formative influences.[26] When, as a result of these processes, people find that traditional socialization mechanisms are no longer operative but have been superseded by new, larger-scale processes shared with a wider population, we can say that a local culture is being lost.

Moreover, in typical cases, the weakening (if not the outright destruction) of historic cultures is consciously encouraged by nation-building policy makers, who aim to integrate all citizens into a statewide national culture. The state designates an official language, imposes a national school system, requires service in the national military, builds national transportation links, supports national broadcasting media, and designs other institutions of the state to integrate members of minority cultures into statewide processes of cultural transmission. In some cases, states have intentionally disrupted processes of familial and community socialization, for example, by taking children from their families and communities and placing them in state-run residential schools. Measures of this kind, which are condemned by the Convention on Genocide's definition of genocide, amount to an especially blatant and brutal effort to extinguish a culture.

By contrast, Kymlicka's case of Quebec in the Quiet Revolution is a good example of cultural continuity in the view being proposed. Even though the character of Quebec society changed dramatically in those years, there was

---

[26] For a classic discussion of how these kinds of social changes lead to cultural loss, see Weber 1976, chap. 6. Weber also discusses deliberate nation-building policies pursued by the French state, of the sort that are discussed in the next paragraph.

never a disruption in the basic processes of cultural transmission. The generation that revolutionized Quebec society was itself socialized mainly by the previous generation of Francophone Quebecers and would itself go on to control the socialization of a subsequent generation of Francophone Quebecers. Despite the enormous changes in Quebec's values, practices, and institutions, there was never a rupture in the Quebecer-to-Quebecer mechanisms of cultural transmission that operated across a wide range of different areas of human life. The proposed account is also confirmed by the kinds of policies that are typically deployed in an effort to revive and protect vulnerable cultures. These policies often involve seeking control over critical transmission mechanisms, such as education and the media, or over factors that impact these mechanisms, such as access to and administration of the territory of the cultural group in question.[27]

Notice, then, that we have managed to identify a conception of cultural continuity that avoids the pitfalls of essentialism. There is no reliance on the idea that certain beliefs, values, meanings, practices, institutions, and so on are somehow constitutive of the culture, or that their maintenance or abandonment is key to determining whether the culture continues or disappears. So long as one generation of a culture is controlling the socialization of a new generation or group of newcomers, there is cultural continuity, even if the later generation engages in dramatic revision of prevailing values, meanings, and practices. There is no reason to think, then, that the idea of cultural preservation is committed to the freezing of cultures in any special form or to the reification of particular ideas or traditions as somehow definitive of culture. As we shall see further below, a case for multiculturalism is not, as the critics contend, irredeemably dependent on an essentialist account of cultural preservation.

2.4 The Social Lineage Account

We have been exploring the conditions under which a culture can be said to continue from one moment in time to another. The key consideration, as we have seen, is an unbroken chain of intergenerational cultural transmission. But we have not said quite yet what it is, exactly, that makes something a distinct culture in the first place. By virtue of what can a person be said to share a culture with some people but not with others?

With so much attention having been devoted to the problem of continuity, however, a possible answer to this question is now staring us in the face.

---

[27] Revivals typically begin with an identity focused on the culture (see the discussion of identity in sec. 2.5). People value the culture and go out of their way to put themselves under the influence of existing members of the culture, and/or (if there are no existing members) to expose themselves to materials (language, texts, practices, etc.) associated with some earlier generation of the culture.

Members of a group that can trace back through time a lineage of cultural continuity do share something that others do not share. They share with one another a common experience of socialization that is distinct from, because historically isolated from, the experiences of socialization undergone by others. This fact suggests the following solution to the individuation problem. *A distinct culture is the relation that people share when, and to the extent that, they have shared with one another subjection to a set of formative conditions that are distinct from the formative conditions that are imposed on others.* Culture, in this proposal, is a kind of precipitate. At any given moment, its content consists in various beliefs, meanings, and practices, but what makes these the beliefs, meanings, and practices of a shared culture is that the people who hold them share a common social lineage.

In defining culture in relation to a set of formative conditions, the point is not that those conditions are *causally* related to the creation of a distinct culture. Rather, the claim is that the existence of a shared culture is *constituted* by the exposure by some group of people to a common and distinctive set of formative conditions.[28] Although this suggestion may seem surprising to some readers, it is structurally parallel to the way in which many biologists understand the concept of species. For exactly the sorts of reasons we explored with regard to cultural essentialism, most biologists avoid defining species in terms of essential sets of traits. There is too much variability of traits within, and commonality of traits across, the species that are taken to exist to support an essentialist account. Instead the tendency among biologists (going back to Mayr) has been to think of species genealogically, as population lineages that are isolated reproductively from other lineages.[29] Although the proposed account of culture is concerned with social and historical rather than reproductive isolation, the structure of the account is the same.

As with all attempts to individuate culture, culture in the social lineage account is both something shared and something distinctive. What is shared, when people share a culture, is exposure to a common set of formative influences. It need not, and generally will not, be the case that everybody sharing a culture has been subjected to *identical* formative influences. Each person's formative environment will typically include some elements that are idiosyncratic relative to the formative experiences of others in the group. The important point is that the environment also includes some encompassing elements, which are imposed, in common, on all members of the group. In other words, for a culture to be in existence, there has to be some set of formative institutions and practices to which all members of the group are subject. If there were no such formative processes at work, there would be no group.

---

[28] Confusion about whether the proposal is causal or constitutive can lead to a number of errors. For discussion, see Patten 2013.

[29] Mayr 1942. See also Kitcher 1999; 2007; Sober 2000, chap. 6.

What is distinctive about a particular culture is the historical lineage of its formative institutions and practices. Those institutions and practices are, to some extent at least, isolated from the institutions and practices that work to socialize outsiders. They are controlled, that is, by a group of people different from those who control the socialization of outsiders. And the members of the controlling group may themselves have been socialized by a distinctive set of practices and institutions, which were, in turn, controlled by people who were socialized under distinctive conditions, and so on.[30]

As noted at the outset, the acceptability of any proposed conception of culture depends on how well it satisfies both empirical and normative criteria. The conception should pick out cultures that accord, at least roughly, with the groups that multiculturalists have in mind when they seek protection for, and fair treatment of, distinct cultures (empirical criterion). And, in at least some range of cases, sharing a culture in the sense specified by the conception should be something that matters normatively (normative criterion). I briefly consider the normative dimension later in the chapter and then explore it in more depth in subsequent chapters.

As for the empirical criterion, a major advantage of the social lineage account is that it is compatible with both internal variation and external overlap of beliefs, values, and meanings. Internal variation is possible because subjection to a common set of formative influences does not imply that people will end up with a homogeneous set of beliefs or values. The most basic reason for this is that formative institutions and practices are themselves likely to be sites of difference and contestation. Their meanings, values, purposes, and so on will be disputed by the people who administer and participate in them, and, predictably, these disputes will reproduce themselves in new generations, and in other newcomers who are brought into their orbit.

Moreover, it would be normal for people who share exposure to even a univocal set of institutions and practices to respond by forming a highly diverse set of beliefs and values. Just as siblings respond differently to a common upbringing, depending on their individual circumstances and characteristics, persons who participate in a common set of institutions and practices also differ in many ways. Some might respond to their upbringing by rebelling against it, others by adopting a stance of studied or ironic detachment toward it, and others by creatively improvising with some of its materials. Indeed, in any typical human group, one would expect to see a great variety of responses to a set of socializing conditions, ranging from a warm embrace of the characteristic beliefs and practices of the previous generation's culture to total alienation from them, and from navel-gazing fascination with the history and distinc-

---

[30] The histories of some cultures may be less continuous than this, punctuated by moments of apparent extinction followed by revival. See Clifford 1988. The italicized proposal above is still valid for such cases. See also n. 27.

tiveness of those beliefs and practices to utter indifference. All these responses are consistent with the idea of a common set of formative influences.[31]

Just as the social lineage account is compatible with internal heterogeneity, it is also compatible with external overlap. As noted earlier, it is not necessary for the account that individuals be subjected only to those formative conditions that generate a shared culture. Individuals are exposed to a set of conditions in common with others in the culture—this is what makes it a culture—but they are also subject to the influence of various idiosyncratic pressures. These include a set of more or less individualized conditions (e.g., particular family upbringings) but also various cross-cutting groups and cultures that persons are shaped by, because nothing in the account requires that individuals be shaped by one and only one encompassing environment.

Once it is allowed that people who share a culture are also subject to various other formative cross-pressures, the overlapping, interactive, hybrid character of cultures immediately becomes predictable. Individuals who participate together in a given set of institutions and practices will also bring to the table various experiences of participating in institutions and practices that unite and apply to different groupings of people. Through their consumption and reading choices, their associational memberships and religious affiliations, their family's and community's migration history, their own travel and migration, and so on, individuals will find themselves under the influence of processes that are idiosyncratic relative to the culture-generating formative influences. In many cases their contributions to the culture may reflect these idiosyncratic influences. As various values and meanings are shaped and negotiated under conditions of multiple affiliation, they predictably acquire an overlapping, hybrid character.

Against these arguments, it might be objected that there is still a sense in which the social lineage account fails to escape the problem of essentialism. According to this objection, by understanding cultures in terms of shared socialization experiences, rather than as shared frameworks of meanings, the proposal transfers the problem up a level without eliminating it. The reasons

---

[31] If a common set of formative influences can elicit such a scattered set of responses, it might be objected that the significance of those influences must be rather slight. But this is a mistake. Consider, as an analogy, the impact that a natural or industrial disaster can have on a community where it occurs. Some members of the community will experience the event as a loss and tragedy, others as an inconvenience, and others still as an opportunity or even an exciting departure from routine existence. Some will lose faith in God; others will cling to their religion for support and comfort. Some will blame the government for not doing enough; others will be defensive about the government's response. And so on. What almost everyone will share in common is the fact that the event makes some, perhaps quite significant, kind of difference in their lives, in a way that it does not for those who were not subjected to it. The disaster exerts a kind of "gravitational pull," one might say, that affects all the objects around it, albeit in different ways. In the same way, the formative influence of culture can be both significant and varied. The shared formative environment exerts a gravitational pull on members of the group that is varied in its impact but an undeniable part of their lives nonetheless.

for skepticism about shared frameworks of meanings are also reasons for skepticism about common socialization experiences. Formative influences are not neatly packaged into sets of institutions and practices that are uniformly subjected on all and only the members of some groups. Among any set of people, there will predictably be too great a diversity of formative influences to allow the identification of groups of persons who share a common formative experience.

But this objection is overstated. The objection would obviously be correct if the account assumed that members of a culture were subjected to an identical set of formative influences. But, as we have seen, this is not the assumption. It is sufficient for the account that there be some significant set of institutions and practices to which, roughly speaking, all and only the members of the group are subject. If there were no such formative processes at work, there would be no group. But to judge that there is a group sharing a culture, the relevant processes just need to reach a threshold level of significance.

Suppose, however, that the objection goes further and challenges the idea that sets of individuals could, and sometimes do, share *enough* exposure to a common set of formative influences to identify them as sharing a culture. The objection is still overstated. Although individuals are subject to a hugely diverse set of formative influences, it will normally be plausible to suppose that among these influences are certain institutions and practices, as well as environmental conditions, that exert an influence on many people at once. Moreover, it is plausible to think that, in typical situations, more than one of these encompassing institutions, practices, and conditions will exert an overlapping influence on one and the same group of people.

As an example of overlapping influence, consider a set of persons who live in a common territory, speak the same language, and share a set of political institutions and hence a legal and bureaucratic framework.[32] Suppose that this framework establishes a common set of educational institutions and a common market for consumer goods, media products, and so on. With these background conditions in place, it makes sense for various forms of media (print, television, etc.) to gear themselves toward the affairs and perceived interests of those same persons and their institutions. Not surprisingly, these media are read and watched with special attention by the same set of people who are

---

[32] Phillips (2007, 44) worries about the tendency to identify cultures with nation-states, "as when a tourist visits India to understand 'Indian culture' and 'Indian society.'" She calls it an "oddity" that "people living on one side of a national frontier are taken as belonging to a different culture from cousins who live on the other." Not so in my view (or, I might add, in my own experience of growing up in Canada and interacting on occasion with my American cousins). Although cultures are not defined so that they are coterminous with states, political and bureaucratic institutions are important encompassing formative contexts, which, in turn, vary according to political boundaries. However, my view does not assume that "everyone who lives in a particular territory" belongs to a "single national culture" (45), because there are significant formative processes (e.g., language) that vary within a given territory.

featured in them.[33] It also makes sense for producers and sellers of consumer goods to orient their production and advertising decisions around the perceived tastes and sensibilities of that same set of people.

With these common institutions in the background, one might also expect to see the emergence of a different kind of common practice, which might be called a "dominant discursive practice." In a group of people who live together in a common territory, speak a common language, and find themselves subject to common political, legal, bureaucratic, economic, and media processes, certain forms of speech and discourse will enjoy considerable prominence at a given point in time. It is not that everyone will speak in the same way. As I insisted earlier, one would expect to find a great variety of responses to the dominant discursive practice. Rather, the suggestion is that there will emerge a common vocabulary of stories, references, and landmarks, as well as a common set of "points of concern," which are widely assumed to be familiar to everyone.[34] To be sure, this common vocabulary will also reflect interactive engagement with other cultures and societies and would thus have a recognizably hybrid character. But if the reflections mentioned above are correct, the institutional and environmental setting will also help to shape the character of the dominant discourse. Someone who was exposed to the dominant discourse over a period of time could be said to have been subject to a formative influence that was distinctive vis-à-vis a discourse that was shaped under different institutional and environmental conditions. The influence will be all the more distinctive, all else being equal, the farther back in time the historical lineage of the culture stretched.

Putting all this together, it is not difficult to suppose that sets of individuals do sometimes share enough exposure to a common and distinctive set of formative influences for us to identify those sets as groups and to say that the members of those groups share a culture. Of course, particular influences are bound to apply with greater or lesser strength to some individuals in the culture. Some will have very few interactions with state institutions; others will be sheltered from the media; and so on. But even people who seem to avoid many of the common formative influences can be shaped by them indirectly. A person might disdainfully resist the media and popular culture in all its forms but still find it hard to escape their influence because of the ways in which they shape the beliefs and values of other people with whom the person interacts. The institutions and practices have certain general social effects that make it hard for anyone in their domain to escape their influence altogether.

Of course, I have picked a particularly stark example of a set of overlapping influences, in which the various common institutions and practices (political, bureaucratic, educational, linguistic, media, entertainment, and so on) all

---

[33] Anderson 1983, chap. 3.
[34] Laitin 2007, chap. 3.

apply to a single set of persons who share a common territory. The inclusion of territory, and of political/administrative institutions, might even suggest a kind of statist view of cultures, in which nation-states are the main species of cultures, a view that would obviously not be congenial to multiculturalism. But even though the example has a stark and "national" character, it is suggestive of how the social lineage account might generate a range of different judgments about which cultures there are. Language is an obvious factor that need not coincide with political or administrative boundaries, as is religion. Common political and administrative institutions may have served as crucial launching pads for distinctive sets of formative conditions, but these conditions may then gain a life of their own and survive the disappearance of the institutions that brought them into existence in the first place. In general, then, the idea of a common and distinctive set of formative institutions retains its plausibility even as we move away from the nation-state cases.

I have been arguing that individuals do sometimes share *enough* exposure to a common set of formative influences to warrant judging that they share a common culture. By insisting on this point, however, perhaps the social lineage account risks falling into the opposite difficulty? Whereas the earlier concern was that the account would not be able to identify any cultures, now the worry is that the account would identify too many cultures. In the United States, for instance, in addition to well-known national institutions, many institutions operate at the state and local levels. Must each state, county, and township be regarded as having its own culture? Because families are also an obvious locus of formative influence, should we also think of each set of family members as sharing their own distinctive culture? Or, to take a particularly hard case, should we say that women and men belong to distinct cultures because they undergo different forms of socialization?

The social lineage account certainly would not want to deny that there are many local and state cultures in a country as vast and diverse as the United States, nor that families are often sites of distinctive formative influence, nor indeed that it might make sense, in some contexts, to talk of "women's culture." As we saw earlier, the account is compatible with the view that persons can have multiple cultural affiliations and thus with the observation, to borrow an example from Scheffler, that a person might be culturally Western, American, Californian, and Northern Californian, at one and the same time.[35] Still, there are a number of reasons for thinking that the account does not imply a limitless proliferation of cultures. One check on this tendency derives from the observation that broader-level discursive practices sometimes shape and structure more local processes. Families and local institutions can often serve as conduits for broader-level social processes as much as distinctive venues of socialization in their own right. Parents and those who adminis-

[35] Scheffler 2007, 100.

ter and populate local practices and institutions are part of a broader social conversation about how those processes should operate, and this conversation may be highly influential on the actual character of the processes. Rather than millions of distinct formative processes at work (each family and local community), it may instead be more accurate to think of there being a single such process (operating quite broadly) with millions of points of application.

Second, it is important to distinguish between two mechanisms by which different people (e.g., men and women) might end up receiving distinct forms of socialization. It may be that they participate in different practices and institutions and thus receive a socialization that is colored by those practices and institutions and by the participants in them. Or it may be that they participate in a common set of practices and institutions, but those practices and institutions socialize their participants in a differentiated manner. It may be integral to the beliefs, values, and norms that are encouraged by a given set of practices and institutions that persons with different ascriptive characteristics are assigned to different roles or treated in different ways. In the social lineage account, only the first of these mechanisms implies the division of the people involved into multiple cultures. The second mechanism is compatible with the generation of a single (gendered, racialized) culture.

A third check on proliferation is that the mere presence of some institution or practice does not, by itself, betoken the existence of a distinct culture. Some institutions and practices will not have sufficient formative impact on individuals to count as establishing a culture. The sufficiency threshold here should be based on the normative reasons for thinking that cultures matter in the first place. The distinctive formative impact has to be great enough so that the reasons for caring about differences of culture (which are introduced toward the end of the chapter) really do register in a morally significant way. An important implication of this last assumption is that there is a pragmatic aspect to the identification of cultures. What entities should be considered as cultures is not a freestanding fact of social reality but is dependent, in part, on the questions that we, the inquirers, find it important to answer.[36]

2.5 Some Related Concepts

To close out the exposition of the social lineage account, let us relate it to several further ideas that are often invoked in discussions of culture: race/ethnicity, identity, language, and societal culture.

---

[36] This is an important theme of Kitcher's (2007) account of race.

RACE AND ETHNICITY

Critics of culture sometimes suggest that the term is little more than a euphemism for race or ethnicity. They reason that, because cultures clearly do not have the levels of homogeneity, boundedness, and determinacy that are apparently assumed by those who believe in them, there must be something else lurking in the background that is doing the work of individuating cultures.[37] Perhaps the unacknowledged premise behind culture-talk is that members of a culture share biological relationships of blood and genealogy? Needless to say, culture in this view becomes highly problematic. Skepticism about the existence of distinct, biologically defined races and ethnic groups is, if anything, even stronger than it is about cultures.[38] And the reduction of culture to race or ethnicity would drain the former concept of much of the normative appeal it might otherwise possess.

The social lineage account does, in fact, share a structural similarity with a racial or an ethnic understanding of distinct groups. In one prominent view, a racial group, if there are such groups, consists of a group of individuals who can all trace themselves back, by a chain of genealogical relations, to some common originary group of families. Like species, race is a "lineage" concept, involving the idea of a reproductively isolated population.[39] Ethnicity also involves the idea of a biological lineage, typically with a coinciding cultural lineage. When race and ethnicity are understood in these terms, the structural similarity to the social lineage account of culture is fairly obvious.[40] For, as we have seen, in the social lineage account, a group of people share a culture if and only if they were subjected to a common and distinctive socialization process. And part of what makes a particular process distinctive is that it extends back in time in a lineage that remains isolated from other socializing processes.

It is easy to conflate genealogical and sociological transmission processes because sometimes they overlap. Consider Iceland, where the population is known for having an unusually pure line of descent from the original Norse settlers. To an uncommon degree, the present population of the country can trace itself back both genealogically and sociologically to a small group of original settlers. Still, the genealogical and sociological processes are distinct, and it is necessary to be clear about the distinction because they come apart significantly once one moves away from extreme cases such as Iceland. Whereas genealogical transmission is primarily a biological relation between parents and their children, sociological transmission works through social practices and institutions. It is a relation in which one group of people socializes another

---

[37] Kuper 1999, 14; Barry 2001, 258–64; Appiah 2005, 136–38; Phillips 2007, 17, 56.

[38] Appiah 1996.

[39] Hardimon 2003; Kitcher 1999; 2007.

[40] Kitcher (1999) also suggests a structural parallel between race and culture and sketches very briefly what an account of the latter might look like.

(children, immigrants, etc.), and more generally in which the members of the group socialize one another through social practices and institutions.

As a general matter, cultural groups as I understand them do not coincide with racial or ethnic groups. In much of the world, migration and the inter-mixing of ethnic populations have been the norm rather than the exception, and these processes tend to compromise the reproductive isolation assumed by concepts of race and ethnicity. One can be skeptical about claims of racial and ethnic distinctness, however, and still think that there are distinct cultures. A gulf opens up between ethnicity and culture in the social lineage account because of the tremendous formative power of social institutions and practices. People coming from the most diverse ethnic origins, arriving from the most far-flung places, can be absorbed into common socializing institutions and practices that were established long ago by somebody else's ancestors, and these institutions and practices will have a profound effect on them. Within a generation or two the process of ethnic transmission—if it is operative at all—may have been entirely disconnected from the process of cultural transmission.

IDENTITY

Another question is how culture, in the social lineage account, relates to identity. Identity is itself a complex notion, which has both subjective and objective dimensions.[41] Both dimensions have to do with the classification of persons and with the beliefs and attitudes that are connected with particular classifications. Subjectively, to have an identity as a member of culture C is to *identify* with C: one thinks of oneself as a member, values one's membership, cares about the success of the culture, and lets one's membership in the culture count as a factor in one's practical reasoning in appropriate contexts. Objectively, identity is a matter of how others classify and relate to a person. In this sense, a person has a particular identity when he or she is identified by others as being a certain kind of person and is evaluated and treated in a distinctive way on that basis. Clearly these two dimensions of identity are not always aligned. For instance, recent immigrants to the United States are sometimes distressed at being classified and treated by others on the basis of prevailing identity categories that have little connection with their own previous experience or avowed attachments.

Understood along these lines, identity is distinct from culture but related to it. There is no necessary conceptual relation between the two ideas because one can think of cases of culture without identity and identity without culture. It is perfectly conceivable that someone could have been shaped in common with others by a set of encompassing formative conditions, and in this

---

[41] My understanding of identity is especially indebted to Appiah 2005, 65–71.

sense be part of the culture defined by those conditions, and yet neither identify him- or herself, nor be identified by others, with the culture in question.
As was noted earlier, one recognizable way in which people respond to the
conditions of their socialization is by adopting an attitude of indifference, or
even disdain, toward the group associated with the formative experience. And,
because identification by others is often based on stereotypes, gaps between
culture and objective identity are to be expected.

Cases of identity without culture are also common. Appiah argues that this
situation has become increasingly typical in the United States.[42] The country's powerful national culture is continuously at work in erasing subnational
processes of cultural transmission. Immigrants arrive in the country with
their own languages, traditions, and attitudes, but the economy and popular culture, and high rates of intermarriage, quickly undermine the transmission mechanisms that would allow immigrant groups to maintain themselves
as distinct cultures. Even while this pattern repeats itself, however, and perhaps, Appiah speculates, because it does so, distinctive cultural identities have
become increasingly salient for people. According to Appiah, Americans
are more likely than ever to identify themselves as members of groups, even
though the groups barely exist as distinct cultural entities.

Although culture and identity are distinct concepts, they are related in
important ways. A common result of sharing a socialization experience with
some group of persons is that one comes to feel a sense of belonging in, and
attachment to, the group. As we shall see later, the value of these feelings of
community is one intelligible reason that people might care about the treatment and preservation of their cultures. Culture does not imply identity, but
it is no accident that they often go together.

In addition, the causal arrow often runs in the other direction too—from
identity to culture. There are cases in which people would never have found
themselves subjected to a set of formative influences if not for the fact that
they felt some attachment to that way of life. Having a certain set of beliefs
and attitudes triggers a willingness to expose oneself to particular influences,
which in turn reinforce the beliefs and attitudes, and so on. For instance, following Anderson we might expect that media institutions will encourage
people to "imagine" their community belonging in certain ways—that is, to
adopt a particular form of subjective identity.[43] And this identity, in turn, will
reinforce the processes of socialization that make up a culture related to that
identity. The objective dimension of identity can also exert a causal impact on
culture. Some of the forms of treatment that ensue from being classified by
others in a certain way leave people—whether they want it or not—subject
to a distinctive set of formative influences. Discrimination and residential seg-

[42] Ibid., 14–20.
[43] Anderson 1983, chap. 3.

regation are familiar examples of identity-related processes that shunt people into formative experiences that are, to some degree, isolated from the broader society.

LANGUAGE

Rather like identity, language, in the social lineage account, is important though not essential to culture. Language is itself a major socializing practice. Although in principle languages are elastic and versatile enough that they could be made to express almost any idea, in practice, at any given time, particular forms of discourse are dominant in a given language, and they privilege certain ways of viewing the world over others. To be a speaker of a particular language is to become entangled in the various ways of organizing and interpreting the world that are current when the language is being learned and used. Since the prevailing discourses of a speech community are often assumed to have a major impact on what tends to be said or thought by a speaker of that language, it seems clear that language is a fundamental part of socialization.

A further reason for thinking that language is fundamental to culture follows from the simple fact that most people can speak at best a few languages and many people can only speak one. Limited linguistic competence imposes a fairly hard constraint on how far individuals can go in exposing themselves to formative influences other than ones that originally socialized them. The realm of cultures thus corresponds, in a rough and ready way, with the realm of languages, both because language is a major socializing influence that corresponds with distinctive ways of thinking about the world and because language acts as a kind of customs barrier that impedes the free flow of people, and, to a lesser extent, of ideas, from one group or environment to another.

For these reasons, it seems correct to think of language as a major reason why cultures as distinctive socialization processes exist and a major factor in explaining how they maintain themselves. When a group abandons its historical language, its culture is weakened and more vulnerable. Having recognized these points, however, we should resist the stronger claim that language is somehow essential to culture. There are examples of groups that abandoned their languages but managed to maintain themselves as distinct cultures; the Irish are a partial case in point.[44] There are also examples of groups that share a language with powerful neighbors and yet still possess distinct cultures. In places such as Canada, Scotland, Ireland, Belgium, and Switzerland, groups share a language in common with larger, more powerful neighbors but still

---

[44] On the Irish case, see Edwards 1985, 53–65. After tracing the decline and continuing marginality of the Irish language, Edwards notes that "the Irish experience indicates that the link between original language and identity is not essential. There exists, today, a strong Irish identity which does not involve Irish, in a communicative sense" (64). Song (2007, 33) cites the Pueblo in the American Southwest as another example of cultural persistence in the face of linguistic loss.

manage to maintain distinct cultures. The neighbors exert an influence, to be sure—through economic ties, popular culture, and so on—but there are political, educational, and social institutions that impart a distinctive socialization experience and thus keep the smaller cultures intact. As we have seen, these processes are boosted by the fact that members of these groups identify with their cultures and thus make certain choices about consumption, reading, attention to the media, place of residence, and so forth, that expose them to the ongoing operation of the distinctive formative influences.

Societal Culture

As Kymlicka has noted, a great variety of entities get labeled as "cultures" in everyday speech.[45] Everything from "Western civilization" as a whole to the lifestyles surrounding particular genres of music, from national traditions to the mores of a particular institution or workplace, is associated with the term culture. The sheer diversity of applications of the term threatens to overload any attempt to theorize about it generally.

Kymlicka's strategy for reducing overload is to distinguish a special class of cultures, which he terms "societal cultures," and which he mainly has in mind when he develops and defends his theory of cultural rights. A societal culture, he says, is "a culture which provides its members with meaningful ways of life across the full range of human activities, including social, educational, religious, recreational, and economic life, encompassing both public and private spheres."[46] Kymlicka argues that societal cultures have special importance for their members and thus have an especially strong claim on the state's recognition and accommodation. Members of distinct societal cultures can legitimately demand self-government rights, as well as rights to the use of their languages by public institutions. In contrast, members of other kinds of cultural groups—notably those formed by recent immigration—can legitimately expect to enjoy only those cultural rights that are compatible with the basic aim of integration into one of the preexisting societal cultures.

There are a couple of different ways of understanding the proposal that societal cultures provide a full range of options. Kymlicka could mean that such cultures generate all the various options included in such a range entirely out of their own resources (their own ideas, traditions, etc.). But then the proposal is vulnerable to Joseph Carens's objection that societal cultures seem excessively homogeneous and totalizing. Carens observes that it would seem more natural to say that there are many sources and traditions that provide options

---

[45] Kymlicka 1995, 18.
[46] Ibid., 76; Kymlicka 2001a, 53.

to Quebecers (to pick one of Kymlicka's examples of a societal culture) than to say that Quebec's culture somehow "provides" Judaism or Islam as options.[47]

Alternatively, however, "provides" might be understood in a more specific and narrow sense. It might be said that a culture provides its members with meaningful options across the full range of human activities if and only if it provides its members, through the socialization and formative processes that make it the culture that it is, with the set of *generic skills and capacities* that they need to access and enjoy those options. If the idea of providing options is restricted to a claim about generic skills and capacities, then societal cultures becomes less homogenizing and totalizing. One can allow that there are many cultural sources of options in a given society and still insist that societal culture provides a foundational set of skills and capacities that are key to accessing all, or at least a great many, of them. When societal cultures are defined by providing in this narrower sense, they fit neatly into the social lineage account.

The background to this approach is a distinction between the generic and the specific skills and capacities that a person needs in order to access a particular option or "way of life." The distinction is drawn from Ernest Gellner, who gives as examples of generic skills and capacities "literacy, numeracy, basic work habits and social skills, familiarity with basic technical and social skills."[48] Chief among these skills, perhaps, is knowledge of (and literacy in) the language in which a society's options are available. On their own, the generic skills and capacities will not qualify people to access many of the ways of life that are on offer. Some more specialized training or preparation is also necessary. Nonetheless, the generic skills and capacities are necessary for accessing options and are presupposed by the further specialized preparation that may be needed to make particular options a genuine possibility.

As an illustration, contrast French-speaking culture in Quebec with Italian-speaking culture in the United States. The former is a societal culture because the socialization provided by French-language institutions and practices leaves people with a basic, generic set of skills and capacities that enables access to an adequate range of options. Someone brought up in Quebec's French-language institutions will have the linguistic and other prerequisites to pursue a variety of careers and economic opportunities, to practice a range of different religions, to enjoy rich popular and high cultures, to participate in formal and informal political life, and so on. To be sure, knowledge of French, and of a few other basic skills, does not, on its own, qualify somebody to be a plumber in Quebec or prepare someone to appreciate the finer points of Québécois theater. But Quebec's French-language institutions leave those who are formed by them with the generic skills they need to pursue the more specific training and preparation that facilitate access to particular options.

---

[47] Carens 2000, 69–70; see also Benhabib 2002, 60–61.
[48] Gellner 1983, 28.

Compare this with someone socialized by Italian-speaking institutions in the United States. These institutions affect such a tiny minority of people, in such a narrow range of contexts, that they could not possibly leave the people they affect with the generic skills needed for an adequate range of options in American society. Whereas a French-speaker in Quebec could access a reasonably full range of options without learning English, the same could not be said of an Italian-speaker in the United States. Someone socialized by Italian-speaking institutions in the United States would also need some further formative experience to acquire the set of generic linguistic skills—involving mastery of English—that are essential in that country. Italian-speaking culture in the United States is not, therefore, a societal culture.

As a general rule, cultures formed by recent immigration will not be societal cultures in this sense, and most societal cultures will be centered around the long-standing, territorially established, national cultures of a society.[49] Not every "national" culture will be a societal culture, however. As Joseph Carens points out, some long-standing, territorially established cultures—such as the Machiguenga and other cultures of indigenous peoples—are arguably too tiny and socioeconomically fractured to provide their members with meaningful options across the full range of areas of human life.[50] To access a full range of options, members of these cultures must also acquire—through additional formation—the generic linguistic and other prerequisites for success in the majority culture.

Kymlicka is right to claim that societal cultures have a special moral importance. In general, citizens ought to possess a set of generic skills and capacities that will enable access to a meaningful array of options across the full range of areas of human life. But, as will become clear in the chapters that follow, there is no reason to think that societal cultures are the only kind of cultures that matter normatively. Indeed, in my view, elaborated in section 6.6, the special importance of societal cultures is just as likely to count as a reason for limiting strong cultural rights as it will a reason for extending them. To enjoy an adequate range of options, members of the Machiguenga may need to integrate into the majority, Spanish-speaking Peruvian society, and promoting this integration may run counter (though it may not) to extending strong cultural rights to them. Much the same is true for Italian Americans.[51]

---

[49] Ibid., chaps. 3–5; Kymlicka 1995, 76.
[50] Carens 2000, 61–64.
[51] I thus follow Carens in decoupling the main case for minority cultural rights from the concept of societal cultures. See ibid., 56, 73.

2.6 The Normative Significance of Culture: A First Glance

The dilemma of essentialism does not rule out the possibility of formulating a nonessentialist concept of culture. What it does claim to rule out is any such concept being serviceable to multiculturalism. For multiculturalism to be a plausible normative demand, two requirements have to be met. First, it has to be possible to identify distinct minority cultures and to make judgments about how they are being treated and whether they are surviving and flourishing. And, second, it has to make sense to think of cultures as mattering to their members. If it did not matter to people how their cultures were faring, the multicultural project would have trouble getting off the ground. A successful response to the dilemma of essentialism has to show how a nonessentialist culture concept can meet these two requirements on which normative multiculturalism depends.

I hope that I have said enough about the concepts of culture and cultural preservation to establish that the social lineage account can satisfy the first of these requirements. The proposed account turns both the identification of distinct cultures and judgments about how they are faring into problems of a largely empirical character, which involve determining how far the socialization experience of some group is isolated socially and historically from that of others, and how robust the transmission mechanisms are whereby new members are socialized by existing members. As for the second requirement, I shall postpone a full-scale exploration of why cultures matter to their members until the next chapter. Here I just want to say enough by way of anticipation of that later discussion to allow us to assess whether there is anything in the social lineage account itself that would make it especially difficult to make sense of culture's value.

The overarching idea that we shall explore in the next chapter is that cultures matter normatively to their members because they are consequential for the options that individuals have at their disposal. The options available to people are worse when their culture is faring poorly than when it is doing well, and the point of strong cultural rights is to prevent this worsening of options. Without getting into the details of the argument, our question for now is whether the social lineage account is compatible with this kind of reason for valuing culture. Does the move from an essentialist culture concept to a nonessentialist one based on social lineage undermine the reasons for valuing culture that will, in subsequent chapters, be deployed to work up a case for multiculturalism?

The discussion in the next chapter will distinguish three different versions of the claim that cultural loss can worsen versions. One version (the "access" argument) holds that members of a deteriorating culture would struggle to access an adequate range of options in the dominant culture, either because they face discrimination or because they lack some of the generic capacities (e.g., language proficiency) necessary to access those options. A second version (the "particular options" argument) claims that the dominant culture would not provide particular options to minority culture members that especially matter to them. Both arguments can be illustrated by returning to our earlier example of Misael. In the access argument, he values his Machiguenga culture because he fears that, should it decline or disappear, he would face discrimination in Peru's dominant culture or lack sufficient fluency in Spanish or mastery of other generic skills needed to enjoy an adequate range of options. With the particular options argument, he values his culture because he expects that particular options that he values (e.g., specific Machiguenga practices and rituals) would no longer be available should his culture be eclipsed by the dominant culture.[52] Finally, a third possible claim about why cultural loss might threaten options (the "intrinsic importance" argument) observes that the survival and flourishing of the culture may be something that people value for its own sake. The culture itself is an "option," the availability of which obviously depends on the culture's preservation.

Clearly these arguments would not show every culture to be valuable. Roughly speaking, the access argument would apply mainly to societal cultures, whereas the particular options argument would apply mainly in contexts where there is a fairly significant discontinuity between the threatened and dominant cultures in the options they can be expected to generate. Moreover, some cultures may be so grossly oppressive or chauvinistic as to lack any value at all. Our purpose here, however, is not to provide a comprehensive examination of arguments for the value of culture but, more narrowly, to consider whether the shift to the social lineage account makes the arguments *less* applicable than they would be on an essentialist view.

One reason to suspect a problem is that culture, in the social lineage account, is no longer defined in terms of any specific beliefs, practices, or options. As we saw in section 2.3, a culture can survive, in the view being proposed, and yet undergo a fundamental revolution in the kinds of values, meanings, and preferences that prevail, and thus in the sorts of options and practices that are available. Given this basic feature of the social lineage account, it might be wondered how it could support an options-based argument for multiculturalism.

However, this challenge overstates the dependence of the options-based argument on an essentialist view of culture. Consider first the access version of the argument. The access argument does not worry about the loss of any option in particular but instead cautions that minority culture members

---

[52] Or that they will *become* available if his culture is revived. In general, some of the considerations canvassed in this section apply to cases of cultural revival, whereas others apply more narrowly to the value of protecting existing cultures.

might lack an adequate *range* of options in the dominant culture. Because there are many different sets of options that would constitute an adequate range (so long as there is a sufficient number, quality, and diversity of options), this version of the argument need not rely on any problematic essentialist understanding of culture. Particular options can come and go, can be contested to greater or lesser degrees, and can overlap to greater or lesser extents with options generated by other cultures, and none of this should affect whether the options available to a member of a culture—given facts about discrimination, generic capacity, and so on—are adequate.

Nor is essentialism about cultures needed for the particular options version of the argument. To be sure, a nonessentialist account does not *define* culture in terms of the existence of particular options or practices, and so there is no necessary connection between cultural preservation and the availability of any particular options. Even if Machiguenga culture is preserved, some of the rituals and practices that Misael cares about the most may disappear. Nonetheless, the *frequency* with which particular preferences and values are affirmed, and particular options made available, will depend greatly on the sorts of socialization processes emphasized by the social lineage account, and this is all the argument needs. Misael can reasonably expect to have better access to the particular options he values in a Machiguenga setting than in a dominant culture setting, not because Machiguenga culture is defined in terms of those options, but because the socialization processes that make it the distinctive culture that it is will generate those options more reliably than will the dominant culture. The particular options reason for valuing culture, then, is fully compatible with the social lineage account.

An analysis of the intrinsic version of the argument produces a similar conclusion. It is true that what attracts certain people in their own culture is some specific set of essential characteristics. Abandoning the essentialist concept of culture and replacing it with the social lineage account will mean that cultural prosperity and preservation do not necessarily guarantee that the characteristics these people value will be present. But the social lineage account still leaves plenty of room for people to feel an intrinsic attachment to their own culture. As we saw in the earlier discussion of identity, people who are socialized as members of a particular culture will often feel a kind of attachment to the culture itself, and/or to fellow members of the culture. An identification with one another, and with the institutions and practices of their joint socialization, grows out of a history of interaction and a common set of experiences and points of reference. In addition, in the social lineage account, there is a straightforward sense in which a person's culture helped to make him or her the individual that he or she is. For people who identify with their culture, it is difficult, as a result, to distinguish disrespectful treatment of the culture from disrespectful treatment of them as individuals. In general, then, far from undermining it, the social lineage account can help to illuminate an argument for multiculturalism grounded in the intrinsic significance that some people attach to their culture.

The aim of this chapter has been to respond to an increasingly common, and deeply troubling, challenge to normative multiculturalism. According to the dilemma of essentialism, *either* culture is understood in an "essentialist" way, in which case multiculturalism is empirically and morally flawed, *or* it is understood in a nonessentialist way, but then it undermines the empirical judgments and normative claims on which multiculturalism relies. Because I agree that an essentialist concept of culture is empirically and normatively unacceptable, the burden of the chapter has been to grapple with the second horn of the dilemma. The chapter has undertaken to develop new conceptions of culture and cultural preservation, and to show that they are compatible with the empirical judgments and normative assumptions that are required by multiculturalism. If the arguments I have advanced are sound, then critics are mistaken when they assert that essentialism plays at the very least an implicit and unacknowledged role in normative multiculturalism. Cultural essentialism can be abandoned altogether without undermining the defense of minority cultural rights.

In focusing on this agenda, the chapter has not undertaken two further tasks. First, it has not sought to develop a new justification of multiculturalism. Instead, on normative matters, it has restricted itself to considering whether the proposed account is compatible with reasons for valuing culture that are frequently cited in the literature on multiculturalism. A full investigation of the justification of multiculturalism would clearly need to go much farther than this. There are other interests and countervailing considerations to be considered, and further principles (e.g., of equal treatment) to be articulated. Responding to the dilemma of essentialism clears away distracting concerns about the concept of culture and thereby sets the stage for a forthright exploration of these questions of justification. That exploration begins in the next chapter.

Second, the chapter has also not considered whether, or how far, the social lineage account is useful in other analytic or empirical contexts besides the normative theory of multiculturalism. Political scientists often debate how to identify and count distinct cultures—for instance, when they are constructing indices such as the Ethnolinguistic Fractionalization Index. Although it would be interesting to explore what the social lineage account could contribute to these debates—my hunch is that it would offer a distinctive approach—these and related questions will have to await another occasion.

CHAPTER 3

Why Does Culture Matter?

3.1 Options Disadvantage

Having explored the concepts of culture and cultural preservation in some detail, I turn in this chapter to the more directly normative question of why culture matters. In posing this question, I am specifically interested in understanding the nature of the burden or disadvantage that individuals would bear in the event that their culture were to fare poorly. In what ways would people be disadvantaged if the preservation or enjoyment of their culture were in jeopardy?

Consider again the story of Misael, the migrant member of the Machiguenga culture whom we encountered in the previous chapter. Suppose that he laments the impending disappearance of his culture, or that those who are sympathetic with his situation lament his culture's loss on his behalf. How can we make sense of this lament? What concrete burdens and disadvantages does Misael risk suffering from?

By focusing on the disadvantages borne by members of the disappearing culture, I am bracketing other interests and values that might be at stake. For the reasons laid out in section 1.3, we are setting to one side the interests of third parties as well as any impersonal value that might be lost if the culture were to disappear. As we saw, these sorts of considerations may provide decent secondary reasons for supporting cultural rights. But, on their own, they seem too weak to justify rights claims by members of a struggling culture. Since I am interested in identifying forms of disadvantage that could carry over into a rights claim, we need to identify some different set of burdens associated with cultural loss. We must explore whether there are particular disadvantages that are borne by members of the struggling culture itself. Do existing members of a struggling culture (like Misael and his children) and/or prospective members (those who are not born yet, but who, foreseeably, will be born and raised in the culture before it has ceased altogether to exist) face any special kind of disadvantage as a result of impending cultural loss? And could that disadvantage help to explain and justify why they have strong cultural rights?

The main answer to these questions focuses on the character of the options that are predictably made available or unavailable to members of the culture depending on whether the culture is preserved. The thesis I consider is that members of a disappearing culture face an "options disadvantage." Their options are significantly worse when their culture fares poorly than they are when the culture survives and flourishes. Avishai Margalit and Joseph Raz offer a clear formulation of the thesis when they write that "the prosperity of the culture is important to the well-being of its members. If the culture is decaying, or if it is persecuted or discriminated against, the options and opportunities open to its members will shrink, become less attractive, and their pursuit less likely to be successful."[1] We shall examine more closely this idea of options disadvantage and assess how far it is relevant to explaining and justifying what I earlier called "strong cultural rights" (sec. 1.2).

In emphasizing the options made available by cultures, I do not mean to exclude or ignore the possibility that the existence of a culture may matter for its own sake to some individuals. I shall allow for this possibility by considering the existence of the culture to itself count as an option that may or may not be available. In this way, familiar attempts to ground cultural rights in considerations of "identity" and "recognition," which typically point to the noninstrumental value of a culture to its members, can be folded into the options-disadvantage account and evaluated within that framework. There are several possible ways, then, of showing that someone faces an options disadvantage when his or her culture fares poorly. One could show that the options that predictably are generated by the culture, and that are valuable to members of the culture, would be less available to those individuals. Or one could show that the culture itself is valuable to individuals, and note that this option would, by definition, become unavailable to people as the culture slides into disappearance. My discussion of the options-disadvantage account of why culture matters is meant to cover both possibilities.

By focusing on the loss of important options, my proposal consciously echoes not only Margalit and Raz but also Will Kymlicka's proposal that culture is valuable to its members as a context of choice.[2] As we shall see more fully in the next section, philosophers who argue that cultures supply contexts of choice to their members are best read as claiming that cultural loss would erode the options available to people in a freedom-compromising manner. My discussion in the present chapter represents a reflection on, and elaboration of, this approach to thinking about why culture matters.

The chapter adds to the existing context-of-choice theory in two ways. The first is that I am interested in a broader range of ways in which options might

---

[1] Margalit and Raz 1990, 449.
[2] Kymlicka 1989b; 1995.

be worsened by cultural loss. Not every case of a loss of options is consequential for freedom. But even where freedom is not implicated, the loss of particular options can represent a significant burden. Ultimately, as I note at the end of the chapter (and explore more fully in the two chapters that follow), the main normative fulcrum of my argument is neutrality rather than freedom.

Second, and more centrally in this chapter, existing context-of-choice accounts do a poor job of handling an important challenge to their claims. The challenge, in a nutshell, is to explain why exactly it is that cultural loss leaves members of the disappearing culture without access to an adequate range of options. Why can members of a struggling culture not access the options associated with the dominant majority culture? The present chapter takes seriously this challenge and devotes much of its attention to exploring two different answers.

According to the first answer, the members of a disappearing minority culture have less *access* to the majority culture's options than do members of the majority themselves. Even if there is a single set of options that, in some sense, is there for everybody, those options are less accessible to the minority than they are to the majority. Cultural loss thus carries with it a risk of options disadvantage for the minority. When their culture was healthy, they had full access to the range of options it provided. With its decline or disappearance, they are forced to rely on the options provided by the majority culture, but they enjoy lesser access to those options than do members of the majority. I call this the "access" account.

The second way of answering the challenge turns not on access but on the *adequacy* of the majority-culture options for members of the minority. The idea is that a single set of options accessible to all could be more adequate to some and less adequate to others, depending on the preferences, beliefs, and values held by each. In this view, cultural loss produces an options disadvantage for members of the disappearing culture because it puts them in a situation in which the options that are available to them (and to everybody else) are less valuable to them than to members of the majority, given the preferences, beliefs, and values that are held by members of the different groups. I call this the "adequacy" account.

We shall see that each of these ways of developing the options-disadvantage approach comes with certain strengths and vulnerabilities. The strength of the access account, I shall suggest, is its evident normative salience. If members of a disappearing minority culture do not have access to important options enjoyed by members of the majority, then this seems like a serious disadvantage the avoidance of which could certainly require some kind of response or remedy by the state. The weakness of the access account, however, lies in its limited scope for justifying minority cultural rights. Cultural rights designed to prevent cultural loss from occurring in the first place might be one way of avoiding or remedying the kind of disadvantage that the argument invokes. But in many cases there are alternative kinds of remedy that go in a very different direction. Far from extending rights to members of minority cultures to prevent cultural loss, the alternatives aim for the fuller integration and acceptance of minorities into the majority culture so that the conditions that give rise to differential access never occur. Given this alternative, as well as other limits on its capacity to justify rights that I shall describe, the access account is an unreliable foundation on which to build a case for minority cultural rights.

The adequacy account, on the other hand, has the opposite mix of strengths and vulnerabilities. It is easy enough to see how cultural rights designed to protect vulnerable cultures would be the main remedy to a problem of inadequacy. A more concerted attempt to integrate the minority into the majority culture would not solve the problem. It is less obvious that inadequacy in the sense that is needed by the account necessarily constitutes a form of disadvantage that is normatively salient or that could form the basis of a rights claim.

One conclusion that might be drawn from this analysis is that any kind of options-disadvantage account of the badness of cultural loss is vulnerable to a dilemma. Options disadvantage occurs either because of differential access, in which case the account will often be insufficient to show why the state ought to extend cultural rights to vulnerable cultures rather than more fully integrating them into the dominant culture, or because the majority's options are inadequate for the minority, in which case the account does not go far enough in explaining why options disadvantage should elicit significant moral concern. There is either a problem of insufficiency or a problem of normative salience.

Much of the chapter is devoted to pressing this dilemma. Ultimately, however, I argue for a slightly different conclusion. The dilemma shows, I think, that there is no general right to cultural preservation. There is no satisfactory account of why culture matters that both requires a general right to cultural preservation and is normatively salient. But, although this conclusion is an important one, it would be a mistake to jump from it to a broader rejection of cultural rights. To do so would be to overlook an important possibility that I mention near the end of the chapter in the course of critiquing the adequacy account. The basic idea is to say that, even if the inadequacy of options would not always ground a valid complaint about one's situation, it would support such a complaint if it occurred in a context of unfair treatment of some kind.

This observation sets the agenda for the chapters that follow. Rather than try to ground the case for cultural rights directly in some account of the badness of cultural loss, those chapters develop an account of the fair treatment of cultures. The argument is that, in a central range of cases, fairness requires a form of "equal recognition" between majority and minority cultures, which entails a set of strong cultural rights.

3.2 Culture as Context of Choice

Let us begin by seeing how the dilemma arises for proponents of the familiar claim that culture provides a "context of choice." Although this claim can be interpreted in several different ways, in the most promising interpretation it refers to the options that a culture provides to its members.[3] As mentioned earlier, theorists who make the claim are best read as claiming that cultural loss would erode the options available to members of the culture in a freedom-compromising manner.

Kymlicka's book *Liberalism, Community and Culture* (1989) was the first to describe culture as a "context of choice" and to defend minority cultural rights on the grounds that culture provides such a context. The same basic argument is restated in Kymlicka's *Multicultural Citizenship* (1995) and is also echoed, with variations in terminology, by several other philosophers writing in the early 1990s, including Joseph Raz, Yael Tamir, and David Miller.[4] In what follows, I focus on the formulations of the position offered by Kymlicka and Raz, which are the most explicitly geared toward a defense of minority cultural rights or what they call "multiculturalism."

Both Kymlicka and Raz attempt to establish a connection between freedom and culture. It is because liberals value freedom, and want to secure the conditions in which individuals can be free, that multiculturalism can be justified by reference to liberal principles. Indeed, Raz goes so far as to suggest that "the justification of multiculturalism becomes obvious" once freedom is analyzed correctly.[5]

The key analytic claim about freedom made by these authors is that it depends on access to an adequate range of options. In *The Morality of Freedom*, Raz calls this requirement the "adequacy of options" and argues that it is one of the three main conditions of autonomy (along with "appropriate mental abilities" and "independence" from coercion and manipulation).[6] Without adequate options, Raz argues, a person cannot exercise actual choice over how her life goes and so cannot be considered the autonomous maker of her own life. She would be in the situation of the "Man in the Pit," who has nothing but trivial options to choose from, or of the "Hounded Woman," who has nothing but horrendous alternatives to the one set of desperate choices that would preserve her life. Kymlicka's version of the requirement calls for a "range of

---

[3] A different interpretation is that cultures provide to their members the beliefs about value that make choice possible. For a discussion of Kymlicka's version of the theory that privileges this interpretation, see Tomasi 1995. I consider this interpretation, as well as the options-based one, in Patten 1999a.

[4] Raz 1994; Tamir 1993; Miller 1995. For discussion of the versions of the argument found in Tamir and Miller, as well as in Kymlicka and Raz, see Patten 1999b.

[5] Raz 1994, 176.

[6] Raz 1986, 373–77.

meaningful options."[7] Kymlicka regards such a range as necessary if individuals are to be in a position to form and revise their conceptions of the good. To think critically about their own life-plans, and to adopt new life-plans if their current ones are found wanting, individuals need to have meaningful alternatives, including exposure to a range of different views about the good life.

The crucial claim about culture, in turn, is that it is essential to making available the adequate range of options that persons need in order to be free. As Kymlicka puts it, "freedom involves making choices amongst various options, and our societal culture not only provides these options, but also makes them meaningful to us."[8] Raz's formulation is fairly similar: "options presuppose culture," he argues, because they presuppose "shared meanings and common practices."[9] Both Kymlicka and Raz emphasize that culture confers value on the various activities that are open to people, thereby helping, when things go well, to make the range of possible options adequate. For Kymlicka, culture plays this role because the meaning of activities is conferred by language, and language in turn is shaped by history, traditions, and conventions. In Raz's slightly different version of the claim, options that are meaningful are constituted, in part, by rules and conventions, which are themselves established and recognized within the practices that make up a culture.

Based on this analysis, both Kymlicka and Raz move directly to the conclusion that liberal principles mandate protections for struggling minority cultures. Kymlicka concludes that "group-differentiated measures that secure and promote" access to a societal culture "may, therefore, have a legitimate role to play in a liberal theory of justice."[10] And Raz suggests that, with this argument, and some additional parallel ones, "the case for multiculturalism" has been made. "Given [the] dependence of individual freedom and well-being on unimpeded membership in a respected and prosperous cultural group, there is little wonder that multiculturalism emerges as a central element in any decent liberal political programme for societies inhabited by a number of viable cultural groups."[11]

Because these conclusions are reached so swiftly, it is difficult to be confident about any specific interpretation of the argument that supports them. It is clear, in both the Raz and the Kymlicka versions, that the argument from context-of-choice starts out from three key premises:

(1) The state has strong reason to embrace policies that secure the conditions of individual freedom.

(2) To be free, individuals must have access to an adequate range of options.

[7] Kymlicka 1995, 83.
[8] Ibid.
[9] Raz 1994, 176.
[10] Kymlicka 1995, 84.
[11] Raz 1994, 178.

(3) Culture plays a role in making available an adequate range of options.

But how does the argument get from these assumptions to its final conclusion?

(C) The state has strong reason to embrace policies that are intended to prevent cultures from being lost ("multiculturalism").

The most plausible interpretation, I believe, is that it does so via an intermediate conclusion, which is meant to follow from (2) and (3):

(4) When a culture is lost, its members are left without one of the necessary conditions of freedom.

Taken together with (1), (4) is said to imply (C).

It should, I hope, be clear why the context-of-choice argument is an example of an options-disadvantage account of why culture matters. The reason cultural loss is bad and ought to be prevented, according to context-of-choice theorists, is that it leaves members of the disappearing culture without access to an adequate range of options. I now want to show how the context-of-choice argument is connected with the dilemma I sketched in the opening section of the chapter. If the argument is to have any hope of success, it will have to make one or other of two possible assumptions about when a person can be said to have, or to lack, access to an adequate range of options. The first of these assumptions corresponds with the access interpretation of options-disadvantage mentioned earlier, and the second with the adequacy interpretation.

To see how we arrive at this choice, it helps to consider a standard objection to the context-of-choice argument, which I shall call the "particularity" problem.[12] In a nutshell, the problem is that, at best, the argument shows that individuals need access to some option-providing culture or other. On its own, the argument is indeterminate with respect to which particular culture it is that performs the option-providing function. An individual might have an adequate range of options because the culture in which he was raised endows the activities that are open to him with the appropriate forms of meaning and value. But it is equally consistent with the argument as laid out that an individual could have an adequate range of options because some other culture confers the requisite meanings on the activities open to her. One cultural context may come, and another may go. So long as *some* culture provides individuals with an adequate range of options, premise (2) is satisfied and there is no freedom-based cause for alarm. The inference from premises (2) and (3) to the intermediate conclusion (4) is flawed, therefore. It is a mistake to think that the loss of any particular culture necessarily undermines the conditions of anybody's freedom. When a minority culture disappears, it is perfectly pos-

---

[12] Early formulations of the objection are in Waldron 1992; Margalit and Halbertal 1994.

sible that some other culture, such as the majority or dominant culture, is able to take up the slack.

The particularity problem need not invoke a merely abstract or hypothetical possibility. Consider, for instance, our earlier example of the Machiguengas. Misael's children risk losing their culture (the culture of their early childhood) because the institutions and practices that transmit that culture are disappearing, replaced instead by institutions and practices associated with the majority culture. Their lives are shaped by the schools, the economy, the media, the social services, the military and policing institutions, and so on, of the majority culture, and not by institutions and practices that are mainly populated and controlled by the Machiguengas. The Machiguenga culture is being undermined, in other words, by a process that involves the majority culture extending its socializing power over the lives of Misael and his children. This characterization of the case does not imply that Misael's children are left without the range of options provided by a culture. To the contrary, they are being socialized as members of the majority culture, who can access and enjoy the options provided by that culture. For that matter, nothing in the context-of-choice argument to this point explains why Misael himself could not be said to have an adequate range of options, or at least the *same* range of options that are enjoyed by his non-Machiguenga neighbors (for perhaps *hardly anybody* in Boca Manu has an *adequate* range of options).

Kymlicka notices the particularity problem in *Multicultural Citizenship* in a passage that runs for several pages.[13] In principle he agrees that people can "switch" cultures and thus do not depend absolutely on the culture in which they were born and raised to provide them with a context of choice. He argues that, in practice, though, switching cultures can be very costly for people, and this is a cost that they have a right not to have to bear. I shall have more to say about the allocation of costs associated with cultural loss in the next section. But for now the puzzle is why there are any costs at all that need to be allocated. Recall premise (2): to be free, individuals must have access to an adequate range of options. We have yet to hear any reason why the condition laid down in (2) is one that would only be met, in certain situations, if some cost is incurred. In one interpretation, at least, (2) states a condition that is social in character. It is either a fact about the society in which an individual lives that it contains an adequate range of options or it is not. If this is the right understanding of (2), then whether a given individual has access to an adequate range of options does not depend on that individual incurring any particular cost.

[13] Kymlicka 1995, 84–93.

We are now in a position to see why the context-of-choice argument leads to the analytic choice between the access and adequacy interpretations of options disadvantage. It is clear that to rescue the argument from the particularity problem, something more needs to be said about the condition laid down in (2). Evidently, having access to an adequate range of options implies more than just the local presence of a range of options that some culture deems meaningful. Otherwise, a community's dominant culture would automatically count as providing options to everyone in that community, and no member of a minority culture would ever be in a position to complain that her options were any less adequate than the options enjoyed by members of the majority. So what more is needed in order to say that persons, or groups of persons, have access to an adequate range of options? Why might we be reluctant to say that Misael (or even his children) enjoy just as adequate a range of options when they move to Boca Manu as do established, majority-culture residents of that same town?

The access approach to answering these questions focuses on the conditions under which a person can be said to have genuine access to options that are present in a community. It adopts a straightforward (or what I shall call a "generic") view of what counts as an adequate range of options and then claims that different individuals in a community will have varying levels of access to those options, depending on culture-related characteristics that they have. The adequacy account focuses on the conditions under which a particular set of options might be considered adequate for a given person. It abstracts away from concerns about differential access and claims that access to a particular set of options may count as adequate for some people, but not for others, depending on culture-related differences in their preferences, values, beliefs, and so on.

The next two sections explore each of these approaches in turn. As we shall see, each of them holds some promise as a response to the particularity problem. If either *access* to or *adequacy* of options depends on culture-related characteristics, then the idea that people rely in a special way on their own culture (the culture in which they were raised) starts to look plausible. I shall argue, however, that both approaches lead to difficulties. If one opts for the access approach, then a major problem arises with the final step of the argument, the inference from (1) and (4) to (C). Policies designed to prevent cultural loss do not look like the only plausible remedy to the problem. An alternative remedy would be to try to remove the conditions that are limiting the access of members of the disappearing culture to an adequate range of options. If one opts instead for the adequacy approach and brackets the issue of access, then the problem is that (1) itself no longer seems unassailable. One can define freedom, or specify its conditions, however one likes. But one should not expect that in just any account of freedom it will continue to enjoy the obvious normative importance that is presumed by (1).

3.3 The Access Account

The general idea of differential access is quite familiar. By almost any standard, New York City contains an adequate range of fine dining options. But these options are not accessible to people who cannot afford them. Even though the city's restaurant options are adequate, it does not follow that all New Yorkers enjoy access to an adequate range of restaurant options.

Our interest is in whether there are culture-related factors that might leave members of a disappearing minority culture with diminished access to the options made available by the dominant culture. If there are, then it seems quite plausible to think that cultural loss might worsen the options available to members of the minority. When their culture is doing well, members of the minority face no cultural impediment to enjoying the full range of options that it offers. When it goes into decline, the options associated with the dominant culture are the only ones left standing, but members of the minority face a cultural impediment to accessing them.

An appealing feature of this form of argument is that it need not rely on any special assumptions about what counts as an adequate range of options. The claim to be considered in the present section is not that the options made available by the majority culture lack value to the minority, but that, for culture-related reasons, they are not available to the minority. For the purposes of this section, then, I shall simply assume that the range of existing options is adequate in a *generic* sense. Its adequacy does not reside in the fact that it corresponds to particular beliefs and preferences, but rather in the fact that it satisfies a preference-independent conception of what range of options people need to have. Such a conception is, I think, quite appealing and bolsters the normative salience of an access account. Even if a person's idiosyncratic preferences are frustrated, we may well judge that his options are adequate, so long as he has a decent range of core options that are plausibly regarded as valuable for people no matter what their preferences are. Such generically valuable options might include a range of education, employment and professional opportunities; opportunities for various kinds of personal relationships, for political participation, for religious, artistic, and intellectual experience; a range of forms of recreation and leisure; access to public spaces and to nature; and so on. Conversely, if a person lacks access to generically valuable options of this sort, then she does seem to be at a serious disadvantage, one that would normally call for some kind of remedy.[14]

[14] A variety of accounts of what makes a set of options generically adequate seem possible. Such an account might be guided by a particular conception of the person, who has certain crucial capacities that

Suppose, then, that some society contains an adequate range of options in this generic sense. Assume that it is home to a struggling minority culture, whose members live alongside the members of a dominant, majority culture. What factors might impede members of the minority culture from enjoying access to the same adequate range of options as do members of the majority? I shall describe two basic exclusionary mechanisms. The first is discrimination; the second I call "incapacity."

Discrimination

One reason why minorities may be unable to access certain options is that they encounter discrimination at the hands of the majority.[15] This mechanism of exclusion becomes significant when three conditions are satisfied.

CONTROL

A significant number of the options that are contained in the society are under the control of members of the majority culture, who occupy key positions of power and authority in the practices and institutions in which those options are made available. They are employers, landlords, government officials, school teachers, bank managers, military officers, influential members of private associations, and so forth and thus are in a position to influence who receives particular benefits, or is admitted to important opportunities, or can obtain the qualifications needed to access those opportunities.

PREJUDICE

Many members of the majority culture have negative attitudes about the minority culture. At the extreme, these attitudes include outright animus toward the group and its members. More insidiously, they include unflattering beliefs, based on negative stereotypes, about the characteristics and capacities of members of the minority. Based on these attitudes, the people who hold them want to harm members of the minority, or they regard members of the minority as (typically) unqualified to participate fully in certain practices and institutions, or at least to hold positions of authority and responsibility in those practices and institutions.

---

need to be developed and exercised. Following this approach, an adequate set of options would be one that made it possible for individuals to develop and exercise the requisite capacities. Or an account of generic adequacy might be guided by a conception of well-being or capabilities. The thought might be that individuals need to have certain sorts of opportunities available to them if they are to be in a position to live good lives. It might be argued, for instance, that human beings have certain innate drives—to exercise their bodies, to stimulate their minds, to form lasting relationships with others, and so on—and that human well-being is likely to be adversely affected if options that allow them to realize these drives are not available. Since my purpose here is not to defend the generic adequacy approach, I will not attempt to develop any particular account of what it is, precisely, that might make a set of options generically adequate.

[15] Gellner (1983, 64–75) describes a mechanism of this sort and relates it to the formation of nationalist movements.

IDENTIFIABILITY

Members of the minority culture typically have certain conspicuous characteristics based on appearance, or accent, or surname, or some other trait. They stand out, and this makes it feasible for those in the majority who occupy positions of power and responsibility to discriminate against them.

Where all three of the conditions are satisfied, a mechanism is in place that can explain how cultural loss brings about options disadvantage for members of a disappearing minority culture. When the minority culture was intact, fellow members of the culture controlled key options. Even if members of the majority harbored prejudices, and even if members of the minority were identifiable, the control condition was not satisfied, and thus cultural discrimination could not block access to those key options. When the minority culture disappears, control over key options shifts away from members of that culture. Increasingly, those who were born and initially raised in the culture are led to look for their options in practices and institutions that are dominated by the majority. Now the control condition is satisfied, and if the prejudice and identifiability conditions are too, discrimination becomes an operative mechanism. When this happens there is an obvious sense in which the options open to members of the minority have worsened. Whereas prior to the loss of their culture they could access a range of key options, once their culture slides into decline the options that they would naturally turn to are partially blocked off to them because of discrimination.

Incapacity

A second reason why minorities are sometimes unable to access majority-culture-based options is that they lack certain of the key capacities needed to participate effectively in the practices and institutions that provide those options. The idea that a person might need particular capacities to participate in certain institutions and practices is a familiar one. Plumbers need special training to practice their trade, as do doctors, lawyers, auto mechanics, childcare workers, and so on. The sort of training that is especially relevant to our current topic, however, is what Ernest Gellner calls "generic training."[16] This is the process of endowing people with certain general skills and capacities that precede, and are more general than, the specialized skills needed to fulfill a particular role. Possession of these generic skills allows a person to be slotted and reslotted into any of a number of particular roles, typically once the individual has obtained the additional specialized training that is peculiar to that role. As we saw in chapter 2, these generic capacities include literacy, numeracy, social skills, technological skills, and, above all, competence in the language in

[16] Ibid., 27–29.

which institutions and practices operate. Persons who lack these generic skills will face both direct and indirect obstacles to participation in many institutions and practices—"direct" ones because the skills are themselves needed for participation in a wide range of institutions and practices, and "indirect" ones because they are needed to acquire more specific skills (e.g., training as a plumber) that are then put to use in particular institutions and practices.

Although some generic skills, such as numeracy and literacy, are fairly universal, others are culturally specific. They are typically acquired through socialization in a particular culture, and, although they are useful for a wide range of activities within that culture (that's what makes them generic), they are of limited use in the institutions and practices associated with other cultures. The cultural specificity of generic skills is particularly clear in the case of language. One typically learns a language through being socialized in it from an early age. And competence in most languages (English and a handful of other languages used as intercultural lingua franca are partial exceptions) is not a generically valuable skill—one that gives access to a variety of options and opportunities—outside of the culture in which it was acquired. The comparison with numeracy is instructive. Whereas numeracy implies mastery of a convention that is universal or near-universal in scope, competence in a language means mastery of a convention that is local to some culture, so that language proficiency is typically a *locally* generic capacity. Social and technological skills occupy an intermediate position between these poles of universalism and specificity. They may seem fairly universal in some settings and quite culturally specific in others. Social norms relating to authority, gender, child-rearing, work, time, friendship, hospitality, and so on, overlap to a considerable extent in many of the world's cultures, but certainly not in all of them. Likewise, the basic skills related to operating motorized vehicles, working with machines, and using digital technology transcend any particular culture, in the sense that they are both acquired in and useful in many different cultures. But there are still a few remote cultures in which such basic technical skills are not in much use, and in which people may not, as a result, be socialized or educated to possess them.

The cultural specificity of certain generic skills means that people in a multicultural society can be excluded from some of the options that their society contains. Most obviously, if minority language speakers are not also competent in the majority language, then they will not be able to participate in practices and institutions that operate in the majority-language medium. This is a well-known challenge facing many new immigrants, but it can also be a problem for members of a long-settled culture that is in the process of disappearing. Their language and other generic skills have been formed in their own culture and prepare them to access options that are available in a particular language and that presuppose particular social and cultural attributes. With the decline of their culture, fewer and fewer of the options that are available will have the cultural characteristics that make them accessible to people with this background.

To be sure, many younger members of a declining culture will experience a bicultural upbringing that leaves them with the generic skills (language, mastery of key social norms, etc.) that they need to access options in either the minority or the majority culture. But there may well be cases in which some members of the disappearing minority culture did not receive such an upbringing. This may be true of middle-aged and older members of the culture (compare Misael's experience with that of his children) and also of younger members of the culture whose geographic or social location left them isolated from the forces of majority-culture socialization. For members of a minority culture who are not equipped with the generic skills needed for participation in the institutions and practices of the majority culture, the decline and disappearance of their culture is a fateful event. They go from a situation in which they were equipped, by their capacities, to access the range of options provided within their own culture to one in which they are excluded by their incapacity from participating in the key options that now remain in their society.

There are other mechanisms as well that can explain why members of a cultural minority might lack access to options offered within the majority culture. Even when there is no discrimination, and when they possess all the relevant forms of cultural capital, members of a minority may find themselves excluded from key majority-culture options because they lack relevant forms of social capital. The social networks they participate in may be geared toward minority-culture options rather than majority-culture ones. In examining the phenomena of discrimination and incapacity, however, we get a good insight into how the access argument is supposed to work, one that can be generalized to other mechanisms of exclusion. Both mechanisms point to reasons for thinking that cultural loss might bring about an options disadvantage for members of the disappearing culture. Moreover, these reasons seem to be of the right kind to justify cultural rights. A person who does not have access to the kinds of options that are associated with a generic conception of adequacy—employment opportunities, opportunities for participation in civil society, and so forth—is clearly facing a significant disadvantage, one that calls out for some kind of remedy. If a lack of access to such options was a voluntary, self-imposed condition, then perhaps no remedy would be called for. But the discrimination and incapacity mechanisms both suggest that such a condition will often not be self-imposed. They point to broader social processes and mechanisms that can leave minorities exposed to disadvantage whatever choices they might make.

The question that now arises is whether this access account of options disadvantage is, in fact, helpful for justifying minority cultural rights. The access considerations seem morally compelling, but do those considerations entail a need for cultural rights? For the account to support minority cultural rights in a given case of cultural loss, four assumptions would have to hold for that case:

1. *Exclusion.* One or both of the mechanisms of exclusion sketched above are operative.
2. *Efficacy.* Minority cultural rights can be expected to improve the range of options open to members of the minority in their own cultural context.
3. *Nonaggravation.* Minority cultural rights would not seriously aggravate the mechanisms that exclude members of the minority from majority-culture options.
4. *No alternatives.* There is no viable alternative approach to reducing or mitigating the mechanisms of exclusion besides minority cultural rights.

All these assumptions have a significant empirical dimension to them. Although I will not investigate the empirical issues here, it does strike me as plausible to think that the assumptions might all hold in at least some cases. In these cases, there is a reasonable argument to be made, on the basis of the access account, in favor of certain minority cultural rights. I describe one such case in section 6.8.

The main point I want to stress here, however, is that the access strategy for defending minority rights is quite limited in scope. The range of cases in which all the assumptions above are satisfied is likely to be quite restricted. If access considerations provided the main argument for cultural rights, then we would be forced to conclude that liberal states are often justified in refusing to recognize such rights. Needless to say, the fact that the argument's scope is limited, or that it does not reliably support a particular policy conclusion, is no criticism of it in those contexts where it does apply. The limits in scope that I point to do suggest, however, that advocates of a fairly robust and general program of minority rights need to look elsewhere for support.

Each of the four assumptions mentioned above is likely not to hold in some range of cases. Let us look at each in turn.

Exclusion

The two mechanisms of exclusion sketched earlier are immediately recognizable as important processes in societies around the world. Despite their familiarity, however, it would be a mistake to assume that those mechanisms are salient to every case in which the members of some minority culture face the loss of their culture or seek rights or institutions that help to protect them against such loss. Some cases of impending cultural loss are characterized by fairly low levels of prejudice and animosity between minority and majority. In these cases, it is not clear that the remaining members of a disappearing minority would encounter especially high levels of discrimination in majority-controlled practices and institutions. Some majority cultures are likely to be proud of their capacity to absorb minorities, seeing it as a sign of their tolerance (and attachment to other liberal values) and as confirmation of the power and prestige of their culture. If Welsh culture were to disappear, for instance, it is not obvious that those who had been socialized into that culture would face high levels of discrimination as they sought out options in Britain's dominant, Anglophone culture. Nor is it obvious that the loss of Catalan culture would expose those who had been raised as Catalan to high levels of discrimination from the Spanish majority. Nor, for that matter, that the loss of Francophone culture in English-majority provinces in Canada (or Anglophone culture in Quebec) would expose the minority in each case to exclusionary levels of discrimination. And even if my conjectures about one or more of these cases are wrong, the general point that cultural loss does not automatically leave the remaining members of the culture victimized by discrimination seems hard to dispute.

The suggestion that cultural loss and discrimination do not move in lockstep with one another may seem surprising to people who assume that discrimination and prejudice are major *causes* of cultural deterioration and loss. In fact, as Jean Laponce and Philippe Van Parijs have both argued, the opposite can be true.[17] The warmer the embrace between majority and minority cultures, the deadlier the implications can be for the survival of the minority culture. For example, intermarriage between members of different cultures often pressures individuals to make pragmatic choices about culture (e.g., which language to school children in) that tend, in aggregate, to work against the maintenance of the minority culture. To the extent that animosity and prejudice discourage intermarriage, they work, in a perverse manner, to protect the minority culture. The point, of course, is not to encourage or justify discrimination but simply to suggest that cultural loss does not always take place under conditions in which members of the disappearing culture can expect to face discrimination at the hands of the majority. Just the opposite may be the case.

A parallel analysis holds for the incapacity mechanism. Cultural loss need not leave anybody stranded without the generic capacities required to access options in the majority culture. One reason for this is that minority and majority may not have been associated with distinct sets of generic capacities in the first place. Minority and majority groups might, for instance, share a common language, as the Scottish and English do, but still count as distinct cultures on the basis of other factors. Given the common language, as well as other commonalities, the disappearance of Scottish culture would not leave Scots stranded without the generic capacities they need for participating in English-dominated options. Even more important, as noted earlier, minorities often receive a kind of bicultural (and bilingual) socialization, in which they

---

[17] Laponce 1984, 145–46; Van Parijs 2000a, 241; 2011a, 143–44.

are brought up in such a way that they end up possessing the generic capacities needed for participation in the minority culture and the distinct set of generic capacities required for the majority culture. Thus, for instance, virtually all Catalans can speak Spanish,[18] the Welsh can generally speak English,[19] most Franco-Ontariens can speak English,[20] and so on. The members of these minorities would not be excluded by their generic capacities from participation in majority culture, and so the access argument (or at least a version of that argument emphasizing the incapacity mechanism) cannot explain why they ought to enjoy rights to cultural preservation.

EFFICACY

From the standpoint of the access argument, the point of minority cultural rights is to protect and expand the range of options available in the minority-culture context so that those options are reasonably adequate even for members of the minority who cannot also hope (because of discrimination or incapacity) to access a full range of options in the majority culture. The idea is to recognize rights that protect opportunities to develop and enjoy the minority culture, thereby making it more appealing for members of that culture to invest their time and energy in that culture and less tempting to "defect" to the majority culture. The recognition of such rights makes it easier, cheaper, and more socially acceptable for members of the minority to maintain the institutions and practices that distinguish their culture from the majority's.

Although it is possible that minority rights may be efficacious in this way, there is certainly no guarantee that they will be. As the rich literature on "reversing language shift" demonstrates, it can be extremely difficult for policy makers to exert a significant impact on cultural outcomes using the tools and measures of public policy (including the recognition of certain rights).[21] And it is likely to be even more difficult to engineer such outcomes if policy makers are committed to respecting liberal values and side-constraints.

[18] According to 2007 data from the Statistical Institute of Catalonia, more than 98 percent of people over the age of two who live in Catalonia can understand Spanish. See http://www.idescat.cat/territ/Ba sicTerr?TC=5&V0=3&V1=3&V3=2523&V4=2569&ALLINFO=TRUE&PARENT=1&CTX=B (accessed May 22, 2012). According to another report produced by the government of Catalonia, approximately 88 percent of all Catalans report having a high level of knowledge of Spanish in all skill areas (understanding, reading, speaking, writing). See Generalitat de Catalunya 2010, 241.

[19] In 1981, the last year in which official data are available, less than 1 percent of the Welsh population were monolingual Welsh-speakers; see Jones 1993.

[20] For instance, according to the 2006 Census of Canada, 88.4 percent of Francophones in Ontario report being French-English bilingual. See http://www12.statcan.ca/census-recensement/2006/as-sa /97–555/p13-eng.cfm (accessed May 28, 2012).

[21] Fishman (1991, 12) argues that "there is no language for which nothing at all can be done." But in general he is forthright about the challenges that face attempts to reverse language shift. Fishman (2001) is entitled, "Why Is It So Hard to Save a Threatened Language?" See also Edwards 1985, chap. 3.

Public-policy efforts to develop and protect minority-culture options face an uphill struggle for a number of reasons. In some cases the lure of the majority culture is particularly irresistible. Its economic opportunities, popular culture, and general status and prestige are such that large numbers of members of the minority are continuously turning to majority-culture options, even as other members of the minority are excluded from those options by discrimination or incapacity. The related point is that some minority cultures are too small, too dispersed, and too economically disadvantaged and marginalized to be in a position to develop their options to the point where those who forgo, or are excluded from, the majority culture can find a reasonable range of options within them. This is often true of minority cultures formed through immigration and is one plausible reason for assigning members of such cultures weaker claims to minority cultural rights than their historically established, territorially concentrated counterparts (see sec. 8.1). Many immigrant cultures are too small and fragmented in the context of the host society to be viable vehicles of opportunity for their members, or even to be developed into such vehicles with the aid of a liberally minded set of public policy measures. However much those immigrants might face exclusion from the majority culture as a result of discrimination or incapacity, the solution is not likely to be found through developing a rich set of options within their own cultures. The same thing seems true of some indigenous cultures. Their size and socioeconomic marginalization makes it hard to imagine how they could be developed to the point where they offer a full enough range of options to serve as an alternative to the majority culture. Tragically, inclusion in majority-culture options has proven no more successful in some of these cases, leaving members of some indigenous cultures with no adequate context of choice of any sort.

Nonaggravation

According to the access account, the point of minority cultural rights is to develop options within the minority culture, so that minorities need not turn to an inhospitable majority culture for a decent range of opportunities. Given discrimination and/or incapacity, who could blame members of the minority for developing their own institutions and practices, and providing themselves with opportunities within their own cultural structure? For this argument to have force, it is not necessary that members of the minority be completely excluded from majority options. Discrimination is not an all-or-nothing barrier to opportunity, nor is incapacity. In fact, if one were to restrict the relevance of the argument only to those situations in which exclusion is total, then the argument would apply to a very limited range of cases indeed. Even though their group is subject to discrimination and is associated with a set of generic capacities that are of limited use in the majority culture, individual members of the minority culture may to greater or lesser extents enjoy certain opportunities in the majority culture. The members of the majority culture will not be uniformly hostile to, or prejudiced against, the minority. And the minority population will include at least some members who are able to acquire the majority's generic capacities to at least some degree, and thus who can access at least some of the majority culture's options.

Once it is conceded that members of the minority are not, in general, totally excluded from majority options, however, then it becomes important to consider whether minority cultural rights might worsen access to the majority culture. Might the institutionalization of such rights aggravate the mechanisms of exclusion that generate the problem of access in the first place? This might seem a remote possibility to worry about. Why would the protection of a minority culture not simply add to the options available to minority culture members? The key point is that cultural rights are likely to introduce a degree of institutional and spatial differentiation into the society in which they are recognized. A scheme of language rights, for instance, will often imply that speakers of different languages receive their public services from different offices and providers and have their children educated in different classes or schools. Regional autonomy for cultural minorities introduces a new set of institutions that operate separately from national institutions and that are meant to be dominated by members of the minority. And so on. This alteration of the institutional landscape may well have consequences for the discrimination and/or incapacity mechanisms that serve to exclude minorities from majority-culture options. Institutional differentiation may frustrate attempts to forge a common sense of nationality among members of a multicultural society, thereby weakening a mechanism that might be counted on to diminish or offset discrimination. And it may also make it less likely that members of the minority will receive the sort of bicultural socialization that equips them with the generic skills they need to access majority-culture options. Either way, and depending on which mechanism was driving the options disadvantage in the first place, the preservation of the minority culture through an extension of minority cultural rights may produce a reduction for some members of the minority in the majority-culture options accessible to them.

It then becomes a largely empirical question whether the gain in minority-culture options that comes about by preserving the minority culture is great enough to offset the loss in majority-culture options. The net effect will depend on a variety of factors, including

- how much of an impact the minority cultural rights, and the institutional differentiation that they imply, do in fact exert on access to majority-culture options;
- the degree to which the minority culture is large and diverse enough that it contains, on its own, an ample range of options; and

- the impact of minority cultural rights on the size and diversity of minority-culture options.

These considerations point to a distinctive third limitation on the scope of the access argument. If the impact of cultural rights on majority-culture access is significant, and the options available within the minority culture are quite limited and/or not much improved by cultural rights, then, from a strictly access perspective, cultural rights are not justified. They would worsen the access to (generically understood) options enjoyed by members of the minority, not improve it. To use a polemical term, cultural rights, under such empirical conditions, would "ghettoize" members of the minority, reinforcing the bonds that tie them into a structure of limited opportunity rather than loosening those bonds.

I do not offer a conjecture here on how widely the nonaggravation assumption is violated. Critics of minority cultural rights frequently charge that such rights foster social exclusion, but, as we shall see in section 6.6, there is no reason to think that this is generally true. What seems most likely is that the nonaggravation assumption holds for some but not all cases. This is one more reason to think that the access argument fails to offer a robust and general justification of minority rights.[22]

No Alternatives

Suppose now that we have isolated a set of cases in which each of the exclusion, efficacy, and nonaggravation assumptions can be expected to hold. There is still a further restriction on the scope of the access argument that has to be recognized. As noted in chapter 1, we want to know, not just whether a scheme of minority cultural rights is permissible, but whether a state that fails to recognize and protect such a scheme would be open to justifiable criticism. For the access account to have this implication, however, it needs to be the case, not just that minority rights would provide minorities with access to a (generically) adequate range of options, but that no alternative policy pursued by the state could bring about the same result. If there was a feasible alternative, then the state could escape justified criticism by *either* protecting minority cultural rights *or* pursuing that alternative.[23]

[22] For related discussion, see Anderson 2010.

[23] In a reply to Forst (1997), Kymlicka (2001a, 55n7) suggests that protecting minority rights (as opposed to integration in the majority culture) is "a way of concretizing our autonomy-based interest in culture." This seems true enough, but it may also be true that integration is a way of concretizing the autonomy-based interest in culture. What the access argument cannot provide is a general reason for thinking that it would be wrong for a state to adopt the integration approach rather than the minority-rights approach. Forst's point—which Kymlicka effectively concedes—is that Kymlicka ends up relying on identity considerations, not autonomy ones, to produce such a reason.

In fact there is a familiar alternative to minority cultural rights that a state might adopt. Instead of introducing rights designed to prevent cultural loss, the state might enact policies designed to eliminate or weaken the mechanisms of discrimination and/or incapacity that connect cultural loss with options disadvantage. This sort of approach occupies an important place in both liberal theory and liberal practice. Liberals have often recognized the ways in which discrimination and incapacity operate to exclude minorities from opportunities that are available to the majority. Instead of concluding that special rights are needed to preserve distinct minority cultures, however, many liberals have reached a quite different conclusion. They have supported a variety of special measures designed to encourage the fuller integration of minorities into an inclusive national culture based on the majority culture.[24]

Liberal states have adopted specific antidiscrimination laws, have pursued various forms of affirmative action and preferential treatment, and have supported various educational initiatives designed to raise awareness of discrimination. More generally, they have pursued nation-building policies, through the schools, the military, the national media, and other public institutions, that seek to define a broad and inclusive sense of shared nationality, thereby encouraging members of the majority to think of the minority as fellow nationals. As far as incapacity is concerned, liberal nation-builders have again advocated the use of public institutions to make sure that every citizen is endowed with the generic capacities that they need to thrive in the society they inhabit. In many liberal countries, these include intensive language classes designed to teach the majority language as a second language in a fairly short period of time.

This repertoire of nation-building measures forms the standard response of liberal states to the integration of new immigrants. Discrimination and incapacity are genuine problems for immigrants. But few people suggest that the appropriate remedy is to extend rights to immigrants that would enable them to opt out of the majority culture and instead re-create their home culture in the host society. To most liberals, it seems obvious that the correct remedy is to try to eliminate or weaken the mechanisms of exclusion themselves. The access argument would be flawed if it failed to explore whether this integrative approach to immigrants could be generalized to other kinds of cultural loss. Just as immigrants lose a significant part of their culture of origin, but are helped to integrate into the dominant culture of their new home, so it might be suggested that members of long-established but now declining cultures can be systematically assisted to integrate into the dominant culture.

To the extent that the integrationist policies are successful at making the majority culture more inclusive, and at giving minorities the generic capacities that are needed for success in the majority culture, cultural loss need no longer

[24]Kymlicka 2001a, 26, 53–54; Barry 2001, 104–9; Stilz 2009; Anderson 2010.

imply an options disadvantage. There may, of course, be other objections to cultural loss—we shall get to some of them in the next section—but, where integrationist policies are a success, minorities cannot say that their generic options are so much worse with the loss of their culture that some further remedy is called for. With full integration, the minority enjoys the same range of options as the majority. If those options are adequate for the majority, then, given the generic view of adequacy assumed in this section, they must also be adequate for the minority.

Of course there may be cases in which integrationist policies are *not* a viable alternative to minority rights. The integrationist approach relies on broad assumptions about the effectiveness of certain policy measures at reducing discrimination and at equipping people with the capacities that enable them to access majority-culture options. It seems plausible to believe that these measures are indeed likely to be effective under certain empirical conditions. There are examples of societies that have made themselves more inclusive over time, and of polyglot societies that have been successful at inducing virtually everyone to learn the majority language (or societal lingua franca). But it also seems plausible to think that integrationist policy measures are *not* likely to be successful under all likely empirical circumstances. In some situations, the conditions that give rise to discrimination may be so deep-seated as to be unresponsive to government policies intended to eliminate them. At a certain point, faced with intransigent prejudice, members of a minority culture might reasonably decide that they are better off developing and strengthening options within their own culture rather than continuing to seek entry into the majority culture. In a similar way, there is no guarantee that policies aimed at promoting language learning, or other forms of capacity building, will meet with success. Second-language education is likely to be effective under some conditions but not under others.

All this serves to remind us that the integrationist alternative amounts to a *limit* on the scope of the access argument, not a decisive, general objection to that argument. Where the state does pursue a viable integrationist alternative, there is no legitimate access-based complaint relating to cultural loss or a failure to extend minority rights. But, as I allowed at the outset, under some empirical conditions, it can be expected that integrationist nation building will be ineffective, and indeed that all four of the assumptions undergirding the access approach will be satisfied. Under these conditions, but only under these conditions, minority rights look like the most promising way of securing access to options for members of struggling minority cultures.

One possible objection to the preceding discussion of the no-alternatives assumption is that it ignores the costs associated with integration. The integrationist, nation-building alternative to minority rights might do an equally good job of securing options for the minority, but it involves costs that are unfairly borne by members of the minority. A program of minority cultural rights is thus the only fair approach to protecting minorities from options dis-advantage induced by cultural loss. As we saw in the previous section, Kym-licka emphasizes this point in his defense of the view that minorities need access to a context of choice based on their own culture. In principle, he allows, people can "switch" cultures, and thus they do not depend absolutely on the culture in which they were born and raised to provide them with a context of choice.[25] In practice, though, switching cultures can be very costly for people, and Kymlicka thinks that this is a cost they have a right not to have to bear, unless they so choose (as immigrants do, in Kymlicka's view). He suggests there is a "legitimate question whether people should be required to pay those costs unless they voluntarily choose to do so," and he compares the "choice to leave one's culture" with a "vow of perpetual poverty": "leaving one's culture, while possible, is best seen as renouncing something to which one is reason-ably entitled."[26]

This objection runs into several difficulties, however. First, it is not clear why the cost in question cannot be subsidized (perhaps entirely) by the state. This possibility, which Kymlicka notes in passing (84), would ensure that mi-norities have access to an adequate range of options without saddling them with the various costs associated with making the switch. If the goals are to provide minorities with an adequate range of options and to ensure a fair al-location of costs, then encouraging and subsidizing assimilation would seem to be no less effective than extending the regime of minority cultural rights advocated by Kymlicka. Second, Kymlicka's response arguably exaggerates the costs associated with "switching" cultures. As I suggested in the previous section, one of the reasons why we think of cultures as in decline is that so many of their members are assimilating into some other more powerful cul-ture. There is no need to assist *them* with a costly "switch." It is because they are already embracing the majority culture that we worry about the loss of the minority culture in the first place. Misael's children illustrate this point. No special assistance or inducement is needed to get them to assimilate into the majority culture. Living in the majority-dominated town of Boca Manu and being subjected to its educational and other institutions should be sufficient to bring such an outcome about. Finally, Kymlicka's analogy with a vow of poverty begs the crucial question. Considerations of distributive justice will normally entitle people to resources that exceed the subsistence level. The fact that some people can lead a perfectly worthwhile life at the subsistence level is irrelevant to what other people are entitled to. But here the analogy with culture breaks down. We cannot *assume* that people are entitled to a context of choice based on their own culture because this is precisely the question we are investigating. It would be circular to assume such an entitlement as part

[25] Kymlicka 1995, 84.
[26] Ibid., 85–86.

of an argument designed to refute the claim that the state can discharge its responsibility to ensure that minorities have adequate options by ensuring that majority-culture options are accessible to all. Some independent reason for thinking that people are entitled to options in their own culture is needed.

The upshot of this section's discussion, then, is neither a clean endorsement nor a clean rejection of the access account of why cultural loss matters in a way that would elicit support for minority cultural rights. What does seem clear is that the access account does not offer a robust and general justification of minority cultural rights. To explore whether such justification can be based on different principles, we should turn now to the adequacy account.

3.4 The Adequacy Account

The access account, as we have seen, rests on a particular conception of what it is for a range of options to be adequate. The idea behind the account is to work with a weak and generic conception of adequacy, such that anyone lacking an adequate range of such options would uncontroversially be in a position of disadvantage. The generic conception of an adequate range identifies such options without reference to the actual aims or preferences or values of the persons whose options they are. The assumption is that certain sorts of options are valuable for people no matter what their particular goals or preferences happen to be. It is valuable for people to have a range of employment options, opportunities for participation in social and political practices, access to art and popular culture, and so on. In the generic conception, all and only those people who do not have a reasonable range of generic options are lacking an adequate range.

The problem we have discovered with this approach, however, is its limited potential to justify minority cultural rights. Someone interested in a robust and general defense of such rights should look for an alternative approach. This section explores one such alternative. The key move is to drop the assumption of "generic" adequacy and, instead, to adopt a conception of adequacy that incorporates a subjective component.

In a fully subjective conception of adequacy, the adequacy of a given range of options for some particular person depends entirely on the degree to which the person is able to realize her actual aims, preferences, and values by choosing from those options. In a mixed view, by contrast, there is a subjective component to adequacy but also a generic component. The adequacy of a range of options depends on both (a) the degree to which the range includes options that any person would have reason to value (even if she does not actually value them), and (b) the degree to which the range allows the person to realize the various aims, preferences, and values that she happens to have. An adequate range is one that does sufficiently well by both (a) and (b).

The fully subjective conception strikes me as implausible. In evaluating the adequacy of a person's options, it fails to do justice to the fact that people often change their minds and revise their ends, and that this is frequently a good thing given that their original judgments are likely to be highly fallible. The mixed view, by contrast, seems more promising. The purpose of this section is to explore whether an options-disadvantage justification of minority cultural rights becomes more plausible if the mixed view of adequacy is substituted for the generic one. Since we have already explored the implications of adopting the generic account, and the main difference between the generic and mixed accounts is the subjective component, I focus on the subjective component. I assume that cultural loss does not deprive anyone of access to an adequate range of generic options and then pose two questions. First, might cultural loss still deprive persons of an adequate range of subjectively valued options? And second, if so, should this be considered a significant form of disadvantage, one that would morally require the state to prevent cultural loss from happening in the first place?

There are two main reasons for thinking that cultural loss might leave members of the disappearing culture with an inadequate set of subjectively valued options (and hence with an inadequate set of options, as that is understood by the mixed view). One focuses on culture's role as a generator of options. The other emphasizes the fact that cultures can come to be valued for their own sakes by their members.

Cultures as Option Generators

The first reason why cultural loss may threaten the subjective adequacy of a person's options has to do with the way in which cultures generate options. The availability of options is often characterized by positive externalities. The more that other people share my values and preferences, the more likely it is that options corresponding to those values and preferences are going to be available to me. These positive externalities derive from the fact that some of the goods associated with a given option are produced with economies of scale, and from the fact that practices and institutions that support a particular option become stronger as more people participate in them.

The members of a community are more likely to share similar values and preferences, in turn, to the extent that they have been subjected to similar socializing influences. To some extent, at least, our values and preferences are formed in response to the environment we have been raised in: its major institutions and practices, its language and patterns of discourse, its geographic and economic characteristics, and so on. Of course, there will be a great variety of responses to a given set of socializing influences (as we saw in sec. 2.4), but this is consistent with thinking that groups of people who experience similar sets of socializing influences are more likely, all else being equal, to end up with similar patterns of values and preferences.

Putting these points about positive externalities and shared socialization together, it follows that a person is more likely to find options that correspond with his values and preferences if his culture is preserved than if it disappears. As we know from chapter 2, when a culture is preserved, an important part of the socialization experience of the new generation consists of their subjection to institutions and practices that are mainly populated and controlled by existing members of the culture. A culture disappears, by contrast, when the institutional processes by which one generation socializes the next are extinguished, and the socialization of the new generation mainly takes place in a context of institutions and practices that are populated and administered by members of some other, more dominant culture. When a culture is preserved, then, the new generation is subjected to similar socializing influences to those experienced by the previous generation, or at least to socializing influences that are administered and controlled by the previous generation and thus grow out of the socializing influences that the previous generation was itself subjected to. When a culture disappears, the new generation's formation is the product of a quite distinct set of forces, which may bear little or no relation to the influences that affected the older generation. Given the influence of socialization on preferences and values, one might expect preferences and values to be more similar across generations when a culture is preserved than when it disappears. And, given the assumption of positive externalities, one should expect that the options valued by the older generation will be more readily available when they, or something approximating them, are also valued by the younger generation.

For an illustration, consider again our earlier example of Misael. Misael was socialized as a Machiguenga and developed certain values and preferences as a result of this socialization. He might quite reasonably expect that he would face a more hospitable set of options, given his values and preferences, if the Machiguenga culture were to survive and flourish than if it were to be eclipsed by the dominant culture. Among the preferences that he might expect a rising generation of members of the Machiguenga culture to have are the ones that he has or that are accessible variations and improvisations on ones that he has. The rites and practices of Machiguenga social life that Misael values—or something like them—will likely be valued by a new generation of Machiguengas and carried on in some form. Indeed, only with the preservation of Machiguenga culture is it predictable that enough others will be socialized into valuing the same rites and practices such that there will be a sufficient core of people interested in carrying them on. If the Machiguenga culture were to disappear, Misael's options may dip below the threshold of adequacy defined by the mixed conception. He may well enjoy a generically adequate range of options in a non- (or post-) Machiguenga environment, if he is able to learn (or already knows) the majority language and culture and is treated with tolerance and respect by members of the majority. But he would not necessarily enjoy a subjectively adequate range of options.

The first reason for thinking that cultural loss threatens to deprive members of the disappearing culture of an adequate range of options, then, is that their culture, when it persists, works as a mechanism that reliably generates options they care about, and having options they care about is part of what it is to have an adequate range of options. This reason, it should immediately be said, is somewhat limited in scope. It assumes, on the one hand, that cultural persistence is accompanied by a fair amount of continuity in the character of the culture. There is no radical break in the culture that makes the institutions and practices favored by the younger generation deeply alien to members of the older generation. And, on the other hand, it also assumes that there is a fairly significant discontinuity between the disappearing culture and the dominant culture by which it is superseded. The practices and institutions of the latter are so different from those of the former that members of the disappearing culture despair of finding options they care about in the transformed world in which they find themselves.

Although these limits on the scope of the first reason are serious, they do not, so far I can see, consign it to irrelevance. They still leave a range of cases of cultural loss in which there is no threat to adequacy in the generic view but there is such a threat in the mixed view. As we shall see, the shift to the mixed view becomes even more consequential once the second reason for thinking that cultural loss threatens access to adequate options is taken into account.

Cultures as Valued for Their Own Sakes

It is a familiar idea that cohorts graduating from a common formative experience often feel a special attachment to one another and to the institutions that gave rise to their common formation. Of course this is not true in every case. Sometimes the formative experience is itself one of distrust and alienation. But it is a recognizable phenomenon that a sense of mutual attachment grows out of a history of interaction and a common set of experiences and points of reference. In some contexts this mutual attachment spills over into an identification with the formative institutions themselves, an identification that is often consciously promoted by those very institutions. Taking a cue from these commonplaces, the second reason for thinking that cultural loss deprives people of subjectively adequate options is that many people value their culture intrinsically, and not just because it is a reliable mechanism for generating other options they value intrinsically. This is the consideration that is highlighted by theorists who emphasize the normative importance of culture as a component of identity.[27]

---

[27] As we have seen, the appeal to identity is sometimes motivated by a recognition that, by itself, the ("generic adequacy" version of the) context of choice argument offers no general reason for preferring

When people are socialized as members of a particular culture, it is not surprising if they come to feel an attachment to the culture itself, and not just to the options they expect it will generate. They may feel a special bond with others who have undergone a similar socialization (fellow members of the culture). They share a history of interaction with these persons in the institutions and practices that provide the common socialization, and they share many common points of reference that those institutions and practices make salient. In addition, as suggested above, they may come to value the institutions and practices themselves that transmit the culture, such as its language, rituals, and other practices. They may feel proud of their culture's achievements, and ashamed of its failures. By virtue of these attitudes, they may want the culture to be preserved in the future and recognize that they, along with other likeminded members of the culture, must do what they can to adapt the institutions and practices that transmit the culture so that they are appealing and choice-worthy to newcomers and new generations. The preservation of the culture becomes something of a project, one that requires the exercise of skill, imagination, and judgment.[28] Invested as they are in this project of making the culture survive and flourish, it seems intelligible that they should want the project to succeed.

All these possibilities suggest that there is an obvious sense in which at least some members of a disappearing culture are likely to be deprived of an option they care about as a result of the loss of their culture. They care about relationships, practices, and projects that are intrinsically connected with the culture itself, and that are, by their very nature, less available as the culture declines and disappears. To be sure, not everyone will value their culture in this way. Many people may be fairly indifferent to the fate of their culture, and some may even welcome its demise. Even people who are generally neutral about their culture's fate, though, may become concerned if they feel that their culture is publicly disrespected. As we know from chapter 2, there is a straightforward sense in which a person's culture helped to make her the individual that she is. For people who identify with their culture, it is difficult, as a result, to distinguish disrespectful treatment of the culture from disrespectful treatment of them as individuals. This last consideration is especially relevant to the theory of minority rights I develop in subsequent chapters, which has more to do with the fair treatment of cultures than with preventing cultural loss per se. The point for now is merely that cultural loss does predictably deprive some people of an option they care about and in this sense affects the subjective adequacy of their options.

---

minority cultural rights over full integration into the majority culture. See n. 23 above. For the appeal to identity, see, e.g., Margalit and Raz 1990, 447–49; Tamir 1993, 41, 71–73; Taylor 1994; Margalit and Halbertal 1994; Kymlicka 1995, 89–90; Forst 1997; Gans 2003; Appiah 2005.

[28] As Scheffler (2007, 108) puts it, "the survival of a culture is an ongoing collective achievement that requires the exercise of judgment, creativity, intelligence, and interpretive skill."

Together the two reasons I have been sketching—that cultures are generators of options, and that they are valued by some people for their own sakes—point to an account of options disadvantage that is more general than the access account explored in the previous section. The class of people who can legitimately complain that cultural loss leaves them with an options disadvantage is no longer restricted just to people who would face discrimination in the majority culture, and to people who lack the generic skills needed for success in the majority culture. It now also includes people who care about particular options that will predictably be less available without their culture (first reason), and people who value their culture for its own sake (second reason). As I have noted, the larger class does not account for all possible cases of cultural loss—there are some in which it would be implausible to advance either of the two reasons—but it is substantially more inclusive than the class of cases swept in by considerations of discrimination or generic incapacity.

An important implication of the mixed view, and of its subjective component in particular, is that an adequate set of options is not, in general, likely to be secured by integrating the members of a cultural minority into the dominant culture. Although the members of a successfully integrated minority may find an adequate range of generic options in the dominant culture—opportunities for employment, political participation, and so on—they will not find some of the particular options that are of value to them. A person will be able to access some of the options that he values only if his own culture is preserved. This is obviously true if one of the things he cares about is the preservation of his culture itself. And it is also fairly clearly the case if what he cares about is the use, in a variety of contexts of life, of the particular language he was raised to speak. But it is also true of a range of other options he might value, where the availability of that option depends on others having similar or complementary preferences and values. Only if their own culture is maintained is it predictable that enough others will be socialized into valuing the same options such that there will be a sufficient core of people interested in carrying them on.

The important question to turn to now concerns the moral salience of complaints about subjective inadequacy. When a minority can argue that they are deprived of access to a generically adequate range of options, they have a complaint that carries obvious moral weight. It is natural to think that a liberal state ought to go to some lengths to ensure that all citizens enjoy access to an adequate range of generically adequate options. As we shall see, however, it is much less obvious that, on its own, being deprived of a subjectively adequate range of options leaves one with a similarly weighty complaint.

To be without a subjectively adequate range of options is to be deprived of options that correspond to certain of one's values, preferences, wants, goals, attachments, commitments, and so forth (I shall simply call these "preferences").

The main objection to subjective adequacy, and thus to the mixed view, questions whether preference frustration, on its own, leaves the preference holder with any sort of morally weighty complaint. According to the objection, the mere fact that one has preferences that cannot be fulfilled in a given environment is not sufficient to establish that there is an injustice or any other morally serious infraction.

One familiar way to develop this objection would be to emphasize the dubious origins and character of many preferences that people hold. Even when they possess fairly good judgment, and arrive at their preferences through fairly reflective processes of thought, people are often deeply misguided about what they want. They suffer from what behavioral economists term "bounded rationality" and are subject to well-known cognitive biases. Compounding these limitations is the fact that most people are not especially reflective about their preferences. They are more concerned with the approval of others than with whether their preferences really merit endorsement. As a result, they fall easily into materialism, a lust for power, an attachment to structures of hierarchy and inequality, and various other unsavory pathologies. Related to this tendency is the fact that the beliefs and preferences of many people are formed in epistemically inhospitable environments, where beliefs and preferences are taken for granted, by family members, local communities, the broader popular culture, and so on, that would be unlikely to survive serious critical scrutiny. The upshot is that a person's preferences often have little basis in her deepest commitments or most clear-headed beliefs about value. And given this characterization of preferences, so the objection goes, it hardly seems to matter whether a person's preferred options are available to her or not. Since preferences are not a reliable tracker of a person's good, she cannot justifiably complain that she is disadvantaged merely by virtue of the fact that an option she cares about is unavailable.

But this form of the objection to subjective adequacy strikes me as overstated. It is true that individual judgment and rationality are often compromised by various cognitive biases and pathologies. This is a reason for not simply equating an individual's good (or advantage) with the satisfaction of whatever preferences he happens to have. It is much more of a stretch, however, to maintain that all, or even most, of a person's preferences are deeply irrational. Although some preferences would disappear if one could (magically) correct for all the relevant biases and pathologies, many would not. Many desires, preferences, attachments, commitments, and so on, are neither deeply rational nor deeply irrational. It would be odd to think that most of the things that Misael actually cares about—the practices he has been brought up to value, the opportunity to use his maternal language, the preservation of his cultural community, and so on—would cease to have any value for him if the biases and pathologies to which he is subject could somehow be made to disappear.

The crucial point, however, is that being able to pursue and fulfill their own preferences is, in general, of some considerable value for individuals, even when those preferences are inferior in value.[29] One reason for this is that, as a general matter, valuable goods and activities do not make a person's life go better unless those goods and activities figure in some positive way in the person's preferences. A standard way of thwarting a person's well-being is to deny him the opportunity to pursue and fulfill his own preferences, and thus to force him into living a life that does not accord with his own values and commitments. A different reason is that being guided by one's own preferences is an aspect of autonomy. An autonomous person shapes and directs her own life according to her own actual values and judgments. I do not claim that this is all there is to well-being or autonomy. But, even when the other conditions are filled in, they do not crowd out the importance of individuals pursuing and fulfilling the preferences they actually hold.

Several variations on the objection are more narrowly targeted at cultural attachments. Some worry that cultural attachments are especially problematic in that they involve the submergence of individuality into a group pattern.[30] Others point out that cultural attachments are the object of a great deal of manipulation and engineering by political elites and "ethnic entrepreneurs." These actors have some political or economic goal, such as state consolidation, tax collection, party formation and competition, or simply elevating themselves into a privileged position of intermediary between state and group. And they find that their goal is well served by measures that consciously, or as a by-product, make particular attachments and identities more salient.[31] People are pushed into attachment to their own group, for instance, because they are provoked by actors for whom it is convenient into fearing that some out-group will pose a threat to them.[32] In this worry, then, cultural attachments have a manipulated or manufactured character to them that make them particularly unsuitable guides to a person's good.[33]

Although these are powerful concerns, I do not think they add up to a decisive objection to the subjective adequacy approach being considered in this

[29] But not when they are worthless. For the distinction between inferior and worthless, see sec. 4.6. The argument of the remainder of this paragraph is elaborated in sec. 4.6 as well.

[30] For a powerful elaboration of this objection, see Kateb 1994.

[31] This kind of instrumental analysis of the construction of identity is quite standard among political scientists. See, e.g., Posner 2005, chaps. 2–3, for a nicely argued example. Moore (2001, 41–44) offers a good assessment of the normative relevance of theories of the social construction of identity and makes a number of points with which I agree.

[32] On this process, see, e.g., Marx 2005.

[33] One theoretical advantage of the account of culture offered in chapter 2 is that it can accommodate the idea that elite actors often engineer and manipulate cultural formations and allegiances. By understanding culture in terms of *subjection* to a common formative context, the account accents the role of power and avoids the dewy-eyed romanticism that sometimes characterizes people's attitudes about their own culture.

section. In a liberal view, there are limits to how far the rights and entitlements of people should depend on facts about the origins or character of individual preferences. We do not think that a particular religion's claims to equal treatment by the state are reduced if it turns out that many members of the religion are compromising their individuality by participating in the collective rituals of the group, or if it turns out that the group itself has some unsavory origins. A group's claims are diminished where there is an impact on other people—we shall get to this in a moment—but it would be paternalistic to condition the accommodation of those claims too strongly on an investigation into the rationality of feeling an attachment to the group. As I argued above, the value of being able to pursue and fulfill one's own preferences, whatever they are, is based on considerations of well-being and autonomy and is not immediately erased by observations about individuality or the etiology of the preferences in question.[34]

One thing that the objection based on the irrationality of preferences does remind us of is the importance of liberal and democratic institutions. There should be rights and institutions that make it possible for people to reflect critically about their ends and to revise them as they judge best. There should be democratic freedoms and practices that check the power of elites to manipulate cultural attachments and identities. And the law should foster an environment in which ideals of the good life are vigorously contested, and in which ideas and information circulate freely. But these familiar core principles of liberal and democratic thought do not imply indifference to the subjective inadequacy of the options that people face.

Let us turn, then, to a different objection to the moral salience of a complaint about the subjective inadequacy of one's options. Unlike the objection that has just been considered, which focuses on the value to the preference holder of having an option that corresponds with her preferences, the objection to be considered now concerns the impact on other people.

The basic point is that the interests of other people can make it quite appropriate for some options to be limited in their availability. This is quite obvious when the options I value involve the participation or cooperation or attitudes of other people. If friendship with Perez is an important priority for me, but Perez has no interest in being my friend, it would be odd to think that I have a complaint of justice (or of a comparable order of moral seriousness) about the situation I find myself in. Certainly nobody thinks that Perez should be *required* to be my friend (assuming this is even possible), as this would presumably violate Perez's rights and might well conflict with his access to the options that he values. Nor would my complaint, or the case for state intervention, be any more weighty if the option I value involved people in my community behaving in certain ways (e.g., practicing abstinence outside of

---

[34] The discussion of perfectionism in secs. 4.5 and 4.6 is relevant to the objection from individuality.

marriage) that they preferred not to behave in. Again, these other people have their own rights, and their own lives to live, and what I can legitimately expect in the way of access to options I care about has to be tailored to these other rights and claims. (Perhaps Perez, or the members of my community, should be left alone but I should be compensated for the subjective inadequacy of the options I am left with? This still strikes me as perverse, treating me, as it does, as a passive victim of my own preferences. But I shall consider a version of this view in section 4.7).

The force of this objection is not confined to preferences that refer directly to other people. Consider competitions for scarce jobs or positions, for example, for places in law or medical school. It is in the nature of those competitions that some person's intense preferences to secure a place will in the end be denied. So long as the competition is conducted fairly, and the background conditions are fair, we do not think that there is any injustice in this outcome. From the mere fact that some failed candidate for medical school does not have available to him an option of great subjective importance, we do not infer that he has any morally salient complaint. It depends on the further question of whether he was fairly treated.

Or consider the much-discussed problem of "expensive tastes."[35] Imagine Martin, whose idea of the good life involves control over a large estate, drinking expensive wine, having household staff at his disposal, possessing a townhouse in the city, flying first class, and so on. In a society that protects basic liberties, promotes equality of opportunity, and seeks to distribute resources fairly, it seems safe to assume that the options corresponding with these preferences will not all be available to Martin. He will likely have to prioritize among his various preferences, trading, for instance, fine wine off against modest living arrangements. But even if the options he ends up abandoning matter a great deal to him, and even if their foreclosure threatens to reduce the options that are available to him below the threshold of subjective adequacy, very few people would judge that Martin has any morally serious complaint about his situation. In some contexts the best characterization of a situation in which some persons are unable to fulfill certain of their preferences has nothing to do with injustice of any sort. Rather, we think it appropriate for the persons who have formed those preferences to put up with the situation themselves.

The objection I have been rehearsing carries an important implication for any attempt to ground minority cultural rights in a view of options disadvantage that conceptualizes adequacy in (partly) subjective terms. From the mere fact that the prospect of cultural loss leaves a person with subjectively inadequate options, it cannot be inferred that she has any strong moral claim, or cultural right, that the loss of the culture be prevented from occurring. As in the previous examples, it may well be the case that the danger of cultural loss arises

---

[35] See the discussion and citations in sec. 4.7.

because of others exercising their rights, or because others use the resources to which they are legitimately entitled in certain ways. And it may be that the only way to prevent the situation from arising, or of remedying it once it has arisen, would involve interfering with those same rights and entitlements. As a result, there is no general right to cultural preservation, or against cultural loss. As far as the adequacy argument is concerned, someone facing the loss of her culture may not have any kind of morally salient complaint at all.

One should not, however, infer from this conclusion that the argument in favor of strong cultural rights has collapsed. In the case of the frustrated medical school applicant, the applicant *would* have a morally serious complaint if he was rejected under conditions of procedural and/or background unfairness. Similarly, Martin would have a reasonable complaint about his frustrated preferences if he could show that he lacks a fair share of resources and opportunities with which to pursue his preferences, or that there is some other sort of relevant background injustice. In the same way, even if there is no general right to cultural preservation, there may well be rights to fairness in the treatment of one's culture (and its options) that are plausibly thought of as strong cultural rights. In this view, the mere fact that one's culture is faring poorly would not entitle one to complain. But if one could show that the culture was faring poorly because of, or in the context of, unfair treatment by the state, one would have a reasonable complaint.

3.5 Cultural Preservation versus Fair Treatment of Cultures

The upshot of the argument is mostly, but not entirely, negative. The chapter has suggested that there is no account of why cultural loss is a bad thing that can justify a general right to cultural preservation. An account that emphasizes the problems of access facing the members of a disappearing culture runs into serious questions about empirical applicability. In some cases, the problem of access would not arise at all. In others, it would arise, but the attempt to avoid or fix it through cultural rights would be unpromising. And in others still, a renewed and intensified effort to integrate the members of the disappearing culture into the dominant culture would be a viable alternative to minority cultural rights.

In one sense, the adequacy argument is more hospitable to minority cultural rights, since the integrationist alternative does not realistically meet its concerns. But the adequacy argument faces a different kind of objection. The disadvantage it highlights—the subjective inadequacy of the options facing members of a disappearing culture—does not, in general, have the moral salience required to ground a case in favor of cultural rights. As I argued in the previous section, one can think of a range of different examples in which a person lacks an option that she cares about intensely, but in which she would have no morally significant complaint about her situation. By itself, the adequacy argument fails to give a reason why complaints about options disadvantage due to cultural loss should not be treated in this light.

The bulk of the chapter develops, then, a dilemma that faces any options-disadvantage account of why culture matters in a way that might be relevant for strong cultural rights. Although the dilemma seems devastating to simple-minded and unqualified assertions of a right to cultural preservation, it is not so fatal to more nuanced and qualified claims about cultural rights. Both the access and the adequacy accounts leave some space in which to develop a positive argument for such rights. Although the access argument will not be applicable in many cases of cultural loss, there may well be some cases in which it is applicable. I explore this possibility in section 6.8.

Even more significantly, our consideration of the adequacy account did not say that considerations of subjective inadequacy are never relevant. Rather it said that they are relevant only when they can be shown to have arisen in a context of unfair treatment. This suggests a new avenue for exploration by would-be defenders of cultural rights. Rather than try to ground the case for cultural rights directly in some account of the badness of cultural loss, one might try instead to develop an account of the fair treatment of cultures.

The next two chapters pursue exactly that agenda. In chapter 4 I step back for a while from the debate about cultural rights and revisit an important, but unfashionable, concept in the liberal lexicon—the concept of neutrality. In chapter 5 I apply a suitably rehabilitated version of this concept back to our concerns about culture. I argue that, in a central range of cases, fairness requires a form of equal recognition between majority and minority cultures, which entails a set of strong cultural rights.

CHAPTER 4

Liberal Neutrality: A Reinterpretation and Defense

4.1 An Unfashionable Idea

In this chapter and the next I develop an account of the moral foundations of minority cultural rights that revolves around two main claims. The first holds that the liberal state has a responsibility to be neutral toward the various conceptions of the good that are affirmed by its citizens. The second claims that, in certain domains, the most promising way for the state to discharge its responsibility of neutrality is by extending and protecting specific minority cultural rights. Although various qualifications and provisos are introduced along the way, and the rights that are justified are constrained in certain important respects, the argument will demonstrate why, in some contexts, specific cultural rights are indeed a requirement of liberal justice.

The present chapter is devoted to the first of the claims, exploring the meaning of neutrality and explaining why it is an important component of liberal justice. Chapter 5 turns to the second claim, considering why neutrality entails a commitment to certain minority cultural rights.

The suggestion that liberal neutrality provides a normative foundation for minority rights claims will immediately strike many readers as unpromising. To the extent that neutrality is possible at all, the idea is often associated with an attitude of indifference or "benign neglect" toward minority cultures.[1] For many, a state that is neutral toward culture is one that takes no notice of culture, which hardly sounds like what proponents of minority cultural rights are after. Moreover, one of the few points that everyone seems to agree on in the literature on culture and justice is that neutrality is impossible or incoherent with respect to culture.[2] Will Kymlicka's formulation of this point is both representative and influential. "The idea that government could be neutral with respect to ethnic and national groups," he argues, "is patently false." "In the

---

[1] Kymlicka 1995, 110–11.
[2] Ibid., 108–15; Carens 2000, 10–11, 77–78; Barry 2001, 107.

areas of official languages, political boundaries, and the division of powers, there is no way to avoid supporting this or that societal culture."[3] One of the primary tasks for the present chapter, accordingly, will be to lay the groundwork for addressing such skepticism about the application of neutrality to culture by articulating a conception of neutrality that can be applied coherently and meaningfully to issues raised by cultural diversity. The payoff from this groundwork will become fully apparent only in chapter 5, which explains why neutrality in the domain of culture does not always entail a policy of benign neglect.

An even deeper source of skepticism concerns the status of the neutrality idea in liberal thought. After a brief ascendancy in the 1970s and 1980s, the idea of liberal neutrality has fallen out of favor in recent years. A growing chorus of liberal writers has joined antiliberal critics in arguing that there is something confused and misguided about the insistence that the state be neutral between rival conceptions of the good. Assuming we can even make sense of the idea of neutrality, these writers contend, it is a mistake to think that there is anything in liberal principles that commits the liberal state to neutrality.[4] With a number of former neutralists softening their support for the idea, the rejection of neutrality is quickly becoming a consensus position, even among liberal political philosophers.[5] According to one writer, all that remains to be done is an "autopsy" on the idea of state neutrality.[6] A major challenge here, then, is to rehabilitate the doctrine of liberal neutrality. I need to explain the sense in which the state ought to be neutral, as well as the scope, strength, and normative basis of the neutrality responsibility.

Much of the literature critical of neutrality has proceeded on the basis of four assumptions. The first contrasts neutrality with perfectionism. To defend state neutrality is to deny that the state can legitimately use its power to encourage ways of life it supposes to be valuable or to discourage ones it regards as worthless.[7] The second standard assumption is that neutrality has the status of a "prohibition."[8] Neutrality is not just one consideration that the state should bring into an appropriate balance with judgments it makes about the good of its citizens. It is a principle that forbids the state from relying on such

---

[3] Kymlicka 1995, 110–11. See also Kymlicka 2001a, 23–27, 43.

[4] Leading critics of liberal neutrality include Raz 1986; Sher 1997; Arneson 2003.

[5] John Rawls and Ronald Dworkin are two prominent neutralists who play down the concept in their later work. See Rawls's reluctant remarks in Rawls 2005, 191; and his restriction of neutrality to "constitutional essentials" (234). On the latter point, see also Rawls 2001, 152. Dworkin (2000, 239, 281–82) still affirms a version of neutrality, but it is less prominent in his thought than it was in Dworkin 1978.

[6] Arneson 2003.

[7] The identification of neutrality with antiperfectionism is extremely common in the literature. See, e.g., Dworkin 1978; Raz 1986, 110–11; Sher 1997.

[8] Sher 1997, 29. This framing of the neutrality debate is quite prominent in Sher's book. Sher sets himself against the view that perfectionist reasons are "in principle inadmissible in politics" (4). See also 72–73, 246.

judgments. The third assumption is that the concept of neutrality can assume one or another of two basic forms: neutrality can be thought of in terms of either the effects of the state's policies or the intentions of the legislators and policy makers who put those policies in place. Although considerable variation in formulation is possible within these basic forms, most philosophers writing about neutrality—whether pro or contra—assume that the concept is best rendered by one or another of them.[9] And, finally, the fourth assumption is that the liberal value of personal autonomy offers a leading reason for thinking that the state should indeed be neutral in the relevant sense.[10]

For reasons I touch on below, the critics have not had too much difficulty challenging the doctrine of liberal neutrality when these various assumptions are in place. The thesis that the state has a strict, autonomy-based obligation to embrace antiperfectionism is difficult to accept. A key claim of this chapter, however, is that none of the four standard framing assumptions is essential to the idea of neutrality. The chapter develops a reinterpretation of neutrality that drops each of the standard framing assumptions and ends up with a view that is more coherent and powerful than the one pictured by critics. If the central argument is correct, then it is plausible to think of neutrality as imposing a significant constraint on the policies of the liberal state.

Thus, first, rather than oppose neutrality exclusively to state perfectionism, the chapter opposes it to a broader range of uses of political power. Departures from neutrality occur not only with state perfectionism but also when the state pursues legitimate, nonperfectionist public goals in a manner that is unequally accommodating of rival conceptions of the good, and, indeed, when, with *no* particularly strong rationale, the state's policies are unequally accommodating of different conceptions of the good. Second, rather than treat neutrality as a strict prohibition, the chapter characterizes it as a significant pro tanto constraint. It is a constraint that has genuine weight and reflects significant liberal values, but it sometimes appropriately gives way to other considerations. When the state has disfavored some particular conception of the good on the basis of considerations that fail to adequately and appropriately grapple with the reason it has to be neutral, it does an injustice to the bearers of that conception. Third, rather than picking between neutrality of effects and intentions, the chapter develops a distinct, third conception of neutrality, which it calls *neutrality of treatment*. According to this third conception, the state is neutral between rival conceptions of the good when, relative to an appropriate baseline, its institutions and policies are equally accommodating of those conceptions. And, fourth, while the justification of neutrality to be sketched in section 4.5 does refer to a dimension of autonomy, which is labeled "self-determination," the argument also emphasizes a fairness consideration. The

---

[9] Influential discussions of different conceptions of neutrality include Raz 1986, 114–15; Larmore 1987, 43ff; Kymlicka 1989a; Waldron 1989.

[10] Raz 1986, 108; Sher 1997, chaps. 2–3.

guiding normative idea is that persons should have a fair opportunity to be self-determining. The importance of fairness in grounding neutrality was recognized in some of the original discussions of the idea but largely dropped out of view in the subsequent critical assessment of neutrality. By reinserting fairness into the justification, it becomes apparent why neutrality imposes a significant constraint on state action.

To be sure, one danger in dropping the various assumptions that have framed the critical literature on neutrality is that a disagreement with that literature can no longer be presumed. Since the chapter does not directly confront the standard critique of neutrality, it might reasonably be wondered whether it is advocating something that anyone has been concerned to deny. For instance, the claim that the state has a pro tanto reason to be neutral is perfectly compatible with the claim that the state ought sometimes to pursue perfectionist aims and, indeed, with the claim that the state also has a pro tanto reason to favor the particular conceptions of the good it regards as valuable. It is not clear that the opponents of neutrality have ever wanted to argue anything stronger than the latter two claims. And the suggestion that neutrality ought to be opposed, not just to perfectionism, but to a broader range of state policies, is again not necessarily venturing onto contested terrain. The key point, for many critics of neutrality, is simply that it is permissible, in some contexts, for the state to pursue perfectionist policies.

Even granting these points, however, the chapter's argument is of genuine theoretical interest. Although proponents of perfectionism have allowed that their preferred policies ought to be limited by various pragmatic and context-specific countervailing considerations, they have not acknowledged anything approaching a general, neutrality-like limit.[11] If the argument of this chapter is correct, there is just such a limit.

The insistence on opposing neutrality to nonperfectionist policies, as well as perfectionist ones, is important for a different reason. Neutrality *is* sometimes invoked in nonperfectionist contexts, including the debates over minority cultural rights that concern us in this book. One prominent liberal theorist, Brian Barry, has argued that neutrality militates against religious and cultural accommodations, while others, as noted above, maintain that claims of neutrality are incoherent and unwarranted in these contexts because there is simply no neutral position to be had.[12] I think that both of these claims about neutrality rest on confusion, and one of the aims of the chapter is to

[11] For instance, Sher (1997, 4) moves from the weak claim that no reasons (including perfectionist ones) are "in principle inadmissible in politics" to the stronger one that "it is no less legitimate for governments than for private individuals to try to promote the good." Although I do not dispute the weak claim, I contend that governments do have special, fairness-based reasons to be neutral, reasons that do not apply in the same way to individuals.

[12] For the first sort of claim about neutrality, see Barry 2001, chap. 2 (though see also 107). On the incoherence of neutrality in the context of debates about the state's role regarding culture, see the references at the start of this chapter.

present a fairly general account of neutrality that can be of use in adjudicating these and other disputes.

4.2 Neutrality as a Downstream Value

One dimension along which views of neutrality vary concerns how far neutrality lies upstream or downstream from other values. In some accounts, neutrality assumes the role of a kind of master principle, which acts as a constraint on all other justification. Rawls's device of the original position is sometimes interpreted as an attempt to formulate a neutral standpoint from which principles of justice can be derived.[13] And his distinction between comprehensive and political conceptions, and the insistence that the former should play no essential role in public justification, is associated with a similar motivation. Critics of neutrality often assume this "upstream" version of the idea and proceed to argue that the supposedly neutral standpoint or values are not as neutral as they appear. Thomas Nagel's early critique of the original position is a well-known example of this argumentative maneuver. "The original position," according to Nagel, "seems to presuppose not just a neutral theory of the good, but a liberal, individualistic conception according to which the best that can be wished for is the unimpeded pursuit of his own path, provided that it does not interfere with the rights of others."[14]

It is equally possible, however, to assign to neutrality a more modest, downstream place in the domain of values. A decision to be neutral in some conflict or contest is sometimes based on nonneutral reasons. The United States might decide to remain neutral in a dispute between Denmark and Norway because of a desire to preserve its friendship with Sweden, which (for its own particular reasons) has decided to remain neutral in the dispute. Or constitution makers might endorse a content-neutral right to free expression for substantive Millian reasons of revealing the truth and maximizing utility—reasons that are not themselves neutral in any deep sense. Neutrality for nonneutral reasons is a familiar phenomenon.[15]

In general, the downstream approach assumes that there is some justifiable set of fundamental values, which make no claim to neutrality. It then argues that these values commit the state, in certain contexts, to being neutral among

[13] Sher 1997, 31.

[14] Nagel 1973, 228–29. For critical discussions of Nagel on this point, see Kymlicka 1989a; Waldron 1989.

[15] See the valuable discussion in Waldron 1989, 164–67. Waldron suggests that all coherent views of neutrality lie at least some ways downstream: "one is always neutral in a particular conflict for a reason, and it is obvious that one cannot then be neutral about the force of that reason." There is no objectionable paradox in this, since "a policy of neutrality in relation to one dispute does not commit a party to a policy of neutrality in all disputes" (165). See also Sher 1997, 14.

different conceptions of the good. It is *because* one accepts certain nonneutral values that one thinks that, in some limited domain, the state ought to adopt a stance of neutrality. The account of neutrality that I shall be defending is of this downstream sort. In my argument, it is by virtue of being guided by a particular, justifiable, liberal value—what I call "fair opportunity for self-determination"—that the state has a weighty, if defeasible, reason to be neutral between conceptions of the good.[16] Because neutrality is a downstream value, certain general challenges to its coherence, exemplified by Nagel's objection to Rawls, can easily be deflected. The account has no ambition to occupy an Archimedean point outside the domain of value and thus is not embarrassed by the observation that its guiding value is in fact quite particular and nonneutral.

The downstream character of neutrality also helps to explain certain restrictions on what I shall term neutrality's "domain" and "strength." By the domain of neutrality I mean the range of conceptions of good with respect to which the state has a pro tanto reason to be neutral. In my view, the state has no reason at all to extend neutrality toward certain conceptions. Some conceptions of the good reject the value of self-determination on which neutrality is based or reject related values of comparable or greater importance. These conceptions, which generally have an illiberal and/or impermissible (because contrary to the rights of others) character, do not fall within the domain of neutrality. States also have no reason, in my view, to be neutral toward *worthless* conceptions of the good. A worthless conception, in my terminology, should be distinguished from an inferior one. A person has a worthless conception of the good when she has a conception that is so lacking in value that she would be better off if she did not pursue and fulfill it, even if she is unable to substitute a more worthwhile conception. A conception is inferior, by contrast, if it is not so lacking in value as to be worthless, but it does suffer from a relative lack of value in that a person who holds it would do better to improve it or replace it with some different conception. Inferior conceptions of the good do belong in the domain of neutrality (here I incline away from perfectionism), but worthless conceptions do not (here I agree with perfectionism).

These exclusions from the domain of neutrality are not ad hoc but are natural implications of neutrality's downstream character. Extending neutral treatment to conceptions of the good that are hostile to the self-determination of others would not leave those others with a fair opportunity for self-determination. Someone who held such a conception, and tried to insist that his conception was owed neutral treatment, would find himself tangled in a contradiction. He would be in the position of saying *both* that

---

[16] The value of self-determination does have an antiperfectionist character. It consists in the pursuit of one's actual conception of the good, not the pursuit of a valuable conception. Self-determination is discussed and defended further in sec. 4.6. I doubt it adds anything useful to call it a "neutral" value.

the state is wrong not to respect his fair opportunity to be self-determining *and* that it should show such respect by adopting policies that deny that very same opportunity to others. The exclusion of worthless conceptions is motivated by a different logic, but again the restriction does not seem ad hoc. By definition, worthless conceptions of the good are conceptions for which self-determination has no value. An account that bases neutrality on the value of self-determination should therefore exclude worthless conceptions from the domain of neutrality.

A quite different kind of case is one in which the neutral treatment of some particular conception(s) of the good would conflict contingently, but not intrinsically, with values such as self-determination. In my view, conceptions of the good covered by this case are *not* excluded from the domain of neutrality. Imagine a state that is successfully protecting liberal values, including the fair opportunity for self-determination. The state is very fragile, however, because it suffers from relatively low levels of allegiance from its citizens. Suppose it is reasonable to expect that, by aligning itself with the majority religion in a nonneutral way, its levels of allegiance would go up, and a liberal framework protecting self-determination would be secured. Then it would seem that the state has a reason, grounded in the value of self-determination, for not extending neutrality to minority religions. At first glance, this sort of case is just like the ones described earlier as falling outside of neutrality's domain. A minority religionist could not reasonably complain about nonneutral treatment if neutral treatment would predictably lead to the destruction of the framework that protects the values underlying neutrality.

But arguably there is a difference between the cases. In the case where a conception is defined, in part, by its hostility to self-determination (or other justifiable values of comparable importance), the bearers of those conceptions lack the standing to complain about nonneutral treatment. It is *their* conception of the good life that conflicts with the self-determination of others. The case of conceptions the neutral treatment of which would contingently weaken liberal institutions seems rather different. There is nothing in the contents of such conceptions that is opposed to the general enjoyment of a fair opportunity for self-determination. It is just that, because of the beliefs of *others* (e.g., the uncertain allegiances of majority religionists), the neutral treatment of such conceptions happens to be on a collision course with the maintenance of liberal institutions. In this latter sort of case, the right thing to say is that the reasons in favor of neutrality may well be defeated by the reasons against, but there are still at least pro tanto reasons in favor of neutrality. The existence of these last reasons is signaled by the various questions we would want to ask about the case before privileging the majority over the minority religions. Is it *really* necessary to do this to secure liberal institutions? How great a threat are liberal institutions, in fact, under? What forms of preference for the majority religion are being proposed? And so on. It is also signaled by the residual goal that a liberal state should retain of establishing the conditions under which it need not sacrifice the neutral treatment of minority religions for the sake of better securing an overall liberal framework. We do not feel the same need to search for a way of accommodating conceptions that are hostile to self-determination. The content of such considerations disqualifies them from even a minimal concern for their neutral treatment.

This discussion brings us to the question of neutrality's "strength." Even for conceptions of the good that fall within neutrality's domain, I do not claim that the state has a general, conclusory, reason to be neutral. Rather the claim is that the state has a defeasible, or pro tanto, reason to be neutral, one that is often quite weighty. Again the point is related to the downstream character of neutrality as a value. Fair opportunity for self-determination is not the only important value, and its claims will have to be balanced against those of other comparably important values. Importantly, however, in cases where the pro tanto reason to be neutral is outweighed, that reason is not erased entirely. Instead, it is deflected into a goal that the state should adopt of establishing conditions in which neutrality can be realized without excessive costs for other values.

Whether the state has a conclusory reason to be neutral in a given case depends on several factors. As we shall see in section 4.5, these factors include the degree to which a possible departure from neutrality would in fact unfairly affect the opportunity for self-determination of some; and the degree to which the countervailing considerations, be they perfectionist considerations or considerations of the public good, are themselves weighty and can be advanced through and only through neutrality-curtailing measures. The relevant factors also include, as I explain in section 4.6, the degree to which self-determination has a heightened importance for persons who are affected by a nonneutral policy because of the special nature of the commitment or attachment that is adversely affected. Policies that deny a person the fair opportunity to fulfill her religious commitments are especially harmful, for instance, and should be adopted only in those situations where they are the least burdensome means of advancing some compelling countervailing consideration.

4.3 Conceptions of Neutrality

Let us move directly now to the chapter's crucial conceptual proposal, which is that there is a distinct third conception of neutrality that has been neglected in the literature. To get a first glimpse of this distinct third conception, consider a schematic representation of state policy-making:

With intentions I, the state adopts policy P, which can be expected to have effects E.

Roughly speaking, proponents of neutrality of intentions are interested in *I*. The state maintains neutrality when and only when its policies are adopted with an appropriate kind of intention. Advocates of neutrality of effects, on the other hand, concentrate on *E*. A policy is neutral when and only when, relative to an appropriate baseline, it is not expected to produce unequal effects on different conceptions of the good.

In contrast with the two traditional approaches, neutrality of treatment focuses its attention on *P*. *P* represents either a form of assistance to one or more conceptions of the good (if it can be expected to promote those conceptions) or a form of hindrance (if its effects are expected to be negative). According to neutrality of treatment, the state maintains neutrality only when, relative to an appropriate baseline, it extends equivalent forms of assistance/hindrance to rival conceptions of the good.

The development of a third conception of neutrality is motivated by certain weaknesses in the first two. Consider, first, neutrality of intentions. The intention behind a policy can be equated with the *aim* of the policy, which is the state of affairs that the policy seeks to bring about. Or it could be thought of as the *justification* for the policy, the fundamental reason why the policy is adopted, which may or may not refer to the intrinsic desirability of the state of affairs to be effected.[17] Conceptions of neutrality featuring these terms would be the following:

> *Neutrality of aim.* The state violates this requirement when it adopts any policy with the aim of making some particular conception of the good more or less successful.
>
> *Neutrality of justification.* The state violates this requirement when its fundamental reason for adopting some policy involves a judgment about the value of a particular conception of the good.

In general, the state maintains neutrality when it restrains itself to pursuing only those policies that are, or could be, supported by appropriate reasons. These reasons must be sufficiently plausible and weighty, and they must not invoke an aim of promoting a particular conception of the good or otherwise rest on a judgment about the value of particular conceptions of the good.

Critics of neutrality of intentions maintain that there is no important liberal value or principle that supports a general prohibition against the state acting on particular judgments about the good. Whether or not the critics are right about this, there is a second, orthogonal problem with the intentions-based view that is more relevant to the contrast with neutrality of treatment. The problem is that neutrality of intentions sweeps too broadly, counting as neutral policies that seem, intuitively, to be nonneutral.

---

[17] Arneson's (1990, 218–19) distinction between "procedure" (roughly what I mean by "justification") and "aim" marks the difference I have in mind here.

To see this problem, consider cases of religious establishment in which the state confers some special advantage on a particular religion that it does not confer on others. In many ways, the establishment of a particular religion or church seems like the paradigmatic example of a departure from neutrality.[18] It is revealing, therefore, that neutrality of intentions does not regard all cases of state establishment as departures from neutrality.[19] It has no difficulty declaring an establishment to be nonneutral in cases where the rationale for the policy lies in the fact that legislators regard the religion in question as true or intrinsically valuable. Suppose, however, that the establishment policy has a different justification. Legislators do not know whether the established religion is true or intrinsically valuable. But they do judge that its establishment will bring desirable social consequences. For instance, they might think that, by associating the state with the majority religion, they will enhance the authority and perceived legitimacy of the state in the eyes of many citizens, thereby making the state more effective at pursuing its other objectives. Now it seems that the intention is a neutral one. The aim is to bring about the relevant social consequences, and the justification is the desirability of those consequences. But the policy still involves an official state preference for one particular religion and would strike many people as plainly nonneutral in character.[20]

The overreach associated with neutrality of intentions provides a reason for considering neutrality of effects. A plausible diagnosis of the nonneutral character of establishment points to the fact that establishment policies can be expected to promote the success of the established religion at the expense of other religions and outlooks. However, neutrality of effects leads into a difficulty of its own.

There are varying ways of formulating neutrality of effects, but all share the following core principle:

> *Neutrality of effects.* The state violates this requirement if it adopts a policy that, relative to an appropriate baseline, has the effect of making some particular conception of the good more or less successful without also adopting offsetting policies that have the effect of making rival conceptions of the good more or less successful to the same degree.

As this statement makes clear, the effects that matter for the view are the success or failure of particular conceptions of the good. If a policy leads a concep-

---

[18] Richard Arneson says with some plausibility that "the ideal of liberal neutrality is constituted by generalizing from practises of religious tolerance. Just as the tolerant state favors no sect or doctrine over any other, so the neutral state adopts this posture of tolerance not just with respect to religious issues but with respect to all controversial ways of life and conceptions of the good" Ibid., 216.

[19] Ibid., 219 (talking about Larmore's "neutrality of procedure").

[20] Raz (1986, 116) makes a related point about the excessive sweep of neutrality of intentions. See the example of arms-sales-for-profit.

tion of the good to be more successful than one or more of its rivals (against the backdrop of an appropriate baseline), then a departure from neutrality has occurred.

Different variations on this principle can be, and have been, proposed. For our purposes, the important variation relates to two different ways of measuring success. One dimension of success might be called "popularity." All else being equal, a conception of the good is more successful the more adherents it has. A second dimension is "realizability." All else being equal, a conception of the good is more successful the easier it is for people to pursue and realize that conception of the good.[21] The distinction between these two dimensions will be relevant in a moment, when we assess the distinctiveness of neutrality of treatment.

If the problem with neutrality of intentions is overreach, the turn to neutrality of effects produces the opposite problem of underreach. Neutrality of effects might help to explain why establishment policies represent a departure from neutrality. But this is mainly because it regards virtually *all* policies as nonneutral. Indeed, even the least controversial liberal principles, if enacted, would bring about nonneutral effects.[22] Legal protections of the basic liberties make it relatively more difficult for boring or unpopular ways of life to flourish than would be the case in a legal system where people are locked into particular ways of life. Policies that seek to establish a fair distribution of material resources make it relatively harder for people with expensive tastes to realize the ways of life they value. And so on. Since liberals are not embarrassed by these implications of their principles and do not think that any special compensation is due to those who are adversely affected, it seems clear that they do not recognize any duty to be neutral with respect to effects.

An examination of the two usual conceptions of neutrality reinforces the sense of neutrality as a deeply flawed idea. If neutrality is interpreted as neutrality of intentions, then it is too sweeping to account for some of the most obvious and paradigmatic cases of nonneutrality. If it is understood as neutrality of effects, then it might just account for such cases, but only because it indiscriminately rejects as nonneutral a wide swathe of policies, including some core liberal ones. Defenders of neutrality thus face a dilemma. But, as I shall now argue, there is a way out of the dilemma, which consists of introducing a distinct third conception of neutrality. Neutrality of treatment can explain why establishment is nonneutral without falling back into an effects-based conception of neutrality.

---

[21] This dual-component conception of success is adapted from Raz 1986, 112, 114–15.

[22] The argument of the remainder of the paragraph follows Kymlicka 1989a, 884–85; and Arneson 2003, 193–94.

If the basic idea of neutrality of effects is to equalize across outputs of the policy process, the idea of neutrality of treatment is to equalize across the state's inputs. The idea can be formulated as follows:

Neutrality of treatment. The state violates this requirement when, relative to an appropriate baseline, its policies are more accommodating of some conceptions of the good than they are of others.

If the state adopts some policy that can be expected, in conjunction with other necessary inputs, to make a particular conception of the good more successful, then, in my terminology, its policy is "accommodating" toward that conception. To maintain neutrality, when the state pursues a policy that is accommodating (or unaccommodating) of some particular conception of the good relative to the appropriate baseline, it must adopt an equivalent policy for rival conceptions of the good. Neutrality of treatment means the state's policies must be equally accommodating of rival conceptions of the good.

I shall consider the baseline issue toward the end of the section. For now, let me try to explain and motivate the basic features of the proposal. Obviously, for the view to get off the ground, there must be some metric of inputs that does not simply reduce back to outputs. If the only way of deciding whether two policies are equally accommodating were to look at whether they had equal effects, then neutrality of treatment would collapse back into neutrality of effects. Indeed, since accommodation, as I just defined it, is identified by a disposition to produce certain kinds of effects, it might seem, at first glance, that neutrality of effects and of treatment are not relevantly distinct.

But, in some cases at least, we do not have trouble identifying a metric of inputs that is distinct from, and independent of, outputs. Consider the case of a philanthropist, who is faced with a decision about how to allocate money between two worthy projects. One possibility would be for the philanthropist to give each project the amount that is calculated to bring the projects as close as possible to equal levels of success. A second would simply be to give each project equal amounts of money. One decision rule equalizes across outputs; the other across inputs. Since, in general, two such rules do not produce equivalent allocations, in this case at least there is an intuitive measure of policy inputs that is both well defined and independent of policy outputs. And this continues to be true even if it is pointed out that what makes the money allocated by the philanthropist an "input" is its disposition (when spent in certain ways and combined with other necessary inputs) to produce the relevant sorts of "outputs." Still we can construct distinct and independent measures of input and output, and equalize one or the other.

The basic idea behind neutrality of treatment is to generalize from cases like that of the philanthropist. In a wide range of different situations, it is possible to identify a sense in which the state might adopt policies toward rival conceptions of the good that are equally accommodating even though they can be expected to have different impacts on the success of those conceptions. The next section will canvas systematically some of the different ways in which state policies can be equally or unequally accommodating. For now, a couple of brief illustrations will suffice to establish the possibility of a distinct third view of neutrality.

A straightforward example of unequal accommodation involves state taxation of goods and services. Suppose that the state taxes the goods that are used in one conception of the good (COG1) at a rate of 15 percent but slaps a 25 percent tax rate on goods used in a rival conception (COG2). Suppose further that both conceptions are permissible and their pursuit imposes limited and roughly equivalent costs on third parties. It seems natural to say that the state's taxation policy is less accommodating toward COG2 than it is toward COG1. This is true even if the state's aim in adopting the policy makes no reference to the desirability of promoting COG1 and even if it makes no judgment that COG1 is superior to COG2. And it is also true even if the tax differential makes no difference at all on the popularity of the rival conceptions. To this extent, neutrality of treatment is both well defined and distinct from neutrality of intentions and neutrality of effects.

Neutrality of treatment is also distinct, in this example, from neutrality of effects when the latter is measured by realizability rather than popularity. But here the difference is quite subtle. All else being equal, the higher tax rate on the goods valued by COG2 means that it is more difficult to pursue and realize that conception. To this extent, unequal accommodation *is* an unequal effect. But, despite this overlap, neutrality of treatment remains a distinct standard from neutrality of effects, even when the latter is measured by realizability. The reason is that the tax differential may trigger further downstream effects on the relative realizability of the two conceptions besides the tax rates themselves. For instance, the tax differential might encourage large numbers of people to exit COG2 and enter COG1. If there are fixed (or lumpy) costs involved in supplying the goods associated with each conception, the per unit pretax prices of goods associated with COG2 might end up rising, and those associated with COG1 might end up falling. None of these further effects matter from the point of view of neutrality of treatment. To the extent that neutrality of treatment overlaps with neutrality of effects at all, it does so only with respect to one special kind of effect, namely, the direct effect that a policy has on making a conception of the good more or less realizable. Neutrality of treatment does not look at the further, indirect effects that arise because of the way in which people react to that relative treatment. Neutrality of effects, by contrast, looks at the whole range of effects that have implications for realizability and requires that the state avoid policies that, on balance, have unequal effects.

The divergence between neutrality of treatment and neutrality of effects (measured by realizability) is less subtle in a second example. Suppose now that the state policy we are concerned with is not a tax but the legal permission to use some particular piece of land. Imagine that a field belongs to a local public authority, which, up to now, has prohibited its use for team sports. The local authority now decides to relax that policy and to allow any group of people to sign up to use the field for the team sport of their choosing. The local community contains people who would like to play softball on the field and people who would like to play cricket. As described, the policy is equally accommodating of these different preferences and is therefore consistent with neutrality of treatment. This is true because the policy extends exactly the same rights to bearers of each sporting preference, and not because of any conjectures about the impact of the policy on the popularity or realizability of the two sports.

To make the point about realizability explicit, imagine that the distribution of preferences for softball and cricket is heavily tilted toward softball. Large numbers of people want to play softball, and only a handful want cricket. With these preferences in the background, the policy can be predicted to have a very unequal impact on softball and cricket lovers. It is now much easier (we might suppose) to play softball: finally there is a suitable place to play. But for the few would-be cricket players, it is not much easier to play their preferred game, at least not a proper game. It is true that they now have access to one of the inputs (a field) that they need to realize their preference. But so few people want to play cricket that there is no realistic prospect of ever getting a game together. Neutrality of treatment clearly diverges, then, from neutrality of effects, even when the latter is measured in terms of realizability.

These examples are suggestive of both the intuitive and distinctive character of neutrality of treatment. In the next section we shall explore more systematically how judgments about equality or inequality of accommodation might be rendered in different contexts, and how these judgments give to neutrality of treatment a distinctive shape that is less problematic than its two traditional competitors.[23]

---

[23] The proposal that neutrality be conceptualized as neutrality of treatment, or equal accommodation, is bound to remind some readers of a similar-sounding suggestion that can be found in Barry 2001. Barry argues that a neutral state is one that is fair, and that fairness in the context of religious and cultural diversity means equal treatment (25, 28). He then suggests that equal treatment amounts to the requirement that the state apply a uniform set of rules to all its citizens (32, 34, 38, 45). Where there is one rule for all, and other background liberal principles are respected, he thinks there is nothing to a complaint made by religious or cultural minorities that the state's policies or institutions are nonneutral. To think that there is such a complaint, Barry maintains, would be to adopt the discredited assumption that neutrality is best thought of in terms of effects.

In the end, my proposal is quite different from Barry's. Despite several of his examples (29–30), Barry's view implies that there is no legitimate neutrality-based objection to religious establishment so long as the rules and policies that constitute the establishment are uniformly applied to all citizens. Under neutrality of treatment, by contrast, there would be such an objection, since establishment means that the state provides some form of assistance to one particular religion that it does not provide to others. The root of the difference with Barry's account is that Barry wrongly assimilates the idea of equal treatment to

Before embarking on this discussion, it is important to clarify the baseline that is being assumed in making judgments about the state's relative treatment of different conceptions of the good.[24] One possible way to think of this baseline is as a kind of "do-nothing" point. In this view, the state treats two conceptions neutrally when it imposes no restrictions on, and extends no benefits to, either conception relative to the baseline position in which it imposes no restrictions at all on, and extends no benefits at all to, either conception. An alternative view would attempt to build into the baseline some of the standard reasons a state might have for regulating or assisting a conception of the good. In the specific version of this alternative view that I shall favor, the baseline reflects the guiding idea of fair opportunity for self-determination. Policies that seek to establish a framework in which this idea is realized—by prohibiting, regulating, taxing, subsidizing, providing, and so on—are not counted as departures from the baseline. Even though such policies may be especially accommodating (or unaccommodating) of particular conceptions of the good, no equivalent, offsetting policies are needed to reestablish neutrality.

To contemplate the implications of these two different views, imagine a public authority that gives permits to groups to hold organized events in a public park. Suppose that, in exchange for a permit, the authority charges the organizers of a classical music concert $1 for each person expected to attend, and the organizers of a rock concert $2 for each person expected. The difference can be explained by the higher level of negative externalities that will be generated by the rock concert. The authority will use the extra money to pay for additional cleanup and/or to compensate local residents for the higher decibel levels. On the do-nothing baseline, the conceptions are not treated neutrally. The public authority is providing a greater benefit to (or imposing a smaller cost on) the classical-music lovers than the rock-music lovers. This departure from neutrality may be justifiable, all things considered, but a departure from neutrality it is. If the $1 per head difference corresponds to the difference in externalities, however, then the fair baseline suggests the opposite result. Once externalities are addressed and a framework of fair opportunity is established, assistance to the two genres of music is equivalent.

As far as I can see, ordinary usage does not favor one of these specifications of the baseline over the other. It seems natural to describe the higher charge to rock organizers as nonneutral (on its face it is), even if justifiable. But once the externalities rationale is noted, the policy also seems intuitively neutral. I shall opt for the fair baseline for theoretical reasons. The fair baseline better aligns with the idea that there is a pro tanto reason to be neutral grounded in the value of a fair opportunity for self-determination. If we worked with

the rule-of-law principle of one-rule-for-all. As the establishment example suggests, there is more to fair treatment than the uniform application of a single law. I return to this point in sec. 4.5.

[24] Discussion of this baseline issue is a significant omission from Patten (2012).

the do-nothing baseline instead, some departures from that baseline (e.g., the higher charge for rock organizers) would not upset the fair opportunity for self-determination at all, and thus there would not even be a pro tanto reason to avoid or offset them.

4.4 Institutions of Neutrality

Broadly speaking, there are three general strategies that a state might adopt if it is committed to remaining neutral, which I shall call "privatization," "generic entanglement," and "evenhandedness." The basic idea of the privatization strategy is to disentangle the state as far as possible from the regulation or provision of the goods and activities that figure in the pursuit of conceptions of the good. Under this approach, the state is equally accommodating of all conceptions of the good because it restricts itself to making a set of general rules that establish a framework of fair opportunity for self-determination, and it otherwise extends no assistance to, and imposes no hindrance on, any goods or activities that might be involved in particular conceptions of the good. The point of departure for the generic entanglement strategy, by contrast, is the recognition that some forms of state intervention are directed at goods and activities that play a role in all, or at least almost all, conceptions of the good. The entanglement of the state in the regulation or provision of these goods and activities is compatible with equal accommodation since no special form of assistance or hindrance is being extended to or imposed on some conceptions of the good but not others. Finally, the main idea behind the evenhandedness strategy is for the state to remain actively involved in providing and/or regulating particular goods and activities that are of special importance to some conceptions of the good and not others, but to do so in a pluralistic fashion such that a roughly equivalent form of regulation or provision is applied to various rival conceptions of the good.[25]

A firm guarantee for the basic liberties is one of the ways that a state implements the privatization strategy. By protecting the basic liberties, the state abjures various neutrality-violating policies such as legal prohibitions on pursuing, or talking about, or associating for, particular conceptions of the good. The state thereby leaves it up to people in civil society to determine for themselves which conceptions of the good they will pursue, or speak favorably about, or associate for the purposes of advancing. A state that allowed people to associate in order to pursue some conceptions of the good but not others, or one that regulated what people could say in criticism of some conceptions

---

[25] My usage of the term "evenhandedness" here follows Carens 2000, 8–14; and Barry 2001, 29. For a comparison of the Carens account and my own, see chapter 1, n. 40.

but not others, would not be equally accommodating of all conceptions of the good.

The idea of separating church from state is another place where one can see the privatization strategy at work. The state has a general responsibility to protect its citizens from harmful practices and to limit the negative externalities imposed by one person's or group's behavior on others. In general, it ought to strike a balance between safeguarding the interests that each person has in self-determination (see sec. 4.6) and protecting the security of each person against harm. Relative to this fair baseline, the state pursues the privatization strategy when it avoids further entanglement with religion, neither assisting nor hindering particular religions or religious groups. It does not provide goods in-kind that are of use to religious conceptions of the good, nor does it subsidize such goods, nor does it use the schools or other institutions or offices of state to instruct people in the value of particular religions. At the same time, relative to a fair baseline, the state does not prohibit or regulate goods or activities that are of use to particular religions, nor subject them to special taxes or encumbrances, nor speak out against them or against religious conceptions of the good. The idea is to make the state equally accommodating of all religious conceptions of the good by applying the same standard of harm to all and otherwise relegating the pursuit and enjoyment of religion to the private sphere of civil society.

The same basic idea can be generalized to nonreligious conceptions of the goods as well and to nonreligious aspects of conceptions of the good. Subject to a fair baseline, the state avoids subsidies, in-kind provision, special regulations and taxes, and so on, for all goods, thereby leaving it to the market to determine what goods will be produced and how they will be allocated. Under this approach, with no particular goods singled out for favorable or unfavorable treatment, the market establishes a process for allocating resources that is equally accommodating of different preferences that people bring to it. This does not mean that market outcomes are equally satisfactory for different preferences or conceptions of the good. Those with expensive tastes, which may include unusual or minority tastes, will find it difficult to satisfy their preferences even if they start from a fair share of initial spending power. Again this is a reminder that neutrality of treatment is not equivalent to neutrality of effects. What it means to say that the market is equally accommodating is that the rules and mechanisms that constitute it show no preference for (extend no special assistance to and impose no hindrance on) some conceptions of the good over others.

Almost nobody would accept the view that resource allocation decisions should be left entirely to the market. There are objections to market outcomes based on both fairness and market-failure considerations not fully captured by the baseline. On their own, these problems do not necessitate the abandonment of neutrality. But they do force us to think about alternative ways of realizing neutrality besides what I have called the privatization strategy.

A leading alternative is for the state to intervene in various ways, but to focus its interventions on goods and activities that are generically valuable, in the sense that they are beneficial or burdensome to a variety of different conceptions of the good. I call this strategy "generic entanglement." Consider, for instance, the state's provision of police, fire, and school-bus services. These services are extended to different facilities associated with a range of different conceptions of the good. By providing fire department services to a local synagogue, a city government extends a form of assistance. But since it provides the same service to facilities associated with all other conceptions of the good, and they are all presumed to value it, there is no departure from neutral treatment.

The state's provision of schools and health-care services are somewhat less pure examples of the same logic. The idea is that there is a core of what is offered in both schools and medical facilities that is useful to, and valued by, persons embracing an extremely broad range of different conceptions of the good. The common school, for instance, need not instruct children in the virtues or truth of any particular conception of the good but instead can seek to equip them with general knowledge and skills they will need for citizenship and for a variety of different conceptions of the good.[26] Although such an approach might be rejected by a few conceptions of the good, it is equally accommodating of a great many, even though it means that the state is not following the privatization strategy.[27]

A different way that a state might try to realize neutrality of treatment is by following a strategy of evenhandedness. In this approach the state involves itself unapologetically with directing and regulating resources and does not insist that its involvement consist only of generic interventions that are equally accommodating of a wide variety of conceptions of the good. Instead, the idea is to make a series of different interventions, each directed at one of several

[26] There are some conceptions of the good that are not neutrally treated by the common school, including those that hold that the general knowledge and skills emphasized by the common school are harmful to children and those that hold that children should be educated in an environment that is suffused by the conception of the good in question. Some of these conceptions of the good are antiliberal or impermissible, but others may not be. The possibility of private education offers at least some relief to permissible conceptions of the good that conflict with the values of the common school. The importance of common school values arguably counsels against any further relief.

[27] As examples of goods that a perfectionist state ought to promote, defenders of perfectionism sometimes mention very general and broad goods such as "quality relationships" (Sher 1997, 246) or knowledge of the natural world, history, literature, music, and athletics (Hurka 1993, 159). At such a level of generality, it is not clear that many conceptions of the good would be excluded. To take Sher's example, so long as the state does not start promoting particular kinds of relationships (e.g., traditional marriage) that are not relevantly dissimilar to other relationships (e.g., same-sex marriage), a state effort to promote quality relationships in general may qualify as neutral in the generic entanglement sense. For an interesting proposal along these lines focused on promoting "caring" relationships, see Brake 2010.

rival conceptions of the good. If a local government provides one form of recreational facility (e.g., a skateboard park) valued by some people, for instance,
then it does its best to provide a range of different kinds of comparable facilities (skating rinks, swimming pools, squash courts, etc.) that others value. The
state equally accommodates different conceptions of the good this way, not
by relegating decisions about their provision to the market, nor by providing
some generic or all-purpose good that is equally useful for them all (e.g., a
voucher valid at any private recreational club), but by positively accommodating all of them in an equal fashion, each in their own way.

In general, privatization is a purer strategy for realizing neutrality of treatment than generic entanglement or evenhandedness. When the state pursues
one of the latter strategies it will at best approximate neutrality. If it opts for
some kind of generic intervention, there are bound to be conceptions of the
good that take a very different view of the value of the assistance or hindrance
or that would prefer, at least, that the assistance or hindrance take some different form. If evenhandedness takes the form of in-kind provision of a variety of
goods corresponding to different conceptions of the good, the state is bound
to fall short. For any given kind of good (e.g., recreation), people are likely to
value different varieties of that good (e.g., different forms of recreation), to
differing degrees (some care more or less about recreation in general) and in
different combinations with other goods. In most areas, the state could not
possibly keep up through in-kind provision with the variety of conceptions of
the good that people endorse. Given the limitations of generic entanglement
and evenhandedness, the only way to achieve neutrality of treatment perfectly
is through privatization. Leave people with all-purpose resources to spend and
let them spend those resources in the way that best reflects their conceptions
of the good.

This is hardly a decisive argument in favor of privatization, however, since
market-failure and fairness considerations may provide powerful reasons not
to leave resource allocations up to the market. Even where there are good reasons for the state not to adopt privatization, however, those reasons do not
prevent the state from trying to approximate, as best it can, neutrality of treatment through either generic entanglement or evenhandedness. The state may
have good reason to provide a particular class of goods itself, but the nature of
that reason may leave space for the state to provide the goods, as best it can, in
a generic manner or in a pluralistic manner that evenhandedly provides different varieties of the good.

The example of public recreational facilities illustrates this last possibility.
There are arguably good reasons for the government to provide such facilities, grounded in values of community and public health. But these reasons
do not dictate that a particular sort of recreational facility should be preferred
over others, or that it is preferable to have just one particular sort. A government can thus be responsive to these reasons *and* try to do its best to honor

the demands of neutral treatment by providing a variety of different kinds of facilities, which accommodates the diverse preferences of its citizens. The achievement of neutral treatment will be far from perfect, but the state is at least trying to be responsive to the range of different values that are in place. As we will see in the next chapter, cases such as this one are crucial for establishing a positive link between neutrality and minority cultural rights.

4.5 The Fairness Justification of Neutrality

The justification of neutrality draws, in part, on some neglected passages in Rawls that discuss the "benefit criterion" of just taxation.[28] According to this traditional criterion, "taxes are to be levied according to benefits received."[29] Rawls argues that, in general, the benefit criterion of tax policy plays no fundamental role in guiding the tax and expenditure policies of the government. Instead, these policies ought to be guided by the two principles of justice.

However, Rawls does assign the benefit criterion a significant subordinate role. Suppose we imagine a situation in which the demanding strictures of the two principles of justice have been satisfied, so that "the distribution of income and wealth that results is just whatever it is."[30] To establish these background conditions, the government is presumably quite active, but Rawls observes that some citizens may want to see the government provide even more in the way of public goods. By assumption, these goods are discretionary, in the sense that they are not necessary to establish just background institutions. They are simply goods that at least some citizens value and that, for one reason or another, are not made easily available on the market. In this special context, Rawls thinks that the benefit criterion *does* apply. Citizens ought to be given the chance to devise schemes of tax and expenditure through an "exchange branch" of government that can provide discretionary public goods. The tax paid by each citizen should be proportionate to the benefits she receives. If taxes to support such expenditures were to run contrary to the benefit criterion, then, in effect the tax system would be recruiting some citizens to subsidize the provision of benefits for others. In a context where we are assuming the justice of the antecedent distribution of income and wealth, this is unfair. As Rawls puts it, "there is no more justification for using the state apparatus to compel some citizens to pay for unwanted benefits that others desire than there is to force them to reimburse others for their private expenses."[31]

---

[28] Rawls 1999a, 247, 250.
[29] Ibid., 247.
[30] Ibid., 249.
[31] Ibid., 250.

When Rawls turns to perfectionism a little later in *A Theory of Justice*, he alludes back to this framework.[32] A government policy in support of the arts, sciences, universities, and so on may well be legitimate, he argues, if it could be shown to promote directly or indirectly the social conditions underlying justice. But if it is just a matter of providing discretionary public goods that some citizens, but not others, take to have value, then the exchange branch, with its governing benefit criterion, is the appropriate forum in which to pursue government action. To fund such goods out of general compulsory taxation would be to risk imposing significant expenditures on some without any compensating benefits.

With these scattered remarks, Rawls offers a simple but powerful framework that helps to explain what is wrong with some of the most obvious departures from neutrality of treatment. As an illustration, imagine a group of citizens who would like to see their local public authority provide an expensive lacrosse facility out of public funds. The local authority does not currently provide major facilities for other conceptions of the good, and no plans to provide other facilities are in the works. It seems clear that the policy departs from neutrality of treatment. A significant benefit is being extended to lacrosse fans and players, without analogous benefits being extended to other conceptions of the good. If proponents of the facility do not plan to reimburse taxpayers, for example, through funds raised from user fees or ticket sales, there is no sense in which the scheme amounts to a roundabout use of a Rawlsian exchange branch: in the long run, the facility is funded out of general tax revenues. Given a just background distribution of resources, it seems evident that the proposed scheme is unfair to citizens who dislike lacrosse or simply are indifferent to it. The scheme consists, in effect, of some people using the coercive power of the state to force others to subsidize their personal sporting preferences. Indeed, it seems possible to go further than this and to say that, even if the background circumstances were unjust, the scheme would still be unfair. It is hard to imagine a set of circumstances in which public provision of the lacrosse facility would represent a reasonable strategy for bringing about justice.

Applied to discretionary public goods, the benefit criterion has a great deal of intuitive force. We might go one step further, however, and ask why exactly it is that violations of the criterion are objectionable. One clue to this explanation is found in imagining a possible response to lacrosse-haters who complain about the policy. Suppose opponents of the policy are told that they have nothing to complain about because the lacrosse facility is meant for everyone to use and enjoy. It is not just the present lacrosse enthusiasts who can benefit from it, but anybody who develops and pursues an interest in the game.

This response draws attention to an account that will *not* work of why violations of the benefit criterion are unjust. The problem with such policies is not

---

[32] Ibid., 291–92.

that they apply different rules to different people (lacrosse enthusiasts versus everyone else) and, in this way, violate the basic rule-of-law principle that the law should be the same for everyone.[33] Formally, at least, it is not particular persons who are given a special benefit by the provision of the facility, but a particular activity. Since any given citizen can enjoy the benefit simply by pursuing an interest in lacrosse, the policy does not single out any class of persons for differential treatment.

A better explanation of the unfairness produced by violations of the benefit criterion is that they conflict with the interest that nonbeneficiaries have in what I call self-determination. This is their interest in being able to pursue and fulfill the conception of the good that they, in fact, happen to hold. In our example, it is true that any citizen could come to value, and be benefited by, the lacrosse facility. In fact, at least some citizens do not value such a facility but instead have other aims, goals, pursuits, and so on, the pursuit and enjoyment of which depend on their having access to resources. When, against a background of justice, the state taxes away some of their resources to spend on advancing somebody else's conception of the good, it denies them a fair opportunity to advance their own conception of the good. It denies them a fair opportunity for self-determination.

Rawls's discussion of the benefit criterion is a useful place to start in building a case for neutrality of treatment, but it needs to be supplemented by other theoretical resources. To see this, consider a variation on the lacrosse example in which, instead of offering a special facility to lacrosse enthusiasts, the local authority imposes a special tax on the sport (e.g., a special user fee on existing facilities, or a surcharge on ticket sales). The purpose of the tax, let us suppose, is not to capture externalities that are peculiarly associated with lacrosse, Rather, the rationale is purely fiscal: lacrosse players and fans are particularly intense in their enthusiasm for the game and are unlikely to diminish appreciably their demand for the game when faced with the tax.

As with the provision of a special lacrosse facility, something seems unfair about the imposition of a special lacrosse tax. In some situations, the benefit criterion helps to identify the source of this unfairness. Suppose that the public authority is using the revenues it raises from the special tax to pay for discretionary public goods the demand for which does not coincide with enthusiasm for lacrosse. The tax then conflicts with the benefit criterion: lacrosse enthusiasts are subsidizing discretionary goods for other people. But imagine instead that the public authority is spending the tax revenues on goods that are essential for maintaining just background conditions (e.g., public education) rather than on discretionary goods. Even in this case, the lacrosse tax seems unfair. Why should lacrosse enthusiasts be singled out to carry the burden of

---

[33] As mentioned in n. 23 above, this principle figures prominently in Barry's (2001) understanding of neutrality.

providing these essential public goods? However, the benefit criterion cannot explain why there is unfairness here, since, in a Rawlsian view at least, it applies only to expenditures on discretionary goods.

Rawls himself has relatively little to say about just taxation in support of essential or nondiscretionary public goods. He registers a mild preference for a proportional expenditure (or consumption) tax over a traditional income tax, both of which would arguably be consistent with neutrality of treatment, since they do not single out particular conceptions of the good for unfavorable treatment. But he does not consider taxes on particular goods or activities (such as lacrosse) or explain whether or why he thinks they are unjust.

Assuming that we do think the lacrosse tax is unjust, we need an alternative to the benefit criterion to explain why this is so. Again I think it would be a mistake to diagnose the unfairness in terms of a violation of the rule of law. The peculiar tax schedule that includes the lacrosse tax does not apply different tax rates to different persons but to different activities. Since any given lacrosse fan or player can avoid the tax by simply opting for a different pursuit, the persons who do opt for lacrosse are not being singled out as persons for differential treatment.

A better explanation of the unfairness produced by the tax is that the tax directly conflicts with the interest that persons have in self-determination. The lacrosse tax is unfair, in this account, because, by attaching special burdens to those who want to enjoy lacrosse, it denies lacrosse enthusiasts a fair opportunity for self-determination. To be sure, since there is no violation of the benefit criterion in the present case, some extra work is needed to show that the limits on the self-determination of lacrosse enthusiasts do, in fact, deny them a *fair* opportunity to realize their preferences. If the limits were somehow essential to the establishment of background conditions of justice, then they might not be unfair at all. Any kind of tax diminishes a person's self-determination to some extent, by reducing the resources they have at their disposal to advance their ends, but not all taxes are an affront to the fair opportunity for self-determination. The key feature of the lacrosse tax, however, is that it singles out a particular activity (valued by some conceptions of the good and not others) that stands in no essential relation to justice and imposes the burden only on those people who pursue that activity.[34] By contrast, other kinds of tax, such as an expenditure or an income tax, are evenhanded in the way they reduce the resources that people have to pursue the various conceptions of the good they hold and thus do not *unfairly* diminish anybody's opportunity for self-determination.

---

[34] At best, it stands in a contingent relation to the promotion of those conditions, for example, because lacrosse enthusiasts are an easy target for the tax collector, and/or because they tend to come from affluent backgrounds.

The lacrosse examples, and the remarks about the benefit criterion and fair opportunity for self-determination, are suggestive of a general argument in favor of neutrality of treatment. That argument might be laid out in three steps.

Equal consideration. The first specifies, in highly abstract terms, the basic obligation of the state toward its citizens. The liberal state is meant to represent all its citizens, and thus it has an obligation to be equally responsive to the interests of each of those citizens. It cannot legitimately single out some favored group, such as a national or religious majority, and act as if the interests of members of this group matter more than the interests of nonmembers.

Fair opportunity for self-determination. The second claim is that self-determination is an important interest of all persons, or at least of all persons who do not have what I earlier called "worthless" conceptions of the good. As a result, the state has a pro tanto reason to adopt policies that leave each of its citizens (except for those with worthless conceptions of the good) with a fair opportunity for self-determination.

Neutrality. The third claim is that departures from neutrality of treatment involve denying holders of disfavored conceptions of the good a fair opportunity for self-determination. In general, the state's pro tanto reason to be neutral derives from the pro tanto reason it has to opt for policies consistent with fair opportunity for self-determination.

I take it that the first step in the argument is not especially controversial, but the second and third steps would require further elaboration and defense. With respect to the second step, it would be necessary to offer some account of *why* self-determination matters, which would explain why people who are denied a fair opportunity for self-determination are being denied something valuable. As for the third step, the case for neutrality of treatment rests on an assumption about fairness that stands in need of defense. Why assume that neutrality of treatment is needed for fair opportunity for self-determination? Perhaps, instead, fairness in this area means contriving to equalize the success of the conceptions of the good that people happen to hold, which would often imply a departure from neutrality of treatment. I shall consider these complicated issues in the next two sections, respectively.

For now, I turn my attention instead to perfectionist alternatives to neutrality. Even with the limited theoretical resources we have already assembled, it should be possible to illuminate why there is a neutralist constraint on perfectionism. As noted at the start of the chapter, a desire to vindicate certain forms of perfectionism lies at the heart of most recent criticisms of neutrality. Since opponents of minority cultural rights do not typically argue on perfectionist grounds, the debate about perfectionism is only obliquely related to the concerns of this book.[35] Still the debate is interesting in its own right and is an important test of the general adequacy of the proposed account of neutrality.

From the perspective of perfectionists, the two lacrosse examples we have been considering may seem beside the point. Since there is nothing especially worthwhile, or worthless, about lacrosse as an end, the critics can remain unfazed by the suggestion that the two examples contain objectionable departures from neutrality. I shall argue, however, that the examples, and the idea of fair opportunity for self-determination that explains our intuitions about them, already give us the tools we need to see why there is a neutralist constraint on perfectionism.

By perfectionism I mean not merely the view that there are objectively better or worse ways of living but also the claim that the state should sometimes adopt policies that favor relatively worthwhile conceptions of the good, and disfavor relatively worthless ones, to encourage people to lead better lives. One general reason why some neutralists have rejected perfectionism stems from skepticism about whether any actual state would adopt policies that reliably track the good. In many cases that one could envision, there is likely to be a gap between the conceptions of the good that are deemed to be worthwhile/ worthless and the ones that are, in fact, so. In fact, the conceptions being promoted will not be relatively valuable at all, or there will at least be reasonable disagreement as to their value. Although this seems like a valid concern to me, in what follows I will set it to one side. I shall grant for the sake of argument that the state's claims about value are well justified and argue that, even based on this improbable assumption, there is still an important neutrality-based limit on perfectionism.

At first glance it might seem that the logic of perfectionism protects it against the kind of fairness objection that was pursued in the lacrosse examples. A key feature of those cases was the allocation of benefits and burdens to different people. This is exactly what the benefit criterion tells the state not to do, and what it does do in the case of the lacrosse facility. The lacrosse tax involved a similar problem. Rather than be guided by the relevant criteria of just taxation, the burden of providing essential public goods was disproportionately placed on the shoulders of citizens who happened to pursue an interest in lacrosse. With perfectionist policies, by contrast, this misalignment of benefit and burden is supposed to disappear. If all goes well, the burden is self-effacing. Insofar as people shift away from the discouraged lifestyle and into the encouraged one, there is no cost to them. They simply enjoy the perks and the status associated with the encouraged way of life.[36]

---

[35] The discussion of perfectionism is relevant to the individuality-based critique mentioned in chapter 3.

[36] Sher (1997, 74) makes an argument along these lines in a slightly different context.

However, the disanalogy between perfectionist policies and the earlier cases is not as stark as this argument suggests. In the case of the lacrosse facility, for instance, it is also true that the burden would be self-effacing if non-enthusiasts could be encouraged by the construction of the new facility to become excited about the game. If their preferences change in the right way, then the taxes would become proportionate to the benefit and there would be no objectionable burden. This possibility is unlikely to change anyone's judgment about the lacrosse facility, however, since it is extremely unlikely that everyone's preferences would change in the direction required to make any legitimate complaint disappear. Things might be a little better with well-judged perfectionist policies, the main purpose of which is to bring about a change in values and preferences. But here too, given the general stickiness of preferences in response to government interventions, it would take a small miracle for a perfectionist policy to have a 100 percent success rate. There are bound to be at least some people who are unresponsive to the set of incentives and disincentives, and the supportive social environment, which are designed to get them to improve their conception of the good. In many cases, the success rate is likely to be disappointingly low.[37]

By assumption, the unresponsive members of the target group are already badly off by virtue of having an inferior conception of the good. The perfectionist policy, however, makes them even worse off. For one thing, they still have to pay the costs associated with the policy, whether it be the costs associated with providing a facility, or giving a tax break, for the encouraged conception of the good, or the penalties that are imposed on the discouraged one that they stubbornly continue to hold.

A second point goes beyond the narrow concern with fiscal fairness that I have emphasized up to this point. (I go even further beyond this concern in the next section.) A perfectionist policy that is neither fully successful nor fully unsuccessful may have a further negative consequence for those for whom it is unsuccessful. By virtue of its partial success, some of the people who had embraced the inferior conception of the good will be induced to abandon it in favor of the more valuable conception. Because of economies of scale, this shift may, in turn, raise the costs associated with the inferior conception for those who continue to hold it, and such a shift may also weaken the institutions and practices that are associated with that conception. As a result of these changes, for people who are stuck with it, the inferior conception becomes harder to realize and perhaps even less rich and valuable than it was before.

The upshot is that perfectionist policies more closely resemble the earlier lacrosse examples than some might think. Assuming that the state's judgments

---

[37] Sher (1997, 66) evinces more optimism that judicious use of incentives and inducements by the state might in fact produce a high level of success. I do not see any reason to share Sher's confidence on this point.

about relative value are justified, then such a policy does produce benefits for some. But it also, predictably, leaves others with a net burden: they do not get the benefit, but they do have to absorb the costs of the policy, and they are left with a conception of the good that is now harder to realize and even less rewarding. For situations that are governed by the benefit criterion, there would be seem to be a clear objection based on this misalignment of benefit and burden. Even for cases that are not governed by that criterion, such as "sin taxes" to finance government expenditures on essential public goods, there would seem to be an objection based on the idea of a fair opportunity for self-determination.

In general, then, I think that there is a fairness objection to perfectionist policies. As I emphasized earlier in the chapter, this objection is merely a pro tanto reason not to adopt such policies, and it does not carry any force at all with respect to certain limited categories of conceptions of the good.[38] The state's reason to endorse antiperfectionism is not always conclusory because, in addition to their interest in self-determination (fulfilling the conception of the good they happen to have), people can also be expected to have an interest in holding a maximally worthwhile conception of the good. It is conceivable that, under some conditions, the prospects for a well-designed perfectionist policy to advance the latter interest, without doing too much damage to the former, will be great enough that, on balance, the perfectionist policy is permissible. Neutrality's critics are fond of pointing to cases in which the perfectionist considerations seem very powerful, and the unfairness involved in the perfectionist policy seems relatively slight. Richard Arneson imagines a case in which the state comes by a windfall that allows it to subsidize opera at no cost to taxpayers.[39] Even setting aside this unlikely scenario, it might be argued that the per taxpayer cost of a modest state subsidy for opera would be so small, and the impact on the success of other conceptions of the good so slight, as to render complaints of unfairness otiose. If the subsidy really would save a valuable option such as opera from vanishing altogether, then, on balance, the policy seems defensible. The important point, however, is that there is some unfairness involved in such a policy, however slight, and thus the state's pro tanto reason to be neutral does not disappear. Moreover, with many perfectionist policies, the balance of considerations between the promotion of the good and the avoidance of unfairness is likely to tilt in the other direction. Just because the state's reason to be neutral is pro tanto, it does not follow that it is easily overridden.

[38] The latter includes "worthless" conceptions, as defined in n. 14 above. This is obviously a concession to perfectionism, albeit a small one given the definition of such conceptions.

[39] Arneson 2003, 198. Even here there might be an objectionable impact on opera's near rivals, such as contemporary musicals. If the state is successful at drawing some fans of musicals into an appreciation of opera, ticket prices for musicals might go up and quality might go down. This is a burden to the ardent fans of musicals who are not tempted by the state-backed opera alternative.

4.6 The Value of Self-Determination

In laying out the fairness justification of neutrality, I made no attempt to explain why, in general, self-determination is an interest that is plausible to attribute to persons. Nor did I justify the suggestion that the state leaves everyone a *fair* opportunity for self-determination by extending neutrality of treatment. The chapter's two concluding sections address each of these difficult issues in turn.

Given that people sometimes have unworthy or mistaken conceptions of the good, why should it matter if they enjoy the opportunity to fulfill the conception of the good that they happen to hold? In section 4.2 I granted that there may be some conceptions of the good that are worthless. Worthless conceptions of the good are ones that a person is better off not fulfilling, even if there is no realistic prospect that he will develop a more worthwhile conception of the good. But the class of worthless conceptions can be distinguished from the class of what I termed inferior conceptions of the good. These are conceptions that could be improved on in one way or another but which, on balance, are not worthless. Someone holding an inferior conception of the good would be better off revising her conception of the good, or even acquiring a wholly different conception, but barring those possibilities, she does better to fulfill the conception that she has than to see that conception frustrated. In the discussion that follows, we should think, not just about why self-determination matters in general, but about why it might be important for people to be able to fulfill their conception of the good, even when it is inferior.

In approaching these questions, it is helpful to distinguish the general reasons that account for self-determination's value from some special considerations. The special considerations apply to certain kinds of commitments that may form part of a person's conception of the good. They augment the value of self-determination with respect to those commitments.

The first general consideration is based on the relationship between self-determination and well-being. As a general matter, valuable goods and activities do not make a person's life go better unless those goods and activities figure in some positive way in the person's conception of the good. A standard way to promote well-being, accordingly, is to give persons the opportunity (the liberty, resources, and so on) they need to pursue and enjoy the conception of the good they happen to have. And a standard way of thwarting well-being is to deny them this opportunity, and thus to force them into living a life that does not accord with their conception of the good.

I say "standard," and not "necessary," because it is possible, in principle, to promote a person's well-being by helping him to acquire a more valuable conception of the good through means that act, in the short run, against his actual conception. This is the possibility that opens the door a crack to perfectionism.

But once the considerations of fairness introduced in the previous section are given their due, the constraints on perfectionism are apparent again. At least some of the policies favored by perfectionists will be disqualified by the indiscriminate character of the costs they entail. If the antecedent situation is just, it seems unfair that those policies will impose costs on people who, predictably, will not benefit. To restate the relationship between well-being and self-determination more exactly, then, we might say that a state seeking to promote well-being *and* concerned to treat its citizens fairly will normally regard self-determination as the value to promote.

The second way in which someone might contend that self-determination matters in general is by arguing that it is intrinsically valuable. Roughly speaking, the claim is that, even setting aside the connection with well-being, it is valuable for people to be autonomous. And an aspect of autonomy is shaping and directing one's own life according to one's own actual values and commitments. In parallel with the previous discussion of well-being, it would be a mistake to reduce autonomy to self-determination. As Raz argues, there are several distinct conditions of autonomy, including the availability of an adequate range of valuable options. Raz's own embrace of perfectionism in *The Morality of Freedom* rests on the claim that an autonomy-regarding state will sometimes act to ensure the availability of adequate options. Since *everyone's* autonomy is presumed to benefit from the presence of an adequate range of options, an advantage of Raz's argument is that it sidesteps the fairness objection that I have been pressing.

There is less to this autonomy-based defense of perfectionism than meets the eye, however. Complex liberal societies are home to thousands of different kinds of options, covering every aspect of life. Normally one might expect such societies to be well over the threshold of adequacy, even without special state support for particularly valuable options. In a later essay Raz himself seems to agree: "But while it is reasonable to surmise that just about all societies have an adequate range of acceptable options available in them, many of them bar sections of their populations—foreigners, the poor, people of colour, people with a disapproved-of sexual orientation—from access to an adequate range of valuable options."[40] The second half of this remark does express doubts about whether certain sections of society enjoy access to an adequate range of options. But the sorts of social reforms that are needed to remedy the problem of blocked access do *not* involve departures from neutrality. They call for inclusiveness, redistribution, nondiscrimination, and the redefinition of certain goods (for example, marriage) so that the benefits they involve (and that are provided, in part, by the state) are available to all. To qualify the earlier claim about self-determination and autonomy, then, we might say that, where the background conditions (including adequacy of options) are secure, the

[40] Raz 1994, 24.

usual way of promoting autonomy is by giving citizens the opportunity to be self-determining.

In addition to these general considerations, the presence of certain special commitments in a person's conception of the good makes self-determination an even more important interest with respect to those commitments. It would be an especially serious setback for an individual to be denied a fair opportunity to fulfill these commitments. As a result, when treating a particular conception of the good neutrally means treating these special commitments neutrally, the state's reason to be neutral is even weightier than it is for more generic elements of conceptions of the good.

There is no space here to develop a full account of what makes a commitment special in this sense. Intuitively, however, there are some areas of life where it seems especially important that a person enjoy the opportunity to conduct her life on the basis of her own values and purposes. A key part of directing one's own life is developing and pursuing one's own religious and moral outlook, for instance. Intimacy, sexuality, friendship, and basic relationships of community with others also seem like areas in which it is especially important for the individual to be able to connect her life's actual course with her own values and commitments.

A variety of factors contribute to the special character of commitments in these areas. Without claiming to offer an exhaustive list, let me mention three such factors.

Pivotal Role

In some cases, it is the central and pivotal position that a particular commitment occupies in a whole set of a person's ends that lends it special significance. If a particular option is not open to people corresponding to such a commitment, then not only will that commitment be frustrated, but other preferences and values that are connected with it will be too. If a person is denied the opportunity to worship as he sees fit, for instance, a number of his other values and preferences may be adversely impacted, and not just his views on how to worship. The denial of worship may prevent him from establishing and maintaining a relationship of religious community with others (coreligionists) and thereby close off to him a set of options he might value that would only be possible in the context of that relationship. Or consider somebody who values the opportunity to use her maternal language. When public institutions elect not to provide that opportunity, the community of speakers of that language may be put in jeopardy. This in turn could lead to the disappearance of options that are typically valued and kept alive by members of that community. In general, a commitment will often have a pivotal role when it involves an attachment to some particular relationship in the context of which distinctive options are made possible. A nonneutral policy that forecloses the relationship also weakens or eliminates the additional options.

NONNEGOTIABLE CHARACTER

Some conceptions of the good, or elements of such a conception, have a nonnegotiable character.[41] A conception has such a character when part of what it is to affirm the conception is to believe that some of the values it includes are binding in a nonnegotiable fashion. One might believe, for instance, that it would be ethically wrong not to be appropriately responsive to some particular value that makes up one's conception of the good. Or one might believe that it would betray or compromise a relationship with others of central importance if one did not act appropriately on a particular value. These beliefs about value present themselves to their bearers as nonnegotiable in the sense that they are taken to have strict precedence over the person's other ends and commitments. A person who thought that a particular commitment could be traded off against money and convenience, for instance, would be regarded as having a different conception of the good than someone who believed such a trade-off to be illegitimate.

There are a variety of reasons for thinking that individuals have an especially urgent interest in being able to pursue and enjoy the commitments they take to be nonnegotiable in character. First, it is likely to be psychologically painful for people to be put in a position where they are unable to honor their nonnegotiable commitments. They may agonize over their situation and be left with a lasting sense of failure or guilt. Second, the position they find themselves in may strain their commitment to the institutions to which they are subject, making it impossible for them to feel fully at home under those institutions and making it harder for others to count on their willing support for those institutions.[42] Third, people may find that their nonnegotiable commitments are socially enforced by members of a community that shares their conception of the good, making them vulnerable to a range of different sanctions if they fail to honor those commitments.[43]

RECOGNITIONAL SALIENCE

In yet other cases, commitments are special by virtue of being implicated in the basic relationships of respect and recognition that a person enjoys with other

---

[41] Rawls emphasizes this in various places when he sketches an account of the liberty of conscience to illustrate some more general points about the basis and special priority of the basic liberties. See Rawls 1999a, 182; 2001, 105; 2005, 311–12. See also Cohen 1998; 2002, 104–6.

[42] Rawls (1999a, 475) mentions the "strains of commitment" in connection with the priority of the basic liberties. See also the discussion of the "first moral power" in Rawls 2005, 315–20.

[43] For this point, see Waldron 2002, 24.

members of society. A decision by the state not to extend a person a fair opportunity to realize such a commitment could reasonably be regarded as denigrating by persons who affirm that commitment. In some cases, such a policy is denigrating because it implies a negative judgment about the person's capacity to direct his own life. By blocking the realization of a particular commitment without a sufficiently compelling reason, the nonneutral policy falsely implies that the commitment in question is worthless or deeply deficient. Where that commitment has special significance to the person who holds it (e.g., he regards it as central to who he is, to his identity), the person may reasonably regard the policy as expressing a judgment about his overall capacity to direct his own life. In other cases, what makes a policy denigrating is the message of exclusion it sends. By failing to treat the frustration of certain commitments as having any real importance, a nonneutral policy suggests that the bearers of those commitments are not full or "real" members of the community, and perhaps, additionally, that their pursuit of the commitment in the environs of the community is a threat to the community's values and way of life.

Again, the exclusionary character of the message seems dependent on the central importance, or special significance, of the commitment for the people who are affected. A state subsidy for local spinach growers may nonneutrally disfavor spinach haters, but, in most contexts at least, it does not convey any disparaging message of exclusion, or any kind of general judgment on the capacity of spinach haters to manage their own lives. By contrast, given the special significance of sexuality for many people, the denial of marriage rights to same-sex couples (even while they are extended to opposite-sex couples) is an example of a self-determination-diminishing, nonneutral policy that sends an unjustifiably disparaging and exclusionary message to gays and lesbians. Restrictions on self-determination are bad, in this kind of case, not just because they leave a person less able to follow his or her values and preferences, but because their imposition involves serious expressive harms.[44]

It should be immediately clear from each of these three considerations—pivotal role, nonnegotiable character, and recognitional salience—that they apply with varying degrees of force to different conceptions of the good and to different elements within particular conceptions of the good. This is particularly obvious in the case of the nonnegotiable character reason. Some preferences and beliefs about value will present themselves to their bearers as having such a character, but many will not. An individual will regard some of her commitments as obligations of conscience, and some as essential to relationships that are of central importance in her life. But other of her commitments will not implicate her conscience or her judgments about important relationships

---

[44] For a helpful discussion of the relationship between neutrality and expressive harms, see Wall 2010, 246–55.

of belonging and affiliation. The case for neutrality is stronger for the former kind of commitment and weaker for the latter. Neutrality of treatment is thus especially robust when it applies to aspects of conceptions of the good that involve religion and conscience, culture, family, sexuality, artistic endeavor, and other goods that are likely to seem nonnegotiable to the individual. Neutrality is less robust with respect to many preferences regarding leisure and ordinary consumption, which are unlikely to have a nonnegotiable character.

The pivotal role and recognitonal salience considerations suggest a very similar conclusion. When a person exercises her judgment about basic relationships of belonging and affiliation, these seem like particularly important ways in which she seeks to shape and direct her own life. When the person's judgments of this kind are blocked, there may be knock-on consequences for her access to other options she values. Likewise a state policy that impedes an individual from pursuing and enjoying a good that is implicated in her conscience, or in her basic relationships with others, has a more damaging expressive message than a policy that merely implicates a person's preferences for ordinary consumption and leisure. Again, then, on the basis of the centrality and respect considerations, we might expect neutrality to be especially robust in the areas of religion and conscience, culture, family, sexuality, and the like, and less robust when it concerns goods that are of mere leisure or consumption value to the individual. This variation is an important feature of my account.

For goods in which these considerations are particularly salient, then, I believe that neutrality should be regarded as a fairly robust commitment. Given what is at stake for the individual in being able to realize his own conception of the good in these areas, and the contribution that neutrality makes to this ability, it would be a mistake to think that just any reason for departing from neutrality that might present itself would be sufficient. As I have stressed, these arguments for the robustness of neutrality do not imply that the state has a conclusory reason to be neutral. Even where neutrality is very robust, there may be sufficiently weighty considerations on the other side that compel the state to depart from neutrality. The exercise of a worthwhile conception of the good may still conflict with legitimate public interests in ways that are relevant to the overall balance of reasons. And, as I have allowed, the state may judge that it has a fairly low-cost but high pay-off opportunity to pursue a perfectionist end. The point of the robustness claim is to establish that the state should not depart from neutrality lightly. Given the values that are at stake, the state should not, for instance, depart from neutrality because of inconvenience, or small financial costs, or slight increases in social friction, or because of highly conjectural and marginal improvements in even important public objectives. These sorts of reasons for action all fail to do justice to the interest that individuals have in self-determination, especially where the special considerations can be invoked.

4.7 Fairness and Neutral Treatment

Suppose it is granted that self-determination is often something of considerable value for individuals. The key problem then becomes how to interpret the suggestion that the state should leave its citizens with a fair opportunity for self-determination. I have suggested that a correct understanding of fairness in this context requires the state to extend neutral treatment to different conceptions of the good. By adopting policies that are equally accommodating of rival conceptions of the good, the state can reasonably claim that it is not taking sides between those conceptions. If one conception is ultimately unsuccessful (in one or other of the senses mentioned earlier), it would be natural to deflect a complaint about that outcome by pointing to the fairness of the background conditions established by the state's observance of neutral treatment.[45] By contrast, if the state was less accommodating toward a conception that is ultimately unsuccessful, then this response is unavailable and a complaint would have at least some prima facie force.

It might be questioned, however, whether the value of self-determination really does support neutrality of treatment in the way that I have been supposing. I have been arguing the following:

Self-determination. Citizens have an important interest in self-determination.

In addition, an important assumption of the whole discussion has been

Equal consideration. The state should give equal consideration to the interests of all its citizens.

These two premises seem to imply the following:

Equal achievement. All else being equal, the state should seek to make people as equal as possible in the degree to which they achieve self-determination.

The problem is that equal achievement implies that the state should *not* observe neutrality of treatment. Under neutrality of treatment, it is predictable that some conceptions of the good will be more successful than others. This is why neutrality of treatment is different from neutrality of effects. In the cricket/softball example developed earlier, for instance, the local authority extends neutral treatment with predictably nonneutral effects. Whereas softball lovers will experience a fairly high level of self-determination—they will be able to pursue and enjoy the sporting preferences that they actually hold—cricket lovers will not be particularly successful at pursuing and enjoying their

---

[45] Rawls 2005, 198–99.

conception of the good. An authority that was really concerned to leave soft-ball lovers and cricket lovers as equal as possible in the degree to which they achieve self-determination would not opt for neutral treatment. Instead, it would tilt its policies in favor of cricket just to the point where the two activities have roughly equal prospects of success.

So, does the argument developed in the preceding sections in fact support some version of neutrality of effects rather than neutrality of treatment? I do not think so. A first point to emphasize is that the argument for neutrality of treatment explicitly invokes fairness. The claim is not that neutrality of treatment leaves people equal in the degree to which they achieve self-determination but that (combined with other conditions) it leaves citizens with a fair opportunity for self-determination. Even if softball lovers and cricket lovers do not achieve equal levels of self-determination in our example, they do enjoy a fair opportunity for self-determination. That, at least, is the claim.

But the objection under consideration might seem to be valid even against the claim that neutrality of treatment offers a fair opportunity for self-determination. If people have an important interest in self-determination, and the state has a duty to give equal consideration to the interests of all its citizens, then why is equalizing the achievement of self-determination, rather than the opportunity for self-determination, not the fair approach to take?

To see why the objection is faulty, it is necessary to take a closer look at the inference from self-determination and equal consideration to equal achievement. Although the premises are not in dispute, the inference is invalid in an interesting and significant way. Once the deficiency in the argument is identified and clarified, neutrality of treatment reemerges as the most plausible implication of accepting the two premises.

To see the structure of the problem, consider a more basic argument:

Care. William has an interest in being cared for.
Duty to promote. Ann has a duty to promote William's interests.
Duty to care. Ann has a duty to ensure that William is cared for.

A problem with inferring duty to care from the two preceding premises is that Ann may not be the only person with a duty to promote William's interests. If she is not, then her duty is not necessarily to ensure that William is cared for, but to do her *fair share* in caring for William. Imagine that William is an ailing elderly person, and Ann is one of several concerned neighbors. The neighbors agree that they will take turns looking in on William. Under this scenario, Ann's duty is to take her turn. Even though William's interest is an important one, and Ann has a general duty to promote those interests, the specific content of Ann's duty is limited to making a discrete contribution to promoting William's interest. The contributions that make up the remainder of the care that is owed to William are the responsibility of other people. It is true that, if one of those other people were to fail to discharge his or her responsibility,

Ann may have a backup duty to step in and do more. But when she does more in such a context, it is understood that she is doing more than fairness requires. As a matter of fairness, Ann is required only to take her turn.

A variation on this example is especially relevant for our problem. Suppose there are no other neighbors but that William is capable of doing certain things for himself. It is still the case that he has an interest in being cared for, and that Ann has a duty to promote his interests. Again we might think that the specific content of Ann's duty in this situation is limited. For instance, it seems plausible to say that William is responsible for caring for himself as far as he can, and Ann's duty is to do whatever else is needed to bring William up to an adequate level of care. This circumscription of Ann's duty is especially intuitive in cases where Ann has duties of care to many people. If Ann were to take on all aspects of William's care and disregard William's responsibility for the aspects of his care that he is capable of handling, then she would have less time and energy to devote to the care of others.

Returning to the objection, we can now see why equal achievement does not necessarily follow from self-determination and equal consideration. It may be that other people share with the state some responsibility for the achievement of self-determination. If that were the case, then the state's obligation would be to do its part. The *importance* of its doing its part would be driven by the importance of the interest that is being served—in this case, the interest in self-determination. But the *content* of the state's obligation is not to fully promote the interest, or to leave people equally situated with respect to the realization of the interest, but to do its part equally for all its citizens.

The main reason to think that the state's responsibility is limited in this way is familiar from liberal political theory. A key assumption of liberal thought is that citizens should be regarded as responsible for their own conceptions of the good. It is the state's responsibility to provide fair background conditions, including the basic liberties, equality of opportunity, a fair distribution of resources, and—if my argument is correct—neutrality of treatment. It is the individual's responsibility to adjust his own conception in the light of these fair background conditions. If the state does its part, by establishing fair background conditions, but an individual ends up with a relatively unsuccessful conception of the good, this is regarded as the individual's own responsibility rather than as an indication that the state has failed to provide him with a fair opportunity for self-determination. This is why the self-determination and equal consideration premises imply neutrality of treatment rather than neutrality of effects.

The case for neutrality of treatment rests, then, on what Rawls calls "a social division of responsibility." As Rawls explains it, this is the idea that

> society, citizens as a collective body, accepts responsibility for maintaining the equal basic liberties and fair equality of opportunity, and for

providing a fair share of the primary goods for all within this frame-work; while citizens as individuals and associations accept responsibil-ity for revising and adjusting their ends and aspirations in view of the all-purpose means they can expect, given their present and foreseeable situation.[46]

As I have said from the outset, neutrality of treatment is a liberal view of neu-trality, and thus it should be no surprise that it rests on one of the core assump-tions of liberal political theory.[47]

Of course, this general strategy for defending neutrality of treatment is only as persuasive as the assumption about responsibility on which it relies. If liberal theorists are wrong to regard persons as responsible for adjusting their own conceptions of the good in the light of fair background conditions, then the state's responsibilities—the responsibilities of society—are correspond-ingly greater. Given the importance of self-determination, this may mean that the state should equalize achievement after all, rather than treatment. Alter-natively, it may be that liberal theory is wrong to consider people *generally* responsible for their conceptions of the good, even if they are responsible in some situations.[48] On such a view, neutrality of treatment would offer a fair opportunity for self-determination in cases where responsibility is appropri-ately assigned to the individual, but in other cases, where the individual can-not reasonably be regarded as responsible, some more active form of assistance for struggling conceptions of the good would be called for by fairness.[49]

My principal aim in the book is to develop a liberal approach to thinking about minority rights, not to vindicate the foundational assumptions of lib-eral thought. If the argument of this chapter has shown neutrality of treatment to be an implication of liberal values and assumptions, then it has prepared the way for the chapters to follow, which seek to articulate a liberal approach to minority rights. Any attempt, in this context, to explore foundational ques-tions about responsibility in response to concerns about liberalism's assump-tion of a social division of labor is bound to seem unsatisfactory. The literature on these complex and difficult issues is large, and the truth about them is not obvious one way or another.

Still, leaving the matter so up in the air also seems highly unsatisfactory. For all that has been said, it could be that the weight of the argument for neutrality of treatment has been made to rest on the least plausible assumption in liberal theory. In addition, it is sometimes suggested that liberal assumptions about

[46] Ibid., 189.

[47] Other liberal theorists who emphasize the assumption include Kymlicka 1989a; 1989b; 1990; Dworkin 2000; Barry 2001; Scanlon 2006.

[48] For this view, see Cohen 1989; 2004; Arneson 1989; 1990.

[49] Wall (2001) explores what neutrality might look like in the event that assumptions about responsi-bility for preferences are relaxed or abandoned.

responsibility are particularly implausible in relation to cultural attachments.[50] With these concerns in mind, let me offer two sets of observations designed to motivate the liberal assumption about responsibility. One emphasizes the assumption's roots in pre-theoretical intuitions and judgments. The other suggests that the assumption's theoretical credentials are respectable as well.

One point in favor of the social division of labor is that it resonates with widely shared intuitions and judgments. Faced with the softball/cricket case described earlier, most people would not view the outcome as unfair or think that the local authority had treated cricket lovers unfairly. They would accept that a local authority that makes a field open for any team sport, without any special restrictions or regulations, is treating lovers of the two sports fairly, even if the existing distribution of tastes in the community make it predictable that one sport will in fact be more successful than another. Implicit in this judgment is the liberal assumption of the social division of labor: the state's responsibility to promote self-determination is limited to providing fair background conditions; it is the individual's responsibility to achieve self-determination within those parameters.

The fit between the social division of labor and everyday intuitions and judgments becomes even tighter once some of the unpalatable implications of rejecting the liberal assumption are exposed. The main point is a familiar one. Where individuals are not responsible for their conceptions of the good, the state is called on to intervene on behalf of relatively unsuccessful conceptions. It becomes a matter of unfairness that cricket lovers cannot get a game together, and the state must do something, either to promote cricket or to compensate the cricket lovers for their disadvantage. But while this implication may seem harmless enough in the case of the disappointed cricketers, it also puts the state on the hook for some extravagantly expensive tastes.

Recall the case of Martin from section 3.4. His idea of the good life involves control over a large estate, drinking expensive wine, having household staff at his disposal, possessing a townhouse in the city, and flying first class. In a society that distributes resources fairly and strives to establish neutrality of treatment, it seems safe to assume that he will not succeed at satisfying all these preferences. Indeed, it seems likely that Martin's conception of the good will be less successful under these conditions than the more modest conceptions affirmed by some of his fellow citizens. If Martin is not responsible for his preferences, then it seems that he is owed a subsidy that might leave him with many times the resources provided to his fellow citizens who have more modest preferences.[51] On pain of leaving Martin without a fair opportunity

[50] Cohen 1999; Mason 2006.

[51] It is possible that Martin deliberately cultivated his extravagant tastes in the way that Louis does in Dworkin's much-discussed example (Dworkin 2000; for discussion, see Cohen 1989; 2004; Dworkin

for self-determination, his fellow citizens will be on the hook for his tastes and preferences, leaving them with a diminished share of secure resources with which to pursue their own ambitions. Since many people would find this consequence deeply problematic, it looks like a good reason to endorse liberalism's social division of responsibility.

This argument about pre-theoretical intuitions offers important support to the liberal idea of a social division of responsibility. It shows that there is cost to rejecting that idea, which consists in having to maintain, with a straight face, that as a matter of fairness certain extravagant preferences ought to be subsidized by people with more modest preferences. The difficult question is whether the social division of labor has a deeper theoretical plausibility to back up its resonance with pre-theoretical intuitions. Can we go further than pointing out the awkward implications of rejecting the liberal assumption, and actually justify the assumption by making and defending a substantive claim about responsibility?

For the reasons mentioned earlier, a proper exploration of these issues is beyond the purview of the present chapter and book. But I do want to offer at least a brief sketch of an affirmative answer. The argument has two main steps. The first relates responsibility to choice, and the second relates choice and preference. As will quickly become apparent, the result is less a watertight argument than an indication of how such an argument might go and of which issues would need to be explored more carefully. It is hoped that enough will be said to dispel the impression that neutrality of treatment is grounded in an obviously flawed assumption about responsibility.

As a prelude to the first step, notice that we are interested in "responsibility" in a very specific sense. We want to know whether an individual who holds a relatively unsuccessful conception of the good (like cricket in our example) should be expected to put up with this disadvantage himself, or whether others should step in to assist him, either by preventing the disadvantage from arising in the first place or by offering some compensation when it does. To regard the individual as responsible, in the sense that interests us, is to opt for the first of these possibilities.[52]

2004). Martin would then be responsible for his tastes, and his case would not be a counterexample to views that are bent on questioning the social division of labor. But, for two reasons, this does not provide a general reason for dismissing the problem raised by Martin. One is that, whatever we assume about Martin, there may be Martin-like cases in which there was no deliberate cultivation of tastes. Second, Martin presumably cultivated his tastes on the basis of an unchosen, higher-order ideal of life; and that ideal would be unsuccessful if he were to opt not to deliberately cultivate the tastes in question. So even Martin would have a claim on additional resources after all. That was Dworkin's point about Louis.

[52] I thus have in mind what Scanlon (1998, 248–49) calls "substantive responsibility." Judgments about substantive responsibility concern what people are required or not required to do for one another. We are interested in whether society is required by fairness to come to the assistance of people by virtue of their having relatively unsuccessful conceptions of the good, or whether instead the social division of labor should prevail.

With this in the background, the first step of the argument simply consists in pointing out a familiar reason for regarding someone as responsible with respect to certain burdens and disadvantages. When, under the right circumstances, some condition is subject to a person's choice, then any complaint the person might have about burdens or disadvantages associated with that condition is diminished or eliminated altogether.[53] Clearly, the circumstances under which choice has this effect are limited in important ways. It might be wrong to make a person choose between X and Y, in which case the fact that she chooses Y does not diminish any complaint she might have about the burdens associated with Y. But choice under fair background conditions does have at least some power to make it appropriate to expect a person to put up with the burdens that result. The intuitive idea is that, where choice under fair conditions is possible, a person has a reasonable opportunity to avoid the burdensome condition and thus has no significant complaint if he does end up facing that condition.

The main question, then, is whether preferences are to be considered as "subject to choice" in the sense that would legitimate the expectation that people put up with their hard-to-realize preferences. Clearly, there are some ways of construing the idea of being subject to choice that would *not* imply that people should be regarded as generally responsible for their preferences. Suppose, for instance, that a condition is considered subject to choice only if the condition was actually chosen by the individual at some point in the past. If this is what being subject to choice implies, then clearly preferences are not, in general, subject to choice. As a matter of fact, for the vast majority of people, many preferences were not consciously chosen at any point in their lives.

This brings us to the second step of the argument, which consists in pointing out that there are alternative ways of understanding being "subject to choice" that are more congenial to the liberal assumption of responsibility for preferences. One approach that seems especially promising is Scanlon's "value of choice" account of responsibility.[54] Scanlon distinguishes, in effect, between having a choice and making a choice. Having a choice is a matter of having an array of reasonable options, having information about those options, and having the capacity for discrimination between and reflection about one's options. It is distinct from making a choice, which involves a more reflective and intentional act of will where one consciously selects one of the options. One can have a choice without making a choice when one possesses the appropriate opportunity to choose but then drifts forgetfully or inattentively into one option rather than others. Scanlon's key thesis about "substantive" responsibility is that—in a range of situations—having a choice is sufficient for responsibility

---

[53] This principle is central to Scanlon's account of substantive responsibility. See ibid., 249, 251, 256–67.

[54] Ibid., 256–67.

and thus making a choice is not necessary. There is value in having choice, and this value makes it reasonable to assign people responsibility for certain outcomes that arise when they have a choice.

If Scanlon's thesis is correct, then the assumption that individuals can generally be regarded as responsible for their preferences starts to gain plausibility.[55] Or at least it does so in the conditions of a liberal society. Under such conditions, one might expect the following empirical generalizations to hold for most people:

> *Capacity condition.* Citizens are socialized into possessing a capacity for a conception of the good, including a capacity to reflect on and revise their conception of the good.
>
> *Pluralism condition.* There is a rich array of valuable options and "experiments in living" available in the society.
>
> *Information condition.* The freedoms of speech, association, and personal mobility mean that the existence and character of the society's different options are widely known.
>
> *Social norm condition.* There is a social norm of responsibility for one's preferences.

When these conditions of a liberal society are in place, it is plausible to think that people have a reasonable opportunity to avoid unsuccessful conceptions of the good should they so choose. They may not actively choose their preferences—most people do not—but they have a choice and could, over the course of their lives, avoid having an unsuccessful conception of the good by choosing appropriately.

Obviously the key question raised by this argument is whether it is true that people *could* avoid having an unsuccessful conception of the good by choosing appropriately. In general, there is very little a person can do to make the conception she actually holds more successful. Remember that success is defined in terms of the number of people who hold the conception and the ease with which the conception is pursued and realized. Since these indicators of success are largely determined by broader social trends (the decisions of thousands, even millions of other individuals), and by other given facts such as material scarcity, there is not much opportunity for a person to avoid a lack of success in this way.

If people can avoid having an unsuccessful conception of the good by choosing appropriately, it is because they can make choices over the course of their lives that will lead them to have a different, more successful conception of the good. This claim, if true, would have to rest on two propositions. The first is that, under the conditions of a liberal society, people have a great many

---

[55] Scanlon (2006) discusses responsibility for preferences. The discussion is more cautious than the suggestion I venture but is compatible with it.

valuable alternatives to their current conception that they can explore. And the second is that experimenting with valuable alternatives is normally a reliable way for people who aspire to a more successful conception of the good to reshape their preferences. Together the two propositions imply that people looking to reshape their preferences will encounter valuable options, and that they have at least some capacity to recognize and respond to value when they find it.

There is an empirical proposition at the heart of this claim, so of course the possibility that the proposition is false cannot be ruled out a priori. In the view of responsibility being gestured at here, our responsibility for our preferences is not a purely conceptual matter but is the empirically contingent implication of certain capacities we have and conditions and opportunities we face. Having noted the empirical character of the claim, however, it is important not to dismiss it too hastily. To defeat the claim, it would be insufficient, for instance, to observe that people do not tend to change their conception of the good whenever they are confronted with an alternative set of ends that are valuable. For one thing, altering one's values and beliefs may require a fairly deep immersion in a new activity or way of life: one is unlikely to see the value in it right away.

Even more important, many people will be loathe to abandon their current conception of the good and embrace the value in new activities and ways of life because they are perfectly content with their current conception of the good, *even though it may be relatively unsuccessful*. As Ronald Dworkin has emphasized in his account of responsibility for preferences, most people tend to identify with their conception of the good; they regard it as an expression of their personality, rather than an externally imposed encumbrance, and they do not wish to be rid of it.[56] We should not expect people with such attitudes to respond to valuable alternatives in the same way as people who really care about having a successful conception of the good and are looking for something different. Not *wanting* a different set of preferences is obviously different from not being *able* to cultivate new preferences by making appropriate choices. It is the latter, not the former, that is relevant to responsibility in the view being proposed.

To recap, then, I have been making two main points in response to concerns that the liberal assumption of a social division of labor represents a shaky foundation on which to rest the case for neutrality of treatment. The first is that rejecting that division leads to a problematic indulging of expensive tastes.

[56] For Dworkin (2000), identification is the basis of responsibility for preferences. In the view being sketched here, by contrast, identification enters into the argument in a more subordinate role. The fact of identification helps to explain why people often do not take up the opportunities they have for revising their conception of the good. It is the opportunities that ground responsibility, not the fact of identification.

The second is that, despite initial appearances to the contrary, a link between choice, preference, and responsibility can be postulated that helps to bolster the social division of labor.

One worry about the foregoing argument is that it may have proved too much. Consider the position of Muslims in a state that officially establishes Christianity. Their conception of the good is unequally accommodated by the state. Suppose that there is no compelling reason for them to be treated in this way, and they lodge a complaint about the situation. Does the account I have been sketching imply that their complaint can easily be dismissed? The critique would have that implication if it licensed the state to make the following response: "If Muslims do not like the way they are being treated in a Christian state, they are welcome to convert to Christianity." At first glance the argument I have been making seems to allow a version of such a response. It is problematic to insist that Muslims are disadvantaged by their convictions since the social division of labor implies that they should take responsibility for their own conceptions of the good. It is true, of course, that some Muslims may not have consciously chosen their religious beliefs or values. But in the view sketched above, the crucial question is whether they had an adequate opportunity to develop alternative convictions, and, in the context of a liberal society at least, it seems plausible to think that they did have such an opportunity. So what is the rejoinder? Since the suggestion that Muslims should convert or accept unequal treatment seems preposterous, the example raises doubts about the whole strategy for defending the social division of labor that I have been pursuing.

If the idea of responsibility for preferences can be manipulated in this way, then other arguments advanced in this chapter also look suspect. Consider a perfectionist state that promotes valuable conceptions of the good over inferior ones. If the earlier analysis was correct, this policy will leave people who cling stubbornly to their inferior conception with a diminished opportunity for self-determination. Rather than acknowledge this as an objection to state perfectionism, however, perhaps the perfectionist could invoke responsibility for preferences? They might say that there is nothing unfair about the costs imposed by state perfectionism so long as those who end up clinging to inferior conceptions had an adequate opportunity to develop a superior conception and thus to avoid those costs.

This line of objection ignores an important qualification in the earlier discussion of responsibility for preferences and thus rests on an oversimplification of that idea. It is a mistake to think that choice always generates responsibility. As I noted earlier, in some situations it would be wrong to make a person choose between two options, in which case the fact that the person does choose one or other option does not justify her bearing the burdens associated with that option. A professor cannot expect students to pay him a special fee for office hours, even if office consultations are optional, because he has no right to leave students with a choice between paying him and going without help. The fact that students have a choice does not legitimate either outcome. The requirement that the opportunity to choose be given against a backdrop of fair background conditions is critical for the account being offered here. Without fair background conditions, it is unreasonable for the policy that produces the burden to expect individuals to choose between the alternatives it leaves, and thus the mere fact that those individuals had a choice is insufficient to render the outcome fair.

Once this feature of responsibility arguments is noted, it is apparent that the objection overlooks an important asymmetry between the different contexts in which the argument is invoked. In considering alternatives to the social division of labor, a crucial part of the argument is that all the relevant parties are assumed to have a fair share of resources and to enjoy the neutral treatment of their conceptions of the good. It was against this baseline that Martin's complaint about unequal success, for instance, seemed unconvincing. Martin has the same set of resources as anyone else, and his conception enjoys the same level of accommodation. Why should he have a claim on *additional* resources simply because his conception is relatively unsuccessful *if* he could have chosen to develop a more modest conception?

When the same arguments are wielded against complaints of unequal accommodation, by contrast, they are drained of their force. My imagined Muslims are not complaining about unequal success in a context of equal treatment. They are complaining about unequal treatment arising because of state establishment of Christianity. Absent some further argument—and it is hard to imagine what that would be—the state establishment of Christianity is not a normatively privileged baseline. A demand for a departure from that baseline is not, therefore, immediately refuted by the observation that the condition giving rise to the demand is in some sense self-imposed.

The same is true, I think, of the perfectionist appeal to responsibility for preferences imagined earlier, although here there may be a real argument to be had. The complaint of those who maintain an inferior conception of the good in the face of perfectionist policies is not one of unequal success in a context of equal treatment. It is a complaint about unequal treatment. It is true that perfectionists might argue that a policy of greater accommodation for superior conceptions of the good is a reasonable enough baseline to make choice relevant for fairness. But this argument is vulnerable to the rejoinder that the perfectionist policy leaves too little space for the self-determination of those who maintain an inferior conception. They are left with a choice between abandoning their conception of the good, which is clearly an affront to their self-determination, and continuing to pursue it but with a cost or penalty that is not imposed on conceptions deemed to be superior.

To summarize: I have been arguing that neutral treatment is plausibly regarded as an implication of fair opportunity for self-determination. I have mainly done so by criticizing a major alternative to this view, which suggests that neutrality of effects (in some form or other) is the more natural implication of fairness. This alternative does not take seriously enough the liberal idea of a social division of labor. The rejection of this idea leads to unpalatable results (the indulging of extravagant tastes), while the idea itself can be given a plausible defense. Moreover, the defense that can be provided is clear about its own limits. It illuminates why responsibility for preferences cannot be invoked to justify arrangements that depart from neutrality of treatment.

CHAPTER 5

Equal Recognition

5.1 Justice and Cultural Decline: Three Views

Consider some minority culture that is faring poorly. It may be that particular practices associated with the culture are disappearing, or that there is some sense in which the culture as a whole has entered into decline. As I suggested in chapter 2, this second scenario would arise if the institutions and practices that had functioned historically to socialize new generations into the culture were being gradually superseded by formative processes associated with the majority culture.

The question that I shall explore picks up where chapter 3 left off. Under what conditions, if any, are there reasons for thinking that people have a complaint based on justice about the decline of the minority culture? More specifically: under what conditions can people justifiably make such a complaint while adopting a broadly liberal account of what justice is?

To further refine the question, recall the distinction I introduced in section 1.3 between "minority-regarding" and "third-party-regarding" reasons of principle that might ground complaints of justice. Since people benefit in various ways from the flourishing of cultures they are not members of, they could conceivably have complaints based on justice when somebody else's culture enters into decline. In general, justice has to do with the distribution of benefits and burdens, and we benefit, all else being equal, from living in a richer and more diverse world. For the reasons I explained in section 1.3, however, my focus here is on the situation of members. I am interested in identifying the conditions under which members of some declining minority culture have a complaint based on liberal justice about the situation in which they find themselves.

We should begin by rejecting the extreme view that says that liberal principles *never* imply that the decline of some particular culture involves an injustice. Cultural decline sometimes occurs as a result of forms of persecution that constitute obvious violations of standard liberal commitments. These forms of persecution, which are all too familiar in the world in which we live, involve everything from genocide and ethnic cleansing, to denials of basic rights and liberties, to racism and job discrimination, to exclusion from the full enjoyment of education, health, or housing benefits. When a minority culture goes into decline because its members are facing one or more of these oppressive conditions, liberals should have no trouble saying that an injustice has occurred.

The difficult theoretical question is whether some further protection against cultural decline is required by liberal principles. To focus on this question, we might imagine a case in which a culture is vulnerable to decline even though its members are not facing any of the oppressive conditions mentioned above. In particular, we might imagine that the members of the cultural minority are secure in their enjoyment of a standard package of liberal rights and entitlements. To fix ideas, I shall assume that this "standard package" includes

— the basic liberties, as defined and defended by Rawls;
— freedom from discrimination in the economy and civil society;
— a "social minimum," consisting of an income floor and/or essential goods and services provided in kind; and
— various programs and policies that promote what Rawls calls "fair equality of opportunity."

Let us also say that this standard package is "secure" for cultural minorities, when people who belong to those minorities (a) have enjoyed the standard package in the recent past, (b) enjoy it currently, and (c) can reasonably expect to enjoy it in the future even if their culture goes into decline.

By securing the standard liberal package for its cultural minorities, a state would go some ways toward safeguarding those minorities against cultural decline. Members of the minorities would not be hounded by oppressive conditions into abandoning their culture. The question I want to explore, however, is whether securing the standard liberal package for minorities is *all* the protection against cultural decline that is owed as a matter of liberal justice.

An affirmative answer to this question provides a useful null hypothesis against which various alternative answers can be tested. I shall call this null hypothesis "basic liberal proceduralism" and understand it as follows:

> *Basic liberal proceduralism.* So long as the decline of a minority culture occurs in a context in which the standard liberal package is secure, members of the culture in question have no justice-based complaint about the outcome.

I call this hypothesis a proceduralist one by virtue of two of its features. First, the hypothesis claims that the fairness of the background conditions under which a culture enters into decline is sufficient to confer justice on the outcome. Justice is not a matter of the outcome having some more immediate right-making quality. Second, the hypothesis does not identify the justice-conferring background conditions by appealing to assumptions about which outcomes it would be desirable to promote. The standard liberal package is derived from a general account of liberal justice, not from claims about desirable cultural outcomes.

If the hypothesis is correct, then we do not say that justice never condemns the decline of particular minority cultures. Instead, we say that it condemns such a decline only if, and because, the decline occurred in a context in which secure enjoyment of the standard liberal package is denied to members of the declining culture. Notice that basic liberal proceduralism is one possible way of following through on the proposal introduced at the end of chapter 3. There I suggested that, even if there is no general right to cultural preservation, members of vulnerable cultures would have a reasonable complaint if their culture is faring poorly because of, or in the context of, unfair treatment by the state. According to basic liberal proceduralism, the members of a struggling culture have just such a complaint when they are denied secure enjoyment of the standard liberal package.

I take it that basic liberal proceduralism is an intuitively attractive position to which many, if not all, liberals would be drawn.[1] One consideration accounting for its appeal relates the standard liberal package to the conditions of voluntariness. When members of the declining culture do not enjoy secure access to the standard liberal package, it is plausible to think that the outcomes that ensue do not necessarily reflect their choices or preferences. The suspicion is that those individuals are driven by oppression, discrimination, or poverty to abandon their culture, rather than by an assessment of the culture's value. By contrast, when the standard liberal package is secured for members of the declining culture, it is easier to imagine that it must have been a set of judgments about the (relative) value of the culture that determined the outcome.[2] We judge that the culture declined because people with reasonable alternatives preferred not to support it, and thus we feel in a strong position to conclude that no injustice has been done.

A further consideration that seems to count in favor of basic liberal proceduralism is more skeptical in tone. It may be impossible to formulate any additional requirement of justice, beyond the basic proceduralist hypothesis, that is not vulnerable to decisive objection. If this were the case, then theoretical modesty would counsel against claims that cultural decline is unjust

---

[1] For versions of the basic liberal proceduralist view on cultural preservation, see Barry 2001, 65, 71; Scheffler 2007, 110–11.

[2] Rawls (1975, 280) suggests that a set of conditions not unlike the standard liberal package satisfy the conditions of Mill's choice criterion. A person who affirms a particular conception of the good under these conditions can be deemed to have compared it with the relevant alternatives and to have found it superior to those alternatives. Rawls (2005, 198) abandons the idea that the conditions in question approximate Mill's criterion but continues to insist that they confer justice procedurally on the outcomes that arise.

in circumstances where the standard liberal package is secured. Such claims might seem intuitive in particular cases, but they cannot be brought under any general principle of justice that is not itself subject to serious objection.

Appealing as it may seem, the thesis of the present chapter is that basic liberal proceduralism does not, in fact, offer a satisfactory account of what is owed to cultural minorities as a matter of justice. In many situations, justice also requires that cultural minorities enjoy a set of specifically cultural rights. For instance, in the view that I shall propose, justice sometimes demands that linguistic minorities be given the opportunity to use their own languages when participating in public institutions, and it sometimes requires that internal boundaries and jurisdictions be settled in such a way as to afford national minorities a measure of self-government.

The thesis that justice requires more than basic proceduralism can be developed in two different ways. The first approach is the one that has been most fully worked out in the existing literature. It focuses on the condition of the persons whose culture has entered, or is vulnerable to entering, into decline. The argument is that this condition is in some way unacceptable, and thus those who are facing it have a morally serious complaint about their situation and a legitimate claim on policies that would prevent the condition from arising in the first place. These policies include the sorts of cultural rights mentioned a moment ago: language rights, self-government rights, and so on.

This first approach rejects the procedural approach to cultural justice in whole or in part. Whether some cultural outcome is considered just or unjust may still depend on the fairness or unfairness of the background conditions under which it came about, but those conditions are themselves shaped by the goal of securing a particular outcome.

By contrast, the second way of developing the thesis that justice requires more than basic proceduralism remains within the broader family of proceduralist views. This approach endorses the view that some form of proceduralism offers the right way to think about the question we are considering but argues that a correct specification of the conditions that confer justice on a given outcome would go considerably beyond the conditions associated with *basic* proceduralism. In the view I am envisioning—call it *full* liberal proceduralism—the standard liberal package is necessary to confer justice but not sufficient. The conditions that are sufficient for justice do not guarantee that no culture will go into decline, but they do mean that a society needs to do more than just provide the standard liberal package if it is to avoid the charge of injustice by cultural minorities that are vulnerable to decline. In particular, the claim is that cultural minorities must sometimes be extended specifically cultural rights if the background conditions under which they strive for the enjoyment and success of their cultures are to be considered sufficiently fair to warrant the judgment that outcomes are just.

Both the nonproceduralist and full proceduralist alternatives to basic proceduralism converge on the conclusion that something more is needed for justice than the standard liberal package, and both suggest that this "something more" will include a set of minority cultural rights. Moreover, both alternatives agree that there is something bad about cultural decline. This is obvious in the case of nonproceduralism, but it is true for full proceduralism as well. If the decline of one's culture were a trivial occurrence, then not much would ride on whether the culture was fairly treated by the background set of rules and institutions.

Although there is substantial and important agreement between them, it is important to note that the two alternatives are not identical. For the full proceduralist, there is a cut-off point determined by an independent standard of fairness beyond which further assistance, accommodation, and recognition for declining cultures is not mandated by justice. Once fully fair background conditions are established, if some culture were still to decline (because many of its members prefer the majority culture), this would not raise any concerns of justice. By contrast, the nonproceduralist focuses on the outcome itself. The reasons for regarding cultural decline as unacceptable do not depend on facts about background conditions, or if they do the background conditions are themselves shaped by the desire to avoid cultural decline. Thus the view has little or no room for an independent cut-off point determined by fairness.

The broad overlap between the two alternatives to basic proceduralism is likely to make them allies in the struggle to articulate a rationale for minority cultural rights. In many contexts, their arguments are mutually supporting and reinforcing. But the theoretical difference between the two alternatives is not without important ramifications. It may be that one of the views is subject to objections or counterexamples that do not disturb the other. If the two alternatives are not properly disentangled, someone might leap from an objection to one of the views to the conclusion that the whole case for minority rights had been driven off the rails. In addition, the two alternatives do not have the same policy implications. As I shall suggest later, full proceduralism lends itself naturally to the idea that public institutions should extend prorated equal recognition to majority and minority cultures alike. If one adopts the nonproceduralist view, by contrast, then it would be contingent whether equal recognition would be the appropriate policy. It might be that the decline of minority cultures could be prevented without extending them equal recognition. Or it might be that preventing such decline would require giving the minority cultures certain privileges (or subjecting the majority culture to certain disabilities) that go *beyond* equal recognition.

Political theorists do not always notice the differences between full-proceduralist and nonproceduralist defenses of cultural rights. In his influential essay "The Politics of Recognition," Charles Taylor fails to notice that

there are two distinct ways in which an account of justice might take identity
seriously. He compares only two alternatives: the "politics of universalism,"
which is roughly equivalent to basic liberal proceduralism and takes no notice
of identity; and the "politics of difference," which supposes that minorities
have a recognition-based complaint when their cultural identity is not accommodated. Taylor argues in favor of the latter position on the grounds that the
former is "inhospitable to difference because it can't accommodate what the
members of distinct societies really aspire to, which is survival" (61). This argument, and the way in which Taylor applies it to the case of Quebec, suggests
that he understands the politics of difference in a "nonprocedural" way. A cultural group has a legitimate complaint whenever its survival is in jeopardy. But
then Taylor's dichotomy excludes what I shall argue to be the most appealing
way of responding to identity and difference, which is full liberal proceduralism. Once this alternative is put on the table, much of the appeal of the "politics of difference" evaporates.[3]

To take a second example, in *Multicultural Citizenship*, Will Kymlicka
defends minority cultural rights with both an argument that appeals to the
conditions of individual autonomy (culture as a "context of choice") and an
argument that appeals to an idea of fairness (minority cultural rights work to
offset certain public benefits that the majority takes for granted).[4] These two
arguments point in broadly the same direction, but it would be a mistake to
suppose that they are the same, or that they are two steps of a single argument,
or, indeed, that they have identical policy implications. The argument from
autonomy presents a reason for thinking there is something bad about cultural
decline per se: cultural decline undermines the context of choice of members
of the culture. By contrast, the argument from fairness follows the logic of
full proceduralism. It suggests that it is unfair for minority cultures to have to
fight for their continued existence under circumstances in which public policy
shows a preference for the majority culture.[5]

---

[3]I develop this critique of Taylor's account in Patten 2008. I also argue that Barry (2001, 63–68)
makes a similar mistake, from an opposing position. He assumes that defenders of minority rights must be
arguing from a nonprocedural, preservationist standpoint and then questions why we should care about
cultural loss if it is the product of choices made by members of the disappearing culture. By avoiding
"nonproceduralism," my position is less vulnerable to this form of critique.

[4]The autonomy argument is developed in Kymlicka 1995, chap. 5. The fairness argument is in chap.
6, 107–15.

[5]The most charitable reading of Kymlicka's theory is that the two arguments are meant as different
steps of a single argument, with the autonomy component explaining why culture matters in a way that
would make us concerned about its fair distribution, and the fairness component explaining what exactly
a fair distribution of such a good consists in. But this seems awkward to me. If culture really is essential to
autonomy in some way, then why stop at a fair distribution of cultural recognition, which will not necessarily provide the conditions of autonomy to all persons? In other domains, liberals seem concerned to
secure individual autonomy. On the other hand, from the standpoint of fairness, why restrict the value of
culture to its autonomy-enabling character? There are other (more straightforward) reasons why people

Faced with a basic proceduralist, who sees no principled case at all for recognizing cultural rights, the difference in normative logic between Kymlicka's two arguments hardly seems to matter. But in other contexts it does matter. By running together these distinct ways of thinking about the case for minority rights, Kymlicka makes it hard for his readers to tell when minority rights are called for, what kinds of policies they would find expression in, and what criteria to apply in judging whether or not they are a success. To the extent that he is arguing within the logic of the autonomy argument, his position is nonproceduralist in form. The aim of minority rights is to protect cultures that are doing a reasonable job of providing a context of choice to their members ("societal cultures") but are vulnerable to disintegration because of the assimilative attraction of the majority culture. The policies needed to protect the culture may require some inequality of recognition between majority and minority—it would only be a special case in which they enjoy equal recognition—and the measure of success of those policies is whether the vulnerable culture is actually protected. By contrast, the fairness argument falls into the full proceduralist paradigm. The argument applies fairly generally to all minority cultures (whether or not they are vulnerable societal cultures); it calls for equal recognition as a matter of course; and its success is not measured by looking at outcomes (which depend, in part, on the choices people make within the framework of equal recognition) but is solely dependent on the degree to which institutions manage to extend truly equal recognition.

The arguments of chapter 3 cast considerable doubt on the viability of nonproceduralism as a strategy for defending strong cultural rights. There may be a narrow class of cases in which the strategy holds some promise. As we saw in section 3.3, these are cases in which the integrationist alternative to minority rights is unavailable for some reason, and a variety of other nontrivial conditions also hold. Apart from such cases, however, the nonproceduralist strategy is forced to base its rights claims on an appeal to the subjective inadequacy of the options facing members of a declining culture. But, as we have seen, that kind of complaint has moral salience only when it is accompanied by the sort of background unfairness that is highlighted by the two proceduralist strategies. Since nonproceduralism makes only a marginal contribution to the justification of strong cultural rights, the main case for such rights will have to rely on some form of proceduralism.

As indicated above, I also believe that basic proceduralism is an unsatisfactory account of what a liberal egalitarian state should do, as a matter of justice, to prevent the decline of its minority cultures. My main argument for this claim will consist of a defense of full proceduralism. I shall argue that full proceduralism provides a more convincing account than does basic proceduralism

---

might value their cultures that seem sufficient to explain why we would care about fairness with regard to cultures.

of what the background conditions would have to be like to confer justice on the outcome. When the various cultural rights called for by full proceduralism are in place, alongside the standard liberal package, then it is more plausible to suggest to minorities who are disappointed with the outcome that they had a fair opportunity to realize their preferred way of life.

The argument I shall develop in favor of full proceduralism builds on the defense of neutrality mounted in chapter 4. Basic proceduralism is an insufficient account of the conditions that confer justice on outcomes because it does not demand that the state attach importance to the neutral treatment of the conceptions of the good embraced by its citizens. The neutral treatment of conceptions of the good implies what I shall call the "equal recognition of cultures." The strong, if not indefeasible, reasons that a state has to extend neutral treatment to conceptions of the good are also strong, if not indefeasible, reasons for extending equal recognition to the different cultures with which its citizens are affiliated. An adequate form of proceduralism, then— "full proceduralism"—would incorporate an appropriate commitment to equal recognition. Members of struggling cultures have a procedural reason for accepting the justice of the outcomes they face only if this condition is added to the standard liberal package. Since the previous chapter offered a general defense of the idea of neutral treatment, the main focus of the present chapter's discussion will be on explaining what exactly is meant by equal recognition and why equality in that sense should be regarded as an implication of neutrality of treatment.

5.2 Recognition

The major difference between full and basic proceduralism is that the former, unlike the latter, incorporates a requirement of "equal recognition" into its understanding of the conditions that confer justice on cultural outcomes. This section explains what I mean by recognition and describes some of the different approaches to recognition that public institutions might adopt, including "equal" recognition. The sections that follow argue that equal recognition ought to be considered an important component of a liberal account of justice.

The concept of recognition is understood in a variety of different ways in contemporary political philosophy, some of which have spawned whole literatures of their own.[6] Compared with these familiar usages, my own understanding of the concept is rather specific and idiosyncratic. At the end of this

---

[6] Some notable accounts include Taylor 1994 [1992]; Tully 1995, chap. 1; Honneth 1996; Fraser 2003; Markell 2003. My own earliest forays into the topic of recognition as it relates to multicultural justice were Patten 1999c; 2000.

section, I return briefly to a comparison of my account with several of the main existing approaches.

At the most general level, I understand recognition to be a form of accommodation extended by the state to particular conceptions of the good. It consists, that is, in some rule or structure or resource that is adopted or provided by the state and that can be expected, in conjunction with other necessary inputs, to have a positive impact on the success of a particular conception of the good. It is important to my view, however, that not every form of accommodation counts as an instance of recognition. For the state to be engaged in recognition, two further conditions must be met. One condition has to do with the character of the accommodation itself; the other, with the character of the particular conception of the good that enjoys the accommodation.

The first condition that is important for isolating instances of recognition relies on a distinction introduced in chapter 4 between two forms of accommodation. To confer recognition on a particular conception of the good, I shall assume, the accommodation must be customized, or tailored, to fit specific features of that conception of the good. Generic accommodations, by contrast, do not confer recognition. We know from the previous chapter that accommodation takes a generic form when it involves the provision of some good, or the adoption of some rule, that is simultaneously beneficial to a range of different, and possibly rival, conceptions of the good. Fire prevention services are a good example of generic assistance in this sense. When the fire department offers its services to the local Catholic church, it has not recognized Catholicism in any way, because it offers the same services to all facilities within its jurisdiction. When a local government shuts down its operations in observance of Good Friday, by contrast, then it is customizing a benefit to fit with the particular beliefs of Catholics (and other Christians). As far as this first condition is concerned, such an accommodation would qualify as a case of recognition.

The second condition that helps to define recognition has to do with the conception of the good that is the object of recognition. In the view of recognition that I shall work with, it is not just any preference or belief about value that can be an object of recognition. When a local government constructs a tennis court in a municipal park, it is providing a customized form of accommodation. But, in general, I do not think that sporting and recreational preferences are the right components of conceptions of the good to be objects of recognition. The government is not recognizing tennis, or tennis players, when it provides the facility.

What, then, gives recognitional salience to some element in a conception of the good? The short answer is that, to be an appropriate object of recognition, a preference or belief about value (an element of a conception of the good) has to be *identity-related*. Since "identity" is one of the most overworked terms in the multicultural lexicon, it is important to be specific about how it is being used here (see also the discussion of subjective identity in section 2.5). I think of a preference as identity-related when it has two main characteristics. First, the preference is connected in a particular way with the other beliefs and preferences that make up a person's conception of the good. The preference is informed by, or an expression of, the fact that the preference holder identifies with a particular group or community and values that identification to at least some degree. Second, the satisfaction, or at least the equal treatment, of the preference matters to the preference holder in a special way. It would be an especially serious setback for the person if the preference went unsatisfied, and/or if the state treated it unfavorably. As suggested in section 4.6, a variety of different factors might endow a preference with special importance in this sense, including its centrality in a person's system of ends, its nonnegotiable character, and its relevance for equal respect.

A person who simply dislikes the taste of pork does not have an identity-related preference. By contrast, someone who refuses to eat pork on religious grounds does have an identity-related preference. The preference is related to, and informed by, the person's identification with a particular religious community and tradition. The person is likely to regard the preference as a nonnegotiable obligation, and its treatment by public institutions as an indicator of the respect given to her community and to herself as an individual. When the state offers alternative menus in public school cafeterias in response to demand by students who do not eat pork because of their religious beliefs, it is extending recognition to the particular conceptions of the good that incorporate those beliefs.

In summary, then, I define recognition as a *customized* form of *accommodation* of an *identity-related* component of a conception of the good. I propose this definition as a stipulation, but the main contours of it are informed by the normative contexts and concerns that situate our interest in the topic of recognition. Our ultimate concern is with how the state ought to relate to minority cultural communities or groups. The proposed understanding of recognition picks up on this concern by stipulating that the objects of recognition are preferences that are informed by, or expressions of, an identification with some group or community. An additional reason for emphasizing the group dimension has to do with aggregation. The contexts we are interested in often involve what I shall later call the "formatting" of public institutions: the endowing of those institutions with particular cultural characteristics in ways that unequally advantage different citizens depending on their beliefs and preferences. It is hard to see how the isolated interests of a single person could ever be sufficient to justify the conclusion that some public institution ought to be formatted one way rather than another. But, as the interests of many people are aggregated, this conclusion becomes more plausible—or so I will argue. The stipulation that the object of recognition consists of preferences that have a special importance for those who hold them is also shaped by a normative concern. As I indicated in the previous section, the argument to come will suggest that equal recognition matters because it is a species of neutral treatment. And, as we know from chapter 4, neutral treatment ought to be given additional weight in the state's deliberations when the commitments that would be burdened by nonneutral treatment have a special importance for those who hold them.

Although, strictly speaking, the objects of recognition in the proposed account are conceptions of the good, I shall sometimes, as shorthand, refer to the recognition of cultures and cultural groups. At first glance this may seem like a problematic elision. A culture is not a conception of the good; as I argued at length in chapter 2, it is best understood as the precipitate of a shared formative context. The shorthand is justified, however, by the train of argument that has brought us to this point. One of the main points made in chapter 3 is that cultural loss is bad for some members of the culture because, predictably, some of the options they value will become unavailable to them. Even if cultures are not defined by shared conceptions of the good, their disappearance matters because of the impact on members who have particular conceptions of the good. These include conceptions of the good that value the culture for its own sake, and conceptions that value options that are more likely to be available when the culture survives than when it disappears. The shorthand references to the recognition of culture highlight this reason for caring about how cultures fare. We care about how they fare because we care about the ease with which people having culture-related preferences can access options that correspond with those preferences.

Recognition, in the sense I have been describing, is a fairly common phenomenon. Consider three areas in which the state often ends up extending recognition to particular conceptions of the good.

> *Holidays.* Many states designate particular holidays and weekly days of rest. Schools and state offices close on these days, and the law may impose special costs on firms who wish to operate on them (e.g., a requirement that they pay their employees on an overtime scale). Very often holidays and days of rest are made to coincide with the important days of worship of one or more religious groups, and sometimes with days that have a special significance for a particular cultural group. Since religion and culture are "identity-related" for at least some people, these customized accommodations of particular religious or cultural preferences count as instances of recognition in the sense I have been describing.
>
> *Language.* Every political community must designate some language or languages for use in public institutions. Governments need to decide which languages to designate for internal use by their employees and

which ones to offer services in to the general public. They need to designate a linguistic medium (or media) of instruction in the public schools and an official language or languages for the courts and legislatures. And so on.[7] Where the state's decisions about language are made to coincide with the preferences of one or more particular groups in the society, then they represent customized forms of accommodation of those preferences. Since such preferences are often identity related, these accommodations should be considered instances of recognition.

Boundaries and jurisdictions. Another decision that states face is how to arrange their own authority internally. In establishing the basic constitutional features of a state, it must be decided whether the state will have a unitary or federal structure. If a state does opt for a federal structure, then a further series of decisions becomes necessary. It will have to be decided where to draw the boundaries of the federal units, how to assign competencies to each jurisdiction, how to structure representative institutions of the central government, and what to do in the event of conflicts concerning one or more of these decisions. The question of recognition arises when these decisions intersect with the sense (or varying senses) of political community, or national identity, of the citizens of the state. The drafters of a constitution might insist on a unitary state on the grounds that such an arrangement of authority best accords with a statewide sense of national identity shared by a majority of citizens. Alternatively, they might opt for a scheme of federalism or devolution in which the boundaries of one (or more) of the substate units are drawn so as to leave a minority with a substate national identity as a local majority. If the state's decisions on internal boundaries and jurisdictions are tailored to fit with particular national identities, then the state is recognizing those identities.

Other examples of recognition could be given as well, although the illustrations above should suffice for the purposes of this chapter's general theoretical argument. Decisions about the school curriculum (which literature and whose history should be taught?) will sometimes involve recognition in the sense I have stipulated, as will decisions about official flags, anthems, uniforms, and other symbols. Any time the state establishes a particular religion, it can be said to recognize that religion in my sense of the term.

Clearly, a state might adopt several different approaches to recognition. It might seek to avoid conferring recognition on any religion or culture (or identity-related conception of the good). A state might, for instance, refuse to designate any particular holidays or days of rest and instead support a sys-

---

[7] For a fuller catalog of various language policy issues that must be settled, see Patten and Kymlicka 2003, 16–25.

tem in which employees are free to choose their own days off. There would be serious difficulties with such a scheme, stemming from the fact that individuals and employers like to coordinate their days off with others, but at least the scheme would not recognize any religion or culture. Alternatively, a state might designate one out of several religions or cultures—typically, the majority one—and recognize it exclusively. It might, for instance, make Sunday the weekly day of rest on the grounds that having some designated day rather than no designated day avoids various problems of coordination, and that having *this* day designated accommodates the preferences of the majority. Or, third, a state might designate several different cultures or religions and try to assist each of them in some relevantly equivalent way. It might, for instance, designate Sundays as the default weekly day of rest but allow individuals to opt out of the default scheme and designate some different day that accords with their religious or cultural commitments.[8]

Among the various strategies a state might adopt, then, are nonrecognition, majoritarian recognition, and equal recognition. Equal recognition is of special salience to my project, so let me say something more about it. The account of even-handed entanglement in the previous chapter provides the basic model. Two or more cultures (or religions, etc.) are equally recognized when a comparable form of customized assistance is extended to each of them. The same kinds of rules, facilities, and resources that are offered to assist one are also offered to assist the other(s).

As I have suggested, a scheme that allows employees to take time off work on particular designated days associated with minority religions would represent a more equal form of recognition, in the proposed account, than would a scheme that gave time off only on days associated with the majority religion. A state that offers public services in one or more minority languages, as well as in the majority language, would come closer to equal recognition than a state that insisted on offering all its services exclusively in the majority language (or that offered minority-language services only on a temporary and transitional basis to people who are in the process of learning the majority language). And a state that establishes a federal system in which national minorities enjoy some degree of self-government is a better approximation to equal recognition than is a unitary system of government in which only the statewide sense of national majority receives any accommodation.

The metric of equality assumed here is broadly "resourcist" rather than "welfarist." By this I mean that equality of recognition depends on facts about the rules that are adopted, the facilities that are made available, the resources that are expended, and so on. It does not depend on the degree to which people who have the relevant conceptions of the good manage to convert these

---

[8] For instructive remarks on weekly days of rest and national holidays, see Carens 2000, 12; Kymlicka 1995, 115 n9.

benefits into a successful way of life. It may be that, in a context where comparable facilities, resources, and so forth are provided to several different cultures, people make choices that leave one of the cultures flourishing and others struggling.

An important complication worth mentioning right away arises when there are great disparities in the number of people affirming rival conceptions of the good. Suppose that 99 percent of citizens speak and value language P and 1 percent speak and value language Q. Do we really want to say that equal recognition of those who value P and those who value Q requires that the state spend the same amount of money on services in each language, or provide the same facilities (same networks of schools, hospitals, etc.) in both P and Q? In fact, there is good reason not to say this. As we shall see in more detail in the next section, the value underlying equal recognition is neutrality of treatment. We know from section 4.4 that neutral treatment can take three major forms, one of which is privatization. When it takes this form it is entirely obvious that there will end up being a higher level of provision of goods figuring in relatively popular conceptions of the good, all else being equal, than of goods that figure in less popular conceptions. This is how people will use their purchasing power in the market. When neutrality takes the form of generic entanglement or evenhandedness, there is less reliance on actual markets to allocate resources, but a hypothetical market can still play a heuristic role. Since neutrality calls for allocations that are responsive to actual preferences, we might model this by imagining that people are given an (equal) budget of purchasing tokens that they could spend on publicly provided goods. The neutrality-satisfying level of provision of various public goods would then depend on how these tokens would be spent. More popular conceptions of the good could expect a higher level of provision of key goods and services, all else being equal, than less popular ones. So, because equal recognition is based on neutrality, and neutrality on the fair opportunity for self-determination of each individual, it is appropriate to interpret equal recognition's idea of "comparable" facilities, resources, and so on in a prorated way.[9] Thus two or more conceptions of the good enjoy equal recognition, not when the same level of resources, facilities, and so forth are devoted to them, but when the same *prorated* level of resources, facilities, and so on are devoted to them. Conceptions of the good that are affirmed only by relatively small numbers of people can expect fewer resources, and less extensive facilities, to be devoted to them.

I explore some of the normative issues relating to equal recognition more fully in the remainder of the chapter. Before doing that, I conclude this section with some brief remarks comparing the understanding of recognition that has just

---

[9] For a suggestion along these lines, see Tamir 1993, 54. Barry (2001, 29) also suggests prorating if the state gets involved in providing religious education.

been sketched with several other usages of the term in the literature on multicultural justice.

One difference is that many authors use the term in a way that is more foundational, and hence more sweeping in its implications, than what I have in mind. Drawing on the Hegelian tradition, for instance, both Charles Taylor and Axel Honneth characterize recognition as a basic moral relation, the elaboration and interpretation of which point to the main principles of political philosophy. In Taylor's account, for instance, the "liberalism of equal dignity" (associated with Rawls and Dworkin) and the "politics of difference" (which supplements the rights and entitlements associated with equal dignity with various group-specific forms of accommodation and assistance) are presented as rival ways of specifying what "equal recognition" might amount to under conditions of modernity.[10] Honneth emphasizes the foundational character of recognition even more explicitly. Arguing that all injustice is experienced by those affected as a violation of well-founded claims to recognition, he claims that a theory of recognition must provide a "unified framework" for thinking about both "material" and "cultural" aspects of justice.[11] In contrast with these usages, my account treats recognition as one fairly specific form of moral and political relation between the state and its citizens, and therefore as a phenomenon that arises well downstream from concerns about the foundations of justice.

Another important account of recognition has been developed by Nancy Fraser.[12] She argues that problems of recognition and misrecognition arise with respect to "institutionalized patterns of cultural value" that confer or deny equal status to citizens. Individuals are misrecognized when those patterns have the effect of subordinating them, thereby denying them "parity of participation." Recognition consists in the elimination of all such subordinating patterns and their replacement with institutional norms that treat all citizens as peers or equals.

Although there are certain similarities between Fraser's approach and my own, there remain some notable differences. My account is, at most, concerned with *one* of the ways in which institutional norms can assign a subordinate status to individuals. It is focused on the ways in which individuals can be disadvantaged by virtue of the state's treatment of their conception of the good (culture, religion, etc.). Unlike Fraser's account, then, my view does not consider recognition to be at issue in institutionalized norms relating to race, ethnicity, gender, sexuality, and the like, except insofar as these categories refer to distinct conceptions of the good or patterns of such conceptions. Of course, norms relating to these categories do raise critical issues of justice, and there

[10] Taylor 1994 [1992], 37–44.
[11] Honneth 2003, 113–14.
[12] Fraser 2003.

is nothing objectionable about a theory of recognition that seeks to address those issues. But my account of recognition is presented in the context of a larger question about whether the "standard liberal package" (which helped to define "basic liberal proceduralism") needs to be supplemented in some way. Standard liberal theories already have plenty of ammunition for condemning state-sponsored racism, sexism, and so forth, and so it is not obvious that we need recourse to an idea of recognition to say what is going wrong in those cases.[13] By contrast, it is much less clear whether standard liberal theories have the resources to criticize state policies that extend special treatment to particular conceptions of the good. I introduce the concept of recognition with this specific question in mind.

A second area of contrast relates to Fraser's idea of "parity of participation." From what she says about this idea, it is not always clear how we can tell whether some particular institutional norm fosters or impedes it. Consider, as an example, a well-designed, successful policy of English-language learning in the public schools, designed to integrate all non-English-speaking children into an English-language-medium public school education as fully and swiftly as possible. Such a policy does aim for a certain form of equality, and its proponents might well defend it as animated by a concern for parity of participation. On the other hand, some parents may prefer that their children be educated in the medium of their home language (perhaps learning English as a subject) and thus would not regard a system of public education that denied them that option as providing for their parity of participation. It is not clear that Fraser's proposal has enough structure to decide between these alternative interpretations. Sensibly enough, she emphasizes the need for a "pragmatic" and "dialogical" application of the parity idea. However, there is a basic issue of principle here that needs to be addressed, which concerns the extent to which people can legitimately expect to have their (minority) conception of the good accommodated by public institutions. My account of recognition zeroes in on this problem and suggests a structure for thinking about it.

5.3 Recognition and Justice

A key feature of basic liberal proceduralism is its general indifference to recognition. The choice between the various approaches to recognition does not, within limits, affect the security of the standard liberal package, and the security of that package is all that concerns basic proceduralism. A liberal state's decisions about recognition are *constrained* by the various conditions making up the standard liberal package. In some situations, for instance, a refusal to

---

[13] There is nothing obviously objectionable about a theory that does use the vocabulary of recognition. There is more than one way to articulate what is going wrong in these cases.

communicate with people in their own language would be tantamount to a violation of their basic rights and entitlements. To secure a monolingual minority-language-speaker's right to a fair trial, a court would need to provide an interpreter. To prevent children who are in the process of learning the majority language from falling too far behind other children in math or reading skills, some instruction may have to be offered in their minority language. In other cases, a decision about internal boundaries may conflict with elements of the standard liberal package. It is conceivable that empowering some particular minority group through self-government arrangements would predictably lead to a spate of rights violations. And the standard package will sometimes rule out certain kinds of decisions about official state symbols. The state should not fly a flag (like the Confederate flag) that is symbolic of slavery and institutionalized racism.

But, although the standard liberal package imposes certain constraints on a state's decisions about recognition, it still leaves ample space for discretion. Subject to constraints like those just mentioned, a state can, in general, opt for multilingualism or monolingualism, for a federal or a unitary constitution, for a single national set of symbols or a plurality of such symbols, and so on—all without disturbing the security of the standard liberal package for minorities or for the majority. Far from defining a complete ideal of government, the standard package lays down a minimal, even if demanding, set of parameters that define a space within which further decisions must be made.

This brings us to the central question of the chapter, which is whether basic proceduralism's general indifference to recognition is justifiable. Is it plausible to think that outcomes produced under the conditions required by basic proceduralism are just no matter what approach to recognition is in force? Or should we think that facts about recognition are important and relevant for determining whether a given cultural outcome could give rise to a legitimate complaint of injustice? As I indicated from the outset, I will argue for the latter of these possibilities. In my view, a member of a declining minority culture *would* have a (defeasible) complaint of justice if the state were to adopt a majoritarian approach to recognition rather than nonrecognition or equal recognition.

The argument for this claim will be delivered in three stages. In the first, I review some basic reasons for thinking that decisions about recognition are consequential. In the second, I argue that the majoritarian approach to recognition is plainly nonneutral. Given the reasons that liberals have for observing neutrality, it follows that liberals have reasons for regarding outcomes produced under majoritarian recognition as unjust to minorities. In the third stage of the argument, I argue that the nonrecognition approach is unavailable and/or unappealing for a central range of cases. The only way in which a state can treat rival identity-related conceptions of the good neutrally is by extending equal recognition. Again, given that neutrality is an important component of liberal justice, the implication is that equal recognition ought, in that central range of cases, to be regarded as a (defeasible) component of justice.

RECOGNITION IS CONSEQUENTIAL FOR MINORITY CULTURES

Although resolving problems of recognition one way rather than another often does not make a predictable difference in the degree to which the standard liberal package is secured, it does have a significant impact on a minority's capacity to enjoy and to maintain its own culture. To appreciate the importance of recognition, consider the case of minority languages. If a state elects to do business and provide services in a particular minority language, then this has a number of salutary effects from the minority's point of view. It makes it possible for minority-speakers to use the language they value and at the same time enjoy the rights and benefits of public institutions. Recognition also makes it more advantageous, and less costly, for parents to pass on the minority language to their children, and for newcomers to adopt it too, thus helping to secure the preservation of the language and culture over time. And such an approach symbolically affirms the language and thus fights against the perception—associated with some minority languages—that the language and its speakers are somehow "low class" or "backward."

By contrast, if a state were to decide not to recognize its minority languages at all (except for accommodations demanded in specific situations to protect basic rights and entitlements), the prospects for linguistic minorities may be much more bleak. In some situations, they will have to choose between using the language they value and fully profiting from the rights and benefits provided by public institutions.[14] The cost/benefit calculus will make it less likely, under this policy, that they will pass their language on to their children, or that newcomers will opt to learn the language, which would be of little use to them in dealing with officialdom. And the exclusion of the language from public institutions may reinforce prevailing views that the language and its speakers have a low status.

Decisions about recognition in other areas are also likely to be consequential for minority cultures. Decisions about boundaries, school curriculums, flags and official emblems, and the like all have symbolic resonance for minorities and affect the capacity of cultural minorities to enjoy their cultures and to reproduce themselves over time as distinct groups. In general under an egalitarian approach to recognition, minority groups are justified in feeling more symbolically included, and they find it easier to express their beliefs and values. In addition, they face more incentives, and fewer disincentives, to pass along their culture to the next generation.

---

[14] For example, a minority-language-speaker might have to choose between a free public education in the majority-language medium and paying for a private education in the minority-language medium.

So long as they are suitably constrained and qualified at the margins, the choice between nonrecognition, majoritarian recognition, and equal recognition is indeterminate from the standpoint of the conditions laid down by the standard liberal package. And yet it is clear that adopting the first or third of these approaches rather than the second would make a significant difference to cultural minorities. Equal recognition does not guarantee that minority cultures will flourish or even survive. Offered recognition of their own culture, cultural minorities may still prefer to assimilate into the majority culture. But it does give members of cultural minorities some of the essential resources and facilities they need if they are to enjoy their cultures and be successful at preserving them over time. Still less does nonrecognition provide any guarantees, though it at least means that minorities do not have to compete against rival conceptions of the good that are given special advantages. Nor, on the other hand, does majoritarian recognition guarantee the demise of minority cultures. A culture may maintain itself in private life, and in the associations of civil society, without official support or assistance from public institutions. But, all else being equal, members of cultural minorities will face a much harder time enjoying and preserving their cultures under majoritarianism than they would under equal recognition or nonrecognition.

Majoritarian Recognition Is Nonneutral

The nonneutral character of majoritarian recognition should be fairly plain to see. Neutrality, as I laid it out in chapter 4, means neutrality of treatment. Neutrality of treatment obtains, in turn, when the state is equally accommodating of rival conceptions of the good. This means that, relative to an appropriate baseline, the state's policies do not extend any assistance to, or impose any hindrance on, a particular conception of the good without an equivalent form of assistance or hindrance for rival conceptions of the good.

It is obvious that majoritarian recognition is not neutral in this sense. Recognition, as we have seen, involves the customized accommodation of an identity-related conception of the good. The majoritarian approach to recognition, by assumption, implies that this accommodation is given only to the majority conception of the good and not to one or more of its minority rivals. Public institutions are tilting in favor of some people's outlook and preferences (members of the majority) over the cultural attachments of others (the minority).

In addition to exploring the concept of neutrality, chapter 4 argued further that neutrality is an important component of liberal justice, especially when it is applied to conceptions of the good having certain characteristics. A liberal approach to justice must acknowledge that at some fairly abstract level the state has an obligation to be equally responsive to all its citizens interests. It must be a state *for* all of its citizens, and not just for a privileged majority. An important part of the state's equal responsiveness consists in the efforts it takes to leave each citizen with a fair opportunity to realize his or her conception of the good. The state's pro tanto reasons to be fair in this sense translate into pro tanto reasons to extend neutrality of treatment to various conceptions of the good. Where the conception of the good (or element of such a conception) has a special importance for the person who holds it, then these pro tanto reasons, while still not absolute, should be regarded as particularly weighty.

Religious conceptions of the good are perhaps the strongest cases in which there is reason to think that the individual's interest in fulfilling his own beliefs is particularly weighty, and thus that neutrality is a particularly exiguous dimension of justice. In general, we think of religious belief as an area in which the individual ought to be left with space in which to exercise a high degree of autonomous judgment. A person's religious beliefs will normally present themselves to him as nonnegotiable. They may play a fairly central role in a person's life. And we recognize that people frequently feel excluded or denigrated by the unequal treatment of their religion by public institutions. Neutrality with respect to religion must still reach a compromise with other values, but it is a compromise in which a fairly heavy weight is given to neutrality itself.

For the same sorts of reasons, we ought to regard the fulfilment of many cultural conceptions of the good (that is, conceptions of the good that include an attachment to some particular culture) as important interests of the individual. It is true that religion has certain special features that mark it out for unusually strong protection. A person may feel that she has committed an absolute wrong, or sin, if she is unable to fulfill certain of her religious convictions. And religion involves an exercise of judgment about ethical and metaphysical questions that seems particularly deserving of protection.[15] But attachments to a culture can be of crucial importance to individuals too in ways that track, if at some distance, the importance of religious convictions. Violating a cultural attachment may not produce a feeling of having sinned, but it may lead to a sense of having betrayed or compromised a relationship of community that is of central importance in an individual's life. Likewise, attachments to culture may not be worthy of autonomous protection because they represent ethical or metaphysical judgments, but they may represent judgments about the basic social relationships that a person wants to be part of which are also worthy of protection. In addition, both religion and culture are matters that can play a central role in a person's ends, and where publicly

---

[15] Scheffler (2007, 119) argues that morality, religion, and philosophy are "perceived sources of normative authority" and thus are properly given special protection in liberal thought. He warns that "it is a mistake to extrapolate from the case of moral, religious, and philosophical convictions to the case of cultural affiliations."

established inequality can be consequential for the respect that minorities feel they are getting from others.[16]

As some of these remarks suggest, and as I argued in detail in chapter 4, I do not think that neutrality is an absolute obligation. The state's reasons for being neutral have genuine weight and reflect significant liberal values, but they sometimes appropriately give way to other considerations. Nevertheless, when the state disfavors some particular conception of the good on the basis of considerations that fail to adequately and appropriately grapple with the reasons it has to be neutral, it does an injustice to the bearers of that conception. I shall return to this question of relative weight in the next section, where I consider the objection that, when it comes to culture, there is *generally* a reason that is sufficiently strong to outweigh neutrality.

THE NONRECOGNITION ALTERNATIVE

Before getting to this issue, however, there is one further claim that has to be defended to cement the case for equal recognition as a component of liberal justice. As we have seen, equal recognition is not the only alternative to majoritarian recognition. From the premise that majoritarian recognition is nonneutral, it does not follow that equal recognition is the only strategy for realizing neutrality. In principle at least, nonrecognition is an alternative. Nonrecognition encompasses the "privatization" and "generic entanglement" approaches to achieving neutrality that I discussed in chapter 4.

A version of the privatization approach is indeed available and appealing in a range of circumstances. In my view, for instance, there are significant limits on how far the state should go in recognizing particular religions at all. Perhaps religion ought to be a factor in designating public holidays, but in general public institutions should not be tailored to fit with the majority religion exclusively nor with a plurality of religions even-handedly. Public institutions achieve neutrality in this area by applying the same standard of harm to all and otherwise relegating the pursuit and enjoyment of religion to the private sphere of civil society.

This privatization solution is not available, however, in contexts where, inescapably, public institutions operate in a particular cultural *format*. They function in some language or languages and not others. They recognize some days as holidays and weekly days of rest and not others. They present themselves to the world—with flags, uniforms, anthems, coats of arms, and so on—through certain symbols and not others. They apply to communities of

---

[16] Recall that, in the social lineage account developed in chapter 2, there is a straightforward sense in which a person's culture helped to make him or her the individual that he or she is. For someone who identifies with his culture, it is difficult, as a result, to distinguish disrespectful or exclusionary treatment of the culture from disrespectful or exclusionary treatment of him as an individual.

people defined in one way rather than another. And so on. Just as an author formatting a document that is ready for distribution has to make various decisions about font, spacing, margins, and the like, an institutional designer has to make decisions about rules, practices, and standards that relate to each of these cultural characteristics. Having no format at all is not an option.

In these contexts, the key question is whether formatting decisions should be responsive to the existing preferences, values, commitments, and so on of citizens who are served by the institutions. As we have seen, when these preferences, values, and so forth are identity-related, then such responsiveness implies that the state is engaging in recognition. The alternative is for the state studiously to avoid formatting its institutions in a way that is responsive to existing preferences and instead to opt for formats that are equally unresponsive to everyone's preferences. Institutional designers might select a weekly day of rest that does not correspond with any major religion (e.g., Tuesday) or allow people simply to choose their own days of rest. Or they might designate a language that is not the first language of any major group in the society (e.g., Bahasa Indonesia in the preindependence archipelago, or Esperanto in contemporary Europe). These would be instances of the nonrecognition approach.

An advantage of nonrecognition is that, depending on the particular formatting decisions that are made, it has the potential to realize a fairly pure form of neutrality. With equal recognition, there are bound to be hard choices about inclusion and exclusion. When there are many claims on recognition, some claims may have to be denied to avoid excessive costs in terms of other values. A single, well-chosen nonrecognition option would be equally unresponsive to the preferences of all and is not deterred by the proliferation of recognition claims.

At the same time, the nonrecognition approach to formatting faces some serious limitations. One problem is that it may be difficult to identify a format that really is unresponsive to everyone's preferences. For instance, prior to being designated as the national language, Malay (which forms the basis of Bahasa Indonesia) was used by maritime traders and for communication with the Dutch. It was not the first language of a major ethnolinguistic group in the archipelago, but it was a language used with some frequency by small segments of the population. A second problem is that there will often be considerable value in adopting a format that responds to existing preferences. Nonrecognition solutions are a bit like equipping the park with facilities for sports that nobody wants to play to avoid having to choose among the sports that people do enjoy playing. They produce institutions that are alien and uncomfortable to everyone, or almost everyone. In some instances, such as letting people choose their own days of rest, they may fail to reap the benefits associated with coordination. Overall, it will often be better to strike a balance between the imperfect neutrality of equal recognition and the realization of other values rather than opting for the purer neutrality of nonrecognition.

I would not go so far as to say that equal recognition is always or even generally superior to nonrecognition. But there will frequently be political pressure from the majority to format institutions in ways that recognize their culture and identity. Members of the majority want to be at home in their institutions: they want to see their own values, traditions, norms, and identity expressed in meaningful ways in those institutions. A state might reasonably resist these demands. As noted above, for the most part I think that institutions are best left without any religious formatting. But, given the political power of the majority, the state will often not resist the demand for at least some recognition. In these instances, the choice will effectively be between majoritarian and equal recognition. The important point for the overall argument, then, is this: *if* a state engages in some form of recognition, and it is granted that neutrality is a pro tanto requirement of justice, then equal recognition should be regarded as a pro tanto requirement of justice.

5.4 Equal Recognition versus Liberal Nationalism

I turn now to two possible objections that might be leveled against the argument I have been sketching. The first, and more obvious, claims that the defense of equal recognition is very weak because, in general, there are powerful considerations pushing institutions to adopt a single format, and these considerations outweigh the reasons that a state might otherwise have to be neutral. The considerations I have in mind invoke various goods that are associated with having a common public culture shared by all citizens. Since liberal nationalists often emphasize these considerations, I shall call this the liberal nationalist challenge. The second objection, which I take up in the section that follows, suggests that the positive, justice-based argument in favor of equal recognition fails to accommodate the important idea in liberal theory that persons should bear the costs of their own preferences. According to this idea, persons are free to form whatever (permissible) commitments they wish, but they should not present these commitments as handicaps or expect that resources will be transferred away from other legitimate uses to enable their pursuit or enjoyment.

Even if the arguments I have been offering on behalf of equal recognition are entirely correct, it would not follow that public institutions should extend equal recognition to any minority cultures. The case for equal recognition is only as strong as the liberal commitment to neutrality, and that commitment, as we have seen, is not absolute. As with any claim about pro tanto reasons, there is a worry that the pro tanto considerations supporting equal recognition might be systematically outweighed by competing reasons. This would render the justification of equal recognition technically valid but uninteresting from a policy- or an action-guiding perspective.

The liberal nationalist believes that the state does, in fact, have general reasons to favor a single culture that are weighty enough to override the justice-based demand for equal recognition. By favoring a particular culture—typically the majority culture—the liberal nationalist argues, the state can bring it about that that culture becomes a common one for all citizens. The goods associated with convergence on a common public culture are sufficiently impressive to justify overriding neutrality.

As this gloss suggests, the liberal nationalist argument rests on both a causal claim about the effects of favoring the majority culture and an evaluative claim about why those effects would be good to bring about. The causal claim is that favoring the majority culture, by adopting a single majority-culture format in public institutions, will promote the integration of all citizens into a common national culture. Integration into such a culture means an ability to speak the common public language, and a sense of attachment to the political community or common sense of nationality. So the suggestion is that when institutions operate more or less exclusively in the national language, this encourages all citizens to become fluent in that language and to develop an identity based on that language. And when states avoid institutional measures (e.g., various forms of federalism and regional autonomy) that foster and reinforce ongoing substate attachments, they encourage everyone to regard the statewide political community as the primary object of their political attachment.

The promotion of a common national culture is desirable, in turn, for a number of reasons. Where the common national culture involves the successful diffusion of the majority language as the national language, nobody would be excluded from economic opportunity or political participation by the fact that they are not fluent in the majority language of the society. In addition, a common language can help to further the common sense of attachment to the political community that is also desirable. Liberal nationalists stress that the existence of a common sense of nationality helps to generate the sort of solidarity, or social cohesion, required for a democratic state to provide public goods effectively and reliably.[17]

The assumption of the liberal nationalist argument, then, is that the most effective way to encourage social integration is for public institutions to adopt a single format based on the majority national culture. Given this assumption, and given the general value of social integration, the objection concludes that institutional designers have compelling reasons not to extend equal recognition to majority and minority cultures alike. These compelling reasons will generally outweigh the pro tanto neutrality-based considerations that justify equal recognition.

---

[17] Miller 1995, 90–99; 2000, chap. 4; 2006. For critical discussion of the idea that a common sense of nationality is necessary for the success of liberal democracy, see Patten 2000; Abizadeh 2002; Müller 2007; and the contributions to Banting and Kymlicka 2006.

One possible response to this liberal nationalist challenge consists in arguing that, in a limited but significant range of cases, there is no major conflict between equal recognition and liberal nationalism. The goods that liberal nationalists highlight do not depend on a *statewide* national culture. For citizens to have adequate opportunities, they need access to a culture that is fairly large and complex, but, as examples such as Quebec, Flanders, and Catalonia verify, it need not be diffused across the whole of the state. Likewise, a successful welfare state and a flourishing democracy may require a common language and shared sense of nationality. But if institutions of the welfare state and of democratic self-government are mainly established at the substate level, then the common language and the shared sense of nationality need not be statewide. It is enough if the linguistic and identity conditions are established in the substate domain where the relevant institutions are operative.

Since the goods associated with liberal nationalism do not depend on a statewide national culture but can also be realized within the institutions and territories of certain kinds of national minorities, a limited reconciliation between liberal nationalism and equal recognition seems possible. If the claims of equal recognition are limited to minority national communities in possession of their own viable, or nearly viable, societal cultures, then the liberal nationalist challenge loses much of its force. There is no liberal nationalist objection to equal recognition in this limited form because the goods that are highlighted by liberal nationalists can be enjoyed by national minorities within their own communities. National minorities with their own viable societal cultures do not need to be proficient in the majority language to avoid social exclusion, since their own linguistic community provides an adequate range of options. Nor is proficiency in the majority language necessary for deliberative democracy so long as the national minority enjoys substantial autonomy to govern their own affairs in their own vernacular. And if national minorities enjoy significant autonomy, then their own internal bonds of nationality should be sufficient to secure the forms of allegiance and solidarity needed for a well-functioning welfare state and for other institutions of liberal democracy.

This limited reconciliation of liberal nationalism with minority cultural rights is suggested in various places by some of Will Kymlicka's remarks about liberal nationalism. In general, Kymlicka finds the concerns of liberal nationalists to be legitimate, and he thinks that liberal states are permitted to engage in nation-building projects designed to bring about liberal nationalist objectives, so long as such projects satisfy various liberal constraints.[18] He squares this acceptance of liberal nationalism with his own defense of minority rights by describing what he calls a "dialectic" between nation building and minority rights. The nation-building projects of the statewide national majority meet

[18] Kymlicka 2001a, 23–29, and chaps. 10–11; 2001b, 21–31.

resistance among national minorities and a determination on the latter's part to engage in their own nation-building projects. If it is legitimate for the majority to engage in nation building, then, as a matter of fairness, it should be regarded as permissible for national minorities to do the same. In this picture, minority cultural rights are paradigmatically claimed by national minorities that aspire to establish and maintain their own substate national communities. The tension between liberal nationalism and equal recognition is alleviated so long as the claims associated with the latter are restricted to national minorities that are suitable vehicles for the goods highlighted by liberal nationalism.[19]

This response to the liberal nationalist challenge does, I think, offer a good reason for thinking that the claims of equal recognition are not inevitably going to be overruled by the concerns of liberal nationalists. One could fully accept the liberal nationalist challenge and still think that there is some space remaining in which accepting or rejecting equal recognition makes a difference.

An implication of the response, however, is to leave minority rights with a rather nationalist complexion. The response consists in saying that one could extend minority rights to groups such as the Québécois or Catalans without running foul of liberal nationalist strictures, since these groups are themselves viable nations capable of supporting their own institutions. Minority rights and minority nationalism start to look suspiciously like the same phenomenon. But many cultural groups do not fit the Quebec/Catalonia model. This is obviously true of immigrant minority groups, but is also the case for certain historically established or national groups that do not form full-scale, sub-state national communities. Many groups are simply too tiny to offer an adequate range of options to their members or to support a comprehensive set of institutions controlled by their members. If one were a convinced liberal nationalist, one might think that extending equal recognition to these cultures is a mistake. Likewise, some groups, while not especially small in size, live scattered amongst the majority society. They are not concentrated in some particular region in which their culture could be made to predominate in the manner of the Quebec/Catalonia model. Internal minorities (members of the state-wide national majority who find themselves in the minority in a particular region where a national minority is locally dominant) often have one or both of these characteristics. They are often small in size and/or live amidst a more numerous dominant culture. Again, the proposed reconciliation of liberal nationalism and equal recognition would not seem to justify strong cultural rights in these cases.

It is possible to go quite a bit farther, however, in defending equal recognition from the liberal nationalist challenge than the modest response considered so

[19] Kymlicka 2001a, chap. 11.

far does. Three main points stand out. Once these points are given their due, the claims of equal recognition are left with significant elbow-room, even in the case of national minorities that do not fit neatly into the Quebec-Catalonia mold. The first point takes issue in several ways with the causal claim of liberal nationalists. The second allows that the liberal nationalist concerns may be valid ones, but insists that equal recognition also has value. And the third point grants the liberal nationalist challenge in its entirety, but insists that in an important way the pro tanto reasons supporting equal recognition do not disappear.

The liberal nationalist challenge assumes that endowing public institutions with a single majority-culture format is an effective way of promoting convergence on the majority culture. But this causal assumption may be flawed in one or both of two respects. Even if the anticipated convergence does occur, it may not be *because* of the decision by public institutions to adopt a single format. There may be all sorts of other incentives and pressures that lead majorities and minorities alike to learn a common national language and to identify with a common political community. Indeed, a shared national framework may exist even under equal recognition, so that a single format for all public institutions is not needed to generate such a framework. Minority-language-speakers often speak the majority language as well, and people with a strong substate cultural attachment often also feel a strong attachment to the political community as a whole, especially when their substate attachment is fairly treated.[20] In short, adopting equal recognition may not have the cost envisioned by the liberal nationalist challenge.

On the other hand, the causal assumption of liberal nationalists may be flawed in roughly the opposite way. It may be that a shared national framework would not be fully attainable even if institutions were to eschew equal recognition and opt for a single format instead. Denying recognition to minority cultures may backfire and lead to a less integrated national framework rather than a more integrated one. In some cases, equal recognition may even outperform uniformity as a means of promoting national integration. The best way to promote a common identity may sometimes be to allow difference to flourish and to let the recognition of difference be a feature of the political community that attracts popular allegiance.[21] In these kinds of cases, as in the cases where convergence is likely to happen anyway, there is limited or no marginal value in insisting on a single format over equal recognition.

The second point is that we should not lose sight of the fact that equal recognition itself has value. In the case of religion, many liberals would be suspicious of the suggestion that the state should abandon nonrecognition (or indeed equal recognition) in order to garner the benefits of having a single,

[20] See the discussion of "nested nationalities" in Miller 2000, chap. 8.
[21] Young 1990, 179; Réaume 2000, 260–61, 269–72; Kymlicka 2001a, 37.

uniform format. In part, the suspicion reflects skepticism about whether uniformity will really produce benefits, for the sorts of reasons I have just been canvassing. It also reflects, however, a sense that the neutral treatment of religion is a great value in a liberal society, one that should be abandoned only for the most pressing of reasons. Although, for the reasons I mentioned in the previous section, neutrality toward culture is less essential from a liberal point of view than neutrality toward religion, a weaker version of the argument still has some force. The values underlying the neutral treatment of culture are significant, and thus the state should not abandon equal recognition for reasons that are marginal in importance or highly conjectural or speculative in nature.

The crucial claim being made here is not that equal recognition outweighs the concerns of liberal nationalists in all cases. Since strong cultural rights are "context-dependent," as I put it in section 1.3, a successful justification of them need not show that their grounds are never outweighed by competing considerations. What we do need is the claim that there exists a significant range of cases in which there is no strong reason to think that the liberal nationalist argument rules out equal recognition. In these cases, the countervailing considerations are insufficient, and we are left with a justice-based requirement to opt for equal recognition.

The third point is one that I have made elsewhere in the book. Even in cases where liberal nationalists are right that it is better, all things considered, to opt for a single format over equality, the pro tanto reasons favoring equality are outweighed rather than erased. In this situation, a state continues to have reasons to aim indirectly for a situation in which equality can eventually be established. For instance, it has reasons to promote the reinterpretation of national identity to make it more capacious and accepting of difference. And it has reasons to promote second-language learning among minorities (at the least possible cost to their first language) so that, eventually, formal rights for the minority language will not conflict with the existence of a lingua franca.[22]

In summary, many theorists agree that there is at least one set of cases in which there is no deep conflict between liberal nationalism and equal recognition. These are cases in which the minorities making claims of equal recognition have their own national communities capable of realizing the goods emphasized by liberal nationalists. If pointing to this set of cases were all that could be said in response to the liberal nationalist challenge, however, then minority rights would end up being highly congruent with minority nationalism. Consistent with this observation, leading theorists of minority rights have tended also to endorse liberal nationalism.

By drawing attention to some additional points that can be made in response to the liberal nationalist challenge, I have sought to disrupt this cozy alliance between minority rights and minority nationalism. None of the addi-

---

[22] Stilz (2009) defends a "least cost principle."

tional points I have made relies on the assumption that groups claiming equal recognition possess their own viable societal culture or national community. Indeed, one point, that minorities may not need much inducement to learn the statewide majority language, is most plausible for minorities that do *not* possess their own complete societal cultures. In general, there is no reason to think that minority rights are limited to viable societal cultures. And there *is* reason to think that, all things considered, minority rights place genuine limits on liberal nationalism, whether it be the statewide nationalism of the majority or the substate nationalism of the minority.

As noted in chapter 1, I do not think that this critical approach toward liberal nationalism commits me to "postnationalism" if that is taken to mean the complete severing of liberal values from nationhood. The account I have just been laying out can grant the legitimacy of liberal nationalist policies in some contexts, even while insisting that, in the long run, a liberal state should strive to remove the conditions that make those policies legitimate. In addition, equal recognition seems compatible with an inclusive, "multinational" form of belonging, which shares some characteristics with nationalism. In contrast with the nationalist model, the multinationalist one does not insist that all speak a common language, or acknowledge the same symbols, or share a sense that citizens of the state constitute a single, unified people. Multinational belonging does involve a sense that one owes it to one's fellow citizens to support a set of institutions that make it possible for cultural and national differences to be respected and accommodated. This implies a common identity of sorts, but one that is defined in part by reference to a common project of recognizing and accommodating difference.[23]

5.5 The Objection from Expensive Tastes

One of Brian Barry's core complaints about theories of multiculturalism is that they operate with a naïve and objectionable conception of equality. He writes:

> The strong claim made by many theorists of multiculturalism is that special arrangements to accommodate religious beliefs and cultural practices are demanded by justice. The argument is that failure to offer special treatment is in some circumstances itself a kind of unequal treatment. For, it is said, the same law may have a different impact on different people as a result of their religious beliefs or cultural practices.[24]

[23] I say more about this form of common identity in Patten 2000, sec. 3.
[24] Barry 2001, 34.

Barry subjects this view to withering criticism. Any conception that condemns a law as unjust simply because it burdensomely affects some citizens, he argues, is obviously indefensible.[25] *Every* law imposes a burden on at least some citizens. The law against rape imposes a burden of sorts on those who would like to engage in nonconsensual sex. Progressive tax laws have a more burdensome impact on the wealthy than on the poor. And so on. The mere fact that a law is more burdensome on citizens with particular beliefs, preferences, or circumstances than it is on others cannot be sufficient for regarding that law as objectionable.

On its own, Barry's objection does not represent an embarrassment to the account I have been developing. I agree with Barry that differential or burdensome impact does not, by itself, provide a reason for identifying some outcome as unjust. This was why I took some pains in chapter 4 to distinguish neutrality of treatment from neutrality of effects, and why I have characterized my account in the present chapter as "proceduralist" in character. If different cultures enjoy equal recognition under the law, and the other conditions of full liberal proceduralism are in place, then, in my view, there is no injustice if one or more cultures ends up doing poorly.

Barry deepens his objection, however, by invoking the problem of expensive tastes.[26] If "inequality of impact is a sign of unfairness," he asks, then would it not follow that somebody with "champagne" tastes would have a claim of justice on additional resources to bring her up to the same level of satisfaction that others get from beer? In Barry's view this implication is "absurd." "The subject of fairness," he says, "is the distribution of rights, resources and opportunities." Inequalities that arise by virtue of unsatisfied preferences should not be counted as unfair.[27]

Although Barry continues here to target the impact-oriented view that I do not defend, it might seem that the objection applies equally to the view that I do defend. To see this, imagine a society in which everybody either worships on Sunday or does not worship at all. To accommodate this pattern, schools and government offices remain closed on Sundays. Over time, however, a social movement forms in which many people freely convert to a new religion. A major tenet of this new religion is that Tuesday should be set aside for worship. Once a significant proportion of the population has converted to this new religion, they start to demand that the state extend the same sort of assistance to them that has historically been extended to Sunday worshippers. They suggest, for instance, that schools and government offices close on Sundays and Tuesdays, rather than Saturdays and Sundays. In the account I have

---

[25] Ibid.
[26] Ibid., 34–35.
[27] Ibid., 35.

been defending, they would seem to have a fairly strong claim.[28] But, if one insists, as Barry does, that fairness is concerned with rights, resources, and opportunities *rather* than with responsiveness to preferences or religious beliefs, then it is not obvious that one would have any claim at all. The Tuesday worshippers have freely developed a new religious belief and now complain that society's institutions do not fit well with their beliefs. But, if the champagne lovers lack a good claim on additional resources to bring them up to an equal level of satisfaction, then why would Tuesday worshippers have a claim in this case on a special accommodation?

Although the challenge here seems to echo the account of responsibility for preferences that I sketched in chapter 4, in fact it makes an important error that I had warned against. Once that error is noted and corrected for, the challenge loses its bite. The argument I have been developing in favor of minority cultural rights does not conflict with the liberal idea of responsibility for preferences when that idea is correctly understood. Nor do the forms of responsiveness to preference that are implied by my account (e.g., in the Tuesday worshippers case) run into difficulty with expensive or "champagne" tastes. One can agree with Barry in withholding compensation from champagne lovers but reject the claim that justice is exclusively a matter of rights, resources, and opportunities if those terms are meant to exclude responsiveness to actual preferences and beliefs about value.

My basic complaint about Barry's challenge is that it fails to grapple with a crucial condition for claims about responsibility and expensive taste.[29] As we saw in section 4.7, responsibility for preferences is based on the notion that, in a liberal society, individuals have, over the course of their lives, the opportunity to make choices that influence their preferences. But, as we also saw, choice makes a difference to responsibility—to the burdens a person can reasonably be expected to shoulder—only when that choice is offered in the context of fair background conditions. Choices taken under unfair or unreasonable conditions do not generate responsibility. Likewise the notion of "expensive" tastes presupposes a context where fair background conditions are assumed. The fact that a person lacks success, relative to other people, at fulfilling his conception of the good does not, by itself, imply that he has expensive tastes. It may be that he has fewer resources than others or is subject to some other unfair condition. The expensive preferences that liberal theory refuses to subsidize consist only of those preferences that are relatively unsuccessful under fair background conditions.

---

[28] To judge whether the claim is decisive, we would need to think about countervailing considerations. One such consideration, for instance, is that the switch from Saturday + Sunday to Sunday + Tuesday as the default days off would make it harder for people to plan leisure activities requiring consecutive days off. The discussion of historical priority in sec. 8.5 is also relevant here.

[29] I have a similar concern about a use that Van Parijs (2011a, 126–27) makes of the expensive-tastes idea.

Barry acknowledges the background fairness requirement but fails to notice an implication of it. In the view I have been defending, a distributive scheme is fully fair only if it is appropriately responsive to the particular conceptions of the good that people happen to hold. If the identity-related conception of the good that they happen to hold does not enjoy (prorated) equal recognition, then bearers of that conception can legitimately complain that the distributive scheme is unfair by virtue of denying the conception neutral treatment. The complaint is presumptive, as we have seen, since neutrality of treatment is not an absolute requirement of justice, although it is a weighty one. The important point to stress here is that the complaint does not run foul of responsibility for preferences or the expensive-taste objection. Those concerns gain traction only in the context of a scheme that is otherwise fair. My account does leave room for the rejection of preference-based demands for accommodation on responsibility or expensive taste grounds, but *only* when those demands are made in a context where a fair distributive scheme is in place.

For an illustration of this point, recall my remarks at the end of chapter 4 about Muslims in a Christian state. It was a misunderstanding of the logic of responsibility for preferences, I argued, to think that Muslims would be left without a complaint about an establishment of Christianity by the considerations that support responsibility for preferences. Those considerations have bite only against preference-based claims that are made in the context of an otherwise fair background. And it is precisely the fairness of the background— its conflict with neutrality of treatment—that Muslims complain about when they reject the establishment of Christianity.

It might be objected that something must have gone wrong here, since one finds in most liberal egalitarian theorists who emphasize responsibility for preferences no trace of the accommodating approach to certain preferences that I am advocating. But, in fact, this is not quite correct. I conclude this section by noting an interesting respect in which my account is compatible with Ronald Dworkin's theory of equality of resources.[30] This discussion should, I hope, underscore how continuous my approach is with a liberal egalitarian theory that is widely regarded as mainstream.

Dworkin's theory is well-known for the central places it assigns to the envy test and to the idea that an auction or, more loosely, a competitive market is the preferred means of producing an envy-free distribution. In several key passages, however, Dworkin notes that the envy test and the imaginary auction do not exhaust the conditions necessary for equality.[31] The envy test and auction are deployed in a "second stage" of analysis. An analytically prior stage

---

[30] Heath (2004, 210–12) overlooks some of the possibilities implicit in Dworkin's theory of equality for defending minority rights.

[31] I mainly follow Dworkin 2000, 145–52. There is a briefer and slightly different sketch of the same argument on 67–68.

consists of specifying a background set of conditions of liberty and constraint that determine what goods are available for auction and what kinds of ownership rights a person would acquire in those goods should she acquire them in the auction.

To illustrate the importance of the first stage, Dworkin mentions several different examples. In one example, the auctioneer decides to put the available land for sale in lots the size of football fields. Although this decision does not prevent an auction from being run that results in a distribution satisfying the envy test, Dworkin does not think that the distribution should be regarded as an equal one. Since not many people will want to spend their scarce resources on such a large lot, those who do want one will pay a relatively low price. Had the lots been smaller, there would have been much more interest in land, and the price of a football field–sized lot would have ended up higher. When the auctioneer insists on such large lots, she is, in effect, allowing those who want large lots to pay too little and forcing those who want small ones to pay too much (since the only way to get a small lot is to buy a large one and use only part of it). If nobody ever wanted small lots, then this would not matter. But if some people do want small lots, then the auctioneer's decision is unfair and compromises equality. An auction is "fairer," Dworkin writes, and "provides a more genuinely equal distribution—when it offers more discriminating choices and is thus more sensitive to the discrete plans and preferences people in fact have."[32]

In a second example, Dworkin imagines an auctioneer who traded all the society's varied resources to another society for a large stock of plover's eggs and vintage claret. Some people may be delighted by this trade, but others are not. If the fancy food and wine are then distributed (in equal shares or by auction), then there is reason to believe that an envy-free distribution could be produced. But the resulting distribution is "offensive to equality," Dworkin says, because it makes the array of resources available to people "much less sensitive—indeed as insensitive as possible—to the plans and preferences of the parties."[33] Someone who does happen to like plover's eggs and vintage claret is paying an artificially low price that is, in effect, subsidized by the forgone opportunities of those with different plans and preferences. Those who have different plans and preferences are forced to set aside their ambitions and put up with something that is less preferred. There would be no unfairness, Dworkin adds, if claret and plover's eggs really were the only resources available for auction. This would be unlucky for people who disliked these goods but not unfair.[34] But if the auctioneer could costlessly trade those goods to another society for a greater mix of goods, "which would have allowed bids

---

[32] Ibid., 151.
[33] Ibid., 151, 67.
[34] Ibid., 69.

in the auction to be more sensitive to the discrete tastes, plans, and ambitions of the bidders," then equality would require the auctioneer to engage in such a trade.[35]

In Dworkin's view, then, a fair distributive scheme does have to be responsive to the conceptions of the good that people actually hold. If it is not appropriately responsive—if the auctioneer puts up a less varied mix of goods for auction than she needs to—then people with conceptions of the good that are disfavored by the auctioneer's decisions can legitimately complain about the burden they are facing.

It is true that Dworkin advances this argument in a somewhat different context from the one that interests me. Dworkin's interest, as I mentioned earlier, is in specifying the background system of rights that ought to be in place so that an auction or market would produce a fair distribution. But there is no reason to think that the same principle of sensitivity to actual plans and preferences (what Dworkin calls the "principle of abstraction") would not also be relevant to thinking about fairness in nonmarket contexts. Thus, for example, in an exchange with G. A. Cohen about fairness in the acquisition policies of public libraries, Dworkin suggests that the right approach would mimic market justice as far as possible.[36] It would be sensitive to the preferences and reading interests of different patrons (which may change over time), as well as to the costs of acquiring different sorts of books. As I explained in section 5.2, the idea of prorated equal recognition is based on this "mimicking" strategy. It is not feasible to solve the problem of cultural formatting through an auction since what is at stake, in part, are the cultural characteristics of the auctioneer (the state). But it is possible to mimic the justice of the market by favoring formatting solutions that are responsive to the cultural attachments of different citizens as well as to the costs of providing the various formats (hence the importance of *prorating* recognition). If these attachments change over time—as with the emergence of the Tuesday worshippers—it is reasonable to expect that the formatting solutions expected by justice would eventually have to change with them.

5.6 Is Full Proceduralism Enough?

The main strategy of this chapter has been to cast doubt on basic liberal proceduralism by defending full liberal proceduralism. Basic proceduralism is flawed because it does not give any place to equal recognition as a component of justice, except insofar as equal recognition happens to coincide with some feature of the standard liberal package. Full liberal proceduralism takes equal

[35] Ibid., 151–52.
[36] Cohen 2004; Dworkin 2004.

recognition seriously and gives it the weight it is due. This does not mean assigning it absolute weight, but does mean that it should be recognized as having significant value that is outweighed only by important countervailing considerations.

As I have suggested with brief illustrative examples, and as I will show more thoroughly in chapters 6 and 7, the equal recognition requirement provides a justification for significant minority rights. More generally, I believe that the argument I have been developing offers a powerful and robust reason for accepting the strong cultural rights thesis. As we saw in chapter 1, this is the thesis that there are basic reasons of principle for thinking that cultural minorities as such are owed specific forms of recognition and accommodation. The case for recognition and accommodation that I have been making is not a pragmatic one. Nor is it derivative from, or an application of, some principle that is already integral to the standard liberal package of rights and entitlements. Nor, again, does the argument appeal to benefits that everyone receives from diversity. Rather, the argument points to something that is specific about culturally defined groups and suggests a distinctively liberal reason of principle for thinking that that something grounds a (defeasible) obligation. Cultural groups are associated with distinctive preferences and beliefs about value, which have special importance to at least some members of those groups. Liberal values, especially the value of a fair opportunity for self-determination, imply that the state has a defeasible reason to extend neutral treatment to various conceptions of the good, a reason that becomes especially weighty for preferences and beliefs about value that have special importance to the people who hold them. For a central range of cases, neutral treatment means equal recognition, and thus the accommodation and recognition of minority cultures.

Although the rights that are justified in this approach are significant, the approach does not guarantee that any particular conception of the good or culture will flourish or even survive. In a context where several cultures enjoy equal recognition, the pattern of individual choices and interactions may be favorable to some cultures and unfavorable to others. This implication of the theory may lead some people to conclude that full liberal proceduralism is something of a letdown. Despite its advantages over basic proceduralism, it might seem to some that it still does not provide sufficiently full and robust protection for struggling minority cultures.

This insufficiency objection might be developed in two different ways. The first sticks with the proceduralist strategy and argues that an even fuller form of proceduralism would provide a more secure foundation for minority cultures, even while stopping short of an absolute guarantee of their success (for this would no longer be a procedural view). A fuller proceduralism might require, in addition to the components that make up full proceduralism, some kind of compensation for past culture-related injustice, and/or some correction for market failures, and/or some mechanism that corrects for the adverse pressures of market forces on minority ways of life. The second way of elaborating the insufficiency objection would abandon proceduralism altogether. In the most plausible version of this view, because the loss of culture is thought to be morally objectionable, fair background conditions ought to specified with the aim of preventing such an outcome from occurring.

For reasons I alluded to in section 4.7, I am skeptical about the "adverse market forces" version of the fuller proceduralist alternative. Someone like Martin (who has extravagantly expensive tastes) faces adverse market forces, and yet very few people would argue that he is owed more than his fair share of resources plus neutral treatment from the state. What people typically have in mind when they complain about markets is the fact that different participants bring to the market dramatically unequal shares of purchasing power. Although this is a reasonable and weighty concern, it is better thought of as a problem of economic inequality not cultural inequality. Economic and cultural inequality do sometimes support and reinforce one another, and there may be cases in which extending cultural rights beyond the point of equal recognition is an effective way of reducing economic inequality. But the underlying concern here is economic justice, not cultural justice, and thus there is no reason to conclude that equal recognition is unsatisfactory as an account of the fundamental requirements of cultural justice.

In addition, some critics of markets may object to the way in which markets price goods on the basis of supply and demand. Is it not unfair to minorities when the goods they prefer are relatively expensive simply because of a conjunction of low demand (by virtue of being minorities) and economies of scale in production? But this variation on the challenge still faces the problem of Martin and, more generally, of responsibility for preferences. It is true that Martin had no realistic opportunity to avoid the fact that the preferences he actually holds are relatively expensive to satisfy: this fact is settled by market and other impersonal forces beyond his control. But the presumption, in a liberal society, is that he did have a reasonable opportunity to avoid holding those preferences, and for this reason he is reasonably held responsible for the (externally determined) costs of holding those preferences. Moreover, as Dworkin has argued, there is a certain moral logic to pricing in this way.[37] When prices are high, this generally means that, relative to supply, many citizens want the goods for their own purposes. If I am going to be the one to get one of the goods, then it is appropriate, given the opportunity costs to others, that I should pay a high amount for it. The high price means that those who go without the good at least get an opportunity to purchase other goods they want without having to compete with the full amount of my purchasing power.

[37] Dworkin 2000, 69–70.

The historical injustice and market failure variants of "fuller" proceduralism do strike me as genuine directions in which full proceduralism needs to be developed. Although I will not attempt it here, a completely adequate formulation of full proceduralism would, in my view, contain some kind of provision for each of these concerns. Adjusting full liberal proceduralism to take account of these considerations would not, I think, require a dramatic revision of the framework I have been developing.[38]

The other standpoint from which one might object to full proceduralism is that of nonproceduralism. One version of nonproceduralism differs from proceduralism in that whether some cultural outcome is considered just does not depend on the fairness of background conditions under which it came about but on justice-making features of the outcome itself. Another, I think more plausible, version allows that the fairness of background conditions is critical for determining whether a cultural outcome is just but insists that what background conditions count as fair for the purpose of such judgments should be influenced by a goal of bringing about particular cultural outcomes.

For the reasons developed in chapter 3 (and alluded to again at the start of this chapter) these alternatives to proceduralism seem generally unpromising to me. Except for a narrow range of cases where nonproceduralism does have some validity (discussed further in section 6.8), such a view leaves too much scope for unreasonable demands the fulfillment of which nobody would regard as a requirement of justice. The interesting debate is between the two versions of proceduralism: basic and full. When liberal political theorists debate the status of cultural rights in liberal thought, this is or should be where the action is. If the argument of this chapter has been successful, then liberals have strong reasons of principle to opt for full rather than basic liberal proceduralism.

---

[38] I say a little more in sec. 6.7.

CHAPTER 6

Equal Recognition and Language Rights

6.1 Linguistic Diversity and Language Rights

Every society in the world is characterized by at least some degree of linguistic diversity. This is obvious in countries such as Canada, Switzerland, Belgium, Spain, India, South Africa, and Nigeria, where more than a fifth of the population are members of historically rooted ethnolinguistic minorities. But even societies that like to think of themselves as having a single national language are home to significant language minorities. In the United States Census of 2000, for example, about forty-seven million residents over the age of five reported using a language other than English in their homes—roughly 18 percent of all people surveyed.[1]

In any context where more than one form of speech is in use, people face the problem of how they should communicate with one another. Although this problem arises in interesting ways in all sorts of informal, nonstate contexts, it presents itself with particular force for public institutions that serve a linguistically diverse citizenry. Faced with linguistic diversity, what norms and practices of language use should public institutions adopt? Should they adopt a policy of institutional monolingualism, in which they designate just one of the languages spoken by their citizens—for example, the majority language—as the sole medium of public communication? Or should they opt for institutional multilingualism and try to conduct business in several (or even all) of the languages used by the citizens they serve?

Suppose that public institutions did make the majority language the sole medium of public communication. Would minority-language-speakers have a serious and principled complaint about this arrangement, and, if so, what exactly would it be? As we have done earlier in the book, we might distinguish between a complaint based on "minority-regarding" considerations, on the one hand, and one based on "third-party-regarding" and "impersonal" con-

---

[1] Shin and Bruno 2003. According to the American Community Survey of 2007 (Shin and Kominski 2010), these figures subsequently grew to 55 million and 20 percent, respectively.

siderations, on the other (sec. 1.3). The speakers of a minority language make a minority-regarding complaint when they object to the monolingual policy in terms that refer to their own interests, either as individuals or as a group. Their complaint is that the monolingual policy fails adequately to take into account the legitimate interests that *they* have in the accommodation of their language. They make a third-party-regarding complaint when their objection refers, not to their own particular interests, but to the interests of some larger entity to which they belong, such as their society as a whole.[2] In this case, the complaint is that the policy fails adequately to take into account the interest that *everyone* has in the accommodation of the minority's language. And they make an impersonal complaint when they appeal to the value of the language, or language community, itself, independent of any contribution that the language or community makes to advancing human interests.

When minority-speakers have a minority-regarding complaint, and that complaint is morally weighty enough to place the state under a duty to use, or to facilitate the use of, the minority language, then the minority-speakers have a (moral) *right* to the public use of their language.[3] Framed in the most general terms, the question I want to explore is whether, and under what conditions, linguistic minorities do have language rights in this sense. When and under what conditions would they have a principled, minority-regarding objection to state monolingualism that would license the conclusion that rights had been violated? I shall consider this question in the present chapter without drawing any categorical distinctions between different kinds of language minorities, such as those formed by recent immigration and those that have a more established presence in the community in question. Chapter 8 is devoted to exploring distinctions of this sort.

The main argument of this chapter draws heavily on the account of equal recognition developed in preceding chapters. I shall argue that equal recognition ought to play a key role in thinking about the justification of minority-language rights, and that disputes about language rights ought to be examined from the perspective of what was called in chapter 5 "full liberal proceduralism." From this perspective, the mere fact that some minority language is doing

---

[2] For the claim that cultural diversity is valuable to third parties, see, e.g., Goodin 2006. The argument that linguistic diversity is valuable for all humanity is frequently made by linguists and language activists, many of whom draw a parallel between linguistic diversity and biodiversity. See, e.g., Nettle and Romaine 2000, 14; Crystal 2000, 32–36.

[3] The relationship between moral and legal rights here is quite complex. On the one hand, not all arguments for legal rights need to appeal to moral rights. Legal rights might be an appropriate policy instrument for responding to legitimate third-party-regarding or impersonal complaints about monolingualism. On the other hand, moral rights need not find their expression in legal rights. A state might, without the prodding of legal rights, adopt a fairly settled policy of serving minorities in their own language, thereby respecting their moral rights. Examining several postcommunist countries in eastern Europe, Csergő and Deegan-Krause (2011, 86) argue that "regardless of whether they 'speak the language' of group rights, new multiethnic democracies have gravitated toward group-based policies."

poorly does not by itself ground a legitimate complaint of injustice by speakers of that language. But minority-speakers do have a complaint—a defeasible one, as we shall see—if their language fares poorly in a context in which it is disfavored by public institutions. There is no right to language preservation, but there is a strong, pro tanto claim for equal recognition, a claim that can be considered a right in the absence of defeating countervailing considerations.

The argument of the chapter unfolds in eight sections. In the next section, I further refine the problem I am interested in by reviewing some key distinctions between different kinds of language rights. The debate that will concern us for much of the chapter is about "promotion" rights, not "toleration" or "accommodation" rights. Section 6.3 then describes two standard models for thinking about promotion rights: the nation-building and language preservation models. In section 6.4, the equal recognition approach is introduced and considered as an alternative to these models. Section 6.5 presents the basic case for equal recognition, a case that borrows freely from the work of previous chapters. Section 6.6 argues that there is no good general reason for preferring the nation-building model over equal recognition, even if the latter will sometimes have to make room for urgent concerns emphasized by the former. And Sections 6.7 and 6.8 defend a similar claim about the relationship between language preservation and equal recognition. Finally, section 6.9 concludes the chapter with a brief exploration of a key policy debate: that between advocates of the personality and territoriality principles.

6.2 Three Kinds of Language Rights

To isolate the issue that will concern us, it is necessary to distinguish between several different categories of language rights. Judged from the standpoint of justice, some of the most important language rights are not especially controversial. In the present section, I briefly consider two categories of such rights, which I call *toleration* rights and *accommodation* rights. Although these rights are not in dispute in the main debate that interests us in the chapter, examining them helps to clarify the nature of the rights that are in dispute.

The category of toleration-based rights derives from the pioneering work of Heinz Kloss, who distinguished between toleration-oriented and promotion-oriented language rights.[4] Toleration rights are protections individuals have against government interference with their private language choices. Rights that permit individuals to speak whatever languages they like—free from government interference—in their homes, in the associations and institutions of

---

[4] Kloss 1977. For adaptations of and critical responses to Kloss's distinction, see Green 1987, 660–62; Réaume 1991, 50–51; MacMillan 1998, 11–14; Rubio-Marín 2003a, 54–55; Patten and Kymlicka 2003, 26–27.

civil society, in the workplace, and so on are all examples of what Kloss meant by toleration rights. Promotion-oriented rights involve the use of a particular language by or in public institutions and are designed to promote the language in question. They are rights that an individual might have to the public use of a particular language—in the courts, the legislature, the public school system, the delivery of public services, and other official contexts.

Clearly many disputes about language rights raise questions that, in Kloss's vocabulary, concern promotion-oriented rights. Should the state adopt a monolingual education policy, designating a single language of instruction in all public schools, or should there be instruction in several languages, according to the needs and preferences of minority-speakers? Should it offer public services in the majority language only or in certain minority languages as well? And so on. At the same time, when states aggressively pursue a policy of monolingualism, they are often tempted to curtail use of minority languages in the private sphere, and this does raise the question of toleration rights. The issue here is whether the state can legitimately seek to restrict or regulate language use away from public institutions: in the economy, civil society, private home, and so forth.

The idea that minority-speakers should enjoy a fairly robust set of toleration rights is easy enough to accept insofar as such rights piggyback on the protection of other important values and rights. If citizens have a morally weighty complaint when they are denied enjoyment of these other values and rights, then they have the same complaint when they do not enjoy toleration rights. Although there are disagreements at the margins about the value and proper scope of freedom of expression, most people would regard that freedom as a key principle to be defended in any free and democratic society. And it is difficult to see how it could be consistent with such a principle for the state to restrict or meaningfully regulate the languages in which people choose to express themselves.[5] The long-standing Turkish policy of banning Kurdish-language newspapers and broadcasts was a straightforward infringement of freedom of expression.[6] Even if one were to maintain that ideas intended for expression in Kurdish could be perfectly translated into Turkish, any defensible principle of free expression would protect not just the content of speech but also its style and form.[7]

A similar argument can be made for privacy and parental autonomy. Clearly the boundaries of rights to privacy and parental autonomy are highly contestable, but again most people would accept that some rights in these areas are

[5] Carens 2000, 77.

[6] Reports by Human Rights Watch suggest that restrictions on Kurdish language expression have been eased somewhat in recent years. Kurdish-language publications and broadcasts are now permitted, and a Kurdish-language state television channel opened in 2009. For a snapshot of the situation in 2009, see http://www.hrw.org/world-report-2010/turkey (accessed February 8, 2012).

[7] Green 1991.

essential in a liberal democracy. The state should not be monitoring speech in the private home, in the associations of civil society, in private enterprises, or on the street, nor should it take away from parents all discretion regarding the moral or communal upbringing of their children.

In arguing that there are fairly straightforward justifications available for toleration-oriented language rights, I do not, of course, mean to suggest that these rights are universally respected, nor do I want to overlook the hard cases where limitations on toleration rights might legitimately be debated. Quebec's famous restrictions on the language of commercial signs, and Belgium's attempts to control the language spoken by children in the schoolyard, are perhaps good examples of borderline cases in which the damage to free speech or personal privacy is relatively mild and the benefits to the public claimed by supporters of the policies are quite significant. The aim here is not to resolve the difficult borderline cases but to observe that there is a set of core cases that are not especially controversial for people attempting to follow the principles of liberal democracy.

The analysis of accommodation rights runs along the same lines. To get a sense of what I mean by "accommodation rights," notice that Kloss's distinction between toleration and promotion rights is too crude. Consider, for instance, the right of an accused person lacking proficiency in the usual language of the court to a court-appointed interpreter. This language right is clearly not a tolerance-oriented right as that term has just been defined.[8] But nor is it obviously a promotion-oriented right either.[9] There is no real attempt to promote the accused person's language: if there were, the right would not be conditional on an inability to understand the usual language of the courts. Rather, the aim is to ensure that the accused can understand the court proceedings.

What is needed, this suggests, is a further distinction: this time between two different sorts of non-toleration-oriented rights, or two different approaches to the treatment of minority languages in public situations. One approach, which might be called the "norm-and-accommodation" model, involves the predominance of some normal language of public communication—typically, the majority language of the jurisdiction concerned. Unless some special circumstance arises, this language is used in the courts and legislatures, in the de-

---

[8] The analysis here departs from Green (1987, 660–62), who groups toleration and (what I am calling) accommodation rights into a single "regime of linguistic tolerance" that "is not restricted merely to negative rights." Green suggests that the general character of tolerance-based language rights is "integrationist" (661–62). This is true of accommodation rights and is plausibly illustrated (as Green says) by the U.S. Supreme Court's reasoning in *Lau v. Nichols*, 414 US 563 (1974). It is not necessarily true of toleration rights, however. As the Court noted in its other major case on language rights, *Meyer v. Nebraska*, 262 US 390 (1923), integrationist goals can militate against toleration of the private use of minority languages.

[9] Green 1987, 661; Rubio-Marín 2003a, 55. For a detailed discussion, see Réaume 2000, 255–58, 262–66.

livery of public services, as the medium of public education, and so on. Special accommodations are then made for people who lack sufficient proficiency in this normal language. These accommodations could take a variety of different forms depending on the circumstances. They might involve the provision of interpreters, the hiring of bilingual staff, or the use of transitional bilingual and/or intensive immersion educational programs to encourage rapid and effective acquisition of the normal language of public communication. The key priority is to establish communication between the public institution and those with limited proficiency in the usual language of public business, so that the latter can exercise the rights and access the benefits to which they are entitled.

The other approach might be called "promotion rights proper" or simply "promotion rights." The point of these rights is to promote the language with which they are associated, and, unlike the special accommodations offered under the norm-and-accommodation approach, their enjoyment is not contingent on a lack of proficiency in a "normal" public language. A person is free to exercise his promotion rights in a minority language even if he is quite fluent in the majority language.

As with toleration rights, the justification of accommodation rights has a piggybacking structure. Accommodation rights are instrumental to the enjoyment of other rights and entitlements, and their justification derives from the justification of those rights and entitlements. The right of a defendant to a court-provided interpreter, for instance, derives from the right to a fair trial. The right to a transitional bilingual program in the public school system derives from the right of children to gain literacy and numeracy even while they are learning the normal language of the society (together with the empirical judgment that transitional bilingualism will best allow children to enjoy the latter right). And so on.

As the discussion should indicate, I believe that the justification of certain toleration and accommodation rights in a liberal democracy is theoretically firm, even if empirically contestable in some cases (such as transitional bilingualism). At the same time, it should also be clear that these categories of rights represent only small subsets of the broader range of possible rights that minority-language-speakers might want to claim. The toleration rights only protect the discretion minority-language-speakers have to use their own language in private contexts of communication. They do not say anything about whether state institutions themselves have an obligation to use or recognize minority languages in any situations.[10]

Accommodation rights do mandate positive state action, but they too are limited in significant ways. Most important, they cannot be claimed by people

---

[10] But see Levy (2003) for an interesting attempt to justify a broad package of language rights as instrumentally valuable in helping to protect toleration rights. I commented briefly on Levy's approach in sec. 1.3.

who could, if they so chose, speak the majority, or normal, language of public communication. In addition, even focusing on cases where the minority-speaker does not understand the majority language, accommodation rights do not invariably imply an obligation on the part of the state to conduct activities in the minority language. The implication may instead be that the state should do a better job of teaching the majority language. In the United States, for instance, the current controversy over bilingual education mainly takes place within the accommodation rights framework.[11] As a result, much of the debate centers on the empirical question of whether transitional bilingual education programs or special English immersion ones do a better job of imparting a basic primary education to English-language learners.

None of this, I should emphasize, is intended to be critical of toleration or accommodation rights. These rights do represent a significant qualification of state monolingualism, and their denial, it should be clear, would give rise to morally weighty complaints on the part of minority-speakers. The point is that these rights do not come close to exhausting the sorts of minority-language rights that someone might want to justify. Minority-language activists often call for rights that are not restricted to the private sphere and that are not conditional on an inability to speak the majority language: they call for promotion rights. The question we shall focus on in the remainder of the chapter concerns the justification of promotion rights.

6.3 Two Models: Nation Building and Language Preservation

Political theorists have given surprisingly little attention to articulating a normative account of promotion-oriented language rights. In the absence of a well-worked-out normative theory, much of the discussion, both in academia and in public debate, has tended to operate implicitly with a simple dichotomy. On the one side, some people assume that language policy should aim to promote linguistic assimilation so as to ensure a common public language within each state or political community. This goal of promoting linguistic convergence, which is associated with nation-building projects of the nineteenth and twentieth centuries, is said to serve a number of important goals. On the other side, there are commentators who assume that language policy should aim to prevent linguistic assimilation and marginalization so as to preserve vulnerable languages. Minority-speakers are assumed to have important interests in the preservation of their languages that make this an appropriate goal of public institutions.

I shall call the first of these standard approaches the *nation-building* model. Harking back to the biblical story of the Tower of Babel, proponents of this

---

[11] See, e.g., the discussions in Crawford 2000; Schmidt 2000.

model regard language diversity as, above all, a problem—one that ought to be ameliorated through the effective use of public policy. For nation builders, the main question to ask in assessing any particular scheme of promotion-oriented language rights is whether it is maximally effective at promoting a common national language. Assuming that the designated common public language is also the majority language of the community in question, the nation-building model implies the rejection of promotion-oriented minority-language rights. Such rights do not encourage convergence on the majority language and will often impede this process.

I already touched on the rationale for this nation-building approach in section 5.4. The main hypothesis is that convergence on a common public language will serve a number of valuable goals. Most obviously, state institutions are more efficient when they operate in a single language only. With a single state language, it is no longer necessary to devote as much money or time to translations, simultaneous interpretation, separate networks of schools and hospitals, and so on. Freed from these costs, public institutions can devote more resources and energy to the core purposes for which they were created.

A common language also helps to ensure that all citizens enjoy an equal opportunity to work in the modern economy.[12] Minority-language communities risk being isolated when their members are unable or unwilling to master the majority language of the society. Their economic opportunities will be limited by the work available in their own language, and they will have trouble accessing the culture of the larger society or participating meaningfully in its political life. Conversely, as Ernest Gellner argued, employers depend on a public education in a common medium to place at their disposal a labor force possessing the linguistic competences necessary for flexibility, trainability, and mobility in the modern workplace.[13]

It can be argued further that a common language facilitates the deliberative dimension of democracy. Democratic decision-making is not just a formal process of voting on the basis of antecedently given preferences. It also presupposes an ongoing activity of deliberation and discussion, mainly taking place in civil society, in which free and equal citizens exchange reasons and are sometimes moved by them to change their opinions and preferences. Too much linguistic diversity may be a barrier to the full flourishing of this informal practice of democracy. If citizens cannot understand one another, or if they seek to deliberate with colinguists only, then democratic politics is likely to be compromised.[14] The nation-building model works against this challenge by encouraging the formation of a common language of democratic dialogue.

---

[12] Carens 2000, 79; Kymlicka 2001a, 26; Barry 2001, 103–9, 220.
[13] Gellner 1983.
[14] Van Parijs 2011a, 28–31.

Closely related to this, a common national language may also help to generate the solidarity, or social cohesion, required for a democratic state to provide public goods effectively and reliably. Fellow citizens must be willing to tolerate and trust each other, to defer to the requirements of public reason, and to accept burdens and sacrifices for the sake of the common good. Where the citizens of a particular community do not share some common political identity, these virtues and dispositions may be absent or weakened. The worry emphasized by nation builders is that an excess of linguistic diversity may fragment citizens into identity groups that do not share the affective bonds of common citizenship and see cooperation with one another solely as an instrument of mutual advantage.[15] They point out that, by contrast, a common language offers an object around which a common identity can be mobilized.

The second of the standard approaches might be called the *language preservation* model. For advocates of this approach, the main evaluative question to ask about a scheme of promotion-oriented language rights is whether it is doing an effective job at ensuring the success of languages that would otherwise be at risk. The success of a language—the degree to which it is surviving and flourishing—can be measured along several dimensions. For vulnerable languages, the two most important are the number of speakers of the language and the language's degree of marginalization. While the first of these dimensions of success is quite straightforward, the second is less familiar. It refers to the "domains," or range of contexts, in which the language is typically used. Highly marginalized languages often form part of a language system characterized by diglossia. Speakers of the marginalized language use their own language in contexts of intimacy—with family, friends, and close associates—but switch to some other, higher-status language in more prestigious public domains.[16] More successful languages, by this metric, are ones that are not marginalized; they are regularly used in prestigious public contexts involving interactions between strangers.

The general principle emphasized by language preservers, then, is that promotion-oriented language rights should promote the success of minority languages along these two dimensions. Different versions of the model correspond to different ways of specifying the optimization problem. For instance, one variant might prioritize maximizing the number of languages spoken in the community that satisfy some bare threshold test of survival. Another might focus on the strongest (and presumably most viable) of the community's minority languages and try to maximize its success along the two relevant

---

[15] Mill 1991, chap. 16; Van Parijs 2000a. This concern, and the related one about the conditions of deliberative democracy, have figured in debates about democratizing the European Union. See, e.g., the exchange between Grimm (1995) and Habermas (1995). For an empirical exploration of the relationship among language, social cohesion, and public good provision, see Miguel 2004.

[16] Ferguson 1959.

dimensions. Other versions of the model might prioritize slightly different preservationist goals or aim at the promotion of some weighted combination of several different goals. Since my ultimate aim is not to defend the language preservation model, I will leave the precise specification of the approach open, allowing its defenders to fill it in in whatever fashion seems most plausible to them or most compatible with their underlying concerns.

Adopting the language preservation model typically implies some kind of commitment to promotion-oriented language rights for minority-speakers, as well as to other forms of assistance for the targeted language(s) (such as corpus planning). Minority-language rights promote the success of minority languages by giving minority-speakers the opportunity to use (and, in the case of schools, to learn) the languages in question in important contexts. Such rights promote minority languages directly by admitting them into prestigious public domains of communication, and indirectly by raising the value of the languages to prospective learners.

Leslie Green has written that ensuring the preservation of vulnerable languages is "the implicit value assumption of nearly every linguistic demographer and sociolinguist" who has written on the subject of language rights.[17] There are several possible rationales for this assumption. One appeals to what I have termed the "third-party-regarding" and "impersonal" values associated with particular languages and with linguistic diversity. When a language disappears, this may be bad for everyone (and not just for those who would have spoken the language in question), and/or it may be bad in itself. Another rationale looks more directly to the interests of members of the disappearing language group themselves. As we shall see in more detail in section 6.8, they may find that their opportunities are diminished by the decline of their language group. And some of them will almost certainly feel that something they value and identify with is being lost.

Nation building and language preservation are often seen as two rival positions on promotion-oriented language rights, and that dichotomous view is supported by the brief pictures of them I have just sketched.[18] There is one interesting exception to this framing of the debate, however, which attracts a fair amount of attention in discussions of language policy. In some cases, speakers of the majority language of some state or political community think of their language as being a vulnerable minority language relative to another, more dominant and widely spoken language spoken outside the community. This is the situation in fairly small nation-states, such as Denmark or the Netherlands, where speakers of the local majority language cannot ignore the more powerful languages of their larger European neighbors, especially English. It is

---

[17] Green 1987, 653.
[18] May (2001) is an example of the dichotomous approach.

also the situation of national minorities that enjoy some degree of autonomy within a multinational state, for instance, Francophone Quebecers within Canada, and Catalan-speakers in Spain. They are in the majority locally but are minorities in a statewide context. In these kinds of cases, the recommendations of the nation-building and language preservation models may converge. From the point of view of the nation-building model, the local political community is well served by having a common public language, and it makes sense to designate the local majority language for this status. And from the standpoint of the language preservation model (in at least some specifications of that model), giving the vulnerable language its own space in which it is the common public language is an effective method of protecting it from (otherwise) more powerful neighboring languages.

As we shall see in the chapter's final section, one of the distinctive features of the equal recognition approach is that it does *not* agree with the nation-building and language preservation models about these cases involving vulnerable national languages. Whereas both the nation-building and language preservation models fit comfortably into a liberal nationalist framework, equal recognition offers a challenge to that consensus.

6.4 The Equal Recognition Model

A striking feature of the nation-building and language preservation models is that they each formulate the fundamental normative standard for evaluating schemes of promotion-oriented language rights in terms of the realization of a preferred outcome. For nation builders, the outcome is one in which a common public language is diffused among all citizens of the political community. For language preservers, it involves the preservation of languages that are vulnerable to assimilation and marginalization. One might say that both approaches work within a "language-planning" framework. The policy maker, or institutional designer, identifies some desirable outcome and then determines how public institutions can best help to realize the outcome.[19]

Once the two approaches are characterized in this way, it should immediately be apparent that a third family of approaches is also available. The approaches I have in mind offer a procedural, non-outcome-based account of the basic normative principles that govern the evaluation of possible schemes of promotion-oriented language rights. In a procedural account, we do not

---

[19] Sociolinguists often use the term "language planning" in a somewhat broader sense to denote "organized efforts to find solutions to societal language problems" (Fishman 1972, 186). Even under the rubric of this broad conception of "language planning," there is a tendency to think of these organized efforts in an outcome-oriented way. For instance, Fishman (1999, 157) writes that "as a result of language planning, policies are adopted and implemented in order to foster (or hamper) and to modernize (or, more rarely, to archaicize) one or more languages of a community's repertoire."

assess a scheme of rights by asking whether it is well calculated to bring about a desirable outcome but by asking whether it is consistent with background conditions that are sufficient to legitimate whatever outcomes should arise.

Both the possibility and the appeal of a procedural approach are obvious in other spheres of life where public institutions must take a stance. A more-or-less settled fact in most places in the world is the presence of a number of different religions and religious viewpoints. This diversity is hardly static, however. With great regularity over the course of history, new religious movements have appeared out of nowhere and risen to levels of considerable social importance, only to stagnate or even to disappear altogether. In the past few decades, for instance, religious denominations such as the Mormons and the Southern Baptists have enjoyed great success in attracting new adherents, while many of the more traditional denominations have struggled to avoid decline.

A historically important set of questions for political theory concerns how public institutions should respond to these facts of religious diversity and religious change. Should the state enforce laws against heresy, apostasy, blasphemy, and proselytization? Should it subsidize the activities of organized religions or give them tax breaks? Should it "establish" certain religions by giving their rituals or officials an official public role, or by making particular religious affiliations a condition of various rights or privileges?

One way in which these questions might be answered is by reference to an objective of promoting a common public religion. Public institutions could adopt rules regarding religious freedom and religious establishment that seek to bring about this outcome. Some might expect such an outcome to have a variety of salutary effects for the political community in question. It might improve social cohesion, for instance, and intensify the patriotic commitment of citizens. Alternatively, the aim of public policy with respect to religion might conceivably be to maintain or protect religions that are vulnerable to decline or disappearance. Committed members of vulnerable religious groups presumably wish to see their religions survive into the indefinite future. And they might value living in a community in which at least some others—and perhaps most others—share their religious beliefs and practices.

I take it that many people would find both these approaches objectionable and that even people who are sympathetic to one or another of them would acknowledge that there is an important third alternative. According to this third view, it is not the business of the state to promote some specific outcome with respect to the success or failure of the different religions adhered to by its citizens. Instead, the appropriate response to religious diversity is for the state to establish a framework of rules that is fair to all individuals, and then to permit individuals to develop their own religious convictions, and choose their own religious affiliations, within the space left to them by these rules. Depending on what convictions individuals develop, and which affiliations they choose, some religions will flourish and others may decline or even disappear.

This third way of responding to diversity and change is articulated at a more general level by Rawls in a section of *Political Liberalism*.[20] Considering the objection that certain ways of life and conceptions of the good may not flourish, or even survive, in the institutions he considers just, Rawls responds by questioning whether public institutions should have as their aim the promotion or maintenance of any particular form of life. Instead, he argues, public institutions should establish "a just basic structure within which permissible forms of life have a fair opportunity to maintain themselves and to gain adherents over time."[21] In this view, the key requirement is not to achieve a particular outcome such as convergence or maintenance. Rather, the responsibility of public institutions is to ensure that different ways of life, and conceptions of the good, struggle for survival and success under "background conditions" that are fair.[22] This requirement that public institutions be fair to conceptions of the good is one part of a larger view about what it is to be fair to the individuals who adopt and pursue those conceptions.

The suggestion I want to explore, then, is that we should think about the normative issues surrounding language rights in procedural terms. The issues that call for exploration are apparent enough. We need to say more precisely what a defensible procedural approach would involve. And we also need to explain why, and how far, such an approach is indeed defensible. Even if proceduralism is the right response to religious diversity, it would not follow that it is the most suitable way of dealing with linguistic diversity. There may be reasons for promoting particular outcomes in the language case that are less salient for the case of religion. In this view, proceduralism may be a coherent position to adopt with respect to language policy but not a very appealing one. I will consider this possibility in the next few sections and partially accept it. Still, I will argue that proceduralism can contribute in a substantial way to a hybrid normative theory of language rights. Before getting to this discussion, however, let us flesh out the procedural alternative to the two language planning models.

There are in fact many different procedural approaches that might be considered. What they all share in common is a rejection of language planning. The task of language policy is not to realize some specific linguistic outcome but to establish non-outcome-based fair background conditions under which speakers of different languages can strive for the survival and success of their respective language communities. What distinguishes different members of the procedural family from one another is the specific understanding of fair background conditions that each assumes.

[20] Rawls 2005, 190–200.
[21] Ibid., 198.
[22] Ibid., 199.

One prominent member of the family might be called the *democratic permission* model. In this model, any linguistic outcome is just so long as the scheme of language rights under which it arises is (a) consistent with standard liberal rights and entitlements and (b) adopted through a legitimate democratic procedure. This model is essentially just an application of the more general approach I termed "basic liberal proceduralism" in the previous chapter. It thus suffers from the same fundamental problem that we discovered in studying that more general approach. While it is easy to accept that standard liberal rights and entitlements (the "standard liberal package") are a necessary condition of procedural justice, it is much less plausible to think of them as sufficient for that purpose. Liberal neutrality is also an important liberal principle, but it goes unmentioned in the conditions required by basic proceduralism. When public institutions show a nonneutral preference for the majority language over the minority, it is hard to avoid the suspicion that people who value the minority language, and care about its use and preservation, have a (defeasible) justice-based complaint about an outcome in which that language fares poorly.

One distinctive feature of democratic permission relative to basic proceduralism more generally is its emphasis on democratic decision-making. Defenders of democratic permission argue that leading normative theories of language rights wrongly neglect democratic procedures, and that this is an especially serious oversight in light of the importance of context in fashioning a satisfactory scheme of such rights.[23] As I argued in chapter 1, however, the appeal to democratic legitimacy in this context involves a conflation of two different questions. There is a question of who should decide, which quite plausibly should be answered in a democratic fashion. But there is also a substantive question—what do those people who are authorized to decide have most reason to decide?—which even the citizens of a democracy ought to consider. Since our question here is the substantive one, the invocation of democratic procedures misses the point. Perhaps language disputes should be settled democratically, but this does not obviate the need for substantive principles that help clarify the choices that citizens are to make.

So democratic permission is not a very satisfactory showcase of the power or appeal of the proceduralist approach. A more promising alternative to democratic permission incorporates the idea of equal recognition. In this view, a variant of what I called "full liberal proceduralism" in chapter 5, a scheme of language rights confers procedural justice on linguistic outcomes if and only if it (a) is compatible with standard liberal rights and entitlements and (b) extends equal recognition to majority and minority languages alike. As with any proceduralist view, this equal recognition model is compatible with a variety of different outcomes. There may or may not be convergence on a

---

[23] See Carens 2000; Laitin and Reich 2003.

common public language. Vulnerable minority languages may or may not be preserved. The key question is not whether these outcomes occur, but whether the outcomes—whatever they are—arise under background conditions that protect standard liberal rights and entitlements and extend equal recognition to majority and minority languages. Where background conditions depart from these standards, those who are disadvantaged by the outcomes have a pro tanto complaint of injustice.

I shall refine and qualify this particular version of proceduralism further in section 6.7. For now, let me a say a little about the policy implications of the unqualified version. Two or more languages enjoy equal recognition from public institutions when those institutions extend roughly comparable forms of assistance to each on a prorated basis. I call the resulting scheme *prorated official multilingualism*. Under official multilingualism, each language spoken in the community enjoys the same benefits of the law. For instance, if a particular public service (e.g., advice about tax matters from a government office) is offered in one language spoken in the community, then that same service is also offered in other languages spoken in the community. Or if a particular piece of public business (e.g., filing a suit in a court of law) can be conducted in one language, then it can also be conducted in the others. Moreover, in the official multilingualism scheme as I shall understand it, there are no significant restrictions on who can access a public institution in a particular language. For instance, a minority-X-speaker would have the right to send his child to a school instructing in the X language even if he and/or his child were perfectly fluent in the majority language Y. The aim of the official multilingualism approach is not to provide special transitional accommodations for those who lack fluency in the majority language but to establish a form of equality—equality of treatment—between speakers of different languages.

In a scheme of *prorated* official multilingualism, some account is taken of the number of people demanding services in each recognized language. The ultimate purpose of equal recognition is to establish fair conditions for individuals who speak different languages, not to be fair to the languages themselves. As I argued in section 5.2, fairness to individuals requires offering the same per capita level of assistance to the different languages those individuals speak. Where there are significant economies of scale in the provision of public assistance, equivalent assistance cannot be provided in less widely spoken languages without departing from this norm of fairness. Thus a more restricted set of public services may be offered in less widely spoken languages, or speakers of such languages might be expected to travel farther to find services in their own language, or the eligibility of such people to receive services in their own language may be constrained by a "where numbers warrant" proviso. Again the underlying principle is equality of treatment, but, with the prorating refinement, this form of equality is said to be realized when people receive services in their own language equivalent in value to their fair claim on public resources rather than when they receive equivalent services.

A scheme of prorated official multilingualism might conceivably be implemented by a planner guided by one or other of the planning models. The planner might judge that, in a particular social context, the (prorated) equal recognition of the different languages would have the effect of producing the outcome associated with the planning model being adopted. It should be obvious, however, that in most contexts official multilingualism would not be the right policy for a planner interested in either convergence on a common public language or language preservation. Official multilingualism may offer too much recognition of minority languages for a planner interested in promoting convergence on the majority language and not enough recognition of minority languages for those interested in preserving those languages. It is in these empirical contexts that equal recognition shows itself to be a distinctive alternative to the planning models. Equal recognition is the model that a policy maker is implicitly or explicitly appealing to when she affirms a commitment—on grounds of equality—to (prorated) official multilingualism, even in the face of evidence that such a policy will lead to neither convergence on a common public language nor maintenance of vulnerable minority languages.

The equal recognition model represents a way of defending minority-language rights that has too often been ignored.[24] Minority-language rights will often turn out to be a necessary part of the institutional framework that establishes fair background conditions under which members of different language communities can each strive for the survival and success of their respective language communities. Unless certain minority-language rights are acknowledged—for instance, in the areas of education and public services—members of the minority language community could reasonably complain that they do not have a fair opportunity to realize their language-related ambitions.

6.5 The Case for Equal Recognition

One kind of argument that will *not* help us make the case for the equal recognition model appeals to the communicative interests that people have in language rights. Undeniably, people have very important interests in being able to communicate both with public institutions and with others in their society more generally. Where communication is possible, an important obstacle is removed to people asserting their rights, participating in decision

[24] For earlier accounts that do refer to fairness, see Green 1987; Green and Réaume 1989; Réaume 1991; 1994; 2000. For discussion, see Patten 2009, 121–24.

making, joining the workforce, and engaging in a rich array of other valuable activities. But, given that we are specifically interested in promotion-oriented language rights, an appeal to communicative interests is of little assistance. We want to know whether minority-speakers have rights to the public use of their language even in situations where they could easily be brought to learn the majority language—indeed, even in situations where they already speak the majority language. It cannot be communication that matters for minority-language rights in this context because communication can occur in the majority language.

So how should one think about the foundations of promotion-oriented language rights? Instead of communication, I think we should focus on two other interests that people have. One is an interest in being able to access the particular options that they value; the other is an interest in the accommodation of their identity. Both can be seen as aspects of the more general interest in self-determination discussed in earlier chapters. Unlike the interest in communication, both interests are most plausibly advanced when a minority-speaker's own language is helped to succeed. Mastering the majority language may be desirable for other reasons, but it does not help with these particular interests.

The idea that people have an interest in being able to access the particular options they value is a straightforward implication of the more general idea that people have an interest in self-determination—in being able to pursue and fulfill the conception of the good that they actually hold. What is less obvious is why this interest is best served for a minority-speaker by a scheme of language rights that promotes the minority language. The explanation draws on the account I sketched in section 3.4 of cultures as "option-generators." It is not unusual for people who belong to the same linguistic community to share preferences for particular options, practices, styles, and so on. Of course, colinguists will not *all* share the preferences in question—in communities of any size, there will be sharp differences and disagreements—but the *frequency* with which certain preferences are held may be much greater within a particular linguistic group than outside of it. (For example, think of tastes for particular musical styles and performers.) This fact about preferences becomes significant once it is recalled that many of the options people care about are likely to be more readily available when more people value them. The goods that are integral to the options are produced with economies of scale, and the practices and institutions in which the options are made available are stronger and richer with more participants. This is not true of all options in all contexts, of course. Some options are subject to scarcity and/or congestion effects when too many people pursue them, and there are options that derive some of their desirability from the very fact that others are not pursuing them (e.g., the enjoyment of unspoiled natural wilderness). But these exceptions aside, people with preferences that are distinctive of their linguistic community have a good reason to care about the ongoing success of that community. The options they care about are more likely to remain available if their language community survives and flourishes than if its members assimilate into another language group.

The connection between the second of the interests I mentioned—the interest in identity—and the promotion of a minority-speaker's own language is even more immediate. To say that language is central to some individual's identity is to say something about her attitudes and preferences. To have an identity based on language X involves, for instance, some or all of the following dispositions. The individual self-identifies with the (local) community of X-speakers. She is proud of the language and the cultural achievements that have been expressed through it. She takes pleasure in using X and encountering others who are willing to use it. She enjoys experimenting with X and discussing its intricacies and subtleties with colinguists. She hopes that the X community will survive and flourish into the indefinite future. She finds that a number of her other preferences are linked with, and may be expressions of, her identification with the X community. In some contexts, she feels respected and affirmed when others address her in X and denigrated when others impose their linguistic preferences on her. And so on. To say that she has an identity interest is to say that she has an interest in the accommodation of some or all of these preferences and attitudes. And if she does have such an interest, it will clearly not be served by assimilation into the majority language. A person who identifies with her own language will be satisfied only by the success or respectful treatment of *that* language.

Having identified two interests that seem relevant to our topic, the next step is to consider how they should figure in a normative argument about language rights. Why think that these interests lend their support to the equal recognition model? One alternative would be to deny that the interests we have been describing are a requirement of liberal justice at all. A very different alternative would be to embrace the importance of the two interests but insist that they support the language preservation model rather than equal recognition.

The bridge between the two interests and the equal recognition model is provided by the account of liberal neutrality developed in chapter 4. Just because the options a person cares about are unavailable does not by itself imply any injustice to that person. Nor need there be an injustice whenever public institutions fail to accommodate some aspect of a person's or a group's identity. But, as I argued in chapter 4, people do have a defeasible complaint of injustice when public institutions treat the things they care about nonneutrally—that is, when they impose more burdens on, or extend fewer benefits to, the pursuit of their conception of the good than they do to the conceptions that matter to other people. The underlying value here that liberals should care about is the fair opportunity for self-determination. The pro tanto obligation of neutral treatment is grounded in the pro tanto obligation to give all persons a fair opportunity to pursue and fulfill the conception of the good that they happen to hold. The strength of the pro tanto obligation depends in part on the way in which the particular options at issue in a given case matter to people. Neutrality is an especially weighty obligation with respect to options and preferences that are connected with identity.

With this concept of neutrality in the background, the case for equal recognition is quite straightforward. There are three basic dispositions that public institutions can adopt with respect to the recognition of languages. They can recognize the majority language only, guaranteeing a limited set of toleration and accommodation rights for linguistic minorities but otherwise conducting all business exclusively in the majority language. They can recognize none of the languages spoken by their citizens, designating some other language for public business. Or they can extend equal positive recognition to some or all of the different languages spoken by citizens, offering public services, and making it possible to conduct public business, in each of those languages.

The first of these approaches conflicts with neutrality. Speakers of minority languages who care about the success of their language will have a defeasible justice-based complaint about such a scheme of language rights. The second is generally unfeasible and undesirable. Although there are some examples of states that have attempted a version of this approach (e.g., Indonesia's adoption of Bahasa Indonesia as the sole official language of the state, and various postcolonial states that adopted the language of the former colonial power), in general the nonrecognition option is a nonstarter. Public institutions have to operate in *some* language(s), and they will typically be constrained by practicality and public preference to choose the public language(s) from the list of languages already spoken fairly widely within the community. So this leaves equal recognition as the only remaining approach. It is the only one that both is consistent with neutrality and has at least some degree of feasibility.

The gist of the argument, then, is to emphasize the importance of neutrality to a liberal view of politics, an importance that is reinforced by the significant ways in which language and language community can matter to people. Unless linguistic minorities enjoy equal recognition of their languages, the background conditions under which they strive for the enjoyment and success of those languages will conflict with liberal neutrality and thus cannot be considered sufficiently fair to warrant the judgment that outcomes are just.

As I have emphasized all along, the claims about fair opportunity for self-determination, liberal neutrality, and thus equal recognition each have a defeasible character. Given the importance of language to some people—as highlighted by the identity interest in particular—the claims should be treated as having considerable weight, but their weight is not absolute. With a sufficiently good countervailing reason, the state is justified in overriding the claims of equal recognition, although a residue of the pro tanto reason survives and should motivate the state to build toward conditions in which that reason can ultimately be satisfied. The question we must now address concerns when, in fact, there is sufficient reason to override equal recognition. We shall see that considerations associated with the nation-building and language preservation models do *sometimes* outweigh the claims of equal recognition, but there is no *general* priority of nation building or language preservation over those claims. The result is a hybrid model of promotion-oriented language rights in which equal recognition has a significant role to play.

6.6 The Nation-Building Challenge

I have already sketched some of the considerations that count in favor of the nation-building model. As we saw in section 6.3, the main arguments emphasize the social utility of a common public language. One argument appeals to the relationship between language and *opportunity*. A second focuses on the function a common language performs of providing a medium for *democratic deliberation*. A third maintains that a common public language can provide the basis for a *common identity* that binds together the citizens of a state and reinforces their civic virtues and sense of mutual solidarity. A fourth way in which a common language is useful is that it can reduce the *cost of public administration*. When a common public language is achieved, it is no longer necessary for public institutions to make significant expenditures on translation and interpretation services, and the resources that are freed up can be devoted to other priorities.

Some of these reasons for thinking that a common public language would be socially useful are more challenging to the equal recognition model than others. For instance, most people do not think that *every* possible measure reducing the cost of public administration should for that reason be implemented. In many areas of public administration, people are willing to tolerate costly or time-consuming procedures aimed at enhancing equality or fairness. The same goes for measures designed to promote a stronger sense of common identity. As I suggested in section 6.4, it is conceivable that a religiously homogeneous society would have a stronger sense of common identity than a heterogeneous society (see also sec. 5.4). But even if this were the case, most liberals would still oppose a policy of state preference for the majority religion designed to bring about greater homogeneity.

As for the appeal to democratic deliberation, it is not clear how much commonality of language deliberative democracy actually requires. If deliberative democracy entails that every citizen should be able to communicate directly with every other citizen, then the absence of a common language would indeed be a problem. But for reasons having to do with scale, and with the limited amount of leisure time that citizens have for deliberation, most deliberative democrats would not advocate such a demanding ideal of citizen deliberation. Citizens can exchange reasons through mediators and go-betweens (the media, elites, and so on), and thus it is not necessary for them literally to be able to speak with every fellow citizen. So long as these mediators and go-betweens are able, through personal bilingualism or reliance on translators and interpreters, to bridge any linguistic divides that they encounter, a common public language is not strictly necessary for deliberative democracy.

In any case, a detailed consideration of each of the different reasons for thinking a common public language to be socially useful is not feasible within a single chapter. Instead I propose to examine in more detail just one of the arguments mentioned above: the appeal to opportunity. The aim is to illustrate the thesis that, even granting the validity of the nation-building approach in some contexts, the equal recognition model still plays an important role in a normative theory of language politics. A complete demonstration of the thesis would require a fuller consideration of the common identity, democracy, and cost-reduction arguments (see also the remarks in sec. 5.4).

As I mentioned in section 6.3, one of the main concerns about language diversity emphasized by proponents of the nation-building model is that the speakers of some languages will end up isolated. This concern reflects the great importance attached to opportunity and social mobility in a liberal democracy. We do not think it is acceptable for an individual's life chances to be significantly constrained by the social position he is born into. Just as public institutions should seek to nullify the effects of class, race, ethnicity, and gender on a person's life opportunities, they should do the same for language. It would violate the spirit, if not the letter, of the principle that Rawls calls "fair equality of opportunity" if one person's life prospects were to be significantly lower than those of fellow citizens for some avoidable reason related to his linguistic capabilities.[25]

As we know from chapter 3, one way of expressing this concern is to say that all individuals need access to what Will Kymlicka calls an adequate "context of choice." They must have at their disposal a variety of valuable options and opportunities embracing the full range of human activities. Being able to communicate with the people around one is a precondition of having access to this context of choice. Without competence in the language spoken by those around her, a person will encounter difficulties in finding a job, doing business, making friends, practicing a religion, and so on.

As we did in section 2.5, we can say that a language supports a "societal culture" when an adequate context of choice is available in that language. There is a Francophone societal culture in Quebec, for instance, because and to the extent that a French speaker in Quebec has access to an adequate range of options and opportunities operating in the French language. There is no Italian-speaking societal culture in the United States, by contrast, because and

[25] Rawls 1999a, 63–64; Van Parijs 2011a, chap. 3.

to the extent that an Italian speaker in that context lacks an adequate range of Italian-language options and opportunities. To enjoy an adequate range of opportunities, an Italian-speaker in the United States must learn English and access the English-language societal culture that dominates the country. As these examples suggest, an individual's interest in adequate opportunity can be satisfied in two different ways: there can be a societal culture operating in the individual's native language, or the individual can integrate into a societal culture by learning the language in which it operates.

The implications for language policy of this concern with opportunity and social mobility are complex and depend on the nature of the case. The argument for the nation-building model highlights one particular kind of situation. In this situation there is only one viable societal culture in the state (operating, we might assume for simplicity, in the state's majority language). Although there are speakers of minority languages, there is no societal culture operating in any minority language. Unilingual speakers of a minority language do not, therefore, have access to an adequate context of choice. Nor, we might further specify, could a minority language societal culture easily be constructed (or revived) by means of public policy.

Under these conditions, a concern for social mobility seems to dictate a policy of getting minority-language-speakers to learn the majority language.[26] Without the majority language, they would be excluded. Unlike their majority-language fellow citizens, they would lack access to an adequate range of economic, social, political, and cultural options and opportunities. Given the great importance we normally attach to social mobility, it seems that the state should not, therefore, be wholly neutral with respect to linguistic outcomes. In some situations, the only way to establish conditions under which all citizens can enjoy social mobility is for the state to aim for a specific language outcome—one in which there is a public language shared by members of the majority and minority alike. Indeed, such is the value attached to social mobility in a liberal democracy that it is tempting to regard this as a knockdown argument in favor of the nation-building model over equal recognition. As I will now argue, however, this conclusion would not be warranted. There remain two important contexts in which equal recognition has a role to play.

The first is connected with the assumption in the argument I have just been sketching that there is only one viable societal culture. This is certainly a fair assumption for some real-world cases, notably including the United States (at least if Puerto Rico is disregarded). But there are many other cases in which several viable societal cultures find themselves sharing a common state or where there are reasons to think that additional societal cultures could establish themselves, perhaps with the assistance of public policy. Canada, Belgium,

---

[26] For this possibility, see Pogge 2000 and Barry 2001, 103–8, 215–20, 226–28, 324.

Switzerland, and Spain are all examples of countries containing several viable societal cultures.

Where a state does contain several viable societal cultures, then from the standpoint of furthering the interest in adequate opportunity there is no need to promote a common public language.[27] An individual's interest in having access to an adequate context of choice would be satisfied by mastering any of the languages corresponding to a viable societal culture. So long as the state is taking measures to ensure that individuals become fluent in at least one of these societal languages, it can otherwise afford to be neutral regarding linguistic outcomes. From the point of view of social mobility, one common public language is no better or worse than several language communities each of which offers an adequate context of choice to its members. In a situation like this, a policy of (prorated) official multilingualism of the sort described in section 6.4 would work to allocate speakers of different languages their fair shares of public resources and attention without jeopardizing anyone's interest in adequate opportunity.

Even if a state does contain only one viable societal culture, there is a second context in which the concern for opportunity still leaves some room for equal recognition. In some circumstances, a common public language may be rather easy to achieve, in the sense that it could be brought about under a range of different language policies. If minority-language-speakers do not enjoy adequate opportunity in their own language, there is already a strong incentive for them to learn the majority language. It is possible that all, or almost all, members of the minority-language community can be made to acquire the majority language with only minimal assistance from public policy. It might be the case, for instance, that a robust curriculum of second-language education in the majority language in a school system that is otherwise available in the minority language would be sufficient to make the majority-language societal culture accessible to minority-language-speakers. Under these circumstances, the interest in social mobility would be compatible with either majority-language official unilingualism or with some form of institutional recognition of the minority language that involved adequate second-language teaching of the majority language.[28]

Suppose, for instance, that, in the context of the U.S. debate over bilingual education, it was the case that both bilingual education and English immersion schemes had roughly comparable levels of success at making English-as-a-second-language students proficient in English. Under these conditions, the nation-building model would not tell us which policy to prefer. It would set

---

[27] This is recognized by Barry (2001, 105, 228).

[28] Even if teaching the majority language as a subject is not by itself a sufficient guarantee that minority-language-speakers will master it, this general approach might be supplemented by other measures that fall well short of rejecting minority rights. For one proposal, see the argument against dubbing in Van Parijs 2011a, 106–13.

a lexical first priority—leaving students proficient in English—but it would not help us to decide among the alternatives as one moves down the lexical ordering.

The indeterminacy of the nation-building model creates a space for equal recognition. Where several different language policies are compatible with realizing a common public language, the equal recognition model indicates that we should prefer the one that comes closest to establishing fair background conditions under which different languages and language-based identities can strive for survival and success.[29] In the U.S. case—assuming the empirical conditions stipulated above—I take it that this would indicate a preference for educational schemes incorporating some form of bilingualism over those that insist on English immersion.

The argument of the previous few paragraphs assumes that the main way in which decisions about the language of instruction in public schools have an impact on opportunity is by influencing the minority-language-speaker's proficiency in the majority language. For people to be equipped for social mobility, however, it is not enough that they leave school proficient in the majority language. They must also have a further range of skills, dispositions, competencies, and so on. Different medium-of-instruction alternatives may have a further, less direct effect on social mobility if they have an impact on the student's propensity to develop these other necessary skills, dispositions, and competencies, or if they leave minority-language-speakers with reduced access to valuable social networks. It is difficult to know whether these indirect effects lend more support for bilingual education or immersion schemes. In the U.S. context, it is often argued that language-minority status correlates strongly with low socioeconomic status. As a result, it is tempting to think that the same arguments that can be made in favor of breaking down class barriers in the public education system can also be made in favor of breaking down linguistic barriers through a single medium of public education.[30] On the other hand, minority children with limited proficiency in the majority language may, in the early years of their education at least, more effectively develop literacy, numeracy, and so on, through instruction in their home language. And it is sometimes argued that developing a positive sense of self-identity is one of

---

[29] It seems to me that presenting the argument this way is enough to dissolve the "puzzle" that Brian Barry (2001, 104) claims to find in Iris Marion Young's discussion of language policy. Barry finds it curious that Young would say both that "many Spanish-speaking Americans have asserted their right to maintain their specific culture and speak their language and still receive the benefits of citizenship" and that "few advocates of cultural pluralism and group autonomy in the United States would deny that proficiency in English is a necessary condition for full participation in American society." There is no contradiction between these propositions if Spanish-language accommodations do not come at the expense of learning English. For Young's own statement of her position, see Young 1990, chap. 6.

[30] For this form of argument (as well as the more straightforward claim that English-medium schooling is more likely to leave minority-language students proficient in English), see, e.g., Rodriguez 1982, chap. 1; Porter 1996, 187–90.

the keys to social mobility, and that this positive sense of self can be effectively encouraged through education schemes, such as bilingual education, which develop and reinforce preexisting social characteristics rather than attempting to negate them. Although these indirect effects of language of education on social mobility seriously complicate the argument I have been making, they do not affect the basic point. They are all consistent with the idea that opportunity considerations may not, on their own, be fully decisive in deciding among various language policy options. Where they are not, the fairness considerations emphasized by the equal recognition model have an important role to play.

An argument from the interest in adequate opportunity, then, only partially vindicates the view that language policy should be guided by the nation-building model. Where a state contains only one societal culture, it is true that a major responsibility of public institutions should be to ensure that everyone is able to speak the language in which that societal culture operates. Some states contain more than one viable societal culture, however, and even states that do contain only one such culture may find that there are several different ways of bringing about a common language and of equipping minority-language-speakers with the skills, dispositions, and competencies they need for social mobility. There is space for the equal recognition model to play a role in both of these scenarios. Since considerations of social mobility do not dictate a policy of exclusively recognizing the majority language, policy makers can seek to give at least some positive recognition to other languages as well. Such a policy would help to leave members of minority-language communities with a fair opportunity to realize their language-related identities and ambitions.

6.7 The Language Preservation Challenge—Weak Versions

The language preserver's challenge starts from the observation that equally recognizing several languages does not guarantee that they will be equally successful or even that they will all survive. Even though public services are offered and public business can be transacted in some language, this does not ensure its health or vitality. It does not guarantee a stable number of speakers of the language or that the language will retain importance in key spheres of language use.

There are numerous determinants of the success of languages, of which public use or recognition is only one.[31] The birthrate within the language community, the language that parents choose to raise and educate their children in, and the language repertoires and choices of newcomers all affect the

---

[31] Laponce 1984; Edwards 1985; Fishman 1991; 2001; Spinner 1994; Laitin 1998; Van Parijs 2011a.

size and degree of marginalization of a linguistic community. Even though a language is designated for public use, it may not be the principal language of work, business, or civil society; some other language may be the de facto medium of economic opportunity and social interaction. In this context, it may be rational for adults to invest heavily in acquiring the more widely used language and for parents to educate their children in, and newcomers to integrate into, this language as well. When these choices to adopt another, economically more powerful language become widespread, even a language that enjoys equal recognition may have difficulty surviving.[32]

These observations lead to the objection that equal recognition is much too formal an approach to language policy. Equal recognition advocates giving the same treatment to all even when it is predictable that some will race ahead and others lag behind. By treating all languages the same, very unequal outcomes result. An alternative would focus on the outcomes themselves. The language preservation model does exactly that, targeting some desirable preservationist outcome and adapting the scheme of language rights to bring it about.

Although the policy implications of the language preservation model can be hard to make out, clearly they may diverge from the ones associated with equal recognition (that is, from prorated official multilingualism). Given that minority languages are subject to pressures of assimilation and marginalization at the hands of the majority language, the most effective way to realize the language preserver's goal may be to extend a better-than-equal set of rights to the minority languages and, by implication, a lesser set of rights to the majority language. The idea is publicly to privilege the more vulnerable language or languages as a means of signaling to people that the language is worth learning and using on a regular basis.

Insofar as the equal recognition and language preservation models pull in opposite directions, it is important to explore how their respective claims should be balanced against one another. As I did with regard to the nation-building model, I want to argue here for a two-part thesis. The first part consists in allowing that there are certain contexts in which it does seem plausible to prioritize the language preserver's concern with unacceptable outcomes over the values that ground equal recognition. In these situations, the claims of equal recognition should be circumscribed to make room for those of language preservation. The second part of the thesis, however, denies that the reasonable claims of language preservation make equal recognition superfluous. These claims still leave plenty of elbowroom for equal recognition. Once again

---

[32] Irish is a good example of a publicly recognized language that would be hard to consider a resounding success. Although around 43 percent of Irish citizens claim to have some knowledge of the language, only around 3 percent report using it as their main community and household language. See Government of Ireland 2006.

we are left with a hybrid normative theory of language rights, one in which equal recognition plays a substantial role.

There are weaker and stronger ways of challenging equal recognition from a broadly preservationist perspective. The weaker challenges point to complicating factors that require a refinement of the account of equal recognition presented earlier. In general, these challenges suggest that the argument from equal recognition to prorated official multilingualism needs to be qualified in certain respects, but they do not imply the rejection of equal recognition itself. By contrast, the stronger challenges would, if valid, imply the rejection of equal recognition itself. Clearly, we need to pay special attention to the stronger challenges (see the next section), but let us begin by noting several versions of the weaker form of objection.

Several of the complicating factors were flagged already in section 5.6. They include economic injustice, historical injustice, and market failure:

> *Economic injustice.* As we have seen, the success of a language is not just a matter of the framework of public rights and entitlements the language enjoys but also depends on the decisions that people make within that framework. Many of these decisions have an economic dimension to them and thus are determined, in part, by the existing distribution of economic assets. Where this distribution is skewed systematically toward speakers of one language and away from the other(s), the result is likely to be a bias against the latter. Speakers of the unprivileged language(s) will feel compelled to learn the language of the economic elite as a ticket to opportunity and advancement. Under conditions like these, equal treatment of the two language groups may be unfair if nothing is done to correct or compensate for the kinds of unfairness that are predictably thrown up by market interactions. It would be hard to argue to members of a disadvantaged language group that a policy of equal treatment leaves them with a "fair opportunity" to realize their identity if, in fact, their lower economic position systematically thwarts the realization of their identity-related goals and projects.
>
> *Historical injustice.* A distinct but often related worry about equal recognition is that it may work as a kind of rubber stamp on historical injustices. A language community may find it hard to flourish under conditions of equal treatment because it is hobbled by injustices it has suffered in the past. The members of the group may have faced significant forms of discrimination, contempt, and denigration in the past, and these past injustices may affect their present capacity to realize their identity. To flourish, a language must have some success at competing with other local languages for speakers and for pres-

tigious domains of language use. Where members of one language group are still dealing with the effects of past injustices, it is hard to be confident that such competition would be "fair" if public institutions make no effort to correct or compensate for the historic damage but instead simply insist on a policy of equal treatment.

Market failure. Even when the distribution of economic assets is fair and there is no legacy of historical injustice, a language regime based on equal recognition may show a bias against languages that are valued by their speakers but require a high level of coordination to be successful. The success of a language is the product of thousands, even millions, of discrete decisions about language use and language acquisition made by speakers and potential speakers every day. No single one of these decisions will make a tangible difference to the overall success of the language, but particular decisions may make a difference to individuals seeking to complete a successful act of communication or to endow themselves or their children with a useful skill. Faced with these incentives, even people who care a great deal about the success of their own vulnerable language may find themselves using the dominant language on a regular basis. The more that speakers of the vulnerable language reason in this way, however, the more it is likely that the success of that language will be seriously impaired. The objection to the equal recognition model, then, is that it leaves too much to be determined by the disaggregated, uncoordinated decisions of individuals. It is all too predictable that vulnerable languages will fare poorly in this environment, and that speakers of those languages may collectively produce an outcome that they disprefer to the outcome that would ensue if all (or at least most) of them stuck to the use and transmission of their own language. Insofar as equal recognition rules out state measures designed to overcome this collective action problem, it seems biased against the vulnerable language.

Obviously more should be said to elaborate each of these objections, but rather than attempt such elaboration here I will content myself with the much more limited suggestion that none of them requires a wholesale jettisoning of the equal recognition model. They require that the model be qualified and complicated in various ways that are likely to be congenial to the general outlook of language preservers, but they do not imply that the model should be abandoned in favor of the language preservation model.

This response is most straightforward in the case of the objection from economic injustice. The objection highlights an assumption of the account that has been stated from the beginning. Equal recognition is a procedural model, but it does not claim that equal recognition alone (or its policy expression in official multilingualism) is sufficient to confer procedural justice on linguistic outcomes. For precisely the reason highlighted by the objection—the interaction between linguistic decisions and economic circumstances—equal recognition is part of a procedural approach (which I have termed "full liberal proceduralism") that insists on *both* equal recognition *and* respect for standard liberal rights and entitlements ("the standard liberal package"). The second of these conditions might be filled out more fully in a number of different ways. Of course, in any actual situation where language rights are being debated, the standard liberal package may not be perfectly implemented, and there will be a real question about how to adjust the overall model in response. It seems possible that, in some cases, the best response might be to give additional rights or protections to the local majority language as a roundabout way of compensating for their economic disadvantage. As far as the objection from economic injustice is concerned, then, the qualification and complication consists in allowing that in nonideal circumstances, where other elements of full liberal proceduralism are not being respected, some sort of offsetting adjustment to the language recognition element, involving a departure from official multilingualism, might be appropriate. Granted there is an indeterminacy that threatens here regarding how much additional assistance to give the disadvantaged language. The right amount of assistance cannot be fixed by estimating what would be necessary to achieve a just outcome, because, in a procedural view, a just outcome is determined by the choices that people would make under just background conditions. Since, by assumption, just background conditions are not in place, a key piece of information is missing.[33] Still, it seems plausible to make *some* adjustment to the assistance given to the disadvantaged language (based perhaps on conservative assumptions about the counterfactual) and then to allow procedures to run their course.

The objection from historical injustice cuts slightly deeper because the objection may still retain its bite even when both of the main conditions of full liberal proceduralism are currently satisfied. It is difficult to know what precisely to say in reply to the objection because we do not yet have a fully satisfying account of how fairness in today's background conditions should be sensitive to unfairness in the past.[34] Liberals widely believe that some kind of affirmative action may be in order as a means of compensating for present disadvantages flowing from past injustices. Where this is applicable to our problem, we would again have a reason for considering a departure from equal recognition. Presumably, as with other forms of affirmative action, the depar-

---

[33] Taylor (2009, 494ff.) clearly formulates this problem (in a somewhat different context).

[34] Again a major problem is the one noted by Taylor (2009): there is no determinate metric of how much additional assistance should be extended to the historically disadvantaged language group given the overall proceduralism of the account. For a broader discussion, see Spinner-Halev 2012.

ture would be temporary (its purpose is to reestablish a level playing field) and calibrated so as not to impose excessive costs on current members of the historically advantaged group (who have the same sorts of interests in self-determination as do members of the historically disadvantaged group).

The objection from market failure cuts even deeper in that it does not depend on there being any present or past injustice at all. As with the objection from historical injustice, full evaluation of the objection is hampered by the absence of a satisfying general theory of market failure and fairness. Standard accounts of market failure emphasize the Pareto suboptimality of outcomes: the collective action problem gives rise to a situation in which at least one person could be made better off without any person being made worse off. But it is not clear what if anything Pareto suboptimality implies about unfairness.

Rawls tries to bridge the concerns of efficiency and fairness through an adaptation of Wicksell's unanimity principle. According to this principle, the costs of any scheme designed to correct the market failure must be allocated in such a way that nobody is a net burden-bearer.[35] While this is plainly consistent with efficiency, Rawls connects it with fairness via the benefit criterion of just taxation.[36] If resources are justly distributed, then schemes of public good provision that leave some as net burden-bearers can be seen as unfair to those persons. It would be as if the state were compelling them to use their justly held resources to pay for consumption goods enjoyed by others.

Followed strictly such a principle would not leave much scope for adjustments to equal recognition in the name of correcting for market failure. It might allow speakers of the vulnerable language to restrict their own language-related decisions in certain ways, if they were unanimous in preferring the combination of costs and benefits that they each end up with under such a restriction over the costs and benefits they face when they each act in an unrestricted fashion. It is sometimes suggested that this is the logic of a key provision of Quebec's language legislation: children of Francophone parents in Quebec are required to send their children to French-medium schools.

But it is hard to see how the unanimity principle could license the imposition of inequalities onto speakers of the stronger language, many of whom, presumably, would not rank the resulting outcome higher than the outcome achieved under equality. Perhaps it could be argued that everyone in the community benefits to some extent from the preservation of the vulnerable language. But, as I argued in section 1.3, these third-party benefits are likely to be limited in magnitude. Given the strict requirements of the unanimity principle, they cannot be expected to justify the imposition of significant costs on speakers of the stronger language. A more promising strategy would be to argue that the unanimity principle is too demanding, and that it is permissible

---

[35] Rawls 1999a, 249–50.
[36] See sec. 4.5.

to impose net costs on some people to save others who are subject to a collective action problem from falling into a dispreferred outcome. No doubt small departures from the unanimity criterion are not seriously unjust and indeed may not be unjust at all if one can point to an overall pattern of subsidies in which net costs and benefits borne by different citizens cancel one another out. But for this line of argument to entail a major qualification of equal recognition, departures from the unanimity principle would have to be significant, and they would have to be *required* by justice and not merely permissible.[37] It would be interesting to explore whether such an argument could be developed, but I am not aware that it has been yet.[38]

6.8 The Language Preservation Challenge—Stronger Versions

Although the objections we have been considering so far suggest that the equal recognition model ought to be qualified in a preservationist direction, they can be accommodated within a broadly procedural approach to language rights. I want to turn now to a pair of deeper objections to equal recognition, which emphasize the badness of the outcomes that would be produced under such a model rather than the unfairness of the conditions associated with it. The first of these objections revisits the account of cultures as "contexts of choice" explored in chapter 3. The second returns us to the language-identity nexus encountered in section 6.5.

---

[37] David Miller (2004) offers a critique of the unanimity principle but is careful to emphasize that he is not arguing that violations of the principle are required by justice.

[38] Laitin (2007, 115–28) argues that language communities and policies should be considered as consumption goods. Groups may try to mobilize to get the state to provide this or that good, and beyond some bedrock liberal principles, the test of legitimacy is simply success in the democratic process: "Communities should be free to provide the public goods its taxpayers demand just so long as fundamental liberal principles are not violated" (117). Clearly, Laitin does not accept the unanimity principle, but he does not explain why. If the distribution of resources is antecedently just, why is it not unfair to citizens who are outvoted in the democratic process that the state is taxing away resources from them to pay for consumption goods that benefit others but not them? In sec. 4.5 I argued that it is unfair because it denies the outvoted minority a fair opportunity for self-determination. Laitin points out that "we may not want a strong national defense, but we pay for it anyways in accord with democratic principles" (119). However, it is problematic to think of national defense as a consumption good, because each of us owes assistance and protection to our fellow citizens (and allies) even if we do not individually benefit. Moreover, excessive national defense spending (as when the main reason for keeping some weapons program is that terminating it would harm a particular region's economy) does seem objectionable for the reason I have mentioned. None of this is to take away from democratic politics the right to make decisions about language. But, as I argued in secs. 1.3 and 6.4, that is a question about authority, not about the substance of what citizens participating in the democratic process should think.

CONTEXT OF CHOICE

To see the first of the objections, consider a scenario in which the members of a language community enjoy an adequate set of options in their own language. They have access to a decent range of jobs and of opportunities for promotion; there is a civil society that operates in the language; there are adequate opportunities to access various forms of culture, to participate informally in the political life of the community, to make social contacts, and so on. In short, the language community forms what was called earlier (following Kymlicka's terminology) a "societal culture."

In the scenario I have in mind, however, the language in question is relatively weak compared with a more dominant language spoken by others in the political community (or perhaps used as an international lingua franca). As a result the societal culture corresponding to the language is vulnerable rather than secure. Even fairly minor adverse changes in demographics, or a modest accumulation of individual decisions to use another language, would leave the language unable to support a societal culture. The processes of assimilation and marginalization that tend to afflict weaker languages have left it in a precarious situation: further setbacks could push the language below the threshold in which the options that it offers can be considered adequate.

In addition, suppose that the language community we are considering contains many people who are monolingual. It need not be the case that everybody is monolingual, and, in fact, given the looming proximity of a stronger language, it is highly likely that many speakers of the weaker language will also have attained proficiency in the stronger language. The important point is that there is some substantial group of people in the community who speak only the weaker language. If the vulnerable societal culture were to deteriorate and to dip below the threshold in which it offers an adequate range of opportunities, then these monolinguals would be stranded. Their limited language capabilities would not allow them simply to turn to the stronger language community for opportunities, and thus their overall set of opportunities would be inadequate. Insofar as adequate opportunity is a condition of freedom, their freedom would be compromised.

The objection we need to consider is that equal recognition does not prevent the scenario I have described from unfolding. As I noted at the beginning of the preceding section, there is nothing in equal recognition that rules out the possibility of very unequal levels of success among the different language groups in the political community. In the scenario laid out above, the implications of a lack of success for the stranded speakers of the weaker language are stark. Given the importance of individual freedom in liberal thought, this possibility should be alarming to proponents of equal recognition. To my mind, it is plausible to think that this is one of the places where equal recognition should relent and concede that some outcomes are unacceptable, even when they arise in the context of procedurally fair conditions. From a liberal perspective, it should be regarded as objectionable if a regime of equal recognition permits a vulnerable language to deteriorate in ways that leave speakers of that language stranded without an adequate context of choice.

How big of a concession is this? The answer, I think, is not very big. The objection to equal recognition is of very limited scope, in fact, because the conditions that would have to hold for the unacceptable outcome to occur are highly demanding. These conditions include the following:

(a) The vulnerable language community currently supports a societal culture: unilingual speakers of the language have access to an adequate range of options in the community.
(b) Under equal recognition, there would likely be demo-linguistic changes that leave the vulnerable language unable to support a societal culture.
(c) These changes would not occur if the political community privileged the vulnerable language in ways that were consistent with the justifiable toleration and accommodation rights of speakers of other languages.
(d) Some speakers of the vulnerable language are unilingual, and they cannot quickly be made proficient in the stronger language.

Although it is not impossible to think of cases in which all these conditions are or could be satisfied, it is not easy to think of many.[39] Condition (a) rules out the numerous minority languages that do not correspond with societal cultures. Speakers of these languages live in the midst of some larger linguistic community, and many key options and opportunities are available to them only in the larger community. Earlier I mentioned Italians in the United States. For a variety of reasons, Italian-speakers in the United States have never established the full set of Italian-language economic, social, and cultural institutions and practices needed to provide an adequate range of options. This absence of a societal culture is typical of linguistic communities established by immigrants, but, significantly, it is also true for many national minorities. Because of small numbers, territorial dispersion, low socioeconomic status, and other factors, many national minorities do not have anything resembling a societal culture as both Kymlicka and I understand it. Joseph Carens has forcefully developed this last point, concluding that "we have good reason to doubt

---

[39] Quebec strikes me as a case in which the conditions are or were satisfied. (a) French in Quebec supports a societal culture. (b) It is plausible to think that Quebec's French-language societal culture is "vulnerable" in the sense explained earlier. (c) Policies that privilege French in Quebec, without violating the basic rights of speakers of other languages, can and do help to secure French. (d) More than 60 percent of Francophones in Quebec report not being able to conduct a conversation in English according to the 2006 Canadian Census (http://www12.statcan.ca/census-recensement/2006/as-sa/97-555/p13-eng .cfm). Note that a complete rejection of the equal recognition model is *not* justified even in this case. A preference for French that leaves some space for meaningful English-language rights may well be sufficient to secure a French-language societal culture.

whether most national minorities have (or could have) a societal culture in Kymlicka's sense of the term."[40] In the all-too-common cases of this type, then, the freedom-based concern for protecting contexts of choice does *not* recommend a departure from equal recognition since there is no adequate context of choice present to protect. If anything, in these cases, the context-of-choice argument suggests that more should be done to encourage minority-language-speakers to learn the majority language: it is in the majority language, rather than in their own minority language, that they will find many of the options and opportunities needed for freedom. As we saw in section 6.6, this is precisely the argument of nation builders.

The other conditions eliminate some possible cases too. Condition (b) filters out language communities that are fairly secure under conditions of equal recognition, and condition (c) does the same for cases of language communities that are so vulnerable that they cannot be rescued without violating basic tenets of liberalism. Condition (d) rules out cases of vulnerable language communities in which there is fairly universal knowledge of the encroaching, more dominant language.[41] For condition (d) to be satisfied, there have to be significant pockets of unilingualism among vulnerable language speakers.

IDENTITY

The second of the deeper challenges to equal recognition returns to the language/identity connection discussed earlier. In setting out the case for the equal recognition model, one of the key assumptions was the importance of language for identity. Many people identify with the community of speakers to which they belong and care about the use and success of their language.[42] As part of having a linguistic identity, they feel respected as individuals when their language is treated respectfully and disrespected when their language is made the basis for exclusion or marginalization. In my account, this link between identity and language provides crucial support for the equal recognition model. Equal recognition is, in general, the best way for the state to remain neutral between the different attachments and preferences of its citizens, and the state's obligation of neutrality is especially weighty when identity is at stake.

The challenge to equal recognition comes from someone who starts from the same assumption about identity and urges an even stronger conclusion. If

[40] Carens 2000, 62.

[41] For instance, knowledge of Spanish among Catalans is extremely high, as is knowledge of English among Welsh-speakers, and knowledge of Romanian among Romania's Hungarian minority. The context-of-choice argument does not work in these cases.

[42] The claim that language is crucial to identity is a commonplace in the literature on linguistic rights. See, for instance, Fishman 1991; Taylor 1994; Kymlicka 1995, 89–90; May 2001; Appiah 2005, 102; Rodríguez 2006, 734–36; Van Parijs 2011a.

identity is so important, according to this challenge, then perhaps a scheme of language rights should promote it directly. Equalizing the recognition of identity-related preferences is consistent with grave inequalities in the actual satisfaction of those preferences. But if identity matters as much as my own argument supposes, why not equalize the actual realization of identity? Or, if this seems too demanding, why not at least adopt a sufficiency standard that guards people against falling below some minimal threshold of identity-related preference satisfaction? The equal recognition model seems to fetishize the public recognition of languages that people care about rather than focus more directly on the underlying interests in identity that actually matter.

This challenge retraces the more general critique of neutrality of treatment that was considered in section 4.7. A premise of the argument for neutral treatment is the importance of self-determination. The critique consisted in asking why it makes sense to stop at the neutral treatment of conceptions of the good when institutions could promote the equal achievement of self-determination itself. Not surprisingly, I think that the response given in section 4.7 to the general critique is valid in the present context as well. Although people do have important interests relating to identity, public institutions do not have sole responsibility for bringing about the realization of these interests. Responsibility is shared with individual citizens—with the identity-bearers themselves— who are assumed to have the capacity and the opportunity, over the course of their lives, to revise their identities if they are unhappy about having an identity with relatively weak prospects of success. Under this social division of labor, the responsibility of public institutions is to establish a fair framework, and it is up to individuals to adjust their identities against the backdrop of this framework. Insofar as the equal recognition model establishes a fair framework, it is a sufficient response to the identity-related interests of individuals.

This response to the objection seems obvious enough when we contemplate a religious analog to the language preservation model. It is possible that a state's policy of equally recognizing different organized religions (or its decision not to recognize any religion) could be powerless to prevent very different degrees of success among the different religions to which it is home. For any number of possible reasons, some religions might be relatively successful (by some measure), whereas others decline in importance. For members of the less successful religions, the plight of their religion might conceivably contribute to a diminished sense of self-esteem and a feeling that a cause that is central to their identity is not faring very well. But we surely do not think that these are good reasons for abandoning the policy of equal recognition (or universal nonrecognition). To some extent, any plausible view of equality or sufficiency has to hold people responsible for the identity commitments they have and not seek to intervene whenever projects those individuals value do not turn out as well as they would like.

To have more success with the identity-based challenge, a critic of equal recognition needs to show that language and linguistic identity are in some relevant sense special. Even though the right approach to other forms of identity is for public institutions to apply a norm of equal treatment, language ought to be handled in a different way. Appropriate regard for linguistic identity requires that public institutions be designed with a view to achieving certain linguistic outcomes, or at least with a view to giving people the tools that would bring those outcomes into reach.

The most impressive attempt to show that language is special in this sense can be found in Philippe Van Parijs's recent book, *Linguistic Justice for Europe and the World*. Van Parijs bases his argument on a normative principle that he calls "parity of esteem." In general, this principle holds that "people must not be stigmatized, despised, disparaged, humiliated by virtue of their collective identity."[43] Van Parijs acknowledges that for many forms of identity—including religious identity—parity of esteem is satisfied by a policy of equal treatment.[44] If a religion goes into decline in a context where it enjoys equal treatment at the hands of public institutions, its members may *feel* a blow to their self-esteem, but they do not have a *legitimate* complaint that they have been denied parity of esteem. However, things are different with linguistic identity. According to Van Parijs, public institutions that carefully abide by the equal recognition model would not necessarily be exempt from legitimate complaints by vulnerable language speakers that they had been denied parity of esteem. Those speakers can justifiably feel that they are denied parity of esteem by public institutions that do not offer them the tools needed for survival.

What explains this difference in the appropriate treatment of linguistic and other forms of identity? Following an approach developed by Jean Laponce, Van Parijs argues that the difference is rooted in a basic and distinctive feature of language.[45] Language is used for communication, and this means that its use always involves a form of coordination between people. When a multilingual person attempts to communicate with some other person or group, she must think, not just about her own preferences for language use, but, crucially, also about the language competences of her intended audience. She must look, in other words, for a lingua franca: a language that *both* she *and* the members of her intended audience can speak.[46] This need to find a lingua franca feeds in turn into choices people make about language acquisition. All else being equal, they are more likely to acquire a language (or arrange for their children

---

[43] Van Parijs 2011a, 119.
[44] Ibid., 119, 145.
[45] Laponce 1984.
[46] Van Parijs 2011a, chap. 1.

to acquire it) if they expect that language to serve as a lingua franca. A person's incentive to learn some additional language is considerably reduced if native speakers of that language are already prepared, when interacting with her, to use the person's own language as the medium of communication.

The fact that language is used as a medium for communication makes it quite unlike religion (or other conceptions of the good) where there is no imperative to coordinate on a common standard with one's neighbors. When neighbors disagree about religion, they have considerable latitude simply to go their own ways and follow their own beliefs and values. Even in the long run, there is no need to adjust one's religious beliefs or practices to conform to a standard adopted by others in the community. In the linguistic case, by contrast, neighbors who want or need to communicate with each other have no choice but to negotiate a medium of communication and, over the longer run, to adjust their language repertoires (or those of their children) in accordance with prevailing patterns. They face a situation in which either they need to adjust to others' way of doing things, or others need to adjust to theirs.

Van Parijs argues further that this elemental characteristic of language— that it is used as a medium for communication—makes weaker languages especially vulnerable to rapid deterioration. It is more likely that speakers of the weaker language will also speak the stronger language than that the reverse will be the case. Given this asymmetry, people will often tend to settle on the stronger language in situations where speakers of each are attempting to communicate. This tendency will then be reinforced by decisions about language acquisition. Expecting that speakers of the weaker language will go to the trouble of learning the stronger language, speakers of the stronger language will not invest the time or resources it takes to learn the weaker language. Speakers of the weaker language, by contrast, will have the opposite set of incentives. The result of this dynamic is that speakers of the weaker language will find themselves systematically deferring to the medium of communication favored by others. The weaker language will be increasingly pushed into marginal domains of language use. New immigrants will not bother learning it, and even native speakers of the weaker language may see little point in passing on the language to the next generation.

Van Parijs thinks that equal recognition is problematic in the linguistic case because it does nothing to prevent this grim outcome from occurring. In many contexts, equal recognition will not stop the logic of convergence on the stronger language as lingua franca.[47] Van Parijs relates this objection back to parity of esteem in two different ways. First, he describes the tendency for one

---

[47] The degree to which the conditions described by Van Parijs will, in fact, lead to the marginalization and eventual destruction of the weaker language depends, in part, on the level of social integration between weaker and stronger language speakers. The more they share a common life (working together, living in close proximity, intermarrying, and so on), the more they will rely on a lingua franca, which will likely be the stronger language. Citing work by Laponce, Van Parijs (2011a, 143) calls this "Laponce's

language—and not necessarily the majority language—to become the lingua franca as involving a kind of "linguistic bowing": "it can easily lend itself to an interpretation analogous to situations in which it is always the members of the same caste or gender that need to bow when meeting members of the other, or to get off the pavement where it is too narrow for two people to walk past each."[48] Second, he suggests that speakers of a weaker language would have a good reason to feel denied parity of esteem by institutions guided by the equal recognition approach once it becomes common knowledge that the dynamic described above is likely to unfold: "once the linguistic communities involved become aware (and aware of everyone's awareness) that accommodation leads to the gradual elimination of one of the languages, it is legitimate for its native speakers to feel denied parity of esteem if they are not allowed to use effective means, consistent with fundamental liberties, to prevent this predictable agony."[49]

What should we make of Van Parijs's identity-based challenge to equal recognition? One problem is that it is hard to see why speakers of the weaker language do in fact have a good reason to feel that they are denied parity of esteem when a scheme of equal recognition is in place. Van Parijs characterizes the routine use of the stronger language as the lingua franca as a kind of linguistic bowing. But this characterization seems questionable. The expectation that the members of one group bow, or give way, to the members of another group presupposes a social hierarchy. The bowing and giving way are means of expressing, or performing, a set of inegalitarian social norms. By contrast, the regular use of another language as a lingua franca need not express any such norms of inequality. It would perhaps express such norms if speakers of the stronger language displayed an arrogant "colonial" attitude to the weaker language and its speakers. But the logic of convergence on a lingua franca described above does not involve any such attitudes. Instead it is driven by the need of interlocutors to settle on a language of communication, the convenience of using a language that all participants can understand, and the significant costs associated with learning a second language.[50] If these factors produce a pattern of linguistic deference, then it is not clear that speakers of the weaker language have a good reason to feel that public institutions deny

---

Law": "the friendlier the relations across language groups, the more savage the competition between their languages."

[48] Ibid., 119; see also 141.

[49] Ibid., 146.

[50] Van Parijs (2011a, 141) anticipates this response: "Of course, grasping the maxi-min dynamics should make both sides aware that sociolinguistic obstacles may have played a greater role than bad will in the persistence of linguistic incompetence." He continues: "But a set of real or imaginary historical episodes or contemporary anecdotes often feeds the suspicion that arrogance is an important factor, if not the main one." Insofar as Van Parijs is developing a normative theory of language rights (one that privileges the territorial over the personality principle, as we see below), appeals to "imaginary" historical episodes and "contemporary anecdotes" seem too weak to be relevant.

them parity of esteem by leaving them in a situation where they end up routinely using the lingua franca. They can and should hold their heads up high, even while employing the stronger language as a convenient, socially low-cost, medium of communication with others in their community.

It is even harder to see why parity of esteem is at stake in the second variant of objection, which simply asserts that parity of esteem is denied to speakers of a vulnerable language whenever it is predictable that the logic of convergence on a lingua franca will threaten the survival of their language (and this is common knowledge). Although Van Parijs insists that the argument does not imply anything about religious survival and parity of esteem, it is hard to see why.[51] It is true that the precise mechanism by which a vulnerable language is driven to disappear is different from the mechanism that would bring about the same outcome for a vulnerable religion. The language case turns on the need for social coordination, whereas the religious case might simply involve people forming negative judgments about the merits of various beliefs and practices. But why should this difference in mechanism make such a difference to judgments about parity of esteem? If, in both cases, an institutionalized public preference for the vulnerable group could prevent a disappearance from occurring, why is the failure to enact such a preference a denial of parity of esteem in the language case but not in the religious case? And if, as I suggested earlier, the reason not to enact such a preference in the religious case is based on an idea of responsibility—the Rawlsian social division of labor—then why does a similar reason not apply to the linguistic case?

I have some questions about Van Parijs's central arguments, then, but I do not want to rule out the possibility that some version of them might ultimately be successful. A defender of the first variant of Van Parijs's challenge might argue that, in many instances, there *are* colonial attitudes on the part of speakers of the stronger language, and these make it reasonable for weaker-language speakers to feel disparaged by the linguistic bowing in which they end up engaging. Or, more subtly, there may have been a history of power relations—of domination and subordination—between the language groups, from which today's linguistic negotiations cannot be entirely abstracted. The argument might be that a pattern of linguistic deference today is reasonably regarded as the latest reenactment of a legacy of subordination and so is grounds for feeling a denial of parity of esteem.[52]

The second variant of the challenge might be recast as well. Even if the mechanism by which the disappearance of a group is brought about is not directly relevant to judgments about parity of esteem, it may be relevant to

---

[51] Ibid., 145.

[52] A legacy of this kind is present in the flagship example that Van Parijs deploys to illustrate his argument: the case of French-Dutch relations in Flanders. As Van Parijs (2011a, 121) reminds readers, French was the sole official language all over Belgium for nearly seventy years after the country's independence.

judgments about fairness. Weaker-language speakers would do much better if they would stop deferring so much in situations where a lingua franca is needed. This would increase the value to stronger-language speakers of learning the weaker language. But, as Van Parijs notes, weaker-language speakers face a form of the prisoner's dilemma.[53] No individual act of deference will have a tangible impact on the preservation of a language, but it might improve the quality of some act of communication or confer on the speaker or his children some tangible advantage. Given this structure, it might be argued that equal recognition is unfair to speakers of the vulnerable language because it forces them into a competition with the stronger language that they will surely lose because they, and not the speakers of the stronger language, are hobbled by a collective action problem. In the earlier discussion of market failure (sec. 6.7), I noted that this sort of claim is hard to evaluate because we lack a good account of the relationship between fairness and market failure. Existing accounts of this relationship seem to imply that the equal recognition model should be qualified rather than rejected. But I do not want to rule out the possibility that someone might mount an argument for a stronger conclusion.

With these concessive remarks in mind, let me offer one further response to the Van Parijs argument. Suppose we accept that it would be objectionable if equal recognition were to permit or facilitate the gradual destruction of a vulnerable majority-language community. Such an outcome would involve too much bowing by members of the majority to members of the minority, and/or it would reflect a structural unfairness that works systematically against the majority.[54] Equal recognition, we might concede, should be compromised in ways that prevent this outcome from occurring, or at least that minimize the likelihood and frequency of the most damaging occurrences. Still this concession does not imply a fundamental rejection of the equal recognition model but rather is consistent with the hybrid thesis I have been proposing all along. Equal recognition is not rendered superfluous but still has an important role to play in the space that is left over once the outcome-based constraint is satisfied.

The continuing relevance of the equal recognition model is secured by the fact that departures from equal recognition are a matter of degree.[55] In between institutional monolingualism and equal recognition lie a range of intermediate possibilities involving a preference for one language that falls short of exclusive recognition. The majority language is given certain privileges and advantages by the law, but minority-language rights are not denied altogether.

---

[53] Ibid., 144. On collective action problems facing speakers of vulnerable languages, see also Laitin 1993; 1998.

[54] The complete elimination of bowing is unrealistic in any diverse community. If linguistic bowing is objectionable, it is mainly so when the majority is bowing to minority. It is this scenario that reminds us of the colonial case.

[55] Van Parijs (2011a, 134–35) makes this point too.

For instance, public institutions might extend equal recognition to majority and minority language alike in the delivery of public services and the organization of public education, while at the same time insisting on a robust curriculum of second-language education in the weaker language (for nonnative speakers) and a set of regulations regarding communication in the workplace and professional qualifications that make knowledge of the majority, weaker language a precondition for success. Depending on the exact empirical circumstances, this limited preference for the majority language may be sufficient to tip the balance in its favor and prevent its rapid disintegration.[56] Ease-of-communication considerations will no longer automatically favor the stronger minority language, and it will not always be the majority speakers who bow to the minority. At the same time, in the delivery of public services and the organization of public education, speakers of the minority language still enjoy some recognition.

Obviously, the calculations and conjectures required to get the balance right between equal recognition and language preservation are bound to prove complex and uncertain. The right balance will depend on numerous factors that vary from one context to the next. Perhaps in some cases the degree of preference needed to tip the balance in favor of the weaker majority language will be very high, consigning the equal recognition model to a very limited role indeed. But, as a general matter, there is no reason to suppose that the values highlighted by the equal recognition model need to be sidelined completely to forestall the patterns of linguistic bowing and disappearance that concern language preservers.

I have been focusing on cases in which the weaker language is the majority language of the population served by the public institutions in question. The relevance of the equal recognition model is even more apparent in cases where the weaker language is also the minority language. Here it would be unrealistic (and inappropriate) to think that a general tendency for speakers

---

[56] Van Parijs (2011a, 135n6) describes a case of this kind. Fluency in Basque is a requirement of some employment in public administration in the Basque country. As a result, Basque-medium and bilingual schools have become popular with parents in the region, despite the fact that Spanish is the stronger language and more obvious lingua franca. In a separate article, Van Parijs explicitly allows that a community with a vulnerable majority language may be able to extend some minority rights to speakers of stronger languages, so long as "granting them these rights involves no serious risk of trapping them in the ignorance of the official language." See Van Parijs 2011b, 55, 63.

The basic pattern that Van Parijs describes here seems quite familiar. A preference is given to the majority language that leaves some room for minority rights but is sufficient to secure the majority language. For instance, Quebec's Anglophones have fairly high levels of English-French bilingualism in a context where they enjoy some minority rights and French is reasonably secure. The local preponderance of French, the law's preference for French (e.g. in the workplace and for professional qualifications), and effective French-as-a-second-language instruction, together provide both the incentive and the opportunity for Anglophones to learn French, even as they enjoy rights to English-language schooling and to receive health-care and other government services in English where local numbers warrant.

of the minority language to defer to the majority language would be reversed. But this dose of realism does not undermine the importance of the equal recognition model. The arguments offered earlier in favor of that model are not diminished by the fact that minority language speakers will also need to learn the majority language and can expect to use it in informal interactions with majority-language-speakers. Even if the long-term prospects of the minority-language community are not especially promising, minority rights can still contribute to the short- and medium-term preservation of the minority-language community, thereby helping to sustain the availability of particular options that minority-speakers care about, and helping to accommodate various identity-related preferences and attitudes they might have. In this way, the equal recognition model serves in a modest but not insignificant way to further important liberal values.

6.9 Equal Recognition versus the Territoriality Principle

The chapter has been contrasting three different normative models of language rights—the nation-building, language preservation, and equal recognition models—and arguing that the third of them should be given a substantial role in evaluating schemes of language rights. I conclude here by considering how the models that we have been exploring can be brought to bear on a difficult problem of public policy that has tended to divide theorists who otherwise share some sympathy for the claims of minority-language-speakers. The problem is an important one in its own right, but it also offers an opportunity to show how incorporating the equal recognition model into a hybrid theory leads to a distinctive approach to language policy.

The debate we shall examine arises in states that have elected to adopt some degree of institutional multilingualism. Looking around the world at some of these states, one quickly notices two different approaches. In some cases, several languages are recognized across the country, so that no matter where a speaker of one of these languages lives, he can interact with public institutions in his own language. A person has the same language rights with respect to education, public services, the courts, and so on, no matter where in the country he resides.[57] In other cases, however, an attempt is made to identify regional patterns of language use within the country, with an eye to varying language rights from region to region according to local conditions. Under this approach, the language rights that you can claim depend on where in the country you happen to be living.[58]

---

[57] Canada and South Africa are notable examples of this approach.
[58] Switzerland and Belgium are prominent examples.

The principle that citizens should enjoy the same set of language rights no matter where they are in the country is commonly referred to as the "personality principle." The opposing principle, that language rights should vary from region to region according to local conditions, is generally labeled the "territoriality principle." In the first principle, language rights follow *persons* wherever in the state they may choose to live; in the second, their language rights depend on what part of the *territory* of the state they find themselves in.[59] Which of these competing principles should be preferred? Supposing that a society has decided to adopt some form of institutional multilingualism, then under what circumstances should it prefer the personality principle, and when should it opt for the territoriality principle?

To focus the discussion on the core issues, I am going to make several simplifying assumptions. The first is that the territory of the state is divided into several provinces or administrative subunits, each of which has its own territory. The second is that there are two main language groups in the country: a statewide majority language (A) and a statewide minority language (B). In a number of regions, the statewide majority language is also the local majority language, but in at least one of them majority and minority status are reversed: in this region, B is the local majority language and A is the local minority.

Proponents of the personality principle argue that citizens of the state should be able to interact with public institutions in either A or B wherever they live in the state, and regardless of whether they form part of a local linguistic majority or minority, subject only to some minimal numbers constraint. By contrast, the territoriality principle recommends that the country be divided into a number of linguistic districts and that public institutions operate exclusively in the language spoken by the local majority. Schools, hospitals, courts, government offices, and so on located in the majority A-speaking districts operate exclusively in A, and those located in the majority B-speaking districts operate exclusively in B. In principle, at least, territoriality in this sense could apply to both local institutions and the local offices and services of statewide institutions. (National institutions operating on a statewide scale, such as the country's legislature and high court, must find an alternative to the territoriality principle since their work applies to the whole of the state's territory.) Mixed approaches are also possible, which blend elements of the personality and territoriality principles, but I set them aside for now to consider the two opposing principles in their purest forms.

The territoriality principle is likely to strike many people as uncontroversial in some contexts. For instance, suppose that the districts described above

---

[59] The distinction between these two principles is now standard in the literature on language rights. See, e.g., Royal Commission on Bilingualism and Biculturalism 1967, chap. 4; Kloss 1971, 264–67; McRae 1975; Laponce 1984; Nelde, Labrie, and Williams 1992; Van Parijs 2000a; 2011a, chap. 5; Réaume 2003; Patten 2003b.

are linguistically homogenous, so that the local linguistic minorities represent only a miniscule fraction of their total populations.[60] Given that numbers play some role in justifying a claim on minority-language rights (see sec. 6.4), the territoriality principle seems quite unobjectionable in these cases. Or suppose that the territories are very small, or that local minorities tend to live near the edge of territories, close to a territory where their language is in the majority. In these cases, the costs of moving to a neighboring territory, or of seeking services from the institutions of a neighboring territory (where this is permitted), may not be particularly high, and so an overall regime based on the territoriality principle does not seem problematic. The harder cases, which I want to focus on, involve local minorities that are fairly numerous and regional units that are fairly sizable.

Another scenario in which the territoriality principle may seem unproblematic is one in which local minorities are themselves territorially concentrated. In this situation, a further subdivision, creating a new linguistic subdistrict, may be a straightforward way in which an overall scheme based on the principle of territoriality can deal with diversity.[61] I shall assume that a subdivision of this kind is not possible (e.g., because local minorities are too dispersed) or not desirable (e.g., because it would make territories too small, or would place key bits of territories, such as the downtown cores of cities, on the "wrong" side of linguistic frontiers).

The real conflict between the personality and territoriality principles arises in cases where some or all of the regions of the country are home to significant local minorities, which cannot easily relocate to another language district or receive their services from institutions of another district, and which cannot easily be provided with their own language district. For some, the presence of such local minorities is a leading reason to prefer the personality approach. Advocates of the territoriality principle, by contrast, argue that the denial of services in the language of local minorities is an acceptable cost to pay in exchange for the benefits associated with territoriality.

Returning to our three models, we find an interesting configuration of recommendations. The territoriality principle has support from *both* the nation-building and language preservation models.[62] When public institutions operate exclusively in the local majority language, a number of the goals emphasized by nation builders may be promoted. Most obviously and directly, institutions will save money and time by operating in a single language. But the nation-building model also anticipates a number of indirect effects, all predicated on the assumption that monolingual institutions will encourage local minorities

---

[60] With one several exceptions, Swiss cantons exhibit very high levels of uniformity of this kind.

[61] Van Parijs (2011a, 166) advocates linguistic subdivision as one response to heterogeneity.

[62] The defense of territoriality in Van Parijs (2011a, chap. 5) mainly draws on preservationist considerations but also invokes some of the benefits of nation building.

to acquire the local majority language. In learning the local majority language, local minorities gain access to the economic activity that is conducted in that language and to the employment and business opportunities that that entails. And when local minorities acquire the local majority language, a lingua franca emerges that can facilitate informal democratic deliberation and foster a sense of solidarity among citizens living together in close proximity.

Proponents of language preservation are attracted to the territoriality principle because it allows for the designation of territories in which vulnerable languages are sovereign. Because the vulnerable language serves as the exclusive medium for the delivery of public services and the conduct of public business, local minorities have little choice but to learn it. The vulnerable language is secured as the local lingua franca, and the linguistic bowing is performed by the local minority rather than the local majority. One influential defender of the territoriality principle, Jean Laponce, goes so far as to argue that minority languages are subject to a "territorial imperative." They must establish themselves as the dominant language in some particular territory or else be faced with extinction.[63]

Against each of these alternative models, the equal recognition approach favors the personality principle over the territoriality principle. In the core case that we are considering, one or more of a country's linguistic districts is home to a sizable local linguistic minority as well as to the local majority. Unlike the nation-building and language preservation models, the equal recognition model offers reasons to entertain and satisfy the claims of such a minority. Equal recognition means that majority and minority alike are able to access, and participate in, public institutions in their own language. It is this access that extends to all a fair opportunity for self-determination. Assuming that the costs of moving to another language district are substantial, a fair opportunity for self-determination is not secured by pointing to some other part of the country where the local minority's language is in ascendance. To secure fairness for local language minorities, public institutions operating in the area where those minorities live must recognize minority rights. The personality principle calls for just such rights.

As I have emphasized throughout the book, public institutions do not have an absolute obligation to leave their citizens with a fair opportunity for self-determination. It is appropriate to balance this obligation against the objectives emphasized by nation builders and language preservers. Sometimes language rights for local minorities ought to give way to allow for the realization of the legitimate objectives of these alternative models. But for the reasons explored in the three previous sections, I do not think that this concession consigns the personality principle to irrelevance. Under a range of realistic empirical conditions, it is possible to satisfy the legitimate aspirations of na-

---

[63] Laponce 1984, 1, chaps. 5–6, conclusion; Van Parijs 2000a; 2011a; Kymlicka 2001a.

tion builders and language preservers without abandoning the language rights for local minorities advocated by the personality principle, or at least without fully abandoning those rights. Even when the local majority language is a relatively vulnerable language, a *preference* of some kind for it may be sufficient to make it the usual lingua franca of the community. Such an approach would award certain rights and privileges to the local majority language even while also continuing to recognize various minority-language rights too.

We see, then, that incorporating the equal recognition model into a hybrid approach to language rights leads to a distinctive policy recommendation. On their own, the nation-building and language preservation models offer strong reasons in favor of adopting the territoriality principle without pointing to comparably strong reasons against. When equal recognition is admitted into the moral calculus, however, the case for the territoriality principle faces some serious resistance. Adopting that principle may still be the best overall approach, under some empirical conditions, but under other conditions the local majority language will have to limit its dominion to leave some room for minority languages.

CHAPTER 7

Democratic Secession
from a Multinational State

7.1 Theories of Secession

When Woodrow Wilson advanced the principle of self-determination in a series of speeches in 1918–1919, he assumed that acknowledging the claims of
self-determination was a simple corollary of respect for democracy. Contemporary secessionists, and many who write and theorize about secession, share
Wilson's intuition about this. It is widely claimed that a people has the right
to determine democratically its own political status, so long as any change is
peaceful and orderly, is consistent with standard liberal rights, and does not
involve any unjust taking of territory or unfair terms of separation.[1] Whatever
the considerations are that count in favor of making decisions democratically
in general—be they equality, autonomy, justice, or so on—count, in this view,
in favor of settling a secession dispute in the same way.[2]

A standard objection to this way of thinking about secession maintains that
the entrenchment of a "democratic" or "plebiscitary" right to secede in international law and practice would have a number of undesirable consequences.[3]
It would lead to a proliferation of secessionist crises and of the outbreaks of
violence and war that sometimes result from such crises. It would also create
perverse incentives for existing states, including an incentive to avoid otherwise beneficial schemes of territorial autonomy where such schemes raise the
probability that secessionists would be able to organize and win a referendum

---

[1] Scholarly defenses of a democratic right to secession can be found in Gauthier 1994; Philpott 1995;
1998; Wellman 1995; 2005; and Copp 1997.

[2] For example, Philpott (1995) bases the democratic right to secede on the considerations of individual autonomy that he thinks ground democracy more generally; Copp (1997, 291–92) pursues a similar
strategy in appealing to considerations of equal respect; and Wellman (2005, 54) argues that "plebiscitary
rights to secede are merely an extension of the principles of democratic governance to the issue of territorial boundaries."

[3] See, e.g., Cobban 1969, 138; Buchanan 1997; 1998a; 2004; Norman 1998. All three arguments
referred to in the remainder of the paragraph are from Buchanan.

on independence. In addition, it is argued, a plebiscitary right to secession would undermine the practice of democracy by making exit too easy and thereby discouraging the exercise of voice.

Those who make these objections against the plebiscitary right typically do not want to prohibit secession outright. Instead, they argue that the right to secede is, in Allen Buchanan's words, a "remedial-right-only": a group should be said to possess such a right only if it is clearly demonstrable that the group has been the victim of injustice at the hands of the state.[4] In Buchanan's influential version of this theory, a right to secede is possessed by only those groups that are subject to at least one of the following forms of injustice:

(1) *Human rights violations.* The group can justifiably complain of a pattern of serious human rights violations at the hands of the state.

(2) *Unjust annexation.* The group can establish that they (and their territory) were unjustly incorporated into the state in the recent or fairly recent past.

(3) *Violation of autonomy agreement.* The group can demonstrate that the state has persistently and culpably failed to honor internal agreements that would provide it with a measure of autonomy.[5]

As Buchanan emphasizes, the ambition of a remedial theory elaborated along these lines is to permit secession in the most pressing cases—where an existing state is failing to discharge its basic duties—without opening the door to a host of secessionist claims in cases where no great improvement in justice is to be expected.

In reply to the objections raised by remedialists, plebiscite theorists emphasize the various qualifications they attach to the plebiscitary right.[6] Groups have a valid claim to independence only when there is reason to believe that the standard liberal rights of all concerned will be respected, when the danger to peace and security is minimal, and so on. One proponent of a democratic right to secession, Daniel Philpott, after noting various qualifications to the right, goes so far as to say, "I doubt that there are many cases to which my own theory would give a green light, but to which Buchanan's would grant a red or yellow light."[7] Plebiscite theorists also point to some of the adverse consequences that might flow from rejecting a plebiscitary right to secede.[8] Groups that (could) organize and win a referendum on secession but are denied independence under the remedial-right-only theory might themselves

[4] Buchanan 1997, 34–37; 2004, 351–53.

[5] Buchanan 2004, 351–59. Note that the third condition is introduced in the 2004 statement of Buchanan's theory. It moves Buchanan's position some of the way toward the view I advocated in Patten 2002, but, as I shall argue in this chapter, not quite all the way.

[6] See, e.g., Philpott 1995, 353, 371–85; 1998, 80–90; see also Nielsen 1998, 110–15.

[7] Philpott 1998, 90.

[8] For example, ibid., 92.

pose a danger to peace and security. And a rule that makes exit too difficult might undermine the practice of democracy on the part of a nonsecessionist national majority. With the threat of secession out of the way, such a majority might feel little incentive to listen to alternative perspectives and legitimate grievances advanced by a minority group.[9]

A further point to consider in assessing the plebiscitary theory is that international law and practice are not the only contexts in which normative questions about secession might be raised. Even if remedial-right-only theorists are correct to insist that a democratic mandate does not by itself generate any international obligations to recognize or support secession, such a mandate may well have domestic implications. It may be that a clear vote in favor of secession by the citizens of some region of a state creates an obligation on the part of the central government and the citizens of the remainder state to negotiate about secession. If, in the course of such negotiations, representatives of the breakaway region can offer credible guarantees concerning rights, territory, and the terms of separation, then the obligation to negotiate may eventually harden into an obligation on the part of the representatives of the remainder state to accept the secession. From the perspective of the international community, a secession that resulted from this process would be consensual rather than unilateral and thus would not conflict with the remedial-right-only theory, which limits its attention to international obligations regarding unilateral attempts to secede.[10]

In this chapter I draw on the account of equal recognition developed earlier in the book to argue that both of the leading theories of secession are overlooking an important consideration. Strikingly, neither approach directly engages with the concerns of nationalists. Although secessionist movements are typically expressions of nationalism, and recent work on secession has to some extent been intertwined with a renewed scholarly interest in the normative questions posed by nationalism, neither approach appeals directly to considerations of nationality either to ground or to limit the right of secession. The present chapter will seek to insert nationality back into our thinking about the relationship among justice, democracy, and secession.[11] An important problem with existing democratic accounts, I will show, is that they permit secessions that have the effect of undermining arrangements for the equal recognition of the different identities found in a multination state. Equally, an objection to leading versions of the remedial-right theory is that they exclude the possibility that secession might be a reasonable response to a failure by

---

[9]This point is made, in a slightly different context, by Weinstock 2001, 203.

[10]See Buchanan 2004, 362–63. As Buchanan observes, the Supreme Court of Canada's 1998 Reference case on Quebec secession contemplated a process of this kind.

[11]For a complementary discussion, which also explores the normative implications of nationality for an account of secession, see Miller 2000, chap. 7; see also Moore 2001, chaps. 6–8.

the state to implement arrangements extending equal recognition to national minorities.

Underlying these objections is a simple idea about how a multinational state should respond to the claims of national minorities. The main claim is that, when a state is home not just to a national majority but also to one or more national minorities, its citizens have a pro tanto obligation to look for arrangements that extend equal recognition to majority and minority alike. When a substate national group is denied recognition, and there is no appropriate justification for this denial, the members of the group suffer from an injustice.

Taking seriously the claims of equal recognition implies a significant amendment to Buchanan's remedial-right-only theory, and a more fundamental revision of the plebiscitary view. The amendment to Buchanan's theory consists in adding a fourth form of injustice to the list of injustices that are considered as giving just cause for a group to pursue secession. As noted above, Buchanan's version of the theory restricts this list to three main forms of injustice: (1) human rights violations; (2) unjust annexation, and (3) violation of autonomy agreements. Drawing on the claim that it is unjust to deny recognition to national minorities (without a sufficiently good reason), I shall argue for an extension of Buchanan's framework to include:

(4) *Failure of recognition.* The state has failed to establish arrangements that extend recognition to a national minority.

If we think of a "minimally just" state as one that respects human rights, is not founded on unjust annexation, and honors the autonomy agreements it has entered into, then Buchanan's thesis is there is no right to unilateral secession from a minimally just state. Against this, I argue that a right to secede can be claimed against a minimally just state in those situations where the state has failed to provide adequate guarantees to its minorities in the first place.

The implications of equal recognition for the democratic approach are more fundamental. When a state does implement and abide by arrangements for the equal recognition of national minorities, then this limits the right to secede. In the standard case, in which diversity is a feature not just of the state but also of the secessionist region, a democratic mandate is not by itself sufficient to legitimate secession. For such a right to be generated, there must be either a violation of Buchanan's conditions of minimal justice or a distinct failure by the state, a denial of recognition. Where a state avoids both of these kinds of flaws, it need not worry about secession: a democratic mandate does not generate a right to secede from a flawless state.

By emphasizing the value of equal recognition, then, I end up charting a middle course between the democratic approach to secession, on the one hand, and the remedial approach, as formulated by Buchanan, on the other. I agree with the remedial view that there is no democratic right to secede from a flawless state. But, at the same time, I adopt a more demanding conception of what a "flawless" state would amount to, thereby enlarging the range of cases in which a democratic mandate would support a valid claim to secede. Although the view I defend lines up in between the leading approaches, clearly I end up much closer to Buchanan's theory. I agree with the basic remedial framework and disagree only with Buchanan's account of what exactly should be considered an injustice for the purposes of the theory. This disagreement might, in turn, be traced back to a difference about the nature of justice or to a difference in pragmatic calculations (or to some combination of both). It may be that we disagree about whether recognition of national minorities is a matter of justice, or about whether incorporating a concern for recognitional justice into a standard meant to guide the evaluation of secessionist claims would be unworkable or otherwise problematic. I will address both of these points in the course of the chapter. Section 7.3 will discuss why equal recognition is a matter of justice, and both sections 7.3 and 7.6 will touch on some of the pragmatic costs and benefits of incorporating a concern for recognitional justice into a normative guide to secession.

The more significant difference is with the plebiscitary theory, and I shall devote much of the chapter to setting out this disagreement and justifying my own position. Taking the plebiscitary theory as my principal opponent, I start by formulating and explaining in the next section the failure-of-recognition condition. I set out the context in which the condition is relevant, and I explain what I mean by "recognition" and give a sense of the kinds of institutional arrangements that recognition involves. Two arguments are then developed in favor of incorporating this condition into a democratic account of secession: the "equality argument" (sec. 7.3) and the "democracy argument" (sec. 7.4). After considering two possible objections to my account (sec. 7.5), I return to some of the institutional issues frequently raised by remedialists (sec. 7.6). Whereas the main body of the chapter sets out the contours of a moral right to secede, I now argue that the entrenchment of my proposal in international law and practice would not generate consequences that are obviously inferior to the entrenchment of a remedial right defined in terms of minimal justice.[12]

Although the argument of the chapter is fairly self-contained, it draws in places on the accounts of culture and equal recognition developed earlier in the book. In doing so, it should serve to illustrate and expand on those accounts by applying them to a specific set of questions about self-government, federalism, and secession that often arise in the real world.

---

[12] Here I follow David Miller's (2000, 112) methodological suggestion that "we should establish the basic principles first, then ask what effect the public promulgation of these principles might have on the behaviour of different political actors."

7.2 The Failure-of-Recognition Condition

In the simplest version of the plebiscitary theory, victory in a referendum held in the secessionist unit on a clear question about independence is sufficient to generate a right on the part of that unit to secede. Following much of the literature on democratic secession, I will assume that this simple plebiscitary theory is too permissive. It fails to account for the possibility that citizens of the secessionist unit may not have a valid claim on the territory of the unit (in which case it is not up to them to decide in a referendum what should happen to that territory),[13] and it ignores the possibility that the terms of secession proposed by the secessionist unit might be unfair. More seriously still, the simple theory implausibly allows secessions that lead to serious violations of standard liberal rights (e.g., the rights of new minorities formed by the secession),[14] as well as secessions the predictable consequence of which would be a significant likelihood of violence and war.[15] Finally, the simple theory departs from an assumption made by almost every plebiscitary theorist: that the right to secede is limited to certain eligible groups. For instance, it ignores the assumption made by some that only "nations" or "peoples" can be holders of the right, and it also clashes with the less demanding view that the seceding unit must be able to form a viable state.[16]

These conditions all raise difficult and interesting issues, which, for the most part, I ignore in this chapter. I am proposing an objection, and then an alternative, to existing democratic accounts of secession, and so it is most appropriate to assume a moderate and plausible version of the democratic view, one that enjoys a degree of actual support in the current literature on secession and among secessionists themselves. With this in mind, I will assume that any rights claimed under the plebiscitary theory satisfy the following conditions:[17] (1) the terms of secession proposed by the secessionists are fair; (2) the cre-

---

[13] Buchanan 2004, 337–38.

[14] For the claim that a democratic right to secession is qualified by a requirement to respect standard liberal rights, see, e.g., Philpott 1995, 372–75; 1998, 83; Nielsen 1998, 111, 115; Wellman 1995, 164, 166; 2005, 37–38, 58, 86–88; Copp, 1997, 280; Beran 1998, 54.

[15] Philpott (1995, 381–82; 1998, 83, 91–92) argues that the democratic right to secede may be restricted in these cases, as does Copp (1997, 280).

[16] For the claim that nonnational groups are ineligible for secessionist rights, see, e.g., Nielsen 1998, 115. For the view that nonviable groups are ineligible, see, e.g., Philpott 1995, 366; Beran 1998, 36–38; and Wellman 1995, 160–64. An even less demanding requirement would be the following: either the seceding group must be able to form a viable state or it must be prepared to join together with another group to form a viable state. Copp (1997, 290–97) proposes an eligibility requirement that combines elements of the nationality and viability views into the requirement that the group form a "society." Wellman (2005, 58) restricts the right to secede to groups that are able and willing to perform the legitimate functions of a state.

[17] Other conditions could be mentioned too. For instance, as Copp (1997, 280) points out, the right to secede may be limited by a duty not to worsen the position of the remainder state in certain ways—e.g., not to cripple its capacity to govern effectively and justly.

ation of the new state is unlikely to generate serious violations of standard liberal rights, or to conflict with the realization of other standard elements of liberal justice; (3) the citizens of the secessionist unit form a group eligible for secession; and (4) the secession will not pose a serious threat to peace and security.

In addition, I shall assume that (5) when a democratic mandate for secession has been given (and conditions 1–4 are met), the citizens of the secessionist unit collectively have a valid claim to the territory of that unit.[18] In making this assumption, I am supposing that one of Buchanan's key theoretical objections to the plebiscitary view can be countered. In Buchanan's view, so long as the state is doing a reasonable job of protecting basic rights, its people have a right to the state's territory, and so no subgroup of that people has a right to make off with part of it and form their own state.[19] I am sympathetic with Buchanan's objection, and the remedialism of the position I end up defending fits comfortably enough with it. But for the sake of exploring the plebiscitary view more thoroughly here, I shall not press Buchanan's objection here but will proceed as if it can be answered. It is useful to consider the plebiscitary view from several different angles, especially as it may play a role in an account of consensual secession, where territorial rights play a less fundamental role. In addition, while Buchanan's view of territorial rights is plausible enough, so is the view of territorial rights implicit in the plebiscitary theory. The latter view agrees that protection of rights is crucial for a well-founded right to territory but leaves a space for democratic preference when there are multiple arrangements that satisfy that important constraint.[20]

My claim is that, even when conditions 1–5 are satisfied, the plebiscitary theory is too permissive. A further condition should also be accepted by plebiscitary theorists as restricting the democratic right to secede: the failure-of-recognition condition. (In fact, as I indicated earlier, my view is that either the failure-of-recognition condition must be met or the state must be violating the conditions of minimal justice. To focus attention on the failure-of-recognition condition, however, I will assume that the state is not violating the conditions of minimal justice.) Adding the failure-of-recognition condition would constitute a fairly fundamental amendment of plebiscitary theories. In their exist-

---

[18] Or, more weakly, no one else has a competing claim on all or part of the territory that is sufficiently strong to defeat the presumption that citizens of the territory collectively have a valid claim on it.

[19] Buchanan 2004, 374–76.

[20] This is Wellman's (2005, 37) view. Copp (1997, 281–82) argues that Buchanan conflates the internal and external implications of having a well-founded right to territory. When a people possesses such a right, they have a right not to be interfered with by *outsiders* in governing their territory. But the valid right to territory possessed by peoples with a legitimate right to govern need not imply the same right against *internal* populations. Because Copp sees no reason why a right to territory implies a right not to be interfered with by an internal population, he rejects Buchanan's claim that nonremedial secession is precluded by a valid right to territory.

ing form, those theories could, in principle, license a secession from a perfect state. By contrast, in my proposal, there is no right to secede from a perfect state: the state must be either violating the conditions of minimal justice or guilty of a failure of recognition.

The failure-of-recognition condition is met when the state has failed to introduce meaningful constitutional arrangements that recognize the distinct national identity of (some) members of the secessionist group. In the remainder of this section, I will try to clarify this condition by setting out the context in which it is relevant and by explaining and illustrating what I mean by constitutional arrangements that recognize a national identity.

The failure-of-recognition condition is relevant to contexts in which there are a plurality of national identities among citizens of the would-be secessionist unit (T). In particular, it is concerned with cases where, although some citizens of T have a strong, even exclusive, substate national identity focused on T, others maintain a national identity focused on the state as a whole (S). To have a national identity focused on S or T, I shall assume, is to have a set of attitudes and dispositions with respect to (a majority of) the group of citizens who live in S or T. These attitudes and dispositions include some or all of the following: identification with the group; a propensity to feel pride and shame about actions on behalf of the group; a tendency to factor one's affiliation with the group into one's practical reasoning; and the identification with some territory (typically the territory of S or T) as the "homeland" of the group.[21] One of the most important attitudes associated with national identity is a more or less settled desire that the group should enjoy some significant degree of collective self-government as a group: it is this desire—shared by most members of the group—that helps to distinguish a national identity from other forms of identity that people might share.[22]

To say that a plurality of national identities are found among citizens of T, then, is to say that some of the citizens of T have these attitudes and dispositions with respect to all citizens of S, and that others have them with respect only to fellow citizens of T (and some will have the relevant attitudes and dispositions with respect to both groups, since it is possible to have multiple identities). Although identity pluralism of this kind may not be found in all regions containing secessionist movements, it is relatively common. For example, in Quebec there are significant numbers of citizens whose national identity is mainly focused on Quebec, but also significant numbers who have a strong sense of Canadian national identity. Likewise, in Scotland and Catalonia, one finds people with Scottish and Catalan national identities, but also

---

[21] See the discussion of "subjective" identity in sec. 2.5, as well as the discussion in sec. 5.2. See also Norman's (2006, 34–36) fuller catalog of the various attitudes and dispositions that are connected with national identity.

[22] Copp 1979, 71–75.

people with British and Spanish national identities. Of course in all these cases it is common for people to have dual identities: they identify with both the national minority and the larger statewide community.[23]

The failure-of-recognition condition involves a failure to adopt an appropriate institutional response to conditions of identity pluralism such as those found in the above-mentioned cases. The condition is triggered when no attempt is made to accommodate minority national identities within a set of multinational constitutional arrangements—arrangements that recognize the substate, as well as the statewide, national identity.

A national identity is recognized, I shall say, to the extent that bearers of that identity enjoy self-government. This in turn requires that the constitutional arrangements of the state provide a democratic forum in which people associated with that identity form a majority and to that extent can think of themselves as making collective decisions together as a group. A multinational constitution is in place, then, when formal and/or informal structures, norms, and practices are established that provide a democratic forum corresponding to each of the national identities found in the political community. When such arrangements are in operation, citizens with different national identities but living together in the same political community can each find and relate to a democratic forum for collective decision making in which their identity finds significant expression. There is a "failure of recognition" when constitutional arrangements fail to provide one of the community's national identities with a forum for self-government.

We should expect multinational constitutional arrangements to take very different forms depending on factors such as the community's political traditions and culture and how the different national identities to be recognized are territorially dispersed. Multinational federalism represents one important example of multinational constitutional arrangements.[24] In a multinational federal system, the federal units are defined in such a way, and given such powers, as to allow bearers of substate national identities their own significant political communities, while at the same time preserving a significant role for the larger state that accords a degree of recognition to those who maintain a statewide identity.

The idea of federalism as an institutional response to substate minority nationalism is a familiar one in the literature.[25] Under multinational federal arrangements, those sharing a substate national identity have a forum—one of the units of the federation—in which they form a majority and to this extent can think of themselves as marking decisions together as a group, decisions

---

[23] The phenomenon of dual identities is emphasized by Miller (2000, chap. 7), who refers to "nested nationalities," and De Schutter 2011.

[24] On the idea of multinational federalism, see Resnick 1994; Kymlicka 1998a, chap. 10; 1998b; Norman 2006, 87–88.

[25] Kymlicka 1995; 1998a; 2001a; Norman 1994; 2006, chap. 5; Levy 2004; 2007.

that apply to the group and its territory. Their identity is recognized in the sense that political boundaries are drawn, and powers assigned, in such a way as to acknowledge the group as a group and give it a space in which to enjoy self-government. A less widely appreciated point is that federalism is also an appropriate response to identity pluralism *within* the federal unit dominated by the national minority. Some of the citizens of this unit will identify not just with (or, in some cases, not at all with) the substate group, but also (or instead) with the statewide population. Under federal arrangements, those who retain a statewide identity also have a forum—the democratic processes of the central state—in which they can make binding collective decisions together with other members of the group with which they identify. As we shall see in more detail in the next section, federalism can thus establish a valuable relation of equality both in the state as a whole (between national majority and minority) and within the minority-controlled federal unit (between those with a substate national identity and those with a statewide national identity).[26] Failure of recognition is significant because it implies the absence of one or both of these valuable relations.

To avoid confusion, let me distinguish the conception of recognition I am proposing from other ways in which we talk of groups enjoying recognition. Most commonly, perhaps, the recognition of a group's national identity is said to involve the provision of government services, and the operation of public institutions, in the language and cultural medium associated with the group. A group is recognized in this important sense, for instance, when there are public schools that offer instruction in the language of the group and employ a curriculum informed by the group's culture and historical experience. In the context of this chapter, I will not understand recognition in this cultural sense, however, because I take it that many proponents of the plebiscitary theory already acknowledge its importance. When moderate and qualified versions of the plebiscitary theory insist that democratic secession is permissible only if it respects standard liberal rights, they often intend this to include minority-language rights and other rights associated with cultural recognition.[27] In any case, this is how I will understand the "standard liberal rights" requirement for the purposes of the present discussion. In the view I will be taking for granted, cultural recognition is already a factor to be taken into account in considering secessionist claims, and the question is whether recognition in the self-government sense is also such a factor.

Recognition can also have a symbolic dimension. We might say that a group's identity is recognized in a set of constitutional arrangements, for instance, when the constitution and other official documents contain specific

---

[26] I have highlighted the latter dimension of equality in Patten 2000; 2001b; 2002. See also De Schutter 2011.

[27] See, e.g., Philpott 1998, 83.

and explicit references to the group and when other aspects of the public face of the state—its flags, coats of arms, national anthem, and so on—incorporate symbols connected with the group. And recognition is sometimes thought to involve the enjoyment of international personality. A group is recognized in this sense when it can have its own direct relations with foreign states and other international bodies, when its leaders can act and speak on behalf of the group in international meetings and forums, when it can field its own sports teams in international competitions, and so forth. Although I will not assume that failure of recognition involves a failure to provide symbolic recognition or international personality, someone who thinks that these forms of recognition are normatively important can reinterpret the failure-of-recognition condition accordingly.[28]

So the failure-of-recognition condition, as I shall understand it, involves a failure by the state to introduce and respect constitutional arrangements that provide space for self-government for members of a national minority. We cannot conclude that a democratic mandate won by a national minority generates a right to secede, I shall now argue, unless this condition is met. Two arguments will be offered in favor of this contention. The first—the equality argument—will contend that the plebiscitary theory can conflict with the equal recognition of national identity and should be rejected on this basis. The second—the democracy argument—will explore the plebiscitary theory's assumption that the secessionist region itself is the appropriate constituency in which to hold a democratic procedure to settle the secession controversy. The best reasons for adopting this assumption, it will be argued, turn out to be even better reasons for acknowledging the failure-of-recognition condition.

7.3 The Equal Recognition of National Identity

The equality argument in favor of the failure-of-recognition condition has three main steps: (1) the recognition of a group is a good for the members of that group; (2) since recognition is a good, arrangements that establish equal recognition ought as a matter of justice to be valued and respected; and (3) the plebiscitary theory is flawed because it would license secessions that dismantle arrangements establishing equal recognition, but this flaw can be repaired by adding the failure-of-recognition condition as a further qualification of the theory.

---

[28] Other powers too might conceivably be identified with recognition. For discussion, see Norman 2006, 156–69. Again someone who thinks some other form of recognition is important might provisionally reinterpret the failure-of-recognition condition accordingly. Of course, recognition is not in the end whatever one wants it to be. It is disciplined by the considerations discussed in sec. 5.2 and ultimately by the underlying normative reason for caring about it, which I argue in the next section is neutrality of treatment.

Although I mainly focus here on developing an objection to the plebiscitary theory, the discussion also has ramifications for the remedial-right-only theory. As I noted earlier, to add a failure-of-recognition condition to the list of injustices that might trigger a remedial right to secession, it is necessary to show both that failure of recognition is a significant injustice and that adding it to the list would not create serious pragmatic difficulties. I will address the second of these conditions in the chapter's concluding section; the present section's discussion will explain why a failure of recognition should be considered a significant injustice.

RECOGNITION AS A GOOD

As we have seen, a group enjoys recognition when boundaries are drawn and jurisdictions are defined so as to leave members of the group in the majority in some context of collective decision making. In asking why recognition is a good, we are asking why it is good for members of the group to be empowered in this way. I shall sketch two main answers to this question. The first highlights the instrumental value of recognition; the second, its intrinsic value.

The instrumental argument relies on the assumption that people who share a national identity also share a culture.[29] Sharing a culture is not inherent in the notion of national identity, but we know from section 2.5 that culture and identity are often connected. On the one hand, a collective identity can easily develop out of a shared culture. Sharing a culture is a matter of common exposure to a set of formative influences, and this experience may foster a common sense of belonging and groupness among those who undergo it. On the other hand, the attitudes and dispositions that constitute an identity may work to accentuate the separateness and distinctness of the formative experience of those who share that identity, thereby helping to endow them with a distinct culture. While nothing rules out the possibility of national identities without national cultures, the standard case is one in which a people sharing a national identity also reasonably think of themselves as sharing a culture. [30]

The reason why sharing a culture matters in the context of our discussion is that people who share a culture are more likely to have similar values and preferences than is the case for people shaped by different cultures. Sharing a culture is a matter of being exposed to a common set of formative influences, and these influences leave an imprint on the values and preferences that people tend to develop. To be sure, not everyone who shares a culture will hold the same values and preferences. It is predictable that there will be many responses

[29] For related versions of the instrumental argument, see Margalit and Raz 1990; Miller 1995, 85–88.
[30] This view of the relationship between national identity and shared culture follows Mill 1991, 427. Mill defines "nationality" by reference to attitudes and dispositions, including common sympathies and a desire for self-government. He observes that nationality, in this sense, is often generated by a shared culture (linguistic, religious, political) but insists that the two ideas can be treated as analytically distinct.

to a common set of formative influences. The claim being made here is about *frequency*. Certain values and preferences will be more prevalent among people who share a culture than they will be among outsiders.

With these points in the background, the instrumental value of recognition comes into focus. When a group enjoys recognition, as we have seen, it has a space in which it can exercise self-government. Self-government makes it easier for members of a group to express their distinctive values and preferences in political decisions and outcomes. When a group is in the majority in a constituency, it has greater power to bring about decisions and outcomes that reflect its beliefs, values, cultural priorities, traditions, and so on than it would if its members are thrown into a collective decision-making process dominated by a culturally distinct majority.[31]

One of the arguments in favor of self-government for certain Native American groups, for instance, refers to the distinctive beliefs about value and approaches to social and political problems shared by members of such groups. Whereas carving out jurisdictional spaces in which such a group can be self-governing helps to ensure that laws and public decisions more fully reflect its distinctive beliefs and approaches, this sensitivity to the group's particular concerns would be much less likely were its members to constitute only a tiny minority in a much larger jurisdiction. A similar argument was often made by Scots in favor of devolution and is echoed again today by Scots who favor full independence. The prodevolution Scots maintained that Scottish political values were systematically thwarted during the Thatcher years (when the vast majority of Scottish members of Parliament were in opposition) and that devolution would make it harder for this to happen again.

So recognition is valuable for members of national groups, then, in the straightforward sense that it allows them to more easily express and realize their distinctive (non-recognition-related) values and preferences. One way to put this point is by saying that, all else being equal, it is good when individuals can be governed by political decisions and outcomes that fit with their own values and traditions. Michael Walzer has referred to this "fit" as "communal integrity."[32] Individuals who enjoy the good of communal integrity are "at home" in their public life and institutions. Public life is understandable and meaningful to them—familiar and comfortable.[33] For Walzer, communal integrity is something that foreigners should respect—one reason that states have some moral standing. The doctrine of state sovereignty, in his view, is partly grounded in the respect foreigners ought to show for the communal integrity of peoples organized into states. While remaining agnostic about

---

[31] In Patten 2010, I suggest that an argument of this form can be traced back to Herder.

[32] Walzer 1980, 211–12.

[33] Tamir (1993, 72) emphasizes a similar point in her defense of what she terms "national self-determination." See also Christiano 1994, 170–71, 175, 186–87; Rawls 1999b, 61, 111.

Walzer's particular use of the community integrity argument to ground state sovereignty, I will be claiming that respect for communal integrity represents a constraint on democratic secession and a consideration that should factor into the interpretation of the remedial alternative.

One obvious worry about this argument is that it may end up catering excessively to values and preferences that are antithetical to liberal democracy. Suppose that the distinctive values that are prevalent in some minority national group are deeply inegalitarian (e.g., with respect to women or to religious minorities). Do we really want to say that members of this group have a good claim to recognition on the grounds that such an arrangement would allow them to more effectively express and realize their values? There may be situations in which empowering the minority is the lesser of two evils because the national majority is also deeply illiberal, and the prospects for improvement are enhanced by recognition. And we might want to allow for cases of nonliberal, decent national cultures whose values represent reasonable alternatives to those of liberal democracy.[34] But, apart from these cases, the fact that recognition would allow some group to better pursue its antiliberal values seems like a reason for rejecting it rather than endorsing it.

In response to this concern, then, I think we should restrict the scope of the argument to cases in which the distinctive values and preferences of the national group in question are broadly compatible with the values of liberal democracy or at least fit into one of the two categories of nonliberal cultures just mentioned. Although this restriction will certainly have some bite, it is important to acknowledge that there are many varieties of liberalism, and many ways that values, traditions, and so on can vary without generating a conflict with liberal values. One question that should be raised is whether the proposed restriction is ad hoc. Although I will not spell the argument out explicitly (having sketched it once already in section 4.2), I do not think that the restriction suffers from this problem. As we shall see in the next subsection, the underlying principle that drives the argument for equal recognition is fair opportunity for self-determination. Given this overarching concern, there is nothing ad hoc about refusing to extend self-determination rights to groups whose dominant beliefs and values are antithetical to fair opportunity for self-determination or to comparatively important liberal values.

Another possible objection to the instrumental argument for the value of recognition is that it tacitly relies on a form of essentialism.[35] Although the concept of culture appealed to by the argument is avowedly nonessentialist,

---

[34] Rawls 1999b.

[35] Waldron (2010, 402–6) argues that "identity-based self-determination" of the sort advocated by Kymlicka (1989, 1995) and by Margalit and Raz (1990) runs foul of the critique of cultural essentialism. In my view, the accounts of culture and cultural preservation developed in chapter 2, and the "adequacy" interpretation of why cultures matter developed in sec. 3.4, offer the resources needed for a rebuttal of Waldron's critique.

the real work might seem to be done by a different concept according to which everyone who shares a culture holds some distinctive set of values and preferences. If essentialism is truly being foresworn, then presumably it is more accurate to say that recognition will help some members of the group and hinder others. Scots with Thatcherite values might have done better in realizing their values in a unitary Britain than under devolution. The decisions and outcomes made in a Britain-wide forum were likely to be a better fit with their values.

This objection raises an important point. It suggests that we should regard the claim that recognition has instrumental value for members of the group as shorthand for the weaker claim that it has instrumental value for *some* members of the group. For our purposes, the weaker claim should suffice. Suppose it is granted that both the majority and the minority in a national group have some claim to a jurisdiction in which their values and preferences are able to flourish. And suppose that the majority preferences do better in a substate jurisdiction (e.g., in decisions made by the Scottish Parliament) and the minority's preferences do better in the statewide setting (e.g., in decisions made in Westminster). An argument for recognition of the group (i.e., recognizing the Scottish national identity by assigning some powers to the Scottish Parliament) could still be made in one or other of two ways. One could argue that it is more important to achieve a fit with the preferences of the majority in the group. Or one could argue that, under a system of devolution or federalism, jurisdictions are assigned in such a way as to fit with the majority in some areas and with the minority in other areas, thereby achieving a kind of equality or evenhandedness. The second of these possibilities anticipates the proposal to be offered below for handling situations in which there is more than one national group present in the territory in which some particular group is seeking recognition.

The intrinsic argument for the value of recognition can be stated more succinctly. Two variants of the argument can be distinguished, one of which relies on the connection with culture described above, while the other makes do without it. The cultural variant starts from the premise that people often value their culture. As Samuel Scheffler reminds us, it is a normal part of valuing something that one wants that thing to be preserved.[36] The preservation of the culture may become something of a project for some people, one that requires that they and other likeminded members of the culture do what they can to adapt the institutions and practices that transmit the culture so that they are appealing and choice-worthy to newcomers and new generations.[37] Invested as they are in this project of making the culture survive and flourish, it seems intelligible that they should want the project to succeed. As Charles Taylor has

---

[36] Scheffler 2007, 106.
[37] Ibid., 108.

emphasized, this notion of survival often figures prominently in the rhetoric and demands of national minorities.[38]

In chapter 2 we examined the concept of cultural preservation in the context of a concern about essentialism. It was argued that a culture's preservation is a matter of members of the culture maintaining some significant degree of control over the socialization of newcomers and new generations. When the present members of some culture largely control the socialization of a new generation, then the culture can be said to be preserved in that new generation even if the substantive values and preferences of the new generation diverge quite markedly from those of their elders. Once control is made central to cultural preservation in this way, it is clear that recognition will be of value for people who value cultural preservation. Recognition consists in being given powers of self-government, and this just *is* a form of control. When these powers include jurisdiction over education, the connection with control over socialization is especially tight.

The second variant of the intrinsic argument maintains that the value of recognition derives simply from the fact that the aspiration to collective self-government is one of the constituting features of a shared national identity. To have a national identity, as we saw earlier, is to have a set of attitudes and dispositions, one of the most important of which is the desire for some degree of collective self-government. The recognition of some particular national identity is a good for individuals in the simple sense that it accommodates, or gives expression to, the desire for self-government shared by (most) people with that identity. The accommodation of this desire may in turn be one of the sources of self-respect for some individuals. Their respect for themselves may, in part, be a function of the respect that is publicly accorded their identity group through the creation of institutional jurisdictional spaces in which the group can be self-governing.[39] Where respect is at stake in this way, the claims to equal recognition considered below should be given added weight.

Equal Recognition

So the recognition of national identity is good for individuals in several different ways. It allows many of them to more effectively realize their values and preferences and to enjoy the Walzerian good of communal integrity. And it offers individuals an essential tool with which to preserve their culture, and an opportunity to participate in collective self-government alongside members of the group with which they identify.

---

[38] Taylor (1994 [1992], 32–33, 38–39, 40n16) emphasizes the desire for cultural survival.

[39] On the connection between self-respect and self-government, see Margalit and Raz 1990; Taylor 1993; Copp 1997, 284–85.

The question we must now explore is how the good of recognition should figure into an account of what is owed to persons as a matter of justice. For the most part, the arguments for the goodness of recognition appeal to ways in which various values and preferences of individuals would be satisfied by recognition. Since there is no general right to have one's values and preferences satisfied (as we saw in section 3.4), clearly the argument that recognition is required by justice awaits completion.

A first step in completing the argument is to observe that recognition is a good that can be distributed more or less equally depending on political arrangements. At one extreme, for instance, political arrangements might not provide any recognition of some national identity at all: boundaries might be drawn, and powers assigned, in such a way as to deny bearers of that identity any meaningful space in which to conduct their affairs alongside other members of their identity group. By contrast, those with a different national identity may, in this situation, readily be able to identify with the political community in which collective decisions are made. It may be the case that they both think of the entire state, and all fellow citizens, as forming their community of belonging and that it is at this statewide level that political decisions are made.

On the other hand, the recognition of national identity need not be so unequally distributed. Constitutional arrangements can be put in place, for example, that give recognition to the substate national identity—through federalism or devolution—while at the same time providing a degree of recognition to statewide national identity holders as well—through the retention of certain democratically controlled powers by the central state. Provided that significant functions and responsibilities are assigned to each level, a kind of rough equality in the recognition of different national identities is worked out.

Consider again the case of Scottish devolution. This arrangement enhances equality in two different respects. First, and most obviously, devolution brings about greater equality between citizens in Scotland with a Scottish national identity and citizens in England who have a British national identity. The Scots enjoy some degree of self-government in the association they value and can expect to enjoy some of the instrumental and intrinsic benefits outlined above that derive from this recognition. Because of the powers retained in Westminster, bearers of a British identity in England enjoy self-government alongside all British citizens, although they do not get to participate in determining for the Scots those questions that are assigned to the Scottish Parliament. This first dimension of equality is especially relevant, as we shall see, to the remedial theory of secession.

Second, devolution enhances equality *within* Scotland between those whose identity is primarily Scottish and those whose identity is primarily British. Whereas the creation of uniquely Scottish institutions, including a Scottish Parliament, gives public expression to the Scottish identity, retaining certain powers and responsibilities in London gives a public, political life to the British identity.[40] This second relationship of equality helps to explain why the goods associated with recognition do not count in favor of a massive delegation of powers to the substate authority. A devolution or a federation that assigned too many powers to the substate authority would end up denying equal recognition to citizens of the substate unit who maintain a statewide identity. Even more important for our current topic, this second dimension of equality helps to explain what is wrong with the democratic theory of secession when it is not qualified by the failure-of-recognition condition. We shall return to this in a moment.

So recognition is a good that can be distributed more or less equally. But why should we think of unequal recognition as a form of injustice? My main answer to this question appeals to the argument developed in chapter 5 and rehearsed again (in the context of a discussion of language rights) in chapter 6. In short, equal recognition is a requirement of justice because neutrality is, and equal recognition is implied by neutrality.

Nobody has a right to the satisfaction of his or her values and preferences. But people do have a defeasible complaint of injustice when public institutions are structured in such a way as to treat the things that they care about nonneutrally—that is, when institutions impose more burdens on, or extend fewer benefits to, the pursuit of their conception of the good than they do to the conceptions that matter to other people. As we have seen, the underlying principle here is fair opportunity for self-determination. The pro tanto obligation of neutral treatment is grounded in the pro tanto obligation to give all persons a fair opportunity to pursue and fulfill the conception of the good they happen to hold.

It is true that nonrecognition would in theory also be a way of extending neutral treatment. Because of this possibility, there is no analytic entailment running from neutrality to equal recognition. Not every good that can be distributed equally ought to be so distributed through political arrangements. The distribution of some goods is appropriately left to the market and civil society. Where these goods are concerned, equality is achieved, not through a direct allocation by the state, but by ensuring that people have equal resources and opportunities to pursue their own ambitions and identity-commitments as they see fit.

It is tempting to think that recognition is one of these goods the provision of which is better left to the market and civil society. One argument for this perspective has already been encountered. Not everyone who lives in the jurisdiction that is empowered by recognition will have the national identity and/or the favored preferences and values that make recognition a good. There are likely to be both internal national minorities (minorities within minorities) as well as members of the recognized group who have minority values and prefer-

---

[40] On the Scottish case, see Miller 1995, 117–18; 2000, 125–41.

ences. Given this diversity, it might seem best for public institutions to avoid taking a stand on recognition, and to leave national identity for mobilization in civil society.

Allen Buchanan has emphasized a second argument. National identity is not the only important form of identity that people have. In a liberal society, individuals can quite reasonably have a plurality of different allegiances. For some, nationality will be of little or no importance relative to other sources of identification. The problem with the recognition of national identity is that it singles nations out and elevates their status above other identities. This, according to Buchanan, represents "nothing less than a public expression of the conviction that allegiances and identities have a single, true rank order of value, with nationality reposing at the summit."[41] It devalues other allegiances and identifications and shows less than equal respect to their bearers.

But neither of these arguments is sufficient to show that nonrecognition should be preferred over equal recognition. The basic reason is that a society must have some set of political boundaries or other. Given that at least some citizens will have a statewide national identity, and that at least some powers will be retained at the statewide level, the positive recognition of at least one identity is inevitable. And once at least one identity is recognized, neutrality does require equal recognition.

Consider this point from the perspective of the Scottish case. It is true that some people living in Scotland do not benefit in the anticipated ways from devolution. They do not have a Scottish identity, and/or they do not have the preferences and values that predictably would be served by such a scheme. But the same thing is true in the unitary British state. There are some people—by virtue of their identity, values, preferences—who do not do well by the metrics we have been discussing in such a context. If there were some way of avoiding the question of boundaries altogether, this might be fairest, but there is not. In practice, the realistic alternatives are a unitary state, an independent Scotland, and some form of devolution or federalism. Of these three options, the last comes closest to realizing neutrality between the different identities, values, and preferences that are in play.

Although nonrecognition is not possible in some situations, it is both possible and attractive in others. For instance, the state can and probably should avoid recognizing any religion, and the same is true of various lifestyles, preferences about consumption and leisure, and the like. It seems quite likely that a liberal state will end up with recognition in the spheres of national identity, language, and a few other areas, but nonrecognition with respect to other aspects of conceptions of the good. This is *not* because it ranks the former set of features higher than the latter, but because nonrecognition is not feasible with respect to the former but is with respect to the latter.

[41] Buchanan 1998b, 294.

The truth in the arguments for nonrecognition lies in the observation that, however boundaries are settled, the jurisdictions that are created are likely to be internally diverse. They will be home to differing senses of national identity, as well as different substantive values and preferences. As I have argued, this diversity is a reason for pluralizing recognition through arrangements that offer some form of recognition to both majority and minority. It is also a reason for recalling that any particular authority created through such arrangements remains subject to the liberal norms and constraints described in this book, including the pro tanto obligation of neutral treatment. The responsibility to be neutral applies to both statewide institutions and substate institutions designed to empower national minorities. Neither the majority nor the minority may regard any particular jurisdiction as "theirs," and thus both face substantial constraints on how far they can go, when exercising their self-governing powers, in asserting their identity and culture in public life.[42] These important points do not, however, lend support to a nonrecognition alternative since in this specific context nonrecognition is a chimera. The recognition of national identity cannot be detached from political institutions and relegated to civil society because those institutions necessarily involve boundaries, the assignment of jurisdictional powers, and so forth, and to make any decision about these matters is already to recognize or fail to recognize some particular national identity

EQUALITY AND SECESSION

It should be obvious that, under certain conditions, secession would upset multinational constitutional arrangements. Where these conditions obtain, secession is objectionable in at least one important way not acknowledged by existing plebiscitary theories: it fails to respect arrangements that establish an equal distribution of recognition among the different national identities found in the community.

To see this conflict more concretely, consider the case of a secessionist unit in which two main national identities are prevalent: a substate minority national identity focused on the secessionist region and a statewide identity

---

[42] There is thus a tension worth noting in the case for equal recognition of national identity. On the one hand, part of the value of recognition for national minorities is that it provides a space in which such groups can more effectively express and realize their distinctive values and preferences. This is the instrumental value of recognition discussed earlier. On the other hand, statewide and substate governments alike are constrained in how far they can go in privileging their majority's identity and culture. Neutrality and other liberal principles constrain each level of government. I do not see this as a problem with the argument so much as a genuine tension in the accommodation of minorities within a liberal-democratic framework. It is not a problem because and to the extent that self-government still has *some* instrumental value for minorities despite the substantial constraints on how self-government may legitimately be exercised.

shared with citizens in other parts of the state. To keep things simple, let us imagine that all the qualifications embraced by plebiscitary theorists are satisfied: the secession of this region would not lead to the violation of standard liberal rights, it would not threaten peace and security, and so on. Let us also assume, for the sake of argument, that multinational constitutional arrangements are in place—for instance, a multinational federation. There is a federal unit with significant powers in which bearers of the substate identity are in the majority and can to this extent collectively make decisions for the group together as a group. At the same time the central state retains enough significant powers to enable those with a statewide identity also to enjoy a degree of collective self-government.

Now suppose that those with a particularly strong substate national identity are able to organize and clearly win a referendum in favor of secession. According to the plebiscitary theory, this result would generate a right to secession since, by assumption, all of the usual qualifications are satisfied. But this implication highlights a clear objection to the plebiscitary theory. In the case being considered, this theory gives the go-ahead to a secession that dismantles arrangements providing for equality in the recognition of the different national identities prevalent in the secessionist region and replaces them with a new set of arrangements that exclusively recognize the substate identity. Prior to the secession, a multinational federation was in place that provided institutional space for the expression of both the substate and statewide identities. By putting together a majority in a referendum on secession, however, those bearing the substate identity are able to obtain a monopoly on the good of recognition and shut the minority statewide identity out completely.

When the specific conditions assumed above obtain, we should question whether there really is a right to secede. Under the stated conditions, there is a direct conflict between the considerations of democracy appealed to by the plebiscitary theory and the equality-disabling outcome of the democratic procedure. Looking at other areas in which this kind of conflict arises, we sometimes come down on the side of equality: we think it legitimate to limit the authority of some particular democratic procedure—through judicial review, for instance, or other checks and balances on the will of the majority—to achieve better, more equal outcomes. More important, the plebiscitary theory already accepts outcome-based limitations on the authority of a democratic mandate in favor of secession. As we saw earlier, in cases where the secession is likely to produce violations of standard liberal rights or conflict with the realization of other standard elements of liberal justice, the more moderate and plausible versions of the theory hold that the democratic decision in favor of secession does not generate a right to secession. Others do not have an obligation to facilitate a profound political change that will lead to violations of individual or group rights, or undermine schemes promoting equality of opportunity or distributive justice, even when a democratic procedure within the secessionist region supports that change.

The equality argument against the plebiscitary theory claims that these outcome-based limitations on the authority of a democratic mandate should be extended to include equality in the recognition of national identity. Just as the authority of a democratic mandate in favor of secession is restricted or nullified when rights violations seem likely, so the authority of such a mandate is restricted or nullified when secession would dismantle arrangements providing for the equal recognition of the different national identities prevalent in the secessionist region.

The situation is quite different if the failure-of-recognition condition is met. If multinational constitutional arrangements have not been established in the first place, and the central state is stubbornly refusing to implement them, then clearly the secessionists cannot be accused of undermining equality in the recognition of national identity. If anyone has undermined equality, it is the central state, with its refusal to recognize the substate identity prevalent in the secessionist region. Were the plebiscitary theory to embrace the failure-of-recognition condition, it follows, it would avoid the kind of equality-diminishing outcome I have been describing. It would not license secessions that fail to respect arrangements establishing an equal distribution of recognition among different national identities.

I have been highlighting the implications of equal recognition for the plebiscitary view. The consequences for the remedial theory are in one way more straightforward, and in another way less so. The straightforward point is that, insofar as failure of recognition is unjust, members of a national minority that are denied recognition have a justice-based grievance against the state. If the central state persistently refuses to implement some form of self-government for such a group and attempts by the group to bring about change within the system have been exhausted, then it seems reasonable for the group to seek self-government through secession as a final recourse. When in such a situation there is clear majority support for secession, domestic and international actors should not simply ignore it. They should pressure the state to reconsider its opposition to self-government arrangements for the minority, and failing that they should support secession as a last-ditch, peaceful remedy to the problem.

As an illustration, imagine that Scottish devolution had never been granted despite repeated indications through the democratic political process that people in Scotland widely supported such a scheme. Having said "no" to devolution, and (let us suppose) to other reasonable schemes of recognition (e.g., federalism), it seems to me that citizens and officials in the rest of Britain have an obligation to consider seriously and with an open mind the secessionist alternative. It may be that, in considering the demand to secede, they are able to respond by pointing to legitimate countervailing considerations. But absent such considerations, it would be unreasonable for the rest of Britain to keep denying substate self-government to the Scots and also to deny the Scots recourse to the secessionist fallback alternative.

The argument for incorporating the failure-of-recognition condition into the remedial-right-only theory, then, boils down to two claims: (1) that failure-of-recognition is unjust (absent sufficiently weighty countervailing considerations); and (2) that when this injustice persists, despite efforts by the national minority to gain recognition, the national minority ought to be permitted to seek a democratic mandate in favor of secession, a mandate that has consequences for the obligations and responsibilities of actors in the remainder state and in the international community.

Although this framework seems clear enough in the Scottish case, in other situations it will be less clear which groups have a good enough claim to self-government to trigger a remedial right to secede in the event that that claim is rebuffed. Some groups will be less numerous, or less territorially concentrated than the Scots, or will have a less pronounced sense of national identity. There is also variation from case to case in the degree to which national minorities have a distinct culture and in the degree to which the dominant values and preferences in that culture diverge from those that prevail in the national majority.[43] Differences along each of these dimensions are bound to make it difficult for domestic and international actors to judge when a group has a well-founded claim to self-government that could, if persistently denied, turn into a well-founded claim to secede.

A further complication arises because of disagreement and indeterminacy concerning the territory implicated in valid claims to self-government and secession. Consider a national minority that, according to the account sketched above, has a valid claim to self-government. In which part of the state's territory exactly should the powers of self-government be granted? A common answer involves the observation that national groups frequently identify with some territory as their "homeland."[44] But this could easily lead to problems and conflicts between various national groups within the state. Imagine a very small national minority (as a percentage of the state's population) that claims a high fraction of the state's territory as part of its historic homeland. One problem that may occur in this scenario is a tension between self-government, as we have defined it, and claims to homeland territory. A group may not be in the majority in the territory it considers its homeland. Even setting aside

---

[43] Buchanan (2004, 381) asserts that "those who seek political independence for Scotland are not united by anything that could reasonably be called a distinct Scottish culture." Based on the social lineage account developed in chapter 2 above, it does seem reasonable to believe that there is a distinct Scottish culture.

[44] On the importance of homeland, see Miller 1995, chap. 2; Kymlicka 2010.

this problem, a second difficulty is that it seems unfair for a group to have a claim to more territory just because it has a historic sense of itself as spread out over a large area. The unfairness becomes especially pronounced if the claim to self-government were to turn into a claim (under the remedial theory) to secede. Why should the territory of the secessionist state be determined in this manner? Another possible solution to the territory problem would be simply to determine where the members of the national minority currently live, and to assign that territory to the group's self-government. But this proposal also faces a difficulty, which is that members of the group are unlikely to be neatly concentrated into some portion of the state's territory. For any given piece of territory that might be demarcated for the group's self-government, there will be nonmembers within and members on the outside.

Although these are some formidable challenges to supplementing existing remedial theories with the failure-of-recognition condition, they do not strike me as insurmountable. It is true that domestic and international actors are required under the proposed account to make some difficult judgments about which groups have weighty claims to self-government and secession. Presumably, decision makers will need to weigh a range of different factors in response to a group that is claiming that it should enjoy self-government. These include the degree to which members of the group can be expected to receive the instrumental and intrinsic benefits associated with self-government, the strength of any countervailing considerations, and the salience of categorical distinctions between different sorts of groups (e.g., immigrants and national minorities) of the sort that will be explored in the next chapter. Since a degree of vagueness accompanies each of these factors, and the need to weigh them against one another produces further indeterminacy, there will be an ad hoc quality to settling exactly where particular lines should be drawn. But it hardly follows that all claims to self-government, or even all such claims that are made in the context of a secessionist effort, should simply be ruled out. There may still be clear cases of strong claims and weak counterclaims. Domestic actors, and international law and practice, might be open to considering cases of this kind, even while generally rejecting cases that fall into the gray area.

Nor does the indeterminacy concerning territory offer a knockdown objection to the account being proposed. Notice that, if it did, this would also be bad news for more minimalist versions of the remedial theory, such as Buchanan's. Buchanan holds that a group has a right to secede when it has suffered persistent human rights abuses at the hands of the state. But with which portion of the territory should the group be permitted to secede? Presumably, the location of the human rights violations does not provide much guidance. The actual rights abuses may have occurred in very specific locations (suggesting too small a territory), while members of the group may quite reasonably feel insecure anywhere in the state (suggesting a claim that is too large). The seceding group's sense of its homeland (if it has one) and the areas in which most of its population live will provide some assistance, but an answer that relies heavily on these factors will suffer from the same shortcomings mentioned above. Intuitively, however, Buchanan's claim that persistent human rights violations can lead to a valid right to secede is a very powerful one and is not defeated by problems determining the precise boundaries of the secessionist territory. That territory will have to be worked out in the course of negotiating secession with reference to a set of imprecise criteria such as numbers, the economic value of the territory and its resources, the present or past existence of administrative or political boundaries, and the historical relationship of the group to the territory. These criteria are themselves somewhat vague and indeterminate and, at best, serve to rule out claims that are obviously excessive. But it seems better to muddle through the question of territory than to give up on even the narrow version of the remedial theory defended by Buchanan.

Roughly the same approach to territory should be adopted by the version of the remedial theory I have been defending. There is no precise formula for determining the territory that goes with a claim to self-government. At best there are a variety of relevant criteria that together rule out some claims and leave open a range of acceptable possibilities. Given how morally arbitrary claims to territory are to begin with, this is perhaps the best that can be hoped for in any case.

7.4 The Democracy Argument

The present section carries on my critique of the plebiscitary theory by developing a second reason why that approach should be amended to include the failure-of-recognition condition. The argument of the previous section appealed to the value of equal recognition. Unless the failure-of-recognition condition is required, the plebiscitary theory may end up licensing secessions that have the objectionable effect of undermining arrangements that establish equality of recognition between the national majority and national minorities. The argument to be developed now appeals to democracy itself rather than to an external equality standard. Rather than confront the plebiscitary theory with such a standard, the proposal is that a constraint is already implicit in the defense of the plebiscitary theory itself.

Consider, to begin with, the following feature of the plebiscitary theory to which attention has not yet been directed. The theory does not just say that so long as certain conditions are met, secession controversies are authoritatively settled by a democratic procedure. It says, more precisely, that so long as the relevant conditions are met such controversies are authoritatively settled by a democratic procedure *involving the citizens of the secessionist unit.*

The italicized qualifier does not itself follow from any principle of respect for democratic procedures. One could affirm the principle of respect for democratic procedures without endorsing the view that the boundaries of the unit of decision making should be drawn in some particular way.[45] For all that the principle of respect for democratic procedures tells us, the boundaries of the unit of democratic decision making could be drawn anywhere: they might coincide with the territory seeking secession, but they might alternatively be defined to include all citizens of the state or to include only citizens of particular subregions of the secessionist territory, each having the authority to determine its own political status.

Depending on how the unit of decision making is defined, the outcome of the secession-determining democratic procedure might be very different. If the secessionist region is the unit of decision making, then a majority might vote in favor of secession. If, on the other hand, the whole state were defined as the relevant unit of decision making, then a majority might vote against secession. Or, if individual subregions of the secessionist region were considered the appropriate units of decision making, then some might decide in favor of secession and others against it. Someone who rejects a democratically mandated secessionist claim cannot automatically be accused of refusing to show respect for democratic procedures. She can always say: "It is not that I refuse to respect democratic procedures. It is just that I do not accept the assumption that the secessionist region is the unit of democratic decision making relevant to settling this issue. If the unit of decision making is defined in some other way, then respect for democratic procedures may actually call for the rejection of the secessionist claim at issue."

A defense of the plebiscitary theory, then, must vindicate the assumption that the democratic procedure to be consulted should involve all and only citizens of the would-be secessionist unit. The most promising way of defending this assumption invokes considerations of autonomy. This is the strategy suggested by Daniel Philpott, for instance, who is one of the few defenders of a democratic right to secession directly to confront the problem. Asking "why everyone in a state should not vote on the separation of a group within its borders," Philpott suggests that the answer is clear:

> The nature of autonomy makes clear the reason: one does not have the autonomy to restrict another's autonomy simply because she wants to govern the other. The larger state's citizens cannot justly tell the separatists: "My autonomy has been restricted because, as a member of our common state, I once had a say in how you were governed—in my view, how we were governed—which I no longer enjoy." A right to decide whether another self can enjoy self-determination would make a mockery of the concept. I am entitled to govern myself with others who govern themselves according to principles of justice; I may not decide who

---

[45] See Barry 1979, 167–70; Brilmayer 1991, 185; Moore 1998.

will and will not be included in my state, or how another group governs its own affairs.[46]

Although Philpott's argument is not as explicit here as it might be, the central thrust of his position is clear enough: to allow the whole state to vote would undermine the autonomy of citizens in the secessionist region. In the remainder of this section, I will explore a version of this argument and argue that it does not provide support for existing plebiscitary theories. In a context of identity pluralism, the argument lends support, not for giving the secessionist region a democratic authority to settle the controversy, but for recognizing such authority only when the failure-of-recognition condition is taken into consideration as well.

Consider, then, the following argument. It is reasonable to suppose that respecting an individual's autonomy means allowing the individual the freedom to associate with whomever he chooses so long, of course, as the chosen associates are willing to associate with him.[47] This freedom of association, in turn, involves the freedom to disassociate from groups to which he no longer wishes to belong. Moreover, it would make a mockery of this latter freedom, the freedom to disassociate, to say that other members of the group could—in the name of their own freedom to associate with whomever they choose— veto an individual's decision to disassociate himself from the group or should even have a say in it. If respect for individual autonomy implies respect for the freedom to disassociate, then it also implies that the act of disassociation is not something the group as a whole should have a right to decide on but is a decision to be left up to the individual whose continued membership in the association is in question. If the individual can govern his own life only in the ways that others allow him to, then he is not really free to govern his own life at all.

I am not sure if this is the argument Philpott intends, but it seems consistent with what he actually says and has a degree of independent appeal. Unfortunately, except for the special case of unanimity that Philpott initially focuses on, the argument breaks down when it is generalized from the single individual to a group of individuals. To see this, consider the secession of T from S. Would it be violating anybody's individual autonomy if citizens of S − T were to be consulted in a referendum meant to settle this question authoritatively? It might seem that it would. Suppose that secession is unanimously supported by citizens of T. Under these conditions, the secession of T does not seem relevantly different from the individual disassociation of each individual member of T with the territory they can validly claim (assuming that the sum total of those territories is the territory of T itself). As has been argued, it would be violating the autonomy of an individual to give other members of an associa-

[46] Philpott 1995, 362–63.

[47] Gauthier (1994, 360) also bases his argument in the idea of freedom of association. See also Beran 1998, 35, 39; Wellman 2005, 61.

tion a veto over her decision to disassociate. But then, by the same logic, it would be violating the autonomy of each individual citizen of T to give a veto, or even a vote, to citizens in S − T over their decision to secede.

The argument of the previous paragraph assumes, as Philpott initially does, that citizens of T are unanimously in favor of secession.[48] The problem arises, however, when there is disagreement about secession among the citizens of T and it is not feasible for territorial reasons for each individual to go his or her own way.[49] Some citizens want to associate exclusively with other citizens of T; others want to be associated with all other citizens of S; and many want to be part of associations at both the S and T levels.

When support for secession is less than unanimous, Philpott thinks that the issue should be settled by a majoritarian democratic procedure involving all and only the citizens of T.[50] Notice, however, that this contention is no longer clearly supported by considerations of individual autonomy and free association. The winners (the majority) get to associate with the people they want (and only those people). But the losers (the minority) are forced to associate with some people they would rather not associate with or are prevented from associating with certain people they would like to associate with. And this is exactly as it would be if the vote were held in all of S rather than only in T. Proponents of holding the vote in T cannot reasonably complain that a vote in S would involve some people deciding for others whom they will associate with, thus violating their individual autonomy. For the same is true of a vote in T: in a vote in T, the majority will decide for the minority.

To this objection, it might be replied that by making T the decision-making constituency, it is at least ensured that a majority of citizens of T can realize their associational preferences. Making S the relevant constituency, by contrast, would open up the possibility that antisecessionist sentiment in S − T could swamp the associational preferences of the vast majority in T. Because of the territorial dimension of secession, it cannot possibly be guaranteed that everyone can realize their preferences with respect to association. But a democratic procedure in T at least gets as close as possible to this ideal, and T should therefore be considered the appropriate constituency for settling the issue.[51]

[48] Philpott 1995, 335.

[49] Beran (1998, 38) suggests that a reiterated use of the majority principle can resolve the problem of disagreement. In general, however, it is unlikely that iterations of the secession process will arrive at a result in which no individual is required to go along with the associational preferences of those around him (Miller 1995, 112). People with different associational preferences are typically territorially intermingled, and no number of iterations will prevent some people from being left on the wrong side of a boundary. This is especially likely if one takes seriously Wellman's (2005, 60) proviso that one must "take care not to divide political states that are subsequently incapable of performing the requisite political functions."

[50] Philpott 1995, 379–80.

[51] Gauthier (1994, 360) is explicit that it is the majority who are able to realize their associational preferences and argues that this is as close as we can get to the ideal in which all are able to do so. See also Philpott 1995, 379; Beran 1998, 39; Wellman 2005, 61.

Although this may be a compelling argument against holding a statewide referendum on secession, it is less persuasive as a defense of existing plebiscitary theories. Allowing a suitably qualified democratic procedure in T authoritatively to settle the secession question does not necessarily come as close as possible to the ideal in which everyone can find themselves in their preferred association. To see this, recall that we are focusing on secessionist claims that are made in a context of identity pluralism. In these cases, some people have an exclusively substate national identity and so desire only to associate themselves with fellow citizens of T. Others have an exclusively pan-state identity and would be happiest belonging to an association that includes all citizens of S. Many people, perhaps, have dual identities: they desire to be part of associations at both the S and the T levels. In this context, a referendum in T might lead to the following kind of result: it might turn out that those having strong substate associational preferences are able to win the majority required for secession, even though a significant minority strongly prefers to remain part of the statewide association and would be shut out of their preferred association by secession.

This kind of result does not come very close to the ideal in which everyone finds themselves in their preferred association. Although it is true that the majority are able to put themselves in exactly the association they most prefer, the minority are excluded from their preferred association altogether. In general, however, a distribution in which all get some of what they want should be regarded as superior to one in which a majority gets all of what they want while the minority gets none.[52] And where this is true, a closer approximation to the ideal would seek to give everyone some degree of membership in their preferred association. But this is exactly what multinational constitutional arrangements seek to do. When such arrangements are in place, each citizen is, in effect, part of two associations: one that includes all and only citizens of T; the other that encompasses all and only citizens of S. Although some might prefer not to be part of one of these associations at all, nobody would be shut out from at least some degree of preferred association.

We have, in effect, arrived back at the main critique of the plebiscitary theory, albeit via a different route from the one taken with the equality argument. With the equality argument, the plebiscitary theory was criticized for ignoring the possibility of a conflict with the ideal of equal recognition of national identity. The argument now—the democracy argument—points to a different problem with such a theory: its assumption that the secessionist region itself is the appropriate constituency in which to hold a democratic procedure to settle the secession controversy. One leading justification for adopting this assumption maintains that defining the constituency in this way best respects the as-

---

[52] This assumption might be supported, in turn, by egalitarian, prioritarian, or utilitarian considerations.

sociational preferences and hence the autonomy of individual citizens of the territory. Under conditions of identity pluralism, however, this justification provides an even better reason for respecting and upholding multinational constitutional arrangements. Such arrangements come closest to achieving the ideal in which all have their associational autonomy fairly respected. As with the equality argument, this conclusion suggests that the plebiscitary theory ought to accept the failure-of-recognition condition. Where the central state has failed to introduce a set of arrangements providing for the recognition of the substate national identity, associational preferences are already being ignored, and secession would not be a setback from that point of view. Where multinational constitutional arrangements are in place, however, the best reason for thinking that the secessionist unit is the appropriate constituency to hold a referendum about secession is also a reason for thinking that such a referendum would not generate a right to secede.

7.5 The Confederal Alternative

Before turning to some of the practical implications associated with the failure-of-recognition condition, let us consider a pair of possible objections to the argument so far. Both objections suggest that taking seriously the equal recognition of national identity would have a broader range of institutional implications than has so far been acknowledged. According to one of the objections, these implications should lead us to reconsider how much priority should be assigned to equality of recognition in the first place. According to the other, it shows that a (somewhat) more permissive approach to secession can be adopted than the one being proposed. In response, I distinguish between the pro tanto reasons generated by equal recognition and the all-things-considered implications of the overall account. I agree that equal recognition does give pro tanto reasons for endorsing the broader range of institutional implications, and I suggest that this is not embarrassing to the view. Once other relevant considerations are factored in, however, I doubt that the institutional implications of the overall account will go much beyond those already laid out, since the countervailing considerations are quite significant in the cases highlighted by the objections.

The first objection draws attention to a difficult case for proponents of equal recognition of national identity: the case of irredentist national minorities.[53] These are groups whose members share a national identity with their perceived kinfolk on the other side of an international boundary. The troublesome feature of groups of this kind is that their recognition cannot be achieved simply

---

[53] I am grateful to Will Kymlicka for presenting this objection to my argument. Wellman (2005, 118–22) presses it further in a discussion of Patten 2002.

through arrangements internal to the state in which they live. Their national identity involves a desire to be self-governing with their perceived kinfolk, and this desire is not accommodated through federalism, devolution, or other such schemes offering local autonomy. Some kind of rough equality of recognition might be worked out through confederal arrangements that create a cross-border democratic forum in which members of the national minority could participate in self-government arrangements with their conationals. But this possibility brings us to the objection. For some will doubt that multinational states have an obligation to enter into such cross-border arrangements. It will normally be permissible, and will sometimes be praiseworthy, for them to do so, but it is not required. And this calls into question whether equal recognition of national identity really should be accorded the high priority presumed by the argument so far.

The second objection also points to the possibility of confederal arrangements, but this time to argue that the failure-of-recognition condition is too restrictive.[54] The argument here is that secession from a state that has equality-respecting multinational constitutional arrangements need not lead to a net loss of equal recognition. It is possible that the postsecession states could enter into confederal arrangements with one another in which the original state-wide national identity borne by some citizens of the secessionist group finds significant expression and recognition. The requirement that there be failure of recognition in the presecession state ignores this possibility of a postsecession reestablishment of equal recognition and to this extent is too restrictive.

Both objections draw attention to significant and difficult issues in thinking about institutional responses to identity pluralism. The first objection raises the interesting question of when, if ever, states have a duty to enter into confederal arrangements with one another. The second objection does, in my view, identify a relevant question to be asked in the moral assessment of a secessionist movement: is that movement willing to enter into postsecession confederal arrangements with the remainder state in order to provide some form of recognition to citizens bearing a statewide national identity?

I do think that the value of equal recognition gives a state that is home to an irredentist national group a pro tanto reason to establish a cross-border, confederal scheme with the neighboring state where the group's conationals live. One of the major strands of the Good Friday Agreement (1998), which helped to bring to an end the decades-long sectarian conflict in Northern Ireland, was the creation of a North/South Ministerial Council designed to co-ordinate and exercise specific government powers on an Ireland-wide basis.[55] Suppose that, in the run-up to the agreement, the government and citizens of the United Kingdom were hesitating about whether to sign on to this particu-

---

[54] Wellman (2005, 118–22) also restates this objection in response to Patten 2002.
[55] See McGarry and O'Leary 2006, 56.

lar provision. Given that the Republic of Ireland supported the provision, and that it does not cut into any of the legitimate, core functions of the U.K. state, it strikes me as quite plausible to think that the United Kingdom had a justice-based obligation, grounded in the value of equal recognition, to accept the proposed cross-border arrangement. Doing so would, and (as things turned out) does, promote (albeit on a small scale) equality between the Unionist and Republican populations of Northern Ireland, with their differing senses of national identity. In the same vein, I think that a well-founded expectation that a new set of confederal arrangements would be established in the aftermath of secession would diminish, and perhaps nullify, the recognition-based objection to plebiscitary secession. Provided that these arrangements are meaningful, they are a valid way of realizing equal recognition and are not obviously inferior to federalism or secession in that respect.

So I concede these points to the two objections, even while denying that they are embarrassing to my account. At the same time, I do not think that the concessions will add up to very much once the full range of factors, including various countervailing considerations, are admitted into the calculus. Viewed from this angle, the problem with the objections is that they ignore the difficulties inherent in constructing meaningful and democratic multinational institutions. To get such institutions up and running requires a degree of genius at institutional design, together with a high level of trust and cooperative commitment on the part of the major parties. There is no guarantee that an intention, however sincere, on the part of one or more of the parties concerned to build institutions providing for the recognition of different national identities will meet with success.[56] Meanwhile, the attempt to build such institutions may have significant costs. It may mean weakening or compromising existing democratic institutions that are working tolerably well (despite failing to establish equality of recognition).

Once the difficulty and costliness of multinational institution building is taken into account, it becomes doubtful that there is an all-things-considered obligation to establish confederal arrangements with a neighboring state in order to recognize an irredentist minority. It is true that the stars may sometimes align, as they did in the Anglo-Irish case, but it seems likely that they will not so align in a significant range of other situations. There will be insufficient will on the part of the neighboring state, or too little trust between the potential partners, or a legitimate fear that a proposed confederal scheme would weaken or undermine established democratic institutions.

---

[56] For instance, as David Miller has suggested to me, multinational institutions seem more likely to succeed where the national identities in question are "nested"—citizens can, and generally do, affirm both at once—than where they are rivalrous (as they would often be in cross-border collaborations). For Miller's distinction between nested and rival nationalities, see Miller 2000, 125–41.

Similarly, once the difficulty of constructing multinational confederal arrangements is acknowledged, the second objection can be faulted for ignoring the significant difference between respecting existing multinational constitutional arrangements and dismantling them with a promise to resurrect equality of recognition later via confederal arrangements. In a critique of an earlier version of my account of secession, Wellman wonders why a secessionist group "could . . . not simply form a confederation with the parent state" and satisfy equal recognition in that way.[57] But whether the group "could" is not the key question. To offer an analogy, we would not want to permit secession by a group with a dark and stormy history of treating its religious minorities on the grounds that it *could* turn a new leaf and respect the rights of its minorities in accordance with liberal norms. Permissible secession ought to be conditional on a well-founded expectation that liberal rights *will* be protected. In the same way, a secession that dismantles a particular scheme for providing equal recognition should not be said to be compatible with equal recognition unless there is a well-founded expectation that a new confederal scheme that reestablishes equal recognition will in fact be adopted. For the reasons mentioned above, I suspect that such an expectation will often be absent. Given the difficulty of establishing successful confederal arrangements, there is simply no guarantee that the promised scheme will ever come to fruition.

7.6 Practical Implications

Up to this point, the focus of the argument has been on articulating and defending a fairly abstract proposal concerning the conditions under which a group ought to be regarded as possessing a right to secession. A great virtue of much recent work on secession is its realization that this exercise in abstract philosophizing does not, on its own, dispose of the question of how the international system (or domestic actors) ought to deal with secessionist claims. To have practical relevance, a theory of secession should, in addition to identifying various abstract normative principles, say something about who has the authority to adjudicate disputes about secession and what rules and procedures they should follow. It ought to consider whether the rules to govern secession should in some way be codified or constitutionalized. And the guidance it offers on these questions should reflect consideration of whether the entrenchment of some abstract proposal into law and practice would have adverse consequences.[58]

---

[57] Wellman 2005, 120. Note that even if Wellman is right about this, a requirement that the group enter into such a confederation represents a significant qualification of his theory.

[58] This "institutional turn" in the literature on secession is promoted by Buchanan 1997; 2004; and Norman 1998; 2006.

To some extent, secessionist disputes are currently resolved by the more or less ad hoc decisions of various international and domestic actors, including individual states and regional bodies. The proposal defended in this chapter offers some concrete guidelines for officials charged with making these decisions. The main implication of my account is that the judgment whether a substate national minority enjoys a plebiscitary right to secede should take into account the degree of recognition enjoyed by the group within the existing state. Where a national minority does enjoy significant recognition, then, in the absence of other rights violations, it should not normally be regarded as possessing a plebiscitary right to secede, at least insofar as the territory that it would take is also home to a significant minority of its own who identify with the statewide national community. Where multinational constitutional arrangements providing for recognition are not in place, a national minority should be regarded as having a plebiscitary right to secede, so long, at least, as the various conditions required by moderate and qualified versions of the democratic account are satisfied.

In general, it is likely to be easier for third parties to determine whether multicultural constitutional arrangements are present than to judge whether a national minority is being denied recognition. Determining the former is a matter of observing the legal and political arrangements that actually prevail in a state, whereas a judgment about whether a group claiming the right to secede is a national minority necessarily involves a set of political, sociological, and historical facts about which there may be considerable indeterminacy and controversy. Once the implementation of the proposed account is considered, then, an asymmetry emerges. It is easier to determine when the account implies a red light for secession than when it implies a green light. Still I do not think that these practical implications mean that the proposed account collapses into Buchanan's version of the remedial theory, which focuses exclusively on whether the conditions of minimal justice are being met. Although there may well be a sizable gray area in which it is hard to say with confidence whether a group that is denied recognition has a good claim to it, there are bound to be cases in which the great preponderance of evidence supports such a claim. In the most obvious cases, many or all of the following conditions are met:

- Members of the group have a strong sense of national identity.
- A distinctive set of traditions and values predominates among the group.
- Members of the group speak a language that is different from the majority's.
- The group has a history of self-government, which may have some present-day echo in the administrative boundaries and practices of the state.

Like many commentators, I think that some of the uncertainty, instability, and arbitrariness that typically surrounds secessionist disputes might be

mitigated by establishing an international adjudicative body with the authority to rule on secessionist claims.[59] The idea would be to take authority away
from actors who are likely to be excessively influenced by a perception of their
own national interests, or biased by their own involvement in the conflict, and
put it into the hands of impartial, third parties who are guided by publicly
promulgated rules and principles. Individual states might consider establishing analogous practices at the domestic level: they might consider constitutionalizing various rules, bodies, and procedures for dealing with secessionist
claims.[60] The proposal defended in this chapter offers some concrete guidelines concerning the kinds of factors that the designers of such international
or domestic institutions, and those who participate in them, should take into
account. It suggests that the rules and procedures for dealing with secession
should be sensitive, as far as possible, to whether or not a secessionist national
minority enjoys recognition within the existing state.

Having drawn these practical implications from my argument, however,
it is now time to consider whether the proposed guidelines for dealing with
secession would generate adverse consequences. As noted at the start of the
chapter, a major advantage claimed by remedial theories over standard plebiscitary theories is that the former, upon entrenchment in international law
and practice, are less likely than the latter to produce such consequences. In
considering whether my proposal is vulnerable to a similar objection, I will
compare it with Buchanan's version of the remedial theory, which allows secession only in those cases where minimal justice has been violated. Focusing
on three kinds of adverse consequences identified by Buchanan, I will argue
that it is far from obvious that Buchanan's proposal is superior to mine.

PROLIFERATION, WAR, VIOLENCE

My proposal is more permissive than Buchanan's since it permits some democratically approved secessions where there is no violation of minimal justice
(i.e., those in which the failure-of-recognition condition is met). To this extent, it might be objected that my account will lead to a (relative) proliferation
of secessions and therefore to more occasions for war and violence. Against
this contention, it is worth emphasizing three points. The first is that recent
plebiscitary theories acknowledge this risk explicitly and seek to counter it by
insisting that any plebiscitary right to secede is conditional on respect for standard liberal rights and the maintenance of peace and security. My proposal
is consistent with accepting these same guidelines. Second, it is also worth
observing that the failure-of-recognition condition reduces the permissibility
of secession (in comparison with existing plebiscitary theories) in precisely

[59] See, e.g., Margalit and Raz 1994, 142; Philpott 1998, 86–88.
[60] On constitutionalizing a right to secede, see Buchanan 1991, 127–49; Sunstein 1991; Norman 1998; Weinstock 2001.

those kinds of cases that are most likely to generate instability and violence: cases, familiar from the breakup of Yugoslavia, in which members of the erstwhile national majority would be "orphaned" in the territory of the seceding unit.[61] Members of the national majority can avoid this potentially explosive scenario, in my proposal, by ensuring that the national minority is adequately recognized in the constitution of the state.

Finally, my proposal should do a better job of limiting extralegal threats to peace and security than a remedial theory focused on minimal justice. A realistic theory of secession should acknowledge that secessionist groups sometimes opt to ignore the legal framework imposed by international (and domestic) law. They try to achieve a de facto secession of their unit in the hopes that, sooner or later, the unit will be recognized as a state by the international community. A full accounting of the consequences associated with the entrenchment in law of a proposed set of rules to govern secession should, therefore, examine not only (a) the consequences for peace and security brought about by actors playing by the rules but also (b) the probability that the proposed rules will be ignored by secessionists and (c) the consequences for peace and security of secessionist attempts outside the proposed legal framework. Although Buchanan's minimal justice remedial theory may perform relatively well under consideration (a), there is reason to suspect it will do less well under (b). A group that has, or could get, a democratic mandate in favor of secession, and whose distinct national identity is not adequately recognized in the constitutional arrangements of the state, does not necessarily have a right to secede in Buchanan's proposal. But it would hardly be surprising if the members of such a group were convinced of the legitimacy of their cause. For them, the "strains of commitment" to Buchanan's proposed legal framework would be great, and the temptation to pursue secession extralegally might be considerable.[62] By contrast, my proposal reduces the strains of commitment to a legal framework for resolving secessionist disputes because it does not shut the door completely on democratic secession, and because it is sensitive to demands for self-government often made by national minorities themselves. It should therefore have a better chance of being accepted by the various parties as a reasonable set of guidelines for handling the dispute in a legal and peaceful manner.

PERVERSE INCENTIVES

Another criticism made by Buchanan against existing plebiscitary theories is that they create an incentive for the state to avoid federalism or other schemes providing for local autonomy for national minorities. This perverse incentive is neutralized in my account by the failure-of-recognition condition. States that are careful to recognize the identity of national minorities through

---

[61] For a good discussion of the dynamics found in these kinds of cases, see McGarry 1998.
[62] The phrase "strains of commitment" is from Rawls 1999a, 153.

federal-style arrangements (and observe the conditions of minimal justice) are inoculated against democratic secession. By contrast, Buchanan's 2004 statement of his position does introduce a perverse incentive. In Buchanan's view, states are liable to a valid secessionist claim when they fail to honor existing autonomy agreements with regionally concentrated minorities but not when they fail to enter into such agreements in the first place. A state looking to minimize the likelihood of valid secessionist attempts will thus be encouraged to avoid autonomy arrangements since then there will be no agreement that it can be found to have violated.

PRACTICE OF DEMOCRACY

Drawing on Albert O. Hirschman's work, Buchanan argues that theories of secession that make "exit" too easy leave insufficient incentive for "voice."[63] Members of a territorially concentrated minority will be less inclined to "invest themselves in the practice of principled debate and deliberation" if they believe that they could secede easily instead.[64] Since secession is somewhat more permissible in my proposal than in Buchanan's, it might seem that my proposal is less attractive from the standpoint of promoting democracy and democratic virtues. In assessing this objection, however, we need to consider not only the incentive of the national minority to invest themselves in the practice of principled democratic participation but also the incentive of the national majority. As Hirschman himself points out, where a minority's threat of exit is absent or very limited, members of the majority have little incentive to take seriously the minority's exercise of voice.[65] The majority can complacently ignore the complaints and perspectives of the minority without any fear that its interests will be compromised. Encouraging principled democratic participation in the face of persistent majority/minority conflicts requires striking a balance between too much exit and too little. My proposal, it is reasonable to believe, gets this balance about right. It allows exit when there are persistent violations of minimal justice or a failure of recognition but not when the state is avoiding both these kinds of problems.

---

[63] Buchanan 1998, 22. For Hirschman's theory of exit and voice, see his *Exit, Voice, and Loyalty* (1970).
[64] Buchanan 1998, 22.
[65] Hirschman 1970, 82–83.

CHAPTER 8

Immigrants, National Minorities, and Minority Rights

8.1 The Immigrant/National Minority Dichotomy

In 2002 an activist named Abou Jahjah gave an interview to the Belgian maga-
zine *Knack* that caused a storm of controversy. Jahjah's organization, the Arab-
European-League, had made notorious remarks applauding the September 11
attacks on the United States and calling for the elimination of the state of
Israel. But this time Jahjah's remarks were much closer to home for his Belgian
audience. Jahjah demanded that Arabic be recognized as Belgium's fourth national language. He argued that, by offering official status to French-, Dutch-,
and German-speakers but not to the country's hundreds of thousands of
Arabic-speakers, Belgium was violating norms of antidiscrimination.[1]

Given Abou Jahjah's notoriety on other issues, many dismissed his demand
as one more example of extremism. But his remarks shine the spotlight on a
genuine puzzle that is both theoretical and practical in nature. How can the
discrepant treatment of national and immigrant groups in the area of language
rights be justified?

This particular puzzle is, in fact, part of a broader set of questions concerning the language rights of immigrants that have become pressing in recent
years. In the United States, questions about language rights and policy have
become intertwined with larger debates about immigration reform. Immigration reform legislation passed by the Senate in May 2006 declared English
to be the "national language," and a number of senators supported a similar
measure as the Senate debated immigration reform in 2013.

The question of immigrant language rights has been particularly vexing for
countries that, *unlike* the United States, extend significant language rights to
national minorities. In Canada during the 1960s, when the enactment of an
official bilingualism law was being debated, the single most common objection
to the policy was that it extended rights and privileges to English and French

---

[1] Osborne 2002, http://www.guardian.co.uk/elsewhere/journalist/story/0,7792,781449,00.html.

but not to the many sizable immigrant communities across the country.[2] As we have just seen, the same form of objection is heard in Belgium today, and indeed it recurs in many European countries. Across Europe, a number of rather small languages of groups considered "national minorities" enjoy official protections of some sort, but the often much more numerous language communities formed through recent immigration do not. The European Charter of Regional or Minority Languages explicitly excludes the "languages of migrants" from the protections it offers, while at the same time encouraging protections for languages as small as Frisian, Sorbian, and Asturian.[3]

From a theoretical perspective, the discrepancy between the treatment of immigrant and national groups is striking. What principles of political morality could possibly make this permissible? Why is it not morally arbitrary to extend one form of treatment to national languages and a different, and symbolically diminished, form of treatment to immigrant languages? Or is the discrepancy merely a matter of luck and power—the principle of "first-come, first-served" applied to rights? If no satisfying answer can be given to these questions, then perhaps the correct conclusion to draw is that *every* language spoken in a community should enjoy a full set of language rights. But this conclusion is unpalatable, a *reductio ad absurdum* of minority-language rights. The implication that many critics of minority rights will draw is that one cannot start assigning cultural or linguistic rights to certain groups without opening up a Pandora's box full of cultural and identity claims that no political community could ever possibly fulfill.[4] A major challenge to political theorists who want to defend a scheme of minority-language rights, therefore, is to explain why such a scheme would not lead to an uncontrolled proliferation of rights claims. Given that in many countries recent immigration is a major contributor to linguistic diversity, a principled defense of the view that it is permissible to limit the language-rights claims of immigrants would be a step in the right direction.

A parallel problem arises for other cultural rights that have been defended in this book. The previous chapter sketched an argument in favor of self-government claims by certain kinds of culturally distinct groups. I referred to these groups as "national minorities," but in light of the problem that is now being introduced, this label looks like an unwarranted presumption. If an immigrant group has a distinct identity and culture and would enjoy the various benefits of self-government outlined in the previous chapter, then why should they not have the same claim to self-government as a more established, "national" group? Again a *reductio* seems to loom. Clearly, self-government claims

---

[2] Laurendeau 1991, 38, 47, 98–99. For discussion, see Patten 2006.

[3] European Charter for Regional or Minority Languages, article 1a, http://conventions.coe.int /treaty/en/Treaties/Html/148.htm.

[4] Weinstock (1999) suggests the Pandora's box image.

cannot be granted to *hundreds* of different groups within a political community. So perhaps we are forced to reconsider whether *any* cultural groups as such have a good claim to self-government.

The best-known attempt to justify differences in the language and cultural rights extended to national minorities and immigrants is associated with the work of Will Kymlicka. In fact, the solution that Kymlicka suggests has been around for a long time and is familiar from everyday discourse.[5] In *Multicultural Citizenship* (1995), Kymlicka maintains that the contrasting ways in which national and immigrant groups come to find themselves under the jurisdiction of the state provide a morally relevant basis for treating their cultural-linguistic claims differently.[6]

National groups, he argues, were typically involuntarily incorporated into the state through conquest or annexation or voluntarily joined the state at some moment of confederation but with the implicit or explicit guarantee that their cultural and linguistic claims would be respected. The members of such groups thus never gave up the rights they may claim to cultural-linguistic protection and recognition. Immigrants, by contrast, "choose to leave their own culture" and thus can be regarded as "waiving" or voluntarily relinquishing their rights to live and work in their own culture.[7] The expectation that immigrants integrate into the host society is not unjust "so long as immigrants had the option to stay in their original culture."[8] The proposal, then, is that it is permissible for a liberal state to extend a restricted set of rights to immigrants, and a full set to national minorities, because immigrants, unlike national groups, became members of the state voluntarily and can be understood to have waived their claim on a full set of cultural and linguistic rights. Immigrants, in short, have voluntarily accepted an arrangement in which their languages and cultures receive less state recognition than do the established, national languages and cultures.

In the recent literature on cultural rights, this *voluntary acceptance* theory, as I shall call it, has been singled out for particularly strong criticism, with some critics suggesting that the weaknesses in Kymlicka's proposal have devastating implications for the whole project of defending minority cultural rights.[9] For the argument to be persuasive, the critics argue, three conditions would have to be satisfied:

[5] The solution is anticipated in Kloss (1971, 245), who observes that it is "frequently held."

[6] Kymlicka 1995, 95–100.

[7] Ibid., 95–96.

[8] Ibid., 96.

[9] Criticisms of Kymlicka's theory can be found in Weinstock 1999, 29; Carens 2000, 81; Bauböck 2001; Choudhry 2002, 61–65; Rubio-Marín 2003b. For earlier and much briefer and sketchier ancestors of the present chapter, see my response to Rubio-Marín in the same volume (Patten 2003c) as well as Patten 2006.

1. *Voluntariness*: In general, immigrants are capable of voluntarily relinquishing their cultural rights.
2. *Alienability*: The fundamental interests of immigrants would not ground a decisive moral objection to treating them as if they had voluntarily relinquished their cultural rights.
3. *Recipient's permission*: The receiving society is morally permitted to make the surrender of cultural rights a condition of admission to immigrant status.

Critics of Kymlicka's theory charge that none of these conditions are generally satisfied. It has been questioned whether (a) immigration is always or generally a voluntary decision; (b) even allowing that immigration is voluntary, a person could waive away their cultural rights; and (c) even allowing that immigration is voluntary and that cultural rights are alienable, it would ever be permissible for a liberal democratic state to expect immigrants to give up their cultural rights.

For some commentators, as I mentioned, these objections are enough to sink the whole project of defending minority cultural or linguistic rights. For others, the failure of Kymlicka's theory motivates the attempt to develop an alternative account of how cultural and linguistic rights should be allocated. The most persuasive of these alternatives seek to articulate certain general criteria for allocating rights—criteria that make no reference to the national or immigrant character of the groups that are claiming rights.[10] A simple version of this approach would allocate scarce rights on the basis of factors such as group size and territorial concentration. A more satisfactory version would look also at the various interests that both figure in, and limit, the case for minority cultural rights. Groups vary in the extent to which their members desire recognition of their cultural differences and in the significance that their members attach to being granted or denied recognition. They also vary in the degree to which their members would enjoy an adequate range of options in their own cultural community, and in the degree to which schemes of recognition would impede their access to options in the wider society.

A "general criteria" approach to allocating cultural rights that paid attention to all these factors might end up, as a contingent empirical matter, supporting differences in the treatment of immigrants and national minorities. Kymlicka suggests, for instance, that the two kinds of groups are characterized by very different aims: "national minorities have resisted integration and fought to maintain or rebuild their own societal culture, while immigrants have accepted the expectation that they will integrate into the dominant so-

---

[10] Carens 2000; Rubio-Marín 2003b.

cietal culture."[11] In addition, national minorities that are large, territorially concentrated, and institutionally well articulated (e.g., the Québécois and the Catalans) can offer their members an adequate range of options and opportunities, whereas most immigrant groups are too small, dispersed, and/or lacking in institutional articulation to be more than a supplemental source of options for their members.

An approach that emphasizes general criteria has the virtue of being continuous with the account laid out in previous chapters. We should not be too satisfied with this solution, however, as it is bound to have some counterintuitive implications. The universe of cultural groups is extremely varied, and there is no reason to expect that all cases will sort neatly into immigrants with weak claims and national minorities with strong ones. There are large, well-established immigrant groups and tiny, quite marginal national minorities, as well as national minorities that have not sought extensive powers of self-government or institutional separateness and immigrant groups for whom a denial of recognition or accommodation gives rise to a significant sense of grievance. Moreover, a satisfactory account of who is eligible to claim which rights should not be tethered too tightly to what various groups or individuals actually want or to the opportunities that are actually available to them. Even if Chinese immigrants in British Columbia, say, do not actually want an extensive range of cultural or linguistic rights, a good account should indicate what to say if they did want such rights. Likewise, even if Spanish-language institutions in the United States do not currently offer an adequate range of options to those who depend on them, a satisfactory account should allow us to assess the claims of people who want those institutions to be developed and promoted further until they do offer a range of options that is adequate.

In the end, the general criteria approach may turn out to be the best we can do in allocating minority rights that cannot be extended to all minorities. But given the weaknesses of such an approach, it is worth at least considering whether some version of Kymlicka's voluntary acceptance theory might be salvaged. The theory holds open the promise of a less contingent, more categorical, distinction between the claims of national and immigrant groups. If such a theory can be validated, then the claims of national minorities might reasonably be given priority even in situations where general criteria, such as those described above, suggest that their claims are relatively weak.

Kymlicka's brief defense of the voluntary acceptance theory barely notices the three conditions mentioned earlier and thus has very little to say to someone who doubts they are satisfied. What is worse, as we shall see, some aspects of his formulation of the theory reinforce the suspicion that several of those

---

[11] Kymlicka 2001a, 156. The idea that immigrants and national minorities have different aims is also stressed in Kymlicka 1995, e.g., 10–11, 15, 97–98.

conditions—the voluntariness and alienability conditions—are likely to be violated. Despite these problems with Kymlicka's account, my aim in this chapter is to offer a defense of the immigrant/national minority dichotomy that draws in a qualified but not negligible way on the voluntary acceptance theory.

The appeal I shall make to that theory is qualified in two different respects. First, I argue that a state is justified in drawing a distinction between immigrants and national minorities even in situations where the voluntary decision to relinquish rights could not have been made. To this extent, voluntary acceptance drops out of the picture altogether, and the basis of the distinction is found elsewhere. Still, I suggest that a voluntary decision to waive the rights in question is a necessary condition where such a decision is possible.

The second respect in which my appeal to voluntary acceptance is qualified is connected with one of the main theoretical claims of the chapter. I argue that the first condition mentioned above (voluntariness) depends in part on factors that are central to the second and third (alienability and recipient's permission). The appropriate criteria for determining whether a person is in position to voluntarily relinquish something make reference to the nature of the thing that is being relinquished and to the benefit that is being provided in return. All else being equal, if it is highly plausible to think that a burden is worth bearing, given the benefits to the individual that accompany it, then we may want to understand the voluntariness condition in a more relaxed manner. Likewise, again all else being equal, if it is highly plausible to think that a recipient of whatever is being relinquished is being reasonable in making that thing a condition of providing some benefit, then we may opt for a more relaxed interpretation of voluntariness. On the other hand, the closer the burdens are to the inalienability end of the spectrum, and/or the closer that imposing them gets to being impermissible, the more we would want to insist on a rigorous interpretation of the conditions of voluntariness. The upshot of this proposal is that much of the weight of the argument for the dichotomy ends up being carried by claims about the modest character of the burden and the reasonableness of the recipient making it a condition of admission. In this respect, the argument follows a pattern seen in some other contexts where the voluntariness of surrendering particular rights is invoked, such as consent theories of political obligation. Consent theory becomes more plausible the less the act of consent is emphasized and the more that the reasonableness of what is being consented to is brought to the fore.[12]

I argue, then, with the above qualifications, that each of the three conditions is or could be satisfied. In response to the first objection, I maintain that even hard choices made under duress can, under specific conditions, make a moral difference to what can be done to, or expected of, a person who makes them. For reasons that I develop, I think it is plausible to think that the spe-

---

[12] See Harrison 2002, 124–31, 190–212.

cific conditions hold in a broad range of immigration cases. Against the second objection, I remind readers of a distinction made earlier in the book between several different ways in which culture is of value to people, and I argue that the value we should focus on does not give rise to concerns about inalienability. And finally, in reply to the third objection, I argue that it is permissible for a liberal democratic state to make the waiving of certain cultural rights a condition of admission to immigrant status. The argument here rests in part on the idea that it is permissible for members of the host society to show some partiality toward their own attachments and projects. In general I intend this reappraisal of the voluntary acceptance theory, not as an interpretation of Kymlicka original intentions, but as a proposal that stands on its own feet and, indeed, as one that gains some of its plausibility from being disentangled from other elements of Kymlicka's theory.

8.2 How Voluntary Is the Decision to Emigrate?

Many critics of the theory under consideration have argued that immigrants do not always satisfy the conditions necessary for a choice to count as voluntary.[13] Certainly, we cannot regard the children of immigrants as having waived their rights: they may not even have been born yet at the moment of immigration. Moreover, "for consent to be morally relevant, it needs to be free and informed."[14] The critics argue that there are reasons to think that neither the freedom condition nor the informational one is satisfied for many immigrants.

For the freedom and information conditions to be satisfied, there must be at least two viable options and the person making the choice must be aware of the options and must have some capacity to make an informed judgment about their relative merits. Very often, the political, economic, and social circumstances faced by people in developing and/or war-torn countries are such as to make emigration the only acceptable option and thus to introduce an element of necessity into the "choice" to leave. This is certainly the case for refugees, whose entitlement to a full set of cultural rights also needs to be considered. There are also reasons for questioning whether the decision to emigrate is generally an informed one. Immigrants may not realize the scale of the cultural adaptation that the receiving society is expecting of them, and they may find it difficult to anticipate the cultural isolation they will experience. "In today's world," one critic concludes, "prosperous countries cannot discharge their obligations to accommodate the cultural demands of those immigrants

---

[13] See, for example, Weinstock 1999, 29; Carens 2000, 81; Choudhry 2002, 61–65.
[14] Rubio-Marín 2003b, 139.

276 | CHAPTER 8

they benefit from economically by simply assuming the consensual nature of immigration."[15]

In evaluating this cluster of objections to the theory, we should concede right away that children and the unborn cannot be said to waive any cultural rights that a member of a national minority would enjoy. When I talk about "immigrants" in this chapter, I have in mind first-generation immigrants— that is, people who are adults at the moment of immigration. In general, it seems to me, the descendants of immigrants should not themselves be thought of as immigrants, and their claims to cultural rights should be analyzed in a different way. It is consistent with this narrow conception of the immigrant, however, to think that educational (and perhaps other) options of children of immigrants might be limited in certain ways while they are still children. If the voluntary acceptance theory can be vindicated in the end, we might envisage that one kind of cultural right that immigrants would waive is the right to have their children educated in an immigrant-language-medium setting. To the extent that children are constrained (by virtue of the rights their parents have waived away) to be educated in one of the national languages, as adults they will typically develop a preference to continue using the national language for official purposes, and they are also likely to develop an identification with institutions of national self-government. To be sure, not all cases will follow this familiar pattern, and the account will eventually have to say something about descendants of immigrants who form an enduring attachment to the culture of their parents and grandparents. But we should begin, at least, by focusing on the more straightforward case of first-generation immigrants.

For the critics, even this more straightforward case is problematic. In their view, there is still reason to doubt that many immigrants are in a position to waive away their rights voluntarily. It is true that many immigrants are not fleeing from dire circumstances of the sort that would give rise to worries about voluntariness. Some immigrants move from one wealthy society to another: think of Britons going to Belgium, or Canadians to the United States. And even immigrants who do move from less prosperous countries often come from the better off and more educated strata of their home societies. They have reasonable alternatives and some insight into the choice they are making, and to this extent it seems fairly unproblematic to characterize their decision to emigrate as voluntary.

There is little doubt, however, that a significant proportion of the world's migrants are escaping from poverty, authoritarianism, and/or extreme social hierarchy in their country of origin. They lack acceptable options if they stay where they are, and they also lack education and accurate information about the wider world. Can we maintain that immigrants in this category are capable of waiving their rights, or should it be conceded that the voluntariness condi-

[15] Ibid., 143.

tion is not satisfied? Kymlicka's own statements about these cases reinforce the suspicion that they will be problematic for his argument: he treats refugees as a pure case of involuntary migration and admits that the line between refugees and poverty-driven emigrants is often hard to draw.[16] Kymlicka's argument here is admirably candid, but it threatens to blow apart his principal justification of the immigrant/national minority dichotomy.

To gain a better perspective on this problem, we need to begin by considering the concept of voluntariness that is at issue. The argument we are considering says that immigrants can voluntarily waive particular rights even when they are exiting from inhospitable circumstances. The critics, on the other hand, say that no rights can be waived under such circumstances, and thus that it would be wrong to deprioritize the claims of the immigrants on the grounds that they had somehow voluntarily relinquished the rights in question. If we think about what exactly is at stake in this disagreement, the salient point of contention seems to concern whether a choice made under a given set of difficult circumstances is sufficient to change the moral rights and permissions of actors at a later time. With this disagreement in mind, I shall understand a choice to be voluntary when it makes a difference to the moral situation of the person whose choice it is. A voluntary choice changes the legitimate rights and claims of the person who makes it and/or the legitimate permissions and claims of agents with whom that person is transacting. An involuntary decision, by contrast, is one that exerts little or no power over the subsequent moral situation. The conditions under which the decision is made are such that few or no new rights, permissions, or legitimate claims are generated.

In conceptualizing voluntariness in this way, I depart from the familiar idea that judgments about voluntariness are mainly concerned with the will. For instance, it is sometimes suggested that a choice is voluntary when it expresses an agent's genuine will, and involuntary when this connection is broken. As we shall see, the notion of voluntariness that I opt for is broader and more holistic than this traditional one in that a range of different factors might influence whether a particular choice makes a difference to the moral situation, including factors that have little to do with the connection between will and decision. The more holistic conception is justified here by the context. The disagreement that interests us is about the moral impact of choice under difficult conditions, and it seems sensible to adapt a conception of voluntariness that is tailored to this concern.[17]

---

[16] Kymlicka 1995, 99.

[17] It might be objected that I am conflating the question of what makes a decision "voluntary" with a question about the moral implications that follow from a choice being voluntary. This may be so, but nothing very much hinges, in what follows, on a correct analysis of the concept of voluntariness: it is the moral implications that really interest us. Readers who are bothered by my conception of voluntariness

For someone to count as having a choice at all, at least two alternatives have to be available to that person. A person who is forcibly removed from his home and taken to a refugee camp does not have a choice in even this most rudimentary sense. Our question, though, is how rich a person's choice set needs to be for his choice to be morally impactful or "voluntary." When a middle-class person from a prosperous liberal democracy makes the decision to emigrate, few would hesitate to call the decision voluntary. But many critics would suggest that voluntariness gives out in cases of poor people exiting from a nondemocratic regime. The fact that such a person still has some minimal, remaining choice makes little or no difference to her subsequent moral situation.

It is important to realize, however, that people facing dire circumstances *are* sometimes considered capable of voluntary choice in the sense that interests us. Consider the case of someone who is gravely ill. Suppose that there is good reason for that person to believe she will die unless she undergoes surgery. It is hard to think of more dire circumstances that a person could face. And yet we still think that she could give her consent to undergo the surgery—at least so long as her medical condition has not deprived her of her mental faculties. Indeed, we would normally regard it as wrong for the surgeon to operate on her unless she gives her consent. Crucially for our interest in immigration, we think that, despite her lack of acceptable alternatives, and even if she is poor and uneducated and has only a rudimentary understanding of what the operation would mean for her future quality of life, she still retains the moral power to make permissible an action (cutting her open with a surgeon's knife) that would otherwise be morally impermissible.

To be sure, we need to be careful about what we infer from this example. While the example suggests that there are at least some situations in which people in dire circumstances are able to give their consent, we should not leap to the conclusion that this is true in general. Consider three situations in which such a conclusion would seem unwarranted. One is a variation on the surgery case, in which this time the surgeon demands an exorbitant fee in exchange for his services. When the surgeon's bill comes, there is a real question about whether the patient has an obligation to pay the full amount. A second is the case of the predatory lender. We might doubt whether people who are desperate for money and ill prepared to understand the terms of a complicated financial arrangement have an obligation to abide by the abusive or unfair financial terms that such a lender imposes. Finally, a third case is the classic one of the highway robber. When the robber threatens to kill a person unless he agrees to a monetary payment, almost everyone would reject the suggestion that there is any subsequent obligation to perform in the event of

---

might substitute a different term (e.g., "morally impactful"). There is precedence in the philosophical literature for the conception of voluntariness I am adopting. See Scanlon 2003, chap. 13.

an agreement to pay. Even though the person's range of options (risk of death, loss of money) may be perfectly identical to the options in the surgery case, any agreement to pay is not voluntary.[18]

What then distinguishes the surgery case from the exorbitant fee, predatory lender, and highway robber cases? Clearly, a number of differences might be noted. In the highway robber example, the robber makes it the case that the victim's no-agreement option is a bad one, whereas in the surgery case the badness of the no-agreement option is part of the background circumstances. But this difference does not explain the divergence between the surgery case and the exorbitant fee and predatory lender cases. Another difference is that, in the surgery case, the patient is agreeing to a burden (the risks involved in surgery) that is integral to the benefit (life-saving surgery), whereas the other three cases involve a financial burden that is ancillary to the benefit to be provided.[19] But I do not think that our intuitions about the surgery case would be dramatically different if the surgeon charged a reasonable fee (or if there was a modest insurance copay) for services offered. Surgeons would have a reasonable complaint about a system that expected them to work for free. A further feature of the surgery case is the urgency of making a decision. But this does not illuminate why a standard fee might be acceptable but not an exorbitant fee. And we might elaborate the predatory lending case to introduce urgency, by stipulating for instance that the borrower needs the loan to pay for life-saving surgery.

It is important that we identify some illuminating difference between the cases if we are to be in a position to understand the immigration case. We need some way of deciding whether the immigrant who waives her cultural rights is more like the patient agreeing to life-saving surgery (and a reasonable fee) or the victims described in the other cases. My suggestion is that the key difference between the various cases lies in how reasonable the terms of agreement are. In the surgery case, the terms seem highly reasonable. There is a strong presumption (we might assume) that the surgery is good for the patient. Indeed, if the patient was unconscious and had left no instructions or proxy, it might be reasonable to go ahead without consent. In addition, the standard fee reflects reasonable demands by the surgeon; anything less, we might suppose, and the surgeon would have a reasonable complaint. By contrast, in each of the other cases the terms of agreement are not reasonable. In the exorbitant fee case, even though surgery is presumptively valuable for the patient, the surgeon's demands are excessive. In the predatory lender case, the benefit may or may not be presumptively valuable (it depends on the

[18] Hume famously compares the surgeon and robber cases in *A Treatise of Human Nature* (2000, sec. III.II.v.). For discussion of the case, see Scanlon 2003, 266–67. Scanlon argues that a will-centric conception of voluntariness has trouble distinguishing these cases and suggests that an understanding of voluntariness in terms of normative implications does better.

[19] Olsaretti 2013.

purpose of the loan), but the demands of the lender are not reasonable (even considering the risks and costs the lender may bear). Finally, in the highway robber case, the benefit is clearly valuable to the victim (having his life spared), but the demand by the robber is morally impermissible and hence obviously unreasonable.[20]

If these judgments are correct, then a more general claim about the possibility of voluntarily relinquishing particular rights and claims suggests itself. Waiving one's rights and claims is possible under dire circumstances in situations where there is a strong presumption that the terms being accepted are reasonable. All else being equal, these terms are more reasonable for an individual facing a hard choice (a) the greater the presumed value of the benefit to that individual, and (b) the more that those terms are framed by the legitimate claims and interests of the party who is imposing them. The surgery case is one in which there is a strong presumption of value to the individual, as in (a), and no cause for doubting the reasonableness of the terms under (b). It is thus plausible to think that the individual's choice to undergo the surgery makes a difference, generating both a permission to proceed on the part of the surgeon and an obligation to pay the standard fee afterward on the part of the patient. In this sense, the conditions of voluntariness are met. By contrast, in the other cases we have looked at, the terms of acceptance are framed by excessive and/or impermissible demands of the recipient. Given the nature of those claims, a person's options and information would have to be considerably better for the person's choice to have the same power to generate permissions and obligations.

In the surgery case, the main work in explaining the possibility of consent is done by the presumption of value to the patient. In other situations, however, the main work will be done by the strength of the recipient's legitimate claims and interests. Imagine that a region's commuter trains have been struck by a series of explosions caused by bombs hidden in passenger bags. Given a paramount concern with passenger safety, it would be reasonable for officials to institute a policy of searching the bags of all passengers. Since such searches are ordinarily considered an objectionable invasion of privacy, it would be appropriate for officials to warn passengers about what will be done, for example, with notices printed on the tickets and announcements made in the station. This way people can be careful about what they pack, and someone who strongly objects to being searched can avoid taking the train. Many passengers will feel they have few alternatives but to continue taking the train under these new circumstances. It may be their only reliable way of getting to work, or of traveling around the area for other important purposes. Despite this limited range of alternatives, it seems plausible to say that, having been duly warned, the choice by passengers to take the train under the circumstances makes a

[20] Scanlon 2003, 267.

difference to the permissibility of the search policy. The reason for this, I am suggesting, lies in the strength of the legitimate interest that officials have in preventing further attacks (consideration (b) above) combined with the sense that the burden on passengers, while hardly trivial, is for most people not intolerable ((a) above).

Returning to the problem of immigration with which we started, we now have a framework in which we can analyze the situation of immigrants departing from dire circumstances such as poverty, authoritarianism, and severe social hierarchy. Does such a situation leave immigrants incapable of a voluntary choice to waive certain cultural rights, or could the fact that they make (or have) a choice make a difference to the rights they would enjoy in the state to which they move? The framework sketched above lays out an agenda for considering this problem. It suggests that we should explore two questions: First, how much of a burden does forgoing the specific rights in question place on the immigrants who waive them? This parallels the issue in the commuter trains case of whether, under the circumstances, the bag searches should be considered a tolerable or intolerable invasion of privacy. Second, how strong are the legitimate claims and interests of the receiving society when it insists that immigrants waive the cultural rights in question? Is this an excessive or impermissible demand, or something that is clearly reasonable for members of the receiving society to expect?

These two questions are closely related to the questions about alienability and recipient's permission I mentioned at the outset. The considerations that inform answers to the second pair of questions are clearly highly relevant to answering the first pair. With this in mind, we shall move on now to considering the issues of alienability and recipient's permission. I will argue in the next section that, for a certain class of cultural rights, forgoing those rights does not place an unacceptable burden on immigrants. I then argue in section 8.4 that members of the receiving society do have a legitimate interest in requiring that immigrants waive certain cultural rights as a condition of entry into the state on a permanent basis. These arguments address the two remaining conditions required for the voluntary acceptance argument. They also take us a long way toward completing our defense of the voluntariness condition. They help us to see why (and under what conditions) immigrants are offered reasonable terms of agreement even when the state offers a fuller set of cultural-linguistic rights to national groups than to immigrants.

8.3 Are Cultural Rights Alienable?

In developing his account of the immigrant/national minority dichotomy, Kymlicka offers the example of an American who emigrates to Sweden, suggesting that he is an unproblematic case of someone who can be taken to have voluntarily waived his cultural and linguistic rights.[21] While the example seems to be aimed at reassuring readers that the voluntariness condition is (or might be) satisfied, it leads to a distinct concern about the argument. For it suggests the question: what if Sweden had made admission to immigrant status conditional on something else? For instance, what if it had demanded that the American surrender his rights to practice core aspects of his religion as a condition of admission to immigrant status? Someone might think that the right to practice the core of one's religion is too precious for anyone to give up, however voluntarily. Religious rights, in this view, should be treated as inalienable: they cannot be given up, in the sense that no agreement in which someone sought to give them up should be enforced afterward. Whatever the American may have thought he was giving up as a price of admission into Sweden, the Swedish authorities would be wrong to deny him his religious rights once his immigrant status had been secured.

If religious rights are inalienable, however, then perhaps, as Joe Carens points out, cultural and linguistic rights are too?[22] Perhaps cultural and linguistic rights are so precious to an individual that she could never be deemed to have waived them? Even if she seemed to waive them in the context of an otherwise voluntary agreement, the authorities should go on treating her as if she had not waived them.

There are components of Kymlicka's view that actually reinforce the suspicion that cultural and linguistic rights might be inalienable in this way. As we saw in chapter 3, Kymlicka's general case for cultural rights rests on the claim that access to a secure societal culture is a necessary precondition of individual autonomy. Since the liberal state has the right and the duty to protect the conditions of individual autonomy, it should take measures to secure the societal cultures to which its citizens are attached. Depending on the context, these measures may involve a range of different cultural rights, including language rights, self-government rights, and rights to special representation.

In some passages, Kymlicka highlights the general importance of culture as a background precondition for individual autonomy by describing it as a kind of Rawlsian "primary good."[23] He also argues, on a variety of grounds, that people have interests in being able to access not just any secure societal culture, but, in particular, their *own* societal culture—that is, the one in which they were born and raised. Encouraged by some of Kymlicka's statements, readers have tended to put these two different claims together to reach the conclusion that access to one's own societal culture is, for Kymlicka, a primary good.[24]

[21] Kymlicka 1995, 96, 99.

[22] Carens 2000, 81.

[23] Kymlicka 1989b, chap. 7; 1995, 84n11.

[24] Kymlicka (1989b, 177) writes: "So it seems that we should interpret the primary good of cultural membership as referring to the individuals' own cultural community." I am grateful to Stéphane Courtois for drawing my attention to this passage.

But, if access to one's own societal culture is such an important and fundamental good, then it is puzzling how immigrants could ever be thought to have waived their rights to re-create their own societal culture in the receiving society.[25] It looks, in Kymlicka's theory, as if they would be renouncing an essential precondition of their own freedom. And we might legitimately question whether freedom is something that anybody could ever be taken to have alienated.

The solution to this problem, however, is not to jettison the voluntary acceptance theory. A better response is to be more careful in describing the way in which access to their own culture is a good for immigrants. We should disentangle the claim that "access to *a* societal culture is a primary good" from the claim that "people *have interests* in accessing their *own* societal culture." It is quite possible to accept both these claims without conflating them into the single proposition that "access to one's own societal culture is a primary good."

The account of why culture matters developed in chapter 3 pointed to a distinction that can help us to avoid this conflation. We saw that there are two distinct reasons why minority-culture members might lack access to an adequate range of options if they are cut off from their culture. It may be that they lack *access* to a generically adequate range of options because they face discrimination in majority culture contexts or because they lack some of the generic skills (language competence, familiarity with cultural norms, etc.) needed to participate effectively in the majority culture. Or it may be that they lack access to an *adequate* range of options because the options they can access in the dominant culture do not include options they particularly care about. The first of these possibilities—the problem of access—does raise a significant problem of autonomy. If waiving cultural rights implies giving up on autonomy in this sense, then there is a genuine question about whether such rights should be regarded as alienable. Certainly, the standard for what counts as voluntarily waiving such rights would need to be set at a high level. We should be troubled by the prospect of people making decisions under duress that resulted in their signing away their own future autonomy.

The second possibility—the problem of adequacy—by contrast is less obviously a matter of autonomy. One can define "autonomy" however one likes, of course, but if the term is stretched to require the presence of the options a person especially cares about, then it no longer stands for a right or a good that is plausibly viewed as inalienable. People may and do give up particular things they care about all the time when they receive or expect to receive some compensating good in return.

In considering whether the alienability condition is satisfied, then, we need to distinguish between these two forms of disadvantage that immigrants might face by virtue of giving up on the possibility of reestablishing their original

---

[25] Weinstock 1999, 30; Bauböck 2001; Choudhry 2002, 61–63.

language or culture in the receiving society. If waiving their cultural or linguistic rights implies that they will face the problem of access, then the concern about inalienability would loom large. I argued in section 3.3, however, that cultural rights are often not necessary to prevent this problem. An alternative is for the receiving society to be aggressive in combating discrimination, and in offering ample, affordable opportunities to immigrants to learn the dominant language and to learn about the dominant culture. When the receiving society successfully follows this "liberal nationalist" approach to immigrant integration, then the objection from inalienability fizzles out. It is true that liberal nationalist integration policies take time to work and that, in the meantime, new immigrants are vulnerable to serious disadvantages. For this reason, we might want to consider "accommodation" rights (as defined in section 6.2) as inalienable in the relevant sense, but again, if the integration policies are reasonably successful over time, immigrants do not need the opportunity to re-create their original culture in the receiving society.

The cultural and linguistic rights that I have mostly focused on in chapters 5 through 7 are not geared to the problem of access. Instead, I have developed an argument for a particular set of minority rights as grounded in the liberal state's pro tanto obligation to be neutral between the various attachments and commitments of its citizens. The concern here is very much with the problem of adequacy. It is, in part, because people care so much about which particular options are available to them that the state has reason to be neutral. Since the concern at issue with these rights is adequacy, not access, it seems plausible to regard them as alienable.

One's own societal culture is a potential source of comfort, familiarity, identity, pride, and a way of talking about, and being in, the world that is to some extent unique. As we have seen, it may also be a reliable generator of the options one cares about. These all point to reasons for thinking that people have interests in being able to access their own societal culture—interests that figure in the state's pro tanto obligation of neutrality. But they are not reasons for thinking that a person's very freedom would be fatally compromised if she were cut off from her own societal culture. It is possible for immigrants (and others) to find the range of meanings and options they need to be free in a new societal culture if they can manage to learn that culture's language and master the rudiments of its way of life, and if the receiving society is willing to accept them with toleration and openness.

So long then as we restrict the immigrant/national minority dichotomy to cultural and linguistic rights grounded in neutrality, the account of waiving such rights can satisfy the alienability condition. Immigrants should be given the same opportunity to access options as national minorities and should enjoy the same set of toleration and accommodation rights as national minorities. But there is no valid inalienability objection to their waiving other cultural or linguistic rights that serve a different, less essential objective.

8.4 Is the Receiving Society Acting Permissibly?

We have been considering two major hurdles to the vindication of the voluntary acceptance argument, but one still remains. To appreciate this final challenge, consider once again the example of a state that makes the surrender of religious rights a condition of admission to immigrant status. Let us assume that the immigrants facing this decision have appealing alternatives and are well informed about the decision they face. Let us also set to one side the worry that they are being asked to give up a right that is inalienable. The receiving society's conditions might still seem objectionable. Just as it was wrong in our earlier example for the surgeon to set an exorbitant fee in response to his patient's misfortunes, someone might think it wrong for a liberal state ever to ask someone to give up their religious rights as a condition of admission to immigrant status. And if it would be wrong in this case, then why, we might wonder, would it not be similarly wrong for a state to demand that immigrants waive cultural or linguistic rights?[26]

One easy way of disposing of this concern would be to deny the antecedent claim that it would be wrong for the state to insist that immigrants waive their religious rights. An argument along these lines might be adapted from Henry Sidgwick. Sidgwick assumed that, as a matter of its sovereignty, the state has a morally legitimate right not to admit any immigrants. Since any decision it does make to admit someone goes beyond what it is morally required to do, it would be permissible for it to attach whatever conditions it likes to offers of admission. As Sidgwick put it, since the state "may legitimately exclude them [immigrants] altogether, it must have a right to treat them in any way it thinks fit, after due warning given and due time allowed for withdrawal."[27] Imagine some particular state whose citizens are concerned to preserve the current religious character of their society. Since many prospective immigrants would bring with them new religious practices, there is little support for admitting any immigrants. However, there would be support for immigration if prospective immigrants agreed to waive their religious rights. And suppose that there are some prospective immigrants who would agree to this deal. Why, the argument goes, should this arrangement be considered objectionable? If a liberal democracy was within its rights to close its borders, then why would it not also have the right to open its border but in this conditional way? Is this not simply a case of *adding* an option to a baseline that, by assumption, is legitimate?[28] Note that this argument, if correct, helps to differentiate the immigration case from the case of the surgeon who charges an exorbitant fee. A surgeon presumably has an obligation to help needy patients (in return for standard compen-

---

[26] Carens 2000, 81.

[27] Sidgwick, quoted in Miller 2008, 374.

[28] I am grateful to Ryan Davis for this way of formulating the argument being sketched.

sation) and thus cannot defend the objectionable terms she offers by claiming that she is simply adding an option beyond what she is morally required to do.

Now, if this argument turns out to be correct, then we will have gotten over our third hurdle rather easily, and we can safely conclude that it would be permissible for a liberal state to make the waiving of cultural and linguistic rights a condition of admission to immigrant status. In what follows, however, I shall not take this easy path. One reason is that it seems to me problematic to assume that a liberal state could permissibly close its borders to all immigration. There might be special circumstances in some states that allow them to do this, but it would be unfortunate for the account being developed here to have to rely on the assumption that states have a general right to close their borders. If states do, in general, have duties to admit a certain number of immigrants, then they can no longer present conditional offers of admission as adding an option beyond what they are morally required to do.

A second reason to avoid the argument sketched above is that liberal citizens may not want to attach conditions to the admission of newcomers that they would not impose on themselves. In this view, to be committed to liberal principles is to be committed to an ideal of equal citizenship that applies to all permanent residents who have lived in the state for a minimal period of time.[29] The conditional offer of admission gives up on this ideal since it implies that some fellow members of society will enjoy fewer rights and freedoms than others on a permanent basis. The idea that immigrants could waive their religious rights seems highly objectionable because it entails the creation of two classes of long-term residents: those who enjoy a full freedom of religion and those who do not. To avoid a situation of this kind, I shall make things difficult for myself by assuming that citizens of the receiving state do not want to attach any conditions to admission that conflict with the principles they apply to themselves.

So let us assume that citizens of a liberal state would indeed regard as impermissible the policy of accepting immigrants on the condition that they surrender their religious rights. Now the question, however, is why the same reasoning does not apply to cultural or linguistic rights. Earlier I suggested that cultural minorities can appeal to the liberal principle of neutrality in support of the demand for such rights. But if this is correct, then it would seem to follow that it would be impermissible for a liberal democracy committed to sticking to its own principles to make admission to immigrant status conditional on giving up the entitlement to claim those rights. The same reason for thinking that limiting immigrant religious rights would be impermissible is also a reason for thinking that limiting immigrant cultural rights would be too.

This argument is flawed, however, because it overlooks a critical disanalogy between cultural rights and religious rights. The judgment that liberal prin-

[29] See Miller 2008, p. 375.

ciples protect freedom of religion is an all-things-considered judgment about the implications of liberal principles. In general, liberals think that religion is potentially so important to people that they ought to enjoy core religious liberties even at considerable cost to others. By contrast, as I mentioned in the previous section (and explained more fully in chapters 5 and 6), the claim that the liberal principle of neutrality supports a fairly robust set of cultural and linguistic rights is not yet an all-things-considered judgment. The pro tanto obligation of neutrality has to be weighed against other obligations of the liberal state. A liberal state must also defend the person and property of its citizens, provide education and health care, promote conditions of equal opportunity, protect the environment, and perform a host of other important functions. It is unlikely to be very effective at performing these tasks if it extends a full set of linguistic-cultural rights to too many languages and cultures. If the state were to try to offer all public services and conduct all public business in more than a small handful of languages, then it would quickly end up devoting a portion of its time and resources to achieving neutrality between speakers of different languages that was disproportionate to the importance this idea has in the principles of liberal democracy. Similarly, if the state were to extend significant powers of self-government to more than a small number of groups, it would face continuous jurisdictional wrangling, and massive negative externalities, that crippled its overall capacity for effective governance.

To be sure, there may be some contexts in which it is possible to extend language rights to a large number of languages. There is nothing unfeasible or absurd about the proposal that government create bilingual neighborhoods (with appropriate street signs, community programs, etc.) in areas with high concentrations of some particular language group, or about the proposal that they offer afterschool (or even in-school) classes in particular minority languages (where there is demand) to help parents to pass on their native language to their children. These forms of language recognition and protection help members of different groups to preserve their heritages and can under the right conditions be extended to an indefinite range of different languages. The neutrality argument sketched above suggests that a state should pursue these policies as a means of making the background conditions somewhat fairer for minority-language-speakers who want to maintain their language. It *would* be problematic for a liberal democracy committed to following its own principles to refuse to extend this restricted set of rights to all languages. Likewise, a rather large number of groups might be able to enjoy limited powers of self-government in a state covering a large territory without any grave damage to the state's governance capacity. There are, for instance, a fairly large number of experiments with indigenous self-government in Canada at the moment, which do not seem to cripple the capacities of federal and provincial governments for effective governance. But, taken as a whole, liberal principles do not require the state to extend a full set of cultural or linguistic rights to every language or culture in all contexts. To extend full status to more than a small handful of groups would undermine the liberal state's ability to pursue its legitimate objectives. The state's duty to be neutral between the different goals and attachments of its citizens has to be balanced against its other important duties.

Drawing attention to this disanalogy between religious and cultural-linguistic rights helps to clarify why it might be both permissible and reasonable for a liberal democratic state to extend a full set of cultural rights to some groups and a restricted set to others. But it still does not fully solve our problem. For we want to know, not merely whether it would be reasonable to extend a full set of rights to some groups but not others, but whether it would be reasonable for liberal citizens to make the national/immigrant distinction the basis for inclusion/exclusion. An alternative, as we have seen, might be to make one or more general criteria the basis for deciding between inclusion/exclusion, that is, one or more criteria that attach no weight to the fact that a group is immigrant or national but instead track considerations that could, in principle, be associated with either sort of group. A state might, for instance, extend a full set of language or self-government rights to the largest cultural groups and a more restricted set to the smaller ones. In the Belgian case with which we started, this might imply extending the full set to Arabic-speakers but only the restricted set to German-speakers. The question we need to answer is whether it would be permissible for citizens of a liberal state to single out immigrant groups as such for restricted status rather than following a general principle like this, which takes no account of the immigrant or national character of the group.

In considering this question, I shall offer two distinct arguments for thinking that it would be reasonable to give national groups some extra priority over immigrant groups in allocating scarce cultural rights. One is situational in character; the other is perspectival. The situational argument points to relevant differences that typically mark the situations of immigrants and national minorities. The perspectival argument draws attention to an asymmetry in decision-making authority between potential immigrants and national groups: it is from the perspective of the latter, not the former, that decisions about cultural and linguistic rights are made. Although neither argument quite suggests that the immigrant/national minority distinction is significant as such, both point to an asymmetry between established groups and newcomers that approximates such a distinction.

The situational argument appeals to the familiar idea that there is a presumption in favor of established practices and institutions insofar as they are functioning well. If general criteria such as size and territorial concentration were to be followed strictly, then there might be considerable jockeying for scarce rights. If the birthrate in one group is much higher than in others, or if there is a wave of immigrants belonging to a particular group, then the eligibility of different groups over time might shift continuously. Some groups that were not eligible for a full set of rights would become eligible, and other groups, which had enjoyed such rights, would lose their eligibility. The problem inherent in this possibility is that dismantling an established practice or institution designed to recognize a group's cultural claims in order to replace it with a new practice or institution designed to recognize a different group's claims will involve various costs and risks. The costs flow from the need to hire and train a new set of people, the need to create or adapt facilities and materials, and the need to communicate with the public about the new arrangement. The risks arise from uncertainty about whether the new practices and institutions will operate effectively and gain a critical mass of participants. Once a maximally accommodating scheme of public institutions is up and running in an effective manner, there is at least some presumption in favor of continuing on with it, even if some different scheme, which recognizes a somewhat different mix of cultures, would do even better by the general criteria.

Even more significantly, dropping an established public practice or institution is likely to be disruptive to the plans and expectations of people who had made plans based around it. The state's earlier decision to recognize some culture or language by establishing an appropriate practice or institution was a signal to people that the state was throwing its support behind the culture or language in question, and that they could go ahead and make decisions and investments (e.g., in language learning) with that in mind. If the state were to withdraw its support as soon as a new group came along with a stronger claim to recognition and accommodation, this would leave the people who are losing support in the lurch. Once it became common knowledge that the state would withdraw support in this way, its interventions on behalf of minority languages and cultures would become gradually less effective.[30]

So there is at least some reason why states should favor groups that already enjoy recognition and accommodation over groups that do not when allocating scarce cultural or linguistic rights. If a state has been conscientious in the past about extending recognition and accommodation to its national minorities, then this consideration will work to favor the claims of such groups over the claims of immigrants. But what if a state has a record of denying recognition and accommodation to its national minorities? Should it now follow general criteria and perhaps privilege the claims of immigrants? Here, I think, a different sort of consideration has to be factored in, which is that national

---

[30] It might be objected that the real concern at issue in this paragraph is with the *abrupt* unsettling of expectations. This would still allow the state to *gradually* phase out the accommodation of cultures that were losing priority based on general criteria and phase in the cultures that were gaining priority. Although there is something to this objection, I think it fails to appreciate the point made in the final sentence of the paragraph. The impact of accommodating minority cultures/languages will be dampened the more it becomes known that such policies will be phased in and out (even gradually) with demographic changes. I am grateful to Javier Hidalgo for raising this issue with me.

minorities may have a legitimate complaint about the past treatment of their group. Such a complaint would be relevant in two different ways: First, it might entail that the group is entitled to some kind of amends, which might take the form of prioritizing their claim on scarce cultural-linguistic rights. Second, the uncorrected injustice may mean that accommodation and recognition now matter to them in a heightened way. To prioritize the claims of immigrants over their claims would be to reinforce their sense of subordination by the state. For both reasons, there is again an asymmetry between the claims of a national group and those of immigrants. These differences, even when they are quite slight, make it reasonable to prioritize the claims of national groups over immigrants, and hence to make acceptance of this priority by immigrants a condition of their admission.

Turning now to the perspectival argument, we can begin by recalling that the point of the cultural rights in question is to provide citizens with assistance in realizing certain goals and projects that they care about, including the survival and flourishing of their language and culture. What is at stake in assigning either a full or a restricted set of rights is the level of public assistance that different people will receive with their pursuit of the objects and projects to which they are attached. For instance, when the state offers a particular language a full set of rights, it provides speakers of that language more opportunities to use the language they value, and more assistance at securing the survival and flourishing of the language, than when it offers a more restricted set.

So our question in effect is whether it would be permissible and reasonable for citizens attached to liberal democratic principles to adopt a policy that gives more help to members of national groups in securing what they care about than it does to speakers of immigrant groups. If one looks at this question as an outsider (e.g., a Canadian examining the Belgian debate), one will likely think that there is no more reason for supporting the national groups in getting what they care about than there is for helping immigrants. From the impersonal perspective of an outsider, the natural stance to adopt is one of impartiality, and this implies attaching equal importance to the projects and attachments of national minorities and immigrants alike. From this perspective, bracketing the situational argument sketched earlier, a blanket policy of favoring national over immigrant groups looks discriminatory in comparison with following a general principle (such as the size principle) that ignores the national/immigrant distinction.

In a democratic context, however, the authority to make cultural and immigration policies for Belgium does not rest in the hands of some benevolent Canadian outsider. Instead, it rests in the hands of Belgian citizens. They are deciding whether to privilege their own national culture and languages or whether to adopt impartial, general criteria for allocating rights. The question then becomes: how much importance should they attach to promoting the success of their *own* culture-related projects and attachments versus the success of the comparable projects and attachments of prospective immigrants? If they are constrained to look at the problem in the same way that a benevolent outsider would, then we should not expect the conclusion to look any different. They would have to be rigorously impartial in the importance they attach to their own projects and attachments and those of prospective immigrants. Again this would suggest that a blanket preference for their own national culture and languages would be impermissible (the situational argument aside) and that something like the size principle would be a better criterion for deciding which groups should enjoy a full set of rights.

It would be unreasonable, however, to constrain Belgian citizens to look at the problem in this way. The Belgians find themselves in a situation that is importantly different from that of an impartial outsider. For the Belgians, several of the languages whose claims are being considered are their own and are, for some of them at least, objects of attachment. We do not normally expect people to adopt the same perspective on their own attachments and projects that an impartial outsider would. We do not, that is to say, expect them to be rigorously impartial between their own attachments and commitments and those of others. The fact that some of the attachments and projects that are competing for support are their own introduces for them a special set of reasons that do not arise for an outsider looking on at the attachments and projects of other people. The existence of these attachment-based reasons to foster their own language make it permissible for Belgians to show some level of partiality to their own languages, and thus to prioritize the national languages over immigrant languages in determining which of them should enjoy full rather than restricted status.

The argument here rests on two general claims about how attachments make a difference to what it is permissible to do.[31] The first is that *my* attachments give *me* reasons for action that they do not give to other people and that other people's attachments do not give to me. If you claim to be attached to some object (e.g., your family, or a project like getting more young people to take up tennis) but then do not recognize any special reasons to advance, protect, or devote yourself to that object, we would wonder whether the attachment was genuine. Indeed one might say that to be attached to something just is for that thing to enter into one's reasoning in a special way, if not with absolute weight then at least with an urgency and degree of priority that differentiates it from things to which one is not attached. At the same time, the fact that you are attached to some object (your family, your favorite sport, etc.)

---

[31] Here I follow quite closely the analysis in Scheffler 2004. See also Nagel 1991; Scheffler 1994; 2001; Raz 2001.

does not normally give anyone else any reasons to support that object, beyond whatever general reasons they would have to do so in the absence of your attachment, or as an evenhanded response to your attachment.

The second key claim is that, insofar as we regard it as permissible and perhaps even essential for leading a worthwhile life that people form and enjoy certain sorts of attachments, we should allow that it is sometimes permissible for people to act on the special reasons that correspond with their attachments. And this implies that it is sometimes permissible for them to act in ways that, bracketing the fact that some of the attachments are *theirs*, would not be permissible were they to be strictly impartial between competing claims on their time and resources. The special reasons corresponding with an attachment generate a moral prerogative to do something that would otherwise conflict with a strictly impartial allocation of the benefit to be extended.

I should hasten to add that the claim is not that attachment-based reasons *always* override the demands of impartiality. An attachment (e.g., to child pornography) might be worthless in itself, in which case it does not generate any genuine special reasons at all and thus nothing that could excuse one from an expectation to behave impartially. Or there may be no reason to doubt the value of the attachment but the special reasons it gives rise to might, if acted on, necessitate a particularly egregious violation of impersonal moral considerations, such that, on balance, it remains impermissible to act against those impersonal considerations. Or a person may find herself in a special role that carries with it a responsibility to be rigorously impartial among some group of people—such as a state official who must be impartial toward all citizens. Still, there are bound to be other cases in which the value of the attachment is unimpeachable and the impersonal moral considerations that would, absent the attachment, make some action impermissible are not overwhelmingly strong. In these cases, it is permissible for people to act on their attachment-based reasons and against the demands of strict impartiality. If there were never any cases in which this were permissible, then individuals would face a significant threat to what Bernard Williams called their "integrity."[32] Since from a strictly impartial standpoint there will almost always be somebody else's projects and attachments that are in more need of assistance than one's own, individuals would be condemned to lead lives in which what they were permitted to do would hardly ever be related to advancing their own personal projects and attachments.

Admittedly, at this level of abstraction, it is hard to see whether a group's decision to prioritize its own national cultures and languages would count as a reasonable exercise of partiality or as one of the cases in which general moral

---

[32] Williams 1973.

considerations should stand firm against the attachment-based reasons. I do not think that it would be permissible for a state official to favor members of his own cultural group over other citizens, but this is not the claim we are considering. Nor for that matter would it be permissible for members of the majority acting in a democratic capacity to favor their own culture over the minority cultures of fellow citizens. In acting as public legislators, they have fairly strict obligations of impartiality to their fellow citizens that leave little room for reasonable partiality. What we are asking is whether the citizens of a state, as a body, can favor the cultures that are found among themselves over the cultures of would-be immigrants in allocating scarce cultural rights. I doubt that political theory can determine this kind of question with any great precision. Often the best that a theory can do is to point to a structure of argument, one that will be more or less persuasive in particular situations depending on the specific features of the situation.

That said, the case of a group deciding to prioritize its own national cultures and languages in awarding full rather than restricted status does strike me as a plausible candidate for a reasonable exercise of partiality. There is no general reason to doubt that one's own culture and language is a worthy object of attachment. There is nothing intrinsically immoral or degrading about such an end and, indeed, people sometimes care about the health and development of their culture and language for very good reasons. At the same time, the general moral considerations in this case do not seem overridingly strong. If what was at stake in the allocation of a full set of rights was an essential precondition of freedom (as would be the case in Kymlicka's theory of cultural rights), then a case might be made that the allocation should be based on the strictest impartial considerations (and hence something like the size principle). But in being asked to waive the minority cultural rights that we have been focusing on, nobody is being made to give up an essential precondition of freedom, nor the right to keep on using and promoting their language in a range of circumstances. They are just being asked to do without something that *somebody* will have to do without (given the cost-based objection to extending rights to all groups)—namely, the state's recognition of, and assistance with, their language or culture. So long as one attaches some genuine weight to attachment-based reasons, it seems plausible to me to regard this as the kind of case in which people might be excused from a requirement to allocate the benefit with strict impartiality.

If one or both of the main arguments of this section are correct, then there is nothing objectionable about a receiving society that makes the waiving of a full set of cultural or language rights a condition of admission to immigrant status. In insisting on this condition, the receiving society is not exacting an extortionate price but is defending legitimate interests in a reasonable manner.

8.5 The Limits of Voluntary Acceptance

We started out with three conditions that any successful attempt to revive the voluntary acceptance theory would have to satisfy: the voluntariness, alienability, and recipient's permission conditions. I have been arguing in the last two sections that the theory can satisfy the alienability and permission conditions. In addition, I argued in section 8.2 that the reasons for thinking that these two conditions are satisfied in a particular instance double as reasons for supposing that the voluntariness condition has been satisfied. In the view I am working with, whether voluntary choice is possible in a particular case is a matter of whether having a choice in that situation makes a difference to the moral situation—to who is permitted or obliged to do what. Voluntariness in this sense depends not just on the availability of options and information but also on the burden that is being accepted, and the legitimacy of the recipient making this burden a condition of whatever benefit is being given in return. Indeed, in some contexts the presumption that an option is valuable to the person, or that a recipient is reasonable in attaching a condition to the provision of that option, is so strong that we are prepared to consider a choice to take that option voluntary even when the alternatives are severely limited.

In focusing on the presumed interests of the different parties, I do not mean to deny that having or making a choice still matters to claims about voluntariness. If a person has no opportunity at all for choice, then there is no moment at which having or making a choice affects the moral situation. Our question has not been whether choice matters at all, but how rich the choice situation has to be for it to matter. My answer has been that it need not be especially rich in the sorts of immigration contexts that interest us.

For reasons alluded to in section 8.2, however, there may be contexts where it is necessary to evaluate the cultural and linguistic claims of immigrants and their descendants but in which there was no real opportunity for choice at all. This is true of children who arrive as immigrants, and it is also true of the descendants of immigrants who come to identify with the culture of their parents or grandparents. I have not said much about refugees in this chapter, a category that covers a range of different kinds of cases. But here too there are cases in which even the most minimal forms of choice are not possible.

I think that it is permissible for a state to give some priority to national groups over immigrants even in these cases where choice is ruled out. The account developed in the two preceding sections explains why this is so. By deprioritizing the claims of immigrants, a state is not denying them rights that are essential to freedom or a worthwhile life but is instead imposing on them a disadvantage that, in any case, will have to be imposed on some people given the impossibility of extending a full set of cultural and linguistic rights to all groups. And in prioritizing the claims of national minorities, a state is recognizing legitimate situational and perspectival differences between the different groups making claims. On balance, the various competing claims and interests suggest that at least some modest degree of priority may reasonably be given to the claims to recognition and accommodation of national minorities over the comparable claims of immigrants.

At this point it might be wondered whether the idea of voluntary acceptance should be dropped from our account of the immigrant/national group dichotomy altogether. If the dichotomy can be justified even in contexts where choice is impossible, then perhaps choice plays no essential role in contexts where it is possible? But this objection moves too fast. Consider again two of the leading examples offered in section 8.2: the surgery and commuter train cases. As I noted in passing, if consent were impossible in the surgery case (e.g., because the patient was unconscious and had left no instructions and designated no proxy) then, given the strong presumption that surgery is beneficial to the patient, it might well be legitimate to go ahead with the surgery without his consent. Something similar can be said in the commuter train case. Suppose that the authorities on board a train receive credible information that one of the passengers has a bomb in a bag and is planning to use it. The authorities would, I think, be justified in searching bags, even though there is now no chance of warning passengers that this will happen and thus no sense in which the right not to be searched has been waived.

The crucial point is that neither of these claims about what would be justified in the event that choice was impossible imply that choice is unnecessary in situations where it is possible. If the patient is in a position to give his consent, then his consent is necessary for the permissibility of the operation. And, if the authorities can warn potential passengers that their bags are liable to be searched, then offering such a warning is necessary for the legitimacy of the searches. In both cases, requiring choice where it is possible helps to make what happens to people as sensitive as possible to their needs and preferences. A patient may have specific preferences about longevity versus quality of life, or specific information about his own medical history, that would be factored into the decision to operate only if his consent is sought. Likewise, a person may have an especially strong objection to what others would regard as a minor invasion of privacy and so might respond to warnings about bag-searches by changing travel plans. More generally, the insistence on choice where it is possible respects the autonomy of the persons concerned, giving them more control over their own lives than would be the case if decisions were simply made on the basis of presumptions about values and interests.

Choice plays a similar role in thinking about the cultural and linguistic rights of immigrants. Where there is no possibility of voluntary acceptance, a state should look at the various interests and claims of groups seeking such rights, including the interests and claims that are highlighted by the situational and perspectival arguments sketched above. On balance, I have suggested, thinking about the problem in this way leads to the conclusion that a modest prioritizing of the claims of national minorities over those of immigrants is reasonable and permissible. But where it is possible for the state to inform potential immigrants about the scheme of cultural and linguistic rights they would face if they decide to immigrate, the legitimacy of favoring the claims of national minorities requires that the state do so. In this way, potential migrants who have a particularly strong attachment to their native culture, and whose options at home are not too unacceptable, might avoid an outcome that is very bad for them by choosing appropriately. And all immigrants are given some added degree of control over their own lives, and to this extent find that their autonomy is respected.

The strategy of this chapter has been to defend the differential treatment of national and immigrant languages by considering and responding to three familiar sets of objections to the theory that immigrants voluntarily accept such an arrangement. The three objections correspond to three different conditions that any such argument has to satisfy: the voluntariness condition, the alienability condition, and the recipient's permission condition. With a few qualifications along the way, I have argued that each of these conditions is satisfied in the case of immigrants waiving certain specific cultural and language rights.

By way of conclusion, let me summarize several of the main policy guidelines implied by the account developed in the chapter. One cluster of guidelines is negative in character and concerns the various kinds of rights that immigrants should *not* be deemed to have waived. These include toleration and accommodation rights, as well as any rights that are relevant to an immigrant's capacity to integrate into the (or a) societal culture of the receiving society. Given the conditions of choice they often face, immigrants should not be treated as if they had voluntarily assumed the weighty burden of forgoing such important rights. Indeed, given the relationship between societal culture and freedom, there is a legitimate question about whether a person could waive such rights even under ideal choice conditions.

In addition, immigrants should not be deemed to have waived cultural and linguistic rights that could easily be extended to an indefinite number of groups without compromising other legitimate functions and purposes of the liberal democratic state. Given the low-cost character of such rights, it is not reasonable for the receiving society to make their surrender a condition of admission to immigrant status.

More positively, the argument suggests that liberal democracies should take steps to make the decision to immigrate more voluntary where choice is a genuine possibility. Receiving states can legitimately impose greater burdens on immigrants the more that those immigrants have decent alternatives to migration. Prosperous liberal democracies thus have one more reason—in addition to the more direct justice-based reasons—to end their complicity in the challenges facing societies burdened by poverty, social conflict, and authoritarian institutions, and to assist those societies in establishing just institutions. More narrowly, receiving states should find ways to make their cultural and linguistic rights and practices as explicit as possible to potential immigrants. The legitimacy of those rights and practices will be enhanced the more that potential immigrants are empowered to choose.

REFERENCES

Abizadeh, Arash. 2002. "Does Liberal Democracy Presuppose a Cultural Nation? Four Arguments." *American Political Science Review* 96 (3): 495–509.

Anderson, Benedict. 1983. *Imagined Communities*. New York: Verso.

Anderson, Elizabeth. 2010. *The Imperative of Integration*. Princeton: Princeton University Press.

Appiah, K. Anthony. 1996. "Race, Culture, Identity: Misunderstood Connections." In *Color Conscious: The Political Morality of Race*, ed. K. Anthony Appiah and Amy Gutmann, 30–105. Princeton: Princeton University Press.

———. 2005. *The Ethics of Identity*. Princeton: Princeton University Press.

Arneson, Richard. 1989. "Equality and Equal Opportunity for Welfare." *Philosophical Studies* 56 (1): 77–93.

———. 1990. "Neutrality and Utility." *Canadian Journal of Philosophy* 20 (2): 215–40.

———. 2003. "Liberal Neutrality on the Good: An Autopsy." In *Perfectionism and Neutrality: Essays in Liberal Political Theory*, ed. Steven Wall and George Klosko, 192–218. Lanham, MD: Rowman & Littlefield.

Banting, Keith, and Will Kymlicka, eds. 2006. *Multiculturalism and the Welfare State: Recognition and Redistribution in Contemporary Democracies*. Oxford: Oxford University Press.

Barry, Brian. 1979. "Is Democracy Special?" In *Philosophy, Politics, and Society*, 5th series, ed. Peter Laslett and James Fishkin, 155–96. Oxford: Blackwell.

———. 2001. *Culture and Equality: An Egalitarian Critique of Multiculturalism*. Cambridge, MA: Harvard University Press.

———. 2002. "Second Thoughts—and Some First Thoughts Revived." In *Multiculturalism Reconsidered*, ed. Paul Kelly, 204–38. Cambridge: Polity.

Bauböck, Rainer. 2001. "Cultural Citizenship, Minority Rights and Self-Government." In *Citizenship Today: Global Perspectives and Practices*, ed. Alex Aleinikoff and Doug Klusmeyer, 319–48. Washington, DC: Carnegie Endowment for International Peace.

Beitz, Charles. 2009. *The Idea of Human Rights*. Oxford: Oxford University Press.

Benhabib, Seyla. 2002. *The Claims of Culture: Equality and Diversity in the Global Era*. Princeton: Princeton University Press.

Beran, Harry. 1998. "A Democratic Theory of Political Self-Determination for a New World Order." In *Theories of Secession*, ed. Percy Lehning, 32–59. London: Routledge.

Blake, Michael. 2002. "Diversity, Assimilation, and Survival." *Journal of Contemporary Legal Issues* 12 (2): 637–60.

Brake, Elizabeth. 2010. "Minimal Marriage: What Political Liberalism Implies for Marriage Law." *Ethics* 120 (2): 302–37.

Brilmayer, Lea. 1991. "Secession and Self-Determination: A Territorial Interpretation." *Yale Journal of International Law* 19: 177–202.

Buchanan, Allen. 1991. *Secession: The Morality of Political Divorce from Fort Sumter to Lithuania and Quebec*. Boulder: Westview.

———. 1997. "Theories of Secession." *Philosophy and Public Affairs* 26 (1): 31–61.

———. 1998a. "Democracy and Secession." In *National Self-Determination and Secession*, ed. Margaret Moore, 14–33. Oxford: Oxford University Press.

———. 1998b. "What's So Special about Nations?" In *Rethinking Nationalism*, ed. Jocelyn Couture, Kai Nielsen, and Michel Seymour, 261–82. Calgary: University of Calgary Press.

———. 2004. *Justice, Legitimacy, and Self-Determination: Moral Foundations for International Law*. Oxford: Oxford University Press.

Callan, Eamonn. 2010. "The Better Angels of Our Nature: Patriotism and Dirty Hands." *Journal of Political Philosophy* 18 (3): 249–70.

Carens, Joseph. 1997. "Two Conceptions of Fairness: A Response to Veit Bader." *Political Theory* 25 (6): 814–20.

———. 2000. *Culture, Citizenship, and Community: A Contextual Exploration of Justice as Evenhandedness*. Oxford: Oxford University Press.

Choudhry, Sujit. 2002. "National Minorities and Ethnic Immigrants: Liberalism's Political Sociology." *Journal of Political Philosophy* 10 (1): 54–78.

Christiano, Thomas. 1994. "Democratic Equality and the Problem of Persistent Minorities." *Philosophical Papers* 23 (3): 169–90.

Clifford, James. 1988. "Identity in Mashpee." In *The Predicament of Culture: Twentieth-century Ethnography, Literature, and Art*, ed. James Clifford, 277–346. Cambridge, MA: Harvard University Press.

Cobban, Alfred. 1969. *The Nation State and National Self-Determination*. London: Collins Clear Type Press.

Cohen, G. A. 1989. "On the Currency of Egalitarian Justice." *Ethics* 113 (4): 745–63.

———. 1999. "Expensive Tastes and Multiculturalism." In *Multiculturalism, Liberalism, and Democracy*, ed. Rajeev Bhargava, Amiya Kumar Bagchi, and R. Sudarshan, 80–100. New Delhi: Oxford University Press.

———. 2004. "Expensive Taste Rides Again." In *Dworkin and His Critics*, ed. Justine Burley, 1–29. Oxford: Blackwell.

Cohen, Joshua. 1998. "Democracy and Liberty." In *Deliberative Democracy*, ed. Jon Elster, 185–231. Cambridge: Cambridge University Press.

———. 2002. "For a Democratic Society." In *The Cambridge Companion to Rawls*, ed. Samuel Freeman, 86–138. Cambridge: Cambridge University Press.

Copp, David. 1979. "Do Nations Have the Right of Self-Determination?" In *Philosophers Look at Canadian Confederation*, ed. Stanley French, 71–95. Montreal: Canadian Philosophical Association.

———. 1997. "Democracy and Communal Self-Determination." In *The Morality of Nationalism*, ed. Robert McKim and Jeff McMahan, 277–300. Oxford: Oxford University Press.

Crawford, James. 2000. *At War with Diversity: U.S. Language Policy in an Age of Anxiety*. Clevedon, UK: Multilingual Matters.

Crystal, David. 2000. *Language Death*. Cambridge: Cambridge University Press.

Csergő, Zsuzsa, and Kevin Deegan-Krause. 2011. "Liberalism and Cultural Claims in Central and Eastern Europe: Toward a Pluralist Balance." *Nations and Nationalism* 17 (1): 85–107.

Danley, John R. 1991. "Liberalism, Aboriginal Rights, and Cultural Minorities." *Philosophy and Public Affairs* 20 (2): 168–95.

Davidson, Donald. [1986] 2006. "A Nice Derangement of Epitaphs" In *The Essential Davidson*, ed. Kirk Ludwig and Ernest Lepore, 251–65. New York: Oxford University Press.

De Schutter, Helder. 2011. "Federalism as Fairness." *Journal of Political Philosophy* 19 (2): 167–89.

Dworkin, Ronald. 1978. "Liberalism." In *Public and Private Morality*, ed. Stuart Hampshire, 60–79. Oxford: Oxford University Press.

———. 2000. *Sovereign Virtue*. Cambridge, MA: Harvard University Press.

———. 2004. "Ronald Dworkin Replies." In *Dworkin and His Critics*, ed. Justine Burley, 337–95. Oxford: Blackwell.

Edwards, John. 1985. *Language, Society, and Identity*. Oxford: Basil Blackwell.

Ferguson, Charles A. 1959. "Diglossia." *Word* 15: 325–40.

Fishman, Joshua. 1972. *The Sociology of Language: An Interdisciplinary Social Science Approach to Language in Society*. Rowley, MA: Newbury House.

———. 1991. *Reversing Language Shift*. Clevedon, UK: Multilingual Matters.

———. 1999. "Sociolinguistics." In *Handbook of Language and Ethnic Identity*, ed. Joshua Fishman, 152–63. New York: Oxford University Press.

———. 2001. "Why Is It So Hard to Save a Threatened Language?" In *Can Threatened Languages Be Saved? Reversing Language Shift, Revisited: A 21st Century Perspective*, 1–22. Clevedon, UK: Multilingual Matters.

Forst, Rainer. 1997. "Foundations of a Theory of Multicultural Justice." *Constellations* 4 (1): 63–71.

Fraser, Nancy. 2003. "Social Justice in the Age of Identity Politics: Redistribution, Recognition, and Participation." In *Redistribution or Recognition? A Political-Philosophical Exchange*, ed. Nancy Fraser and Axel Honneth, 7–109. London: Verso.

Gans, Chaim. 2003. *The Limits of Nationalism*. Cambridge: Cambridge University Press.

Gauthier, David. 1994. "On Breaking Up: An Essay on Secession." *Canadian Journal of Philosophy* 24 (3): 357–72.

Geertz, Clifford. 1973. *The Interpretation of Cultures*. New York: Basic Books.

Gellner, Ernest. 1983. *Nations and Nationalism*. Ithaca: Cornell University Press.

Generalitat de Catalunya. 2010. "Language Policy Report Concerning Catalan Language."

Glazer, Nathan. 1998. *We Are All Multiculturalists Now*. Cambridge, MA: Harvard University Press.

Goodin, Robert. 2006. "Liberal Multiculturalism: Protective and Polyglot." *Political Theory* 34 (3): 289–303.

Government of Ireland. 2006. "Statement on the Irish Language."

Green, Leslie. 1987. "Are Language Rights Fundamental?" *Osgoode Hall Law Journal* 25 (4): 639–69.

Green, Leslie. 1991. "Freedom of Expression and Choice of Language." *Law & Policy* 13 (3): 215–29.

Green, Leslie, and Denise Réaume. 1989. "Education and Linguistic Security in the Charter." *McGill Law Journal* 34 (4): 777–816.

Grimm, Dieter. 1995. "Does Europe Need a Constitution?" *European Law Journal* 1 (3): 282–302.

Habermas, Jürgen. 1995. "Remarks on Dieter Grimm's 'Does Europe Need a Constitution?'" *European Law Journal* 1 (3): 303–7.

Hardimon, Michael O. 2003. "The Ordinary Concept of Race." *Journal of Philosophy* 100 (9): 437–55.

Harrison, Ross. 2002. *Hobbes, Locke, and Confusion's Masterpiece: An Examination of Seventeenth Century Philosophy*. Cambridge: Cambridge University Press.

Heath, Joseph. 2004. "Resource Egalitarianism and the Politics of Recognition." In *Adding Insult to Injury: Nancy Fraser Debates her Critics*, ed. Kevin Olson, 196–220. London: Verso.

Hirschman, Albert O. 1970. *Exit, Voice, Loyalty: Responses to Declines in Firms, Organizations, and States*. Cambridge, MA: Harvard University Press.

Honig, Bonnie. 1993. *Political Theory and the Displacement of Politics*. Ithaca: Cornell University Press.

Honneth, Axel. 1996. *The Struggle for Recognition: The Moral Grammar of Political Conflict*. Cambridge, MA: MIT Press.

———. 2003. "Redistribution as Recognition: a Response to Nancy Fraser." In *Redistribution or Recognition? A Political-Philosophical Exchange*, ed. Nancy Fraser and Axel Honneth, 110–97. London: Verso.

Hume, David. 2000. *A Treatise of Human Nature*, ed. David Fate Norton and Mary J. Norton. Oxford: Oxford University Press.

Hurka, Thomas. 1993. *Perfectionism*. Oxford: Oxford University Press.

Johnson, James. 2000. "Why Respect Culture?" *American Journal of Political Science* 44 (3): 405–18.

Jones, R. O. 1993. "The Sociolinguistics of Welsh." In *The Celtic Languages*, ed. M. J. Ball, 536–605. London: Routledge.

Kateb, George. 1994. "Notes on Pluralism." *Social Research* 61 (4): 511–37.

Kitcher, Philip. 1999. "Race, Ethnicity, Biology, Culture." In *Racism*, ed. Leonard Harris, 87–117. Amherst, NY: Humanity Books.

———. 2007. "Does 'Race' Have a Future?" *Philosophy and Public Affairs* 35 (4): 293–317.

Kloss, Heinz. 1971. "Language Rights of Immigrant Groups." *International Migration Review* 5 (2): 250–68.

———. 1977. *The American Bilingual Tradition*. Rowley, MA: Newbury House.

Kluckhohn, Clyde. 1950. *Mirror for Man*. London: George G. Harrap.

Kukathas, Chandran. 1992. "Are There Any Cultural Rights?" *Political Theory* 20 (2): 105–39.

———. 1997. "Multiculturalism as Fairness: Will Kymlicka's *Multicultural Citizenship*." *Journal of Political Philosophy* 5 (4): 406–27.

———. 2003. *The Liberal Archipelago: A Theory of Diversity and Freedom*. Oxford: Oxford University Press.

Kuper, Adam. 1999. *Culture: The Anthropologists' Account*. Cambridge, MA: Harvard University Press.

Kymlicka, Will. 1989a. "Liberal Individualism and Liberal Neutrality." *Ethics* 99 (4): 883–905.

———. 1989b. *Liberalism, Community, and Culture*. New York: Oxford University Press.

———. 1990. *Contemporary Political Philosophy: an Introduction*. New York: Oxford University Press.

———. 1995. *Multicultural Citizenship*. Oxford: Oxford University Press.

———. 1998a. *Finding Our Way: Rethinking Ethnocultural Relations in Canada*. Toronto: Oxford University Press.

———. 1998b. "Is Federalism a Viable Alternative to Secession?" In *Theories of Secession*, ed. Percy Blanchemains Lehning, 111–50. London: Routledge.

———. 2001a. *Politics in the Vernacular*. Oxford: Oxford University Press.

———. 2001b. "Western Political Theory and Ethnic Relations in Eastern Europe." In *Can Liberal Pluralism Be Exported? Western Political Theory and Ethnic Relations in Eastern Europe*, ed. Will Kymlicka and Magda Opalski, 13–105. Oxford: Oxford University Press.

———. 2010. "Minority Rights in Political Philosophy and International Law." In *The Philosophy of International Law*, ed. Samantha Besson and John Tasioulas, 377–96. Oxford: Oxford University Press.

Laden, Anthony Simon. 2007. "Negotiation, Deliberation and the Claims of Politics." In *Multiculturalism and Political Theory*, ed. Anthony Simon Laden and David Owen, 198–218. Cambridge: Cambridge University Press.

Laitin, David. 1993. "The Game Theory of Language Regimes." *International Political Science Review* 14 (3): 227–39.

———. 1998. *Identity in Formation: The Russian-Speaking Populations in the New Abroad*. Ithaca: Cornell University Press.

———. 2007. *Nations, States, and Violence*. Oxford: Oxford University Press.

Laitin, David, and Rob Reich. 2003. "A Liberal Democratic Approach to Language Policy." In *Language Rights and Political Theory*, ed. Will Kymlicka and Alan Patten, 80–104. Oxford: Oxford University Press.

Laponce, Jean A. 1984. *Langue et Territoire*. Québec: Presses de l'Université Laval.

Larmore, Charles. 1987. *Patterns of Moral Complexity*. Cambridge: Cambridge University Press.

Laurendeau, André. 1991. *The Diary of André Laurendeau*. Toronto: Lorimer.

Laurin, Camille. 1977. *White Paper: Quebec's Policy on the French Language*. Government of Quebec.

Levy, Jacob. 2000. *The Multiculturalism of Fear*. Oxford: Oxford University Press.

———. 2003. "Language Rights, Literacy, and the State." In *Language Rights and Political Theory*, ed. Will Kymlicka and Alan Patten, 230–49. Oxford: Oxford University Press.

———. 2004. "National Minorities without Nationalism." In *The Politics of Belonging: Nationalism, Liberalism, and Pluralism*, ed. Alain Dieckhoff, 257–73. Lanham, MD: Lexington Books.

———. 2007. "Federalism, Liberalism, and the Separation of Loyalties." *American Political Science Review* 101 (3): 459–77.

Lincoln, Abraham. Letter to Horace Greeley. August 22, 1862.

Macedo, Steven. 1995. "Liberal Civic Education and Religious Fundamentalism: The Case of God v. John Rawls?" *Ethics* 105 (2): 468–96.

MacMillan, C. Michael. 1998. *The Practice of Language Rights in Canada.* Toronto: University of Toronto Press.

Mallon, Ron. 2007. "Human Categories Beyond Non-essentialism." *Journal of Political Philosophy* 15 (2): 146–68.

Margalit, Avishai, and Moshe Halbertal. 1994. "Liberalism and the Right to Culture." *Social Research* 61 (3): 491–510.

Margalit, Avishai, and Joseph Raz. 1990. "National Self-Determination." *Journal of Philosophy* 87 (9): 439–61.

———. 1994. "National Self-Determination." In *Ethics in the Public Domain: Essays in the Morality of Law and Politics,* ed. Joseph Raz, 125–45. Oxford: Oxford University Press.

Markell, Patchen. 2003. *Bound by Recognition.* Princeton: Princeton University Press.

Marx, Anthony W. 2005. *Faith in Nation: Exclusionary Origins of Nationalism.* Oxford: Oxford University Press.

Mason, Andrew. 2006. *Levelling the Playing Field: The Idea of Equal Opportunity and its Place in Egalitarian Thought.* Oxford: Oxford University Press.

———. 2007. "Multiculturalism and the Critique of Essentialism." In *Multiculturalism and Political Theory,* ed. Anthony Simon Laden and David Owen, 221–43. Cambridge: Cambridge University Press.

May, Stephen. 2001. *Language and Minority Rights.* Harlow/London: Longman/ Pearson Education.

———. 2003. "Misconceiving Minority Language Rights: Implications for Liberal Political Theory." In *Language Rights and Political Theory,* ed. Will Kymlicka and Alan Patten, 123–52. Oxford: Oxford University Press.

Mayr, Ernst. 1942. *Systematics and the Origins of Species: From the Viewpoint of a Zoologist.* New York: Columbia University Press.

McGarry, John. 1998. "Orphans of Secession: National Pluralism in Secessionist Regions and Post-Secession States." In *National Self-Determination and Secession,* ed. Margaret Moore, 215–32. Oxford: Oxford University Press.

McGarry, John, and Brendan O'Leary. 2006. "Consociational Theory, Northern Ireland's Conflict, and Its Agreement: Part 1. What Consociationalists Can Learn from Northern Ireland." *Government & Opposition: An International Journal of Comparative Politics* 41 (1): 43–63.

McRae, Kenneth. 1975. "The Principle of Territoriality and the Principle of Personality in Multilingual States." *International Journal of the Sociology of Language* 4:33–54.

McRoberts, Kenneth. 1997. *Misconceiving Canada.* Oxford: Oxford University Press.

Miguel, Ted. 2004. "Tribe or Nation? Nation Building and Public Goods in Kenya Versus Tanzania." *World Politics* 56 (3): 327–62.

Mill, John Stuart. 1991. *Considerations on Representative Government.* In *On Liberty and Other Essays,* 203–467. Oxford: Oxford University Press.

Miller, David. 1995. *On Nationality.* Oxford: Oxford University Press.

———. 2000. *Citizenship and National Identity.* Cambridge: Polity Press.

———. 2004. "Justice, Democracy and Public Goods." In *Justice and Democracy: Essays for Brian Barry*, ed. Keith M. Dowding, Robert Goodin, and Carole Pateman, 127–49. Cambridge: Cambridge University Press.

———. 2006. "Multiculturalism and the Welfare State: Theoretical Reflections." In *Multiculturalism and the Welfare State: Recognition and Redistribution in Contemporary Democracies*, ed. Keith Banting and Will Kymlicka, 323–39. Oxford: Oxford University Press.

———. 2008. "Immigrants, Nations, and Citizenship." *Journal of Political Philosophy* 16 (4): 373–90.

Moore, Margaret. 1998. "The Territorial Dimension of Self-Determination." In *National Self-Determination and Secession*, ed. Margaret Moore, 134–57. Oxford: Oxford University Press.

———. 2001. *The Ethics of Nationalism*. Oxford: Oxford University Press.

Moreno, Luis, Ana Arriba, and Araceli Serrano. 1998. "Multiple Identities in Decentralized Spain: The Case of Catalonia." *Regional and Federal Studies* 8 (3): 65–88.

Müller, Jan-Werner. 2007. *Constitutional Patriotism*. Princeton: Princeton University Press.

Nagel, Thomas. 1973. "Rawls on Justice." *Philosophical Review* 82 (2): 220–34.

———. 1991. *Equality and Partiality*. New York: Oxford University Press.

Nelde, Peter H., Normand Labrie, and Colin H. Williams. 1992. "The Principle of Territoriality and Personality in the Solution of Linguistic Conflicts." *Journal of Multilingual and Multicultural Development* 13: 387–406.

Nettle, Daniel, and Suzanne Romaine. 2000. *Vanishing Voices*. Oxford: Oxford University Press.

Nielsen, Kai. 1998. "Liberal Nationalism and Secession." In *Self-Determination and Secession*, ed. Margaret Moore, 103–33. Oxford: Oxford University Press.

Norman, Wayne. 1994. "Towards a Philosophy of Federalism." In *Group Rights*, ed. Judith Baker, 79–100. Toronto: University of Toronto Press.

———. 1998. "The Ethics of Secession as the Regulation of Secessionist Politics." In *Self-Determination and Secession*, ed. Margaret Moore, 34–61. Oxford: Oxford University Press.

———. 2006. *Negotiating Nationalism: Nation-Building, Federalism, and Secession in the Multinational State*. Oxford: Oxford University Press.

Okin, Susan Moller. 1999. *Is Multiculturalism Bad for Women?* Princeton: Princeton University Press.

Olsaretti, Serena. 2013. "Scanlon on Responsibility and the Value of Choice." *Journal of Moral Philosophy* 10 (4) 465–83.

Osborne, Andrew. 2002. "Arabic: a Language for Belgium?" *Guardian*, August 27.

Owen, David, and James Tully. 2007. "Redistribution and Recognition: Two Approaches." In *Multiculturalism and Political Theory*, ed. Anthony Simon Laden and David Owen, 265–91. Cambridge: Cambridge University Press.

Parekh, Bhiku. 2002. *Rethinking Multiculturalism: Cultural Diversity and Political Theory*. Cambridge, MA: Harvard University Press.

Parfit, Derek. 1984. *Reasons and Persons*. Oxford: Oxford University Press.

Patten, Alan. 1999a. "Liberal Egalitarianism and the Case for Supporting National Cultures." *The Monist* 82 (3): 387–410.

Patten, Alan. 1999b. "The Autonomy Argument for Liberal Nationalism." *Nations & Nationalism* 5 (2): 1–17.

———. 1999c. "Conception Libérale de la Citoyenneté et Identité Nationale." In *Nationalité, Citoyenneté et Solidarité*, ed. Michel Seymour, 232–56. Montréal: Éditions Liber.

———. 2000. "Equality of Recognition and the Liberal Theory of Citizenship." In *The Demands of Citizenship*, ed. Catriona McKinnon and Iain Hampsher-Monk, 193–211. London: Continuum.

———. 2001a. "Political Theory and Language Policy." *Political Theory* 29 (5): 683–707.

———. 2001b. "Liberal Citizenship in Multinational Societies." In *Multinational Democracies*, ed. Alain-G Gagnon and James Tully, 279–98. Cambridge: Cambridge University Press.

———. 2002. "Democratic Secession from a Multinational State." *Ethics* 112 (3): 558–86.

———. 2003a. "Liberal Neutrality and Language Policy." *Philosophy and Public Affairs* 31 (4): 356–86.

———. 2003b. "What Kind of Bilingualism?" In *Language Rights and Political Theory*, ed. Will Kymlicka and Alan Patten, 298–321. Oxford: Oxford University Press.

———. 2003c. "Can the Immigrant/National Minority Dichotomy Be Defended? Comment on Ruth Rubio-Marín." In *Self-Determination and Secession: NOMOS XLV*, ed. Stephen Macedo and Allen Buchanan, 174–89. New York: NYU Press.

———. 2006. "Who Should Have Official Language Rights?" *Supreme Court Law Review* 31: 103–15.

———. 2008. "Beyond the Dichotomy of Universalism and Difference: Four Responses to Cultural Diversity." In *Constitutional Design for Divided Societies: Integration or Accomodation?*, ed. Sujit Choudhry, 91–110. Oxford: Oxford University Press.

———. 2009. "Survey Article: The Justification of Minority Language Rights." *Journal of Political Philosophy* 17 (1): 102–28.

———. 2010. "'The Most Natural State': Herder and Nationalism." *History of Political Thought* 31 (4): 657–89.

———. 2012. "Liberal Neutrality: A Reinterpretation and Defense." *Journal of Political Philosophy* 20 (3): 249–72.

———. 2013. "Cultural Preservation and Liberal Values: A Reply to William James Booth." *American Political Science Review* 107 (4): 875–82.

Patten, Alan, and Will Kymlicka. 2003. "Introduction: Language Rights and Political Theory: Context, Issues and Approaches." In *Language Rights and Political Theory*, ed. Will Kymlicka and Alan Patten, 1–51. Oxford: Oxford University Press.

Phillips, Anne. 2007. *Multiculturalism without Culture*. Princeton: Princeton University Press.

Philpott, Daniel. 1995. "In Defense of Self-Determination." *Ethics* 105 (2): 353–85.

———. 1998. "Self-Determination in Practice." In *Self-Determination and Secession*, ed. Margaret Moore, 79–102. Oxford: Oxford University Press.

Pogge, Thomas. 2000. "Accommodation Rights for Hispanics in the U.S." In *Hispanics/Latinos in the United States: Ethnicity, Race, and Rights*, ed. Jorge J. E. Gracia and Pablo de Greiff, 181–200. New York: Routledge.

Popper, Karl. 1976. *The Myth of the Framework*. New York: Routledge.

Porter, Rosalie Pedalino. 1996. *Forked Tongue: The Politics of Bilingual Education*. Second edition. New Brunswick, NJ: Transaction.

Posner, Daniel N. 2005. *Institutions and Ethnic Politics in Africa*. Cambridge: Cambridge University Press.

Rawls, John. 1975. "Fairness to Goodness." *Philosophical Review* 84 (4): 536–54.

———. 1999a. *A Theory of Justice*. Revised edition. Cambridge, MA: Harvard University Press.

———. 1999b. *The Law of Peoples*. Cambridge, MA: Harvard University Press.

———. 2001. *Justice as Fairness: A Restatement*. Cambridge, MA: Harvard University Press (Belknap Press).

———. 2005. *Political Liberalism*. Expanded edition. New York: Columbia University Press.

Raz, Joseph. 1986. *The Morality of Freedom*. Oxford: Oxford University Press.

———. 1994. *Ethics in the Public Domain: Essays in the Morality of Law and Politics*. Oxford: Oxford University Press.

———. 2001. *Value, Respect, and Attachment*. Cambridge: Cambridge University Press.

Réaume, Denise. 1991. "The Constitutional Protection of Language: Survival or Security?" In *Language and the State: The Law and Politics of Identity*, ed. David Schneiderman, 37–57. Cowansville: Éditions Yvon Blais.

———. 1994. "The Group Right to Linguistic Security: Whose Right, What Duties?" In *Group Rights*, ed. Judith Baker, 118–41. Toronto: University of Toronto Press.

———. 2000. "Official-Language Rights: Intrinsic Value and the Protection of Difference." In *Citizenship in Diverse Societies*, ed. Will Kymlicka and Wayne Norman, 245–72. Oxford: Oxford University Press.

———. 2003. "Beyond Personality: The Territorial and Personal Principles of Language Policy Reconsidered." In *Language Rights and Political Theory*, ed. Will Kymlicka and Alan Patten, 271–95. Oxford: Oxford University Press.

Reich, Rob. 2002. *Bridging Liberalism and Multiculturalism in American Education*. Chicago: University of Chicago Press.

Resnick, Philip. 1994. "Toward a Multinational Federalism: Asymmetrical and Confederal Alternatives." In *Seeking a New Canadian Partnership: Asymmetrical and Confederal Options*, ed. F. Leslie Seidle, 71–89. Montréal: Institute for Research on Public Policy.

Rodríguez, Cristina M. 2006. "Language and Participation." *California Law Review* 94 (3): 687–767.

Rodriguez, Richard. 1982. *Hunger of Memory: The Education of Richard Rodriguez*. New York: Bantam Books.

Royal Commission on Bilingualism and Biculturalism. 1967. *Book I: The Official Languages*. Ottawa: Report of the Royal Commission on Bilingualism and Biculturalism.

Rubio-Marín, Ruth. 2003a. "Language Rights: Exploring the Competing Rationales." In *Language Rights and Political Theory*, ed. Will Kymlicka and Alan Patten, 52–79. Oxford: Oxford University Press.

———. 2003b. "Exploring the Boundaries of Language Rights: Insiders, Newcomers, and Natives." In *Self-Determination and Secession: NOMOS XLV*, ed. Stephen Macedo and Allen Buchanan, 136–73. New York: NYU Press.

Scanlon, T. M. 1998. *What We Owe to Each Other*. Cambridge, MA: Belknap Press of Harvard University Press.

———. 2003. *The Difficulty of Tolerance: Essays in Political Philosophy*. Cambridge: Cambridge University Press.

———. 2006. "Justice, Responsibility, and the Demands of Equality." In *The Egalitarian Conscience: Essays in Honour of G.A. Cohen*, ed. Christine Sypnowich, 70–87. Oxford: Oxford University Press.

Scheffler, Samuel. 1994. *The Rejection of Consequentialism: A Philosophical Investigation of the Considerations Underlying Rival Moral Conceptions*. Oxford: Oxford University Press.

———. 2001. *Boundaries and Allegiances: Problems of Justice and Responsibility in Liberal Thought*. Oxford: Oxford University Press.

———. 2004. "Projects, Relationships, and Reasons." In *Reason and Value: Themes from the Moral Philosophy of Joseph Raz*, ed. R. Jay Wallace, Philip Pettit, Samuel Scheffler, and Michael Smith, 247–69. New York: Oxford University Press.

———. 2007. "Immigration and the Significance of Culture." *Philosophy and Public Affairs* 35 (2): 93–125.

Schildkraut, Deborah. 2005. *Press "One" for English: Language Policy, Public Opinion, and American Identity*. Princeton: Princeton University Press.

Schmidt, Ronald, Jr. 2000. *Language Policy and Identity Politics in the United States*. Philadelphia: Temple University Press.

Sher, George. 1997. *Beyond Neutrality*. Cambridge: Cambridge University Press.

Shin, Hyon B., with Rosalind Bruno. 2003. *Language Use and English Speaking Ability: 2000*. Census 2000 Brief, C2KBR-29. Washington, DC: U.S. Census Bureau.

Shin, Hyon B., and Robert A. Kominski. 2010. *Language Use in the United States: 2007*. American Community Survey Reports, ACS-12. Washington, DC: U.S. Census Bureau.

Sniderman, Paul, and Louk Hagendoorn. 2007. *When Ways of Life Collide*. Princeton: Princeton University Press.

Sober, Elliott. 2000. *Philosophy of Biology*. Second edition. Boulder: Westview.

Song, Sarah. 2007. *Justice, Gender, and the Politics of Multiculturalism*. Cambridge: Cambridge University Press.

Spinner, Jeff. 1994. *Boundaries of Citizenship: Race, Ethnicity and Nationality in the Liberal State*. Baltimore: Johns Hopkins University Press.

Spinner-Halev, Jeff. 2012. *Enduring Injustice*. Cambridge: Cambridge University Press.

Stilz, Anna. 2009. *Liberal Loyalty: Freedom, Obligation, and the State*. Princeton: Princeton University Press.

Sunstein, Cass. 1991. "Constitutionalism and Secession." *University of Chicago Law Review* 58 (2): 633–70.

Tamir, Yael. 1993. *Liberal Nationalism*. Princeton: Princeton University Press.

Taylor, Charles. 1993. "Why do Nations Have to Become States?" Reprinted in *Reconciling the Solitudes*, by Charles Taylor, 40–58. Montreal: McGill/Queens University Press.

———. 1994. "The Politics of Recognition." In *Multiculturalism and "The Politics of Recognition,"* ed. A. Gutmann, 23–73. Princeton: Princeton University Press.

Taylor, Robert S. 2009. "Rawlsian Affirmative Action." *Ethics* 119 (3): 476–506.

Terborgh, John. 2002. "Vanishing Points." *New York Review of Books* 49 (20): 78–80.

———. 2003. "Reply." *New York Review of Books* 50 (6): 93.

Tomasi, John. 1995. "Kymlicka, Liberalism, and Respect for Cultural Minorities." *Ethics* 105 (2). 580–603.

Tully, James. 1995. *Strange Multiplicity: Constitutionalism in an Age of Diversity*. Cambridge: Cambridge University Press.

Van Parijs, Philippe. 2000a. "Must Europe Be Belgian? On Democratic Citizenship in Multilingual Polities." In *The Demands of Citizenship*, ed. Catriona McKinnon and Iain Hampsher-Monk, 232–56. London: Continuum.

———. 2000b. "The Ground Floor of the World: On the Socio-economic Consequences of Linguistic Globalization." *International Political Science Review* 21 (2): 217–33.

———. 2011a. *Linguistic Justice for Europe and the World*. Oxford: Oxford University Press.

———. 2011b. "On the Territoriality Principle and Belgium's Linguistic Future: A Reply." In *The Linguistic Territoriality Principle: Right Violation or Parity of Esteem*, Lead Piece and Reply by Philippe Van Parijs. Re-Bel e-book 11:53–74.

Waldron, Jeremy. 1989. "Legislation and Moral Neutrality." In *Liberal Neutrality*, ed. Robert Goodin and Andrew Reeves, 61–83. London: Routledge.

———. 1992. "Minority Cultures and the Cosmopolitan Alternative." *University of Michigan Journal of Law Reform* 25: 751–94.

———. 2002. "One Law for All? The Logic of Cultural Accomodation." *Washington and Lee Law Review* 59 (1): 3–36.

———. 2004. "Tribalism and the Myth of the Framework: Some Popperian Thoughts on the Politics of Cultural Recognition." In *Karl Popper: Critical Appraisals*, ed. Philip Catton and Graham Macdonald, 203–30. New York: Routledge.

———. 2010. "Two Conceptions of Self-Determination." In *The Philosophy of International Law*, ed. Samantha Besson and John Tasioulas, 397–413. Oxford: Oxford University Press.

Wall, Steven. 2001. "Neutrality and Responsibility." *Journal of Philosophy* 98 (8): 389–410.

———. 2010. "Neutralism for Perfectionists: The Case of Restricted State Neutrality." *Ethics* 120 (2): 232–56.

Walzer, Michael. 1980. "The Moral Standing of States: A Response to Four Critics." *Philosophy and Public Affairs* 9 (3): 209–29.

Weber, Eugen. 1976. *Peasants into Frenchmen: The Modernization of Rural France*. Stanford: Stanford University Press.

Wedeen, Lisa. 2002. "Conceptualizing Culture: Possibilities for Political Science." *American Political Science Review* 96 (4): 713–28.

Weinstock, Daniel. 1999. "Le Problème de la Boîte de Pandore." In *Nationalité, Citoyenneté et Solidarité*, ed. Michel Seymour, 17–40. Montréal: Éditions Liber.

———. 2001. "Constitutionalizing the Right to Secede." *Journal of Political Philosophy* 9 (2): 182–203.

———. 2003. "The Antinomy of Language Policy." In *Language Rights and Political Theory*, ed. Will Kymlicka and Alan Patten, 250–70. Oxford: Oxford University Press.

Wellman, Christopher. 1995. "A Defense of Secession and Political Self-Determination." *Philosophy and Public Affairs* 24 (2): 142–71.

———. 2005. *A Theory of Secession: The Case for Political Self-Determination*. Cambridge: Cambridge University Press.

Williams, Bernard. 1973. "A Critique of Utilitarianism." In *Utilitarianism: For and Against*, ed. J.J.C. Smart and Bernard Williams, 77–150. Cambridge: Cambridge University Press.

Williams, Melissa. 1995. "Justice toward Groups: Political Not Juridical." *Political Theory* 23 (1): 67–90.

Young, Iris Marion. 1990. *Justice and the Politics of Difference*. Princeton: Princeton University Press.

Yu, Douglas W., and Glenn Shepard, Jr. 2003. "Vanishing Cultures." *New York Review of Books*, 50 (6): 92.

INDEX